Criminal Law

Criminal Law

L B Curzon

Barrister

Seventh Edition

THE M+E HANDBOOK SERIES

Pitman Publishing
128 Long Acre, London WC2E 9AN

A Division of Longman Group Limited

First published in Great Britain 1973
Second edition 1977
Third edition 1980
Fourth edition 1984
Fifth edition 1987
Sixth edition 1991
Seventh edition 1994

© Macdonald & Evans Ltd 1973, 1977, 1980, 1984
© Longman Group UK 1987, 1991, 1994

ISBN 0 7121 0860 2

Typeset by ROM-Data Corporation Limited, Falmouth, Cornwall
Printed and bound in Singapore

Contents

Part three Offences against property

Appendices

Preface to the seventh edition

Preparation of this new edition of *Criminal Law* has been guided by the established objectives of the Handbook series, namely, the provision of a structured, concise series of study notes and progress tests intended for the use of students making an initial acquaintance with principles of criminal law and for examination candidates requiring material which can be utilised for purposes of planned revision. The book is not intended in any sense as a replacement for a standard text; it has been planned as an adjunct only and should be used accordingly.

Recent legislation and case law have necessitated considerable revision of the previous edition. Some material which featured in that edition (such as traffic offences) is omitted; several chapters have been partly rewritten; tables of cases and statutes have been brought up to date; a selection of recommendations from the 1993 *Report of the Royal Commission on Criminal Justice* is presented as an appendix. References are made to the Criminal Justice and Public Order Bill, published in December, 1993.

Important recent decisions of the House of Lords are noted throughout the text: these include *R. v. R.* (1992) (marital rape), *R. v. Gotts* (1992) (duress and attempted murder), *R. v. Savage* (1992) (foreseeability and intent in assault), *R. v. Brown and Others* (1993) (consent to infliction of violence), *R. v. Gomez* (1993) (appropriation and theft). Court of Appeal decisions which are noted include *R. v. Lebrun* (1992) (coincidence of *mens rea* and *actus reus*), *R. v. Thornton* (1992) (provocation and domestic violence), *R. v. Rook* (1993) (withdrawal from participation in an offence), *R. v. Sulman* (1993) (basis of involuntary manslaughter), *R. v. Kingston* (1993) (defence of involuntary intoxication).

Students are expected to know the criminal law *as it is* at any given time; hence a regular and methodical perusal of periodicals such as *Criminal Law Review, Current Law, New Law Journal,* and *Student Law Review,* is recommended. The authoritative reports in the columns of *The Times, The Guardian, The Independent,* are of much value and ought to be read and analysed frequently.

A planned course of study based on the text used as an adjunct might take the following form for *beginners*.

(a) The *first reading* should be swift, and designed for the acquisition of a *general view* of the nature and content of the criminal law. At this stage the progress tests need not be attempted.

(b) The *second reading* constitutes the main part of this scheme of study and involves a *detailed, methodical study of the text*. Each chapter must be studied very carefully and the appropriate progress test should be completed and checked. Definitions should be comprehended; principles and their application in leading cases should be examined.

(c) The *third reading* should be in the nature of a *general revision* based on principles, definitions and leading cases.

(d) *Finally*, the *test paper* in Appendix 3 should be attempted under examination conditions.

A swift course of *revision* based on the text might take the following form.

(a) *First*, read through each chapter and attempt the progress test. Answers should be checked before moving on to the next chapter.

(b) *Next*, attempt the test paper in Appendix 3 under examination conditions.

(c) *Finally*, check your answers to the test paper by working through the relevant parts of the text.

I acknowledge with thanks suggestions as to content and presentation of the text made by tutors and students. I am grateful to the Senate of the University of London for kind permission to reprint in Appendix 3 a selection of questions from LLB examination papers.

L.B.C.

NOTE: The cross references in the text of this book consist of the relevant chapter number followed by the section number in bold type.

Table of cases

Table of statutes

Part one
Preliminary matters

1

The nature and classification of criminal offences

General considerations

1. The nature and province of the criminal law

The broad purpose of the criminal law is the prevention of harm to the community, 'the protection of the security of individual interests, and the assurance of the survival of the group.' Specifically, it is concerned with the definition, trial and punishment of those acts and omissions which are recognised as crimes (*see* **14–18** below). The criminal law has been interpreted as 'an expression of social and moral criticism governed by highly-authoritative social rules . . . essentially prohibitive, restrictive, and coercive'.

(a) Gross (in *A Theory of Criminal Justice*, 1978) comments: 'The criminal law provides a *set of rules* to fix the limits of socially tolerable conduct and to prohibit those acts that are out of bounds. It also includes rules requiring that certain things of social importance be done . . . At the core of any body of criminal law are rules that prohibit certain acts whose harm is plain, grave and universally unwelcome . . . In contrast there are crimes in which conduct is generally thought to be wrong but not criminal unless the law says so . . . A third group of rules makes certain acts criminal, although they would not even be thought wrong, much less criminal, except for the law.'

(b) George, writing in 1968 on the *social basis* of criminal law, suggested that in modern society criminal law should be seen as a body of norms, formally promulgated through specified governmental organs, contravention of which warrants the imposition of punishment through special proceedings maintained in the name of the people or state.

(c) Rawls, writing in 1969 on punishment as the primary sanction of the criminal law, enumerated the features of that law as follows: 'A person is said to suffer punishment whenever he is legally deprived of the normal rights of a citizen on the ground that he has violated a rule of law, the violation having been established by trial according to due process of law, provided the deprivation has been carried out by the recognised legal authorities of the State, that the rule of law clearly specifies both the offence and the established penalty, that the courts construe statutes strictly, and that the statute was on the books prior to the offence'.

2. The plan of this Handbook
This is based on a traditional division of the subject matter:

(a) *Part one*: Preliminary matters. Topics to be treated include: the nature of a crime, with emphasis on problems of definition; the basis of criminal responsibility, with reference to conduct and state of mind; strict and vicarious liability; general defences; the so-called 'preliminary crimes' of incitement, conspiracy and attempt.

(b) *Part two*: Offences against the person. This part comprises a discussion of a number of specific offences, including those arising from unlawful homicide, assault and battery, and sexual crimes.

(c) *Part three*: Offences against property. 'Property' is considered in its wide sense, and the offences treated include theft, blackmail, burglary, criminal deception, criminal damage and forgery.

(d) *Part four*: Offences against the state, public order and morals and the administration of justice. This very wide heading embraces a variety of offences, including treason, riot, terrorism, criminal libel and obscenity, misuse of drugs, perjury and contempt of court.

3. The vocabulary of the criminal law: a caveat
As in the case of other branches of English law, the criminal law has acquired its own highly specialised vocabulary. Words in general, everyday use – such as 'crime', 'intention', 'assault', 'steal' – have been defined with precision on the basis of case law and statute, and so transmuted, that, in many instances, their meaning, when employed in the terminology of the criminal law is at variance with their everyday meaning. Note, for example, the comments of Lord Simon in *DPP for N. Ireland* v. *Lynch* (1975), in referring to *mens rea* (*see* 3:1): 'A principal difficulty in this branch of the law is the chaotic terminology . . . Will, volition, motive, purpose, object, view, intention, intent, specific intent or intention . . . such terms, which do indeed overlap in certain contexts, seem frequently to be used interchangeably, without definition, and

regardless that in some cases the legal usage is a term of art differing from the popular usage.'

(a) Confusion of legal and everyday vocabularies must be avoided. 'The law in action compiles its own dictionary. In time, what was originally the common coinage of speech acquires a different value in the pocket of the lawyer than when in the layman's purse': *per* Lord Edmund-Davies in *R* v. *Caldwell* (1982). Terms employed in the criminal law must be used with precision.

(b) The vocabulary of the criminal law often changes: note, for example, the introduction of terms and phrases such as 'automatism' (*see* 6:**20**) and 'diminished responsibility' (*see* 9:**34**). Shifts in the meaning of technical terms, e.g. 'burglary' (*see* 16:**9**), are common.

The sources of the criminal law

4. General
The major sources of criminal law are to be found in:

(a) the common law (*see* **5**), and

(b) statute and delegated legislation (*see* **6–7**).

5. Common law sources
Blackstone speaks of: 'the chief cornerstone of the laws of England, which is general and immemorial custom, or common law, from time to time declared in the decisions of the courts of justice. . . .' Some sources of our criminal law are to be found in early custom as developed on the basis of judicial decision and precedent.

(a) Among the earliest common law offences were those serious violations of standards of behaviour which struck at the very foundations of society and which were usually punished with death and forfeiture of property. Examples of such acts are murder, rape and theft.

(b) The development of the common law produced the practice of deciding cases by interpretation and reference to earlier decisions. New crimes were often created as the result of judicial decisions.

(c) Although written statements of the criminal law in early textbooks now have no binding authority, some are considered as having *persuasive* authority. Examples are: Coke's *Third Institute* (1642), Hale's *History of the Pleas of the Crown* (1736), Foster's *Crown Law* (1762) and Blackstone's *Commentaries* (the fourth volume: *Public Wrongs*) (1765).

(d) Some common law crimes have now been codified and defined in statutory form, e.g. Offences against the Person Act 1861, Sexual Offences Act 1956 (*see* Chaps. 12, 13).

6. Statute

Parliament is now the major source of innovation and reform in the criminal law. (Note, too, the work of the Royal Commissions on, e.g. Criminal Justice: *see* Appendix 4.)

(a) Today, the great majority of crimes are defined by statute: *see*, for example, 'insider dealing' (Criminal Justice Act 1993, s. 52).
(b) Some statutes entirely replace the common law with regard to certain offences, e.g. the Theft Act 1968 (*see* Chap. 14).
(c) An entirely *new* crime may be created by statute, as, for example, 'tipping-off' (Criminal Justice Act 1993, s. 18).
(d) Where statute does not alter the common law, either in express terms or by implication, the common law continues in effect.

7. Delegated legislation

Criminal offences may be created also under statutory instruments and by-laws, which result from powers conferred by Parliament.

8. Codification of the criminal law

Attempts at codifying some aspects of statute and case law have been made, e.g. the Offences against the Person Act 1861. The acceptance by Parliament of a *unified code* of the English criminal law remains an important objective for many lawyers, jurists and social reformers. For a recent, comprehensive draft of a suggested criminal code, *see* **28–30** below.

English criminal law is now to be found, therefore, in no single code, but in the common law, in statutes, in instruments resulting from delegated legislation, and in case law (which is of considerable significance today).

The problem of judicial law-making

9. The problem stated

Reference was made in **5** to the part played in the development of the criminal law by judicial interpretation. The problem is: is there today a residual judicial power to declare new law, and, if so, how wide is this power?

10. The 'principle of legality': *Nullum crimen sine lege*

(a) This fundamental principle (no crime except in accordance with the law) is implied in many judgments. It is illustrated in the words of Stephen LJ, in considering whether a certain act (the burning of a corpse) might be declared a criminal offence in the absence of a statutory basis (*see R.* v. *Price* (1884)):

> 'Before I could hold that it must be a misdemeanour . . . I must be satisfied . . . that it is, on plain, undeniable grounds, highly mischievous or grossly scandalous . . . but I cannot take even the first step . . . *The great leading rule of criminal law is that nothing is a crime unless it is plainly forbidden by law.* This rule is no doubt subject to exceptions, but they are rare, narrow, and to be admitted with the greatest reluctance and only upon the strongest reasons. '

> (Note *R.* v. *Horseferry Road Magistrates' Court, ex p. IBA* (1986): when Parliament wishes to create criminal liability it almost invariably does so expressly.)

(b) It has been suggested that the 'principle of legality' necessitates recognition of other, allied, principles: non-retroactivity, maximum certainty, and the precise, strict construction by the courts of penal statutes. The rules of the criminal law should be, in the words of Raz (*The Authority of Law*, 1979), 'fixed, knowable and certain'.

11. The basis of the creation and extension of offences at common law

In 1616, the Court of King's Bench declared:

> 'To this court belongs authority, not only to correct errors in judicial proceedings, but other errors and misdemeanours extrajudicial, tending to the breach of the peace or oppression of subjects. '

In *Jones* v. *Randall* (1744) Lord Mansfield stated: 'Whatever is *contra bonos mores et decorum*, the principles of our law prohibit, and the King's court, as the general censor and guardian of the public manners, is bound to restrain and punish.' In *R.* v. *Higgins* (1801), Lawrence J stated: 'All offences of a public nature, that is, all such acts or attempts as tend to the prejudice of the community are indictable.' (Note the Justices of the Peace Act 1361, allowing for the binding over of persons to be of good behaviour if their conduct is *contra bonos mores* (contrary to a good way of life): *see Hughes* v. *Holley* (1987).)

12. Judicial law-making in the criminal law.

The 'declaratory theory' suggests that the judge's task involves *declaring*, or interpreting, the law; but he may not *make* it. The judge 'throws off the wrappings, so that what is concealed in the body of the common law is exposed to view'. The later 'creative theory' (formulated by Bentham) indicates that judges do much more than 'declare' the law; in effect, they *produce* it, just as Parliament does.

(a) In *R.* v. *Manley* (1933), X alleged falsely that she had been robbed. Police wasted their time in an investigation and she was convicted of effecting a 'public mischief'. She appealed on the ground that no such offence was known to law. (*See* now the Criminal Law Act 1967, s. 5(2).) Her appeal was *dismissed*; the Court of Appeal held that there *was* a misdemeanour of committing an act tending to the public mischief, and X's acts constituted such an offence. Following much criticism of the judgment, Lord Goddard stated in *R.* v. *Newland* (1954), that the safe course was not to follow *R.* v. *Manley*. 'It is surely now the province of the legislature and not of the judiciary to create new offences.'

(b) *Advantages* of judicial law-making have been said to include: the possibility of a swift development of law so as to take into account changing social attitudes and conditions; the possibility of doing justice in individual cases. *Disadvantages* are said to include: the by-passing of the democratic processes of Parliament; the conscious or unconscious reflection in a decision of a judge's personal 'hidden agenda'. Critics of judicial law-making include those who view the wide, clear and precise statement of the criminal law as being of greater significance than 'the *ad hoc* proscription of particular abuses'.

13. The position today

The decision in *Shaw* v. *DPP* (1962) (*see* **22**) suggests that the courts retain a very wide power to conserve the 'moral welfare' of the state against conduct which might be considered as intrinsically criminal. Note also *Knuller (Publishing)* v. *DPP* (1973) at **22** below.

(a) In *DPP* v. *Withers* (1975), the House of Lords stated clearly that there is no separate class of criminal conspiracy called 'conspiracy to effect a public mischief', although conduct already recognised by the law as criminal may be so described. '*The judges have no power to create new offences': per* Viscount Dilhorne.

(b) Nevertheless, 'judicial creativity', particularly the judges' power to modify the scope and pattern of existing offences, remains. See, for example, *R.* v. *Soul* (1980), in which it was held, on a charge of conspiracy to commit a public nuisance (within the Criminal Law Act 1977, s. 1(1)), that the prosecution need prove only that the danger to the public was 'potential' rather than 'actual'. (The case concerned a conspiracy to effect the escape of a Broadmoor patient.) Note the comments of Lord Scarman in *DPP for Northern Ireland* v. *Maxwell* (1978), concerning a decision of the Court of Criminal Appeal in Northern Ireland: 'I accept it as good judge-made law in a field where there is no statute to offer guidance.'

(c) May the phrase 'judicial law-making' (and its implications) be applied correctly to recent decisions of the House of Lords, such as *R.* v. *R.* (1992) in which it was declared that there is no marital rape immunity (*see* 13: **8**), and *R.* v. *Gomez* (1993), in which it was held that, for the purposes of the Theft Act 1968 (*see* 14:**9**), an act done with consent can constitute an 'appropriation'? Have the Lords, in these cases, 'made' new law?

(d) It may be that the principal function of a judge should be 'the disinterested application of the known law', but, as Lord Radcliffe has noted, before the law can be applied it has to be interpreted, and interpretation is itself a 'creative activity'.

The definition of a crime

14. The popular concept
A typical general dictionary definition of 'crime' is 'any act of wickedness or sin'. In everyday use, the word often carries overtones of immorality and wrongdoing. The links between religious morality and the criminal law have been very strong; common lawyers accepted that a crime was, *in essence*, an offence against morality, manifesting itself in the violation of a legally-protected interest.

But the popular definition of a crime carries its own difficulties; thus, while murder and robbery are condemned as obvious examples of criminal conduct which is clearly injurious to the public welfare, there is disagreement on the 'criminal nature' of, say, failure to purchase a licence for a television receiver; yet this omission is a criminal offence. (It is significant that, from time to time, popular demands lead to legislation withdrawing certain categories of conduct from the ambit of the criminal law: *see*, for example, the Sexual Offences Act 1967, s. 1 (under 13:**24**), which decriminalises certain homosexual activities.)

15. The difficulty of definition
The popular concept of crime, as noted above, lacks precision; terms such as 'sin', 'wrong-doing', can have no place in the terminology of the criminal law for that very reason.

(a) Some jurists, influenced by contemporary developments in the study of linguistics, draw attention to the difficulty of definition in general. Hart writes of 'the cardinal principle that legal words can only be elucidated by considering the conditions under which statements in which they have their characteristic use are true'. Thus, an appropriate definition of 'crime' will emerge from a consideration of 'whole sentences' in which the word plays its 'characteristic role'.

(b) An acceptable definition of a crime must cover a variety of seemingly disparate acts or omissions: treason, burglary, falsifying an income tax return, publishing an obscene article. Is it possible for one definition to embrace the *essence* of these and many other widely differing acts and omissions?

(c) Is it possible to avoid circularity in definition? Thus, statements such as, 'a crime is an offence against the criminal law', or 'a crime is an offence for which the law awards punishment' (*per* Littledale J in *Mann* v. *Owen* (1829)) are tautologous. Note, similarly, Jescheck's definition of a crime as: 'the intentional commission of an act usually deemed socially harmful or dangerous and specifically defined, prohibited and punishable under the criminal law.' But can circularity be avoided, save by a definition in highly abstract terms?

16. Some definitions of 'a crime'
A few of the many definitions which have been put forward from time to time are given below.

(a) 'A violation of the public rights and duties due to the whole community considered as a community' (Blackstone).

(b) 'A wrongful act of such a kind that the state deems it necessary, in the interests of the public, to repress it; for its repetition would be harmful to the community as a whole' (Odgers).

(c) 'Wrongs whose sanction is punitive and is no way remissible by any private person, but is remissible by the Crown alone if remissible at all' (Kenny).

(d) 'Any act done in violation of those duties which an individual owes to the community, and for the breach of which the law has provided that the offender shall make satisfaction to the public' (Bell).

(e) The House of Lords, in *Board of Trade* v. *Owen* (1957), adopted as a correct definition of a crime that given in Halsbury's *Laws of England*: 'A crime is an unlawful act or default which is an offence against the public and renders the person guilty of the act liable to legal punishment.'

17. Some more recent definitions
The search for a precise definition continues to exercise legal writers, and recent definitions include the following:

(a) 'Any undesirable act which the state finds it most convenient to correct by the institution of proceedings for the infliction of a penalty, instead of leaving the remedy to the discretion of some injured person' (Keeton).

(b) 'A legal wrong that can be followed by criminal proceedings which may result in punishment' (Williams).

(c) 'Any behaviour punished at public expense and through the criminal process' (Friedman).

(d) 'Conduct which, if duly shown to have taken place, will incur a formal and solemn pronouncement of the moral condemnation of the community' (Hart).

A comment in *Proprietary Articles Trade Association v. A. -G. for Canada* (1931) is appropriate at this point: 'The criminal quality of an act cannot be discerned by intuition; nor can it be discovered by reference to any standard but one: *is the act prohibited with penal consequences?*': *per* Lord Atkin.

18. A working definition

For the purpose of this text the following definition is presented for consideration: *a crime is any state of affairs ensuing directly from an act or omission resulting from human conduct which is considered in itself or in its outcome to be harmful and which the state wishes to prevent, which renders the person responsible liable to some kind of punishment, generally of a stigmatic nature, as the result of proceedings which are usually initiated on behalf of the state and which are designed to ascertain the nature, the extent and the legal consequence of that person's responsibility.*

(It is suggested that this definition be kept in mind throughout the reading of this text.)

Criminal law and social change

19. Social and legal evolution

Criminal law emerges in society at a relatively late stage of its development. It evolves as that society evolves, so that, in a sense, it mirrors social change. Developments in social attitudes towards liability for an offence, and towards the characteristics and extent of punishment for the crimes, are reflected in legislation. Thus, the introduction of the defence of diminished responsibility (*see* 9:**34**), the Murder (Abolition of Death Penalty) Act 1965 and the Abortion Act 1967 (*see* 11:**7**), exemplify society's changing attitudes towards certain controversial aspects of conduct.

Typical examples of recent social pressures for change may be discerned in the public concern which led to the prohibition of commercial dealings in human organs intended for transplant, and the restriction of transplants between persons not genetically related (*see* Human Organ Transplants Act 1989), and in the general desire to achieve a coherent and comprehensive approach to sentencing by the courts (*see* Criminal Justice Acts 1991 and 1993).

Developments in the economic and political basis of society also affect the scope and content of the criminal law: thus, the contemporary growth in road transport is reflected in the Road Traffic Acts 1972–91 and the creation of entirely new offences, such as dangerous driving; acute problems concerning the disposal of some of the by-products of industry resulted in the Clean Air Act 1993. Political development is mirrored in legislation such as the Public Order Acts 1936 and 1986, and the Race Relations Acts 1965 and 1976.

The evolution of social attitudes and economic and political changes affect the criminal law, but it may be argued that changes in society's *concepts of morality* have a more profound effect. (It has been said that our law reflects 'the community ethic' and that a fraction of it lags behind that ethic, while another projects ahead of it.) (*See Law and Morals* by S. Lee (OUP, 1986).)

20. Morality and criminal law

Concepts of morality, generally derived from religious beliefs, and the substance of English criminal law are inextricably interlocked. ('It would not be correct to say that every moral obligation involves a legal duty; but every legal duty is founded on a moral obligation': *per* Lord Coleridge in *R. v. Instan* (1893).) In the development of our criminal law Christian ethics have played an important role from very early times. *See*, for example, the *Laws of Alfred* (*c*.890), in which a scriptural introduction commences with the Ten Commandments. Note Lord Denning's assertion (*The Changing Law*, 1953) that the common law has been moulded by judges who have been brought up in the Christian faith, and who, consciously or unconsciously, have been guided in the administration of justice by the precepts of religion. Consider, for example, the statement of Lord Coleridge CJ, in *R. v. Dudley and Stephens* (1884) (*see* 6:**11**), in which, in rejecting the concept of 'any absolute and unqualified necessity to preserve one's life', he affirms: 'It is enough in a Christian country to remind ourselves of the Great Example which we profess to follow.'

Changes in the interpretation of religious principles and the modification of their ethical scope have often stimulated shifts in social and legislative attitudes towards the perception of what is, or is not, 'criminal conduct'. Thus: incest became a statutory offence only in 1908; suicide ceased to be a crime in 1961; some homosexual conduct, which at one time carried the dire penalties considered appropriate to the commission of *crimen innominatum* ('the nameless crime'), is no longer a crime in certain circumstances (*see* 13:**24**).

21. Criminal law and the 'moral sentiment of the community'

The *Wolfenden Report 1957*, which recommended changes in the law concerning homosexual behaviour, was followed by a public debate which touched on the fundamental relationship of the criminal law and morality. The Report saw the function of the criminal law, thus: 'To preserve public order and decency, to protect the citizen from what is offensive or injurious, and to provide sufficient safeguards against exploitation and corruption of others, particularly those who are specially vulnerable . . .' Further, the Report emphasised: 'It is not the function of the law to intervene in the private lives of citizens, or to seek to enforce any particular pattern of behaviour, further than is necessary to carry out the purposes we have outlined.'

(a) Lord Devlin (1905–92), who opposed the general philosophy of the Report, argued that the State has a claim to legislate on matters of morals *when it has a need to preserve itself.*

> 'A recognised morality is as necessary to society's existence as a recognised government . . . and although a particular act of immorality may not harm or endanger or corrupt others, for we must not view conduct in isolation from its effect on the moral code . . . it might threaten one of the great moral principles on which society is based. . . . In this sense the breach is an offence against society as a whole . . . this is why the suppression of vice is as much the law's business as the suppression of subversive activities.'

(b) The jurist, Professor HLA Hart (1907–92), supported the findings of the Report.

> 'No doubt we would all agree that a consensus of moral opinion on certain matters is essential if society is to be worth living in. Laws against murder, theft, and much else would be of little use if they were not supported by a widely diffused conviction that what these laws forbid is also immoral. So much is obvious. But it does not follow that everything to which the moral vetoes of accepted morality attach is of equal importance to society; nor is there the slightest reason for thinking of morality as a seamless web: one which will fall to pieces carrying society with it, unless all its emphatic vetoes are enforced by law.'

(c) Lord Devlin was reminded by some jurists of the warning of Spinoza: 'He who tries to fix and determine everything by law will inflame rather than correct the vices of the world.' Gross noted: 'Whenever the public force has been used to give teeth to morality, and the State has become an avenging angel bent on punishing moral wrongs, the State has done things in the name of morality that turn out to be far more serious than the wrongs that prompted them.' Hart was urged by critics to recall Holmes' warning that a sound body of law must correspond with the community's actual feelings and demands, whether right or wrong, and to remember that legal and moral rules 'are in symbiotic relation – people learn what is moral by observing what other people tend to enforce'. The debate continues.

22. The courts and public morals: *Shaw* v. *DPP* (1962)

In recent years there has been further development in the position of the courts as 'guardians of society's morals' against whatever is *contra bonos mores et decorum*, as exemplified by the much-criticised judgment of the House of Lords in *Shaw* v. *DPP* (1962).

(a) *The facts.* X was charged with, *inter alia*, a conspiracy to corrupt public morals by publishing an obscene article, i.e. a magazine (*The Ladies' Directory*), which listed names, addresses and other information concerning prostitutes. X's conviction was upheld in the Court of Criminal Appeal and the House of Lords.

(b) *The judgment. Per* Lord Simonds, in the House of Lords:

> 'In the sphere of criminal law I entertain no doubt that there remains in the courts of law a residual power to enforce the supreme and fundamental purpose of the law, to conserve not only the safety and order but also the moral welfare of the state, and that it is their duty to guard it against attacks which may be the more insidious because they are novel and unprepared for.'

(c) *The opposite approach. Per* Lord Reid: 'Notoriously there are wide differences of opinion today on how far the law ought to punish immoral acts which are not done in the face of the public. Some think the law already goes too far, some that it does not go far enough. Parliament is the proper place, and, I am firmly of opinion, the only proper place, to settle that.'

Shaw v. *DPP* has been interpreted as supporting those who argue that the courts have a continuing fundamental duty to enforce moral standards through the criminal law. In *Knuller* (*Publishing*) v. *DPP* (1973) (concerning the publication of advertisements in a magazine inviting readers to meet advertisers for purposes of homosexual activity), it was held that the decision in *Shaw* v. *DPP* must still be applied, and that an offence of conspiring to corrupt public morals can be committed by the encouraging of conduct which, although in itself not illegal (i.e. in this case certain homosexual practices), might be calculated to result in corruption of that kind. *Per curiam*: the courts have no general or residual power at common law to create such offences, and *Shaw* v. *DPP* is not to be taken as affirming or supporting such a doctrine. 'What the courts can and should do (as was truly laid down in *Shaw*) is to recognise the applicability of established offences to new circumstances to which they are relevant': *per* Lord Simon.

> NOTE: An attitude common to many American jurists is encapsulated in the following extract from the Tentative Draft No. 4, relating to the American Model Penal Code: 'The Code does not attempt to use the power of the state to enforce purely moral or religious standards. We deem it inappropriate for the government to attempt to control behaviour that has no substantial significance except as to the morality of the actor. Such matters are best left to religious, educational and other social influences. Apart from the question of constitutionality which might be raised against legislation avowedly commanding adherence to a particular religious or moral tenet, it must be recognised, as a practical matter, that in a heterogeneous community such as ours, different individuals and groups have widely divergent views of the seriousness of various moral derelictions'. (See, in this context, 'The Nature of Crime and Punishment' in *The Nature and Process of Law*, edited by Patricia Smith (OUP, 1993).)

The classification of criminal offences

23. General

Criminal offences may be classified in several ways. The classifications outlined below are:

(a) *treasons, felonies and misdemeanours* (now of historical interest only): *see* **24**;

(b) *indictable and summary offences* (essentially a procedural classification): *see* **25**;

(c) *offences triable only on indictment, triable only summarily, and triable either way* (related to modes of trial): *see* **26**;

(d) *arrestable and non-arrestable offences*: *see* **27**.

Classification by subject matter (as in **2** above) has no authoritative or other significance; it does no more than provide a convenient division of topics. Classification by source (e.g. common law and statutory crimes) is no longer important.

24. Treasons, felonies and misdemeanours

This old common law classification is now of historical interest only, but is included here so that the terminology of pre-1968 cases may be understood.

(a) *The position before 1967.* All offences were felonies or misdemeanours. (Treason, although technically a felony, was in a separate category.) Since the Treason Act 1945, procedural differences between trials for treason and felony have disappeared (but note **(c)** below).

(*i*) A *felony* was an offence which had been made such by statute, or which, at common law, carried on conviction the penalties of death and forfeiture of property. (Forfeiture was abolished by the Forfeiture Act 1870; the death penalty was abolished in almost all cases after 1827, and exists today only in some cases of piracy and treason.)

(*ii*) All the other offences were *misdemeanours*.

(b) *The position following the Criminal Law Act 1967, s. 1.* 'All distinctions between felony and misdemeanour are hereby abolished': s. 1(1). 'On all matters on which a distinction has previously been made between felony and misdemeanour, including mode of trial, the law and practice in relation to all offences . . . shall be the law and practice applicable at the commencement of this Act in relation to misdemeanour': s. 1(2).

(c) *Treason.* In Part I of the 1967 Act 'references to felony shall not be taken as including treason; but the procedure on trials for treason or misprision of treason shall be the same as the procedure as altered by this Act on trials for murder': s. 12(6). (This makes it possible, therefore, to classify crimes as 'treasons and other offences'.)

25. Indictable and summary offences

This division is of a procedural type.

(a) *Indictable offences.* An indictment is a written accusation of one or more persons of a crime, made at the suit of the Sovereign. Indictable offences are the more serious crimes (eg murder, theft, perjury), the trial of which takes place in the Crown Court. 'An "indictable offence" without any qualifying context can mean nothing else but an offence in respect of which an indictment would lie . . . it is none the less "indictable" because, if the prosecution chose, it could proceed in respect of it summarily. . . . The measure of gravity is to be sought, in my opinion, in what can happen to persons guilty of that class of offence, not what does happen': *per* Asquith LJ in *Hastings Glassworks* v. *Kalson* (1949).

(b) *Summary* (or petty) *offences.* Summary offences are those which must be tried summarily, i.e. before a magistrates' court, where there is no jury.

26. Offences triable only on indictment, summarily, or either way

The Magistrates' Courts Act 1980, ss. 17–28, set out details of this classification which is based on modes of trial.

(a) *Offences triable only on indictment.* This category refers to the more serious offences, e.g. murder, manslaughter, rape, robbery, blackmail, causing grievous bodily harm with intent. Such offences usually necessitate committal proceedings followed by a trial in the Crown Court by judge and jury.

(b) *Offences triable only summarily.* Such offences are designated by statute (as where it is enacted that an offence is punishable on summary conviction). *See* e.g. the Criminal Law Act 1977, s. 15 and Sch. 1, the Magistrates' Courts Act 1980, s. 22 and the Criminal Justice Act 1988, ss. 37, 38. Note that magistrates have exclusive jurisdiction in summary trials.

(c) *Offences triable either way. See* the Magistrates' Courts Act 1980, s. 17 and Sch. 1. Offences of this nature include common assault, bigamy, most indictable offences under the Theft Act 1968. The accused may opt for trial on indictment or summarily. The court can insist on trial on indictment; it may not impose a summary trial where the accused objects. *See* the 1980 Act, ss. 18, 19. Under s. 25, the court has the power to change from summary trial to committal proceedings and vice versa. *See* also *Practice Note: National Mode of Trial Guideline* (1991) 92 Cr. App. R. 142.

27. Arrestable and non-arrestable offences

By the Criminal Law Act 1967, s. 2(1), a new class of offence was created – the 'arrestable offence' – for which the sentence is fixed by law or for which a person (not previously convicted) may under or by virtue of any enactment be sentenced to imprisonment for a term of five years, and any attempt to commit such an offence. 'Non-arrestable offences' were offences other than those referred to in s. 2(1). This section of the 1967 Act was repealed by the Police and Criminal Evidence Act 1984, Sch. 7. Part III of the 1984 Act now states the law.

(a) An 'arrestable offence' under the 1984 Act, s. 24, means one in which the sentence is fixed by law (murder, treason, piracy with violence), one for which a person of 21 or over (not previously convicted) may be sentenced to imprisonment for a term of five years (or might be so sentenced but for the restrictions under the Magistrates' Courts Act 1980, s. 33, or one listed in the 1984 Act, s. 24(2) (such as an offence under the Sexual Offences Act 1956, ss. 14, 22, 33, or under the Theft Act 1968, s. 2(1)).

(b) The 1984 Act introduces a new category of 'arrestable offence' – the 'serious arrestable offence'.

  (*i*) The following arrestable offences are always 'serious' (*see* s. 116): offences (whether at common law or under any enactment) specified in the 1984 Act, Sch. 5, Part I (including, e.g., treason, murder, manslaughter, rape, carrying firearms with criminal intent (under the Firearms Act 1968, s. 18)); offences under an enactment specified in the 1984 Act, Sch.5, Part II (e.g. under the Sexual Offences Act 1956, s. 13, the Aviation Security Act 1982, s. 80); offences the commission of which is intended to lead, or has led, to certain consequences specified in the 1984 Act, s. 116(6), including, e.g., serious harm to state security, serious interference with the administration of justice or the investigation of offences, death or serious injury to any person. (*ii*) Some police powers under the 1984 Act may be exercised only if there are reasonable grounds to believe that the offence in question is a 'serious arrestable offence', e.g., the use of road checks (s. 4), delay in permitting access to a legal adviser (s. 58). (*See also* the Criminal Justice Act 1988, s. 99(3).)

NOTE: See the Criminal Justice Act 1993, s. 1, for a division of offences essentially related to the jurisdiction of the courts.

Codification and the Draft Criminal Code

28. Essence of codification
Codification involves a systematic collection in comprehensive, statutory form of the laws, or a substantial part of the laws, of a state. It seeks to produce written general principles from which specific deductions may be made. Attempts to codify English criminal law have 'a long but chequered history'. Note, for example, the code formulated by Sir James Stephen in 1879, which failed to be adopted when introduced into Parliament as the Indictable Offences Bill (but which became the model for some colonial legal systems, e.g. in New Zealand). The drive to codification of the criminal law continues. It is based on dissatisfaction with the unsystematic, uncertain and highly complex nature of the existing law and the desire to produce a compact, coherent and comprehensible system.

29. Advantages and disadvantages of codification
For an outline, *see 'The Case for a Criminal Code'* in Law Comm. No. 177, Vol. 1, Part 2.

(a) *Advantages.* A criminal code, it is claimed, will be accessible to all: its logical, systematic arrangement will ensure this. It will replace the archaic verbiage of the old common law with a precise vocabulary attuned to contemporary society and will be more comprehensible than the present difficult amalgam of statute, common law and regulations. In place of the equivocal, often-contradictory nature of some areas of the criminal law will be consistency and relative certainty. Flexibility is guaranteed, since judges will continue to interpret the code, and case law will continue to flourish; in any event, amendment of the statutory code is always possible. But the code will be supreme and will not lend itself to decisive alteration against the declared intentions of Parliament, in the guise of mere interpretation.
(b) *Disadvantages.* A criminal code, it is claimed, will, by its very character and format, be rigid and fundamentally immutable. It will be no more

'accessible to all' than is the present system. By its very nature and design a criminal code must reduce the creative role of the courts and lead to a loss of the virtues of the case system. The complexities of a changing society cannot be mirrored accurately in its content; at best, no more than an oversimplified pattern will be reflected. A code lends itself to 'endless embroidery, commentary and explanation, with resulting obscurity.' The immediate aftermath of its introduction is likely to involve, it is suggested, much confusion, many difficulties in interpretation, and a considerable growth in the number of appeals. Above all, perhaps, a code involves a dramatic break with the past, and the history of English law suggests that such breaks tend to be rejected.

30. Draft Criminal Code: Law Comm. 177 (1985)
The Law Commission formulated in 1968 the objective of a comprehensive examination of the criminal law with a view to its codification. A report was published in 1985, consisting of the draft of a Criminal Code Bill and a commentary.

(a) The Law Commission recommended that *there should be a criminal code* for England and Wales. The Draft Bill comprises 220 sections and 10 Schedules. It is divided into two parts, General Principles and Specific Offences (including offences against the person; sexual offences; theft, fraud and related offences; other offences relating to property; and offences against public peace and safety).

(b) The Code is far-reaching in its proposals and their implications.

(*i*) It gives statutory form to a number of common law offences, e.g. murder, manslaughter, kidnapping, false imprisonment (replaced by unlawful detention): *see* s. 4(1) and Sch. 8.

(*ii*) It re-defines with precision some statutory offences, e.g. handling: s. 172.

(*iii*) It attempts to deal with some difficult problems of terminology in the criminal law: *see* 2:**7(a)**.

(*iv*) It embodies in statutory form some fundamental common law principles as they relate to the criminal law. 'No offence shall be created except by, or under the authority of, an Act of Parliament': s. 3. (The Commentary on the Code points out (Vol. 2; **4.8**) that the existence of a power in the courts to create new offences, 'with the resulting uncertainty as to the scope of the criminal law, is incompatible with the fundamental aims of a criminal code.') Under s. 11, a person is not to be tried for an offence in respect of which he has formerly been convicted or in peril of conviction. The Commentary states (Vol. 2; 5.**24**): 'This substitutes a reasonably simple statutory statement for a mass of common law materials. '

Selected sections of the Draft Criminal Code Bill will be set out in the final paragraphs of some of the following chapters.

Progress test 1

1. Outline the general province of the criminal law.   **(1)**

2. What problems may emerge from the use of a highly-specialised vocabulary in the criminal law? **(3)**

3. Summarise the major sources of the criminal law.   **(4–7)**

4. 'Judicial law-making has no place in the criminal law.' Comment. **(9–13)**

5. Why is the defining of 'criminal law' a difficult process? **(14–16)**

6. Comment on the nature of the links between social evolution and the criminal law. **(19)**

7. In what sense is *Shaw* v. *DPP* (1962) of importance for the criminal law in general? **(22)**

8. Outline the principal advantages and disadvantages of a codified criminal law. **(29)**

2

Criminal responsibility (1): *actus reus*

General considerations

1. The problem of criminal responsibility
Assume that X's act or omission results in a state of affairs which the law seeks to prevent. Does criminal responsibility under the law *invariably* attach to X?

(a) Consider the following: X draws a pistol from his pocket, points it at Y and presses the trigger. Y is killed by a bullet fired from the pistol. It might seem, on these few facts, that X is responsible for the murder of Y and ought to be convicted of that crime.

(b) Consider, next, in conjunction with the facts above, the following sets of surrounding circumstances:

(*i*) X, intending only to frighten, and not to harm, Y, presses the trigger as the result of an involuntary action.

(*ii*) X genuinely believes that the pistol is not loaded, *or* that it will not fire, having been told incorrectly that the trigger mechanism is ineffective, *or* that the bullets are blanks.

(*iii*) X is a soldier on active service. Y is an enemy soldier attacking him.

(*iv*) X acts under the insane delusion that Y intends to harm him and that he (X) must shoot Y so as to prevent this.

The question of criminal responsibility (or, as it is also known, criminal liability) is often more complex than that posed by the few facts in (*a*) above. Lack of intent to kill, insanity, accident, may transform a seemingly simple event into sets of intricate circumstances, or consequences, which raise the complex problem of liability for a crime.

2. The problem further exemplified
The following cases illustrate further aspects of the problem of criminal responsibility:

(a) X, a mother, threw a piece of heavy metal at her child with the sole intention of frightening him. The metal struck and killed another child: *see R. v. Conner* (1835). X was found guilty of manslaughter.

(b) X was charged with 'being concerned in the management of premises used for the purpose of smoking cannabis'. X did not know, and had no means of knowing, that the smoking was taking place: *see Sweet* v. *Parsley* (1970). *See also* 3:**4**.

(c) X was charged with taking an unmarried girl under the age of sixteen out of the possession and against the will of her father, contrary to the Offences against the Person Act 1861, s. 55. X honestly believed that the girl was eighteen: *see R.* v. *Prince* (1875). *See also* 4:**4**; 13:**35**.

(d) X, a foreigner, was charged with committing a sexual offence on board a ship in an English port. He pleaded that the act was not considered an offence in his country and that he was ignorant of English law: *see R.* v. *Esop* (1836). X was convicted: ignorance of the law is no excuse. *See also* 6:**6**.

These cases will be considered later in their place; at this point it suffices to note that they illustrate some of the difficulties of attempting to attach criminal liability without a full understanding of the nature of the crime alleged, a consideration of whether all the elements of that crime were present, and a knowledge of other surrounding circumstances.

3. Matters to be considered
The following matters require consideration in relation to criminal liability:

(a)   the elements of a crime;
(b)   *actus reus* and *mens rea*;
(c)   strict and vicarious liability;
(d)   parties to a crime;
(e)   general defences to criminal responsibility.

The elements of a crime

4. General
'Every wrong is an act which is mischievous in the eye of the law – an act to which the law attributes harmful consequences': Salmond. In the early development of English law a person was generally liable for harm resulting from his conduct. The state of his mind (i.e. his 'moral blameworthiness') was rarely a relevant consideration in attaching liability. *Performance of the act alone which led to a prohibited event created liability; the presence or absence of criminal intent was usually disregarded.* Thus, X, who injured Y accidentally and without any negligence, would be held liable for the harm caused, as if he had *intended* that injury to Y. By the thirteenth century, influenced by the teachings of the Church, which drew attention

to, and emphasised, the importance of *the mental element in evil conduct,* the law came to recognise the significance of *criminal intention* and its role as an essential feature of many crimes.

5. *Actus non facit reum nisi mens sit rea* (an act does not itself constitute guilt unless the mind is guilty)

This maxim contains a cardinal doctrine of English criminal law: *see Fowler* v. *Padget* (1798); *Younghusband* v. *Luftig* (1949).

(a) The maxim draws attention to the two essential elements of a crime:
  (*i*) the physical element (the *actus reus*), i.e. the *conduct* (*see* **7** below) (the so-called 'condition of illegality');
  (*ii*) the mental element (the *mens rea*), i.e. the *condition of mind* (*see* Chap. 3) (the so-called 'condition of culpable intentionality').
(b) Some writers suggest a third element – absence of a valid defence, i.e. a defence which would reduce or negate a defendant's criminal liability.
(c) The practical effect of the doctrine is that if X is to be convicted of a crime, the prosecution must usually prove *beyond reasonable doubt* (*see Woolmington* v. *DPP* (1935)):
  (*i*) that as a result of X's *conduct* there has been created a *state of affairs* which the law desires to prevent, *and*
  (*ii*) that X's conduct was accompanied by a *certain condition of mind* (i.e. that the *actus reus* and *mens rea* coincided so as to constitute one forbidden 'event' in law and time).
(d) Coincidence of *actus reus* and *mens rea* in point of law was discussed by the House of Lords in *R.* v. *Taafe* (1984). The facts emerge from the certified question put by the Court of Appeal: 'When a defendant is charged with an offence, contrary to the Customs and Excise Management Act 1979, s. 170(2), of being knowingly concerned in the fraudulent evasion of the prohibition on the importation of a controlled drug, does the defendant commit the offence where he (a) imports prohibited drugs into the United Kingdom; (b) intends fraudulently to evade a prohibition on importation; but (c) mistakenly believes the goods to be money and not drugs; and (d) mistakenly believes that money is the subject of a prohibition against importation?'
  (*i*) In the Court of Appeal Lord Lane construed the relevant subsection as creating an offence in which an essential ingredient was a guilty mind. To be 'knowingly concerned' meant, in his judgment, not only the existence of a smuggling operation but also that the substance being smuggled into the country was one the importation of which was prohibited by statute. Respondent thought he was concerned in the smuggling of currency; but the importation of currency was not subject to prohibition. Respondent's mistake of law

did not convert the importation of currency into a criminal offence; importing currency was what it had to be assumed that respondent believed he was doing.

(*ii*) *Per* Lord Scarman: 'I agree with Lord Lane's construction of s. 170(2) of the 1979 Act; and the principle that a man must be judged on the facts as he believes them to be is an accepted principle of the criminal law when the state of a man's mind and his knowledge are ingredients of the offence with which he is charged.'

(e) The importance of a temporal coincidence of *actus reus* and *mens rea* is discussed in the cases mentioned below.

(*i*) In *Fagan* v. *MPC* (1969), X accidentally drove his car on to Y's foot; he then deliberately left it there for a few minutes. X was charged with assault (*see* Chap. 12) and claimed that there was no coincidence of act and intent. It was held that X's conduct in driving the car on to Y's foot and allowing it to remain there constituted a continuing act; the assault was committed when X decided to leave the car on Y's foot. James J stated: 'It is not necessary that *mens rea* should be present at the inception of the *actus reus*; it can be imposed on an existing act. On the other hand, the subsequent inception of *mens rea* cannot convert an act which has been completed without *mens rea* into an assault.'

(*ii*) In *Thabo Meli* v. *R.* (1954), X had planned to kill Y in a hut and then to throw his body over a cliff so as to suggest accidental death. X beat Y over his head while he was in the hut and then rolled him over a cliff, believing him to be dead. Medical evidence established that, in fact, Y died from exposure, having been left at the bottom of the cliff. X argued that the first act (beating Y) had been accompanied by *mens rea*, but the act had not caused Y's death; the second act (rolling Y off the cliff top) had not been accompanied by *mens rea* since X believed Y to be already dead. The Privy Council *rejected* X's appeal against conviction of murder; X's argument could not be sustained. *Per* Lord Reid: 'It appears to their Lordships impossible to divide up what was really one series of acts in this way. There is no doubt that the accused set out to do all these acts in order to advance their plans, and as part of their plans; and it is too much refined a ground of judgment to say that, because they were at a misapprehension at one stage and thought that their guilty purpose was achieved before it was achieved, therefore they are to escape the penalties of the law.'

(*iii*) In *R.* v. *Lebrun* (1992), X argued with his wife, Y, in the street in the early morning and struck her unlawfully although not intending to do her really serious harm. Y fell unconscious and X, in an attempt to conceal the assault moved her. Y slipped from X's grasp and struck her head on the pavement, sustaining a fatal injury. X was charged with murder and convicted of manslaughter. He appealed against his conviction. *Per* Lord Lane, in dismissing the appeal: 'It seems to us that where the unlawful application of force and the eventual act causing death are parts of the same sequence of events, the same transaction, the fact that there is an appreciable interval of time between the two does not serve to exonerate the defendant from liability. That is certainly so where the appellant's subsequent actions which caused death, after the initial unlawful blow, are designed to conceal his commission of the original unlawful assault. . . . In short, in circumstances such as the present . . . the act which causes death and the necessary mental state to constitute manslaughter need not coincide in point of time.'

(f) Thus, if X is to be convicted of theft (*see* 14:1), the prosecution must prove *beyond reasonable doubt* that he appropriated property belonging to Y *and* that the appropriation had been carried out by X dishonestly *and* with the intention of permanently depriving Y of that property: *see* the Theft Act 1968, s. 1(1). If X is to be convicted of the rape of Y (*see* 13:3), the prosecution must prove *beyond reasonable doubt* that X had unlawful sexual intercourse with a female, Y, without Y's consent. (These so-called 'external features' of the offence constitute the *actus reus* of rape.) *Further*, the prosecution must show (*see* 13:3) that, at the time of the alleged act, X *either* knew that Y was not consenting, *or* that he was reckless as to whether she was or was not consenting. (These so-called 'internal features' of the offence constitute the requisite *mens rea* of rape.)

(g) The vital importance of the doctrine has been stated thus:

'It is of the utmost importance for the protection of the liberty of the subject that a court should always bear in mind that, unless a statute, either clearly or by necessary implication, rules out *mens rea* as a constituent part of a crime, the court should not find a man guilty of an offence against the criminal law unless he has a guilty mind': *per* Lord Goddard CJ in *Brend* v. *Wood* (1946).

6. Proof 'beyond reasonable doubt'

In a *criminal case* the proper standard of proof is generally proof *beyond reasonable doubt*: *see R.* v. *Winsor* (1865); *Woolmington* v. *DPP* (1935).

(a) 'The degree is well settled. It need not reach certainty, but it must carry a high degree of probability. Proof beyond a reasonable doubt does not mean proof beyond the shadow of a doubt. The law would fail to protect the community if it admitted fanciful possibilities to deflect the course of justice. If the evidence is so strong against a man as to leave only a remote possibility in his favour, which can be dismissed with the sentence "of course it is possible but not in the least probable", the case is proved beyond reasonable doubt, but nothing short of that will suffice': *per* Denning J in *Miller* v. *Ministry of Pensions* (1947).

(b) 'One would be on safe ground if one said in a criminal case to the jury: "You must be satisfied beyond reasonable doubt", and one could also say, "You, the jury, must be completely satisfied", or better still, "You must feel sure of the prisoner's guilt" ': *per* Lord Goddard in *R.* v. *Hepworth and Fearnley* (1955).

(c) No precise formula in a direction to the jury is necessary. It will suffice that the direction is in accordance with the principle stated in *Walters* v. *R.* (1969) by Lord Diplock: 'If the jury are made to understand that they have to be satisfied and must not return a verdict against the defendant unless they feel sure, and that the onus is all the time on the prosecution and not on the defence, then whether the judge uses one form of language or another is neither here nor there.'

(d) In the unusual event of a *civil claim* for damages for *murder*, the standard of proof should be the criminal one because no one should be declared guilty of murder unless a tribunal was sure that there was no other sensible conclusion: *see Halford* v. *Brookes and Another* (1992).

> NOTE: Where the burden of proof falls *on the accused*, it may be satisfied by proof on a *balance of probabilities*; it does *not* require proof beyond reasonable doubt. (For proof on a balance of probabilities, *see* the statement of Denning J in *Miller* v. *Ministry of Pensions* (1947): 'If the evidence is such that the tribunal can say: "We think it more probable than not", the burden is discharged, but, if the probabilities are equal, it is not.') *See R.* v. *Carr-Briant* (1943); *R.* v. *Patterson* (1962). For reversal of burden of proof, *see DPP* v. *Williams* (1989). For situations in which the burden of proof lies on the accused, *see* e.g.: the need for the defence to prove (where insanity is pleaded) that at the time of commission of the alleged offence, the accused was insane within the M'Naghten Rules (*see* 6:**28**); the defence of diminished responsibility to a charge of murder under the Homicide Act 1957 (*see* 9:**34**); the defence of lawful authority or reasonable excuse to a charge of carrying an offensive weapon in a public place (*see* the Prevention of Crime Act 1953, s. 1(1), at 12:3**(1)**). *See also* the Police and Criminal Evidence Act 1984, s. 74(1)–(3); the Magistrates' Courts Act 1980, s. 101.

Actus reus

7. Meaning of the phrase

Actus reus refers not only to an 'act' in the usual restricted sense of that term; it has a much wider meaning. It involves the *conduct* of the accused person, its *results* and those relevant surrounding circumstances and consequences or *states of affairs*, i.e. the 'external elements', which are included in the definition of the offence and which must be proved. The *actus reus* comprises, therefore, *all the elements of the definition of the offence, save those which concern the condition of mind of the accused*. It is *not merely conduct;* it is the *result of conduct,* and, as such, should be differentiated from the conduct which brought about the result. (In Turner's words: 'The crime is constituted *by the event,* and not by the activity . . . which caused the event.') In essence, therefore, *the* actus reus *is a 'deed', the result of human conduct, which, if accompanied by* mens rea, *is contrary to the law.*

(a)   Consider the following summary, given in the Commentary on the Draft Criminal Code Bill (Vol. 2, para 7.4): 'A person may commit an offence by doing something; or (less often) by omitting to do something. Or he may be guilty of an offence because a state of affairs arises, or because something occurs and he occupies a given position; examples are possession offences. . . . The definition of an offence commonly refers to circumstances that must exist if there is to be liability, or to a result that the person's act or omission must cause or fail to prevent, or to both.' *See,* further, **15** below.

(b)   Note, for example, the 'definition' of the common law offence of *false imprisonment,* at 12:23. The *actus reus* is constituted by X's unlawful infliction of bodily restraint on Y.

(c)   It will be for the prosecution to prove beyond reasonable doubt that X unlawfully restrained Y's freedom of movement from a particular place, that X's act was intentional, or reckless. Hence the prosecution, in establishing the *actus reus,* must show:

(i)   positive *conduct* on X's part (e.g. the intentional locking of a room which he knew Y to be occupying);

(ii)   certain *circumstances* (i.e. lack of a lawful basis for X's conduct);

(iii)   certain consequential *results* (i.e. Y was unlawfully prevented from moving from the room).

(d)   Should the prosecution be unable to show the existence of *all* the elements of the *actus reus,* then the offence has not been committed. If, for example, X is able to show that his reason for locking Y in the room was lawful – the event may have been related to X's lawful arrest of Y – there is no *actus reus* which can be used as the basis of a charge of false imprisonment.

(e)   Note the remarks of Lord Diplock in *R.* v. *Miller* (1983): 'It would be conducive to clarity of analysis of the ingredients of a crime . . . if we were . . . to think and speak about the conduct of the accused and his state of mind at the time of that conduct, instead of speaking of *actus reus* and *mens rea.'*

8.   Voluntary basis of the *actus reus*

In general, where the *actus reus* involves some *act* on the part of X, that conduct must usually have been willed by him. (*See* **10.**) (Note an early formulation of the essence of this matter: 'The only objects which can be called acts are consequences of volitions. A voluntary movement of my body, or a movement which follows a volition is an *act* . . . Volitions are desires of those bodily movements which immediately follow our desires of them': John Austin, 1862. Later jurists, such as Hart, emphasised the significance of man's *conscious control* of his actions: 'the controlling agency is not a desire for muscular movements but the mind of a man bent on some conscious action'.) *See R. v. Charlson* (1955); *Blayney* v. *Knight* (1975) – a person who accidentally set in motion another's motor car did not 'take it' within the meaning of the Theft Act 1968, s. 12(1) (*see* 16:**25**). But note the 'situation offences' at 14 below.

9. No *actus reus*, no crime
Proof of actus reus is essential; if this proof is impossible, then the crime cannot be shown to have been committed by the accused person.

(a) X seizes Y, intending, initially, sexual intercourse with her against her will. Y then consents *freely*, and intercourse follows. There is here no *actus reus* of rape: *see* the Sexual Offences Act 1956 and the Sexual Offences (Amendment) Act 1976, at 13:**3**. *See* 5(**d**) above.

(b) In *R. v. Deller* (1952), X told Y that his (X's) motor car was free from any mortgages and induced Y to purchase it. X believed that a document which he had previously executed had resulted in the car's being mortgaged to a finance house. X believed, therefore, that he was lying to Y. It was found later that the document was void in law and that, as a result, X had been (accidentally and dishonestly) telling the truth to Y. X's conviction on a charge of false pretences (*see* the Larceny Act 1916, s. 32) was quashed on appeal. He certainly had *mens rea*, but, since there was no *actus reus*, there was no crime.

(c) In *R. v. Runting* (1989), X, a newspaper photographer, persistently attempted to photograph Y during Y's trial. Y tried to prevent this and ran off, colliding with scaffolding. X was later found guilty of contempt of court (*see* Chap. 24). His appeal was allowed by the Court of Appeal which held that X's acts were *not of sufficient gravity to constitute a contempt*, so that the necessary *actus reus* had *not* been proved.

10. Causation
Where the *actus reus* of a crime includes specific consequences of conduct, it must be shown that those consequences have been *caused effectively* by the accused. In general, X will not be held to have caused a particular event unless it is possible to establish a sufficiently direct 'link' between X's conduct and that (prohibited) event.

Consider the following cases which illustrate, in ascending degrees of complexity, the problem of causation; in each case the question is: did X cause the death of Y, thus creating the *actus reus* of unlawful homicide? (*See* Chap. 9.)

(a) X, intending to kill Y unlawfully, moves towards him and deliberately shoots him. Y dies. Here there is no apparent problem of causation; the link between X's physical act and Y's death can be established without difficulty.

(b) X assaults Y who is riding a horse. Y, intending to escape, spurs the horse which rears in fright, throwing Y. Y dies. It was held, on these facts, that Y's death was caused by X: *see R. v. Hickman* (1831).

(c) X, intending to murder a child, Y, gives a bottle of poison to Y's nurse, stating that it is a medicine to be administered to Y. The nurse decides that Y does not need it and leaves the bottle on a shelf from which her daughter, aged five years, later takes it and administers it to Y. Y dies. A sufficiently direct link was established between X's conduct and Y's death, so that X was convicted of murder: *see R. v. Michael* (1840).

(d) X unlawfully wounds Y in a finger. Y refuses advice to have the finger amputated, lockjaw sets in and he dies a fortnight later. 'The real question is whether in the end the wound inflicted by the prisoner was the cause of death'; *per* Maule J. X was convicted of murder, a sufficiently direct connection having been traced between the wounding and Y's subsequent death; *see R. v. Holland* (1841).

11. The chain of causation and the *actus reus*

Proof of *actus reus* may be complicated by the existence of a chain of events (as in 10(c) and (d) above), making difficult the proof of the causal nature of that chain and a link between an act (or omission) and apparent consequences

(a) In general, where the event in question is not caused *solely* by the conduct of the accused, this will not necessarily exempt him from liability for that event:

(i) X, a colliery engineer, left his post, leaving in charge of the engine a boy who, to X's knowledge, was incompetent to control it. The boy failed to control the engine, as a result of which Y was killed. X was held guilty of manslaughter (*see* Chap. 10): *see R. v. Lowe* (1850).

(ii) X, the governor of a colony, was convicted of the murder of Y, who had been sentenced by X to an illegal flogging. Evidence was given which showed that Y had worsened his condition by drinking spirits in hospital: *see R. v. Wall* (1802). *Per* Macdonald LCB:

'. . . there is no apology for a man if he puts another in so dangerous and hazardous a situation by his treatment of him, that some degree of unskilfulness and mistaken treatment of himself may possibly accelerate the fatal catastrophe. One man is not at liberty to put another into such perilous circumstances as these, and to make it depend upon his own prudence, knowledge, skill or experience what may hurry on or complete that catastrophe, or on the other hand may render him service.'

(b) Where the cause of an event can be traced partly to X's conduct and partly to the conduct of another person, the court may hold, in certain circumstances, that X's conduct is *too remote or indirect* a cause for criminal responsibility to be attached to him. Note, however, the following decisions.

(*i*) X, in charge of a steam engine, stopped the engine and went away. In his absence an unauthorised person started up the engine, as a result of which Y was killed. X was charged with manslaughter and acquitted, the court holding that Y's death was 'the consequence not of the act of [X] but of the person who set the engine in motion after [X] had gone away': *see R. v. Hilton* (1838).

(*ii*) X stabbed Y, who died in hospital. X was convicted of murder. On appeal, further medical evidence established that Y's death was caused, not by the wound (which had almost healed), but by the administration in hospital of drugs to which Y was intolerant. X's conviction was quashed: *see R. v. Jordan* (1956). (The Court of Criminal Appeal stated in *R. v. Smith* (1959) (*see* (*iii*)) that *R. v. Jordan* was 'a very particular case depending upon its exact facts'.)

(*iii*) In a barrack room brawl, X unlawfully wounded Y. On the way to a medical reception station Y was dropped twice on the ground, and, on arriving at the station, he was given incorrect and 'thoroughly bad' treatment. Y died. X's appeal against his conviction on a charge of murder was rejected: *see R. v. Smith* (1959). *Per* Lord Parker CJ:

'It seems to the court that if at the time of death the original wound is still an operating cause and a substantial cause, then the death can properly be said to be the result of the wound, albeit that some other cause of death is also operating. Only if it can be said that the original wounding is merely the setting in which another cause operates can it be said that the death did not result from the wound.'

(*iv*) X stabbed Y, a Jehovah's Witness, who was taken to hospital where she refused a blood transfusion, which would have saved her life. X was acquitted of murder, but convicted of manslaughter on grounds of diminished responsibility (*see* 9:**34**). His appeal was dismissed on the grounds that it does not lie in the mouth of an assailant to say that his victim's religious views, which prevented the acceptance of certain types of medical treatment, were not reasonable; X had to take the victim 'as he found her', and this referred to her mind (i.e. her religious beliefs) as well as her body. X's stabbing was an operative cause of Y's death and 'the fact that Y refused to stop this end coming about did not break the causal correction between the act and death': *per* Lawton LJ in *R.* v. *Blaue* (1975).

(*v*) X struck Y on the head with a stone, causing severe brain damage. On admission to hospital, electro-encephalogram tests on Y proved negative, and the life-support system to which Y was attached was disconnected by the doctors. X was convicted of Y's murder and appealed on the ground of the judge having withdrawn the question of causation from the jury. The appeal was dismissed. There was no evidence on which the jury could conclude that the assailant did not cause Y's death: *R.* v. *Steel* (1981).

(*vi*) X shot Y in the arm and leg during an argument. Y was taken to hospital where he developed respiratory problems requiring a tracheotomy. Two months later he died in hospital following a complication arising from the tracheotomy. X was convicted of murder and his subsequent appeal was dismissed. The Court of Appeal held that it was sufficient for the jury to be told that they must be satisfied that X's acts need not be the sole or even the main cause of Y's death; it was sufficient that X's acts contributed *significantly* to that result. Even though negligence in Y's treatment may have been the immediate cause of death, the jury should not regard it as excluding the responsibility of X unless the negligent treatment was so independent of X's acts and in itself so potent in causing death that they regarded the contribution made by X's acts as *insignificant*: *R.* v. *Cheshire* (1991).

(*vii*) *See also R.* v. *Malcherek* (1981) at 9:**11**; *R.* v. *Mitchell* (1983) at 10:**6**; and *R.* v. *Pagett* (1983) at 9:**12**, in which Goff LJ stated: '. . . Generally speaking, causation is a question of fact for the jury . . . But that does not mean that there are no principles of law relating to causation, so that no directions on law are ever to be given to a jury on the question of causation. On the contrary, we have already pointed out one familiar direction which is given on causation, which is that the accused's act need not be the sole, or even the main, cause of the victim's death for his act to be held to have caused the death.' *See also R.* v. *Williams* (1992); *R.* v. *McKechnie* (1992).

Causation and the *actus reus* of unlawful homicide are considered further in 9:**10–12**.

12. *Actus reus* as the result of omission to act
There are circumstances in which an *actus reus* may stem from an omission to act (*see R.* v. *Dytham* (1979)). In general, the harmful effects of X's omission to act in given circumstances will result in criminal responsibility *only* where the law has imposed *a duty* on X to act in those circumstances. Thus, if X, who has no special relationship with Y, stands

by passively and watches Y drown in circumstances in which he could have saved him, then, no matter how morally reprehensible X's omission to act may be, no crime results from that omission. *See* 10:7; *R.* v. *Miller* (1983) at 19:9.

Under common law there were very few circumstances in which an omission to act was punishable. Note, eg, misprision of a felony, i.e. the concealment of knowledge of commission of a felony (now abolished by the Criminal Law Act 1967, although misprision of treason still exists).

Examples of the circumstances in which omission to act may create criminal responsibility are given below. (Such circumstances may arise from a duty imposed by statute, by contract, by office, or as the result of a special relationship, or conduct.)

(a) Parents are under a statutory duty to take care of their children and to provide them with food, clothing, and medical attention: *see R.* v. *Watson and Watson* (1959); Children and Young Persons Act 1933, s. 1(2); *R.* v. *Sheppard* (1981). (In this case, Lord Diplock explained the requirements for a conviction on a charge of wilful neglect of a child under s. 1 by stating that the jury must be satisfied that there was an *actus reus*, i.e., that the child did in fact need medical aid at the time at which the parent was charged with failing to provide it; *and* that there was *mens rea*, ie, either that the parent was aware at the time that the child's health might be at risk if it were not provided with medical aid, or that the parent's lack of awareness of this fact was the result of his not caring whether the child's health was at risk or not.)

(b) Where X undertakes (whether by contract or not) to look after Y, and Y is unable to look after himself properly (because, say, he is infirm), X is under a duty to take all reasonable steps to care for Y: *see R.* v. *Marriott* (1838); *R.* v. *Instan* (1893), in which X omitted to give food to a helpless invalid. 'There was a common law duty imposed upon the prisoner which she did not discharge.' *See also R.* v. *Stone* (1977) at 10:**13**.

(c) Where X conceals his knowledge of a treasonable offence committed by Y (*see* 23:**7**).

(d) Where X undertakes a duty upon the proper performance of which the safety of other persons may depend: *see R.* v. *Lowe* (1850) under **11**(*a*) above; *R.* v. *Pittwood* (1902), in which a railway crossing keeper omitted to close a gate, so that a person was killed when a train collided with a cart – the crossing keeper was held guilty of manslaughter, since he owed a duty of care to all users of the crossing.

(e) Under some statutes omission may be a crime, e.g. failure to stop in the event of a road accident: *see* the Road Traffic Act 1988, s. 170. *See also DPP* v. *Drury* (1989).

(f) Note the comments of Lord Diplock in *R.* v. *Miller* (1983) (*see* 19:9): 'I see no rational ground for excluding from conduct capable of giving rise to criminal liability conduct which consists of failure to take measures that lie within one's power to counteract a danger that one has oneself created, if at the time of such conduct one's state of mind is such as constitutes a necessary ingredient of the offence.' *See R. v. Ahmad* (1986).

(g) In *R. v. Dytham* (1979), X, a police officer, made no attempt to stop an attack on a person who was being beaten to death. He had driven away from the scene, saying that he was due to go off duty. He was charged with 'misconduct of an officer' and convicted. It was held on appeal that such an offence requires that the police officer's offence involved neglect which is wilful, not merely inadvertent, and culpable, that is without reasonable excuse or justification. The Court of Appeal, in *rejecting* X's appeal, cited with approval Stephen's statement (*Digest of the Criminal Law*, 9th edn): 'Every public officer commits a misdemeanour who wilfully neglects to perform any duty which he is bound either by common law or by statute to perform, provided that the discharge of such duty is not attended with greater danger than a man of ordinary firmness and activity may be expected to encounter.'

(h) In *R. v. Firth* (1990), X, a consultant, had avoided being billed for NHS hospital services by omitting to inform the hospital of the patients' private status. He was convicted under the Theft Act 1978, s. 2(1)(c). It was held that the offence of evasion of a liability by deception can be committed by *an act of commission or omission.*

13. The withdrawal of medical care leading to death

The problem of withdrawing medical care from a person in a persistent vegetative state was discussed by the House of Lords in *Airedale NHS Trust v. Bland* (1993) (a civil proceeding of much importance to the criminal law in that the Official Solicitor contended that the withdrawal of life support constituted a criminal offence).

(a) *The facts.* Following his injuries received in a crowd disaster, X (aged 21) remained in a persistent vegetative state after some three and a half years, resulting from hypoxic brain damage which had destroyed all the higher functions of his brain. The health authority responsible for X's care applied to the court for a declaration that all life-sustaining treatment be withdrawn from X, allowing him to end his life and die peacefully 'with the greatest dignity and the least pain, suffering and distress'. The President of the Family Division granted the declaration.

(b) *Court of Appeal.* The Official Solicitor appealed to the Court of Appeal. The President's decision was *affirmed*, and the Official Solicitor then appealed to the House of Lords.

(c) *House of Lords.* The appeal of the Official Solicitor was *dismissed. Per* Lord Goff:

(i) '. . . We are concerned with circumstances in which it may be lawful to withhold from a patient medical treatment or care by means of which his life may be prolonged. But here too there is no absolute rule that the patient's life must be prolonged by such treatment or care, if available, regardless of the circumstances. . .'

(*ii*) '. . . I am of the opinion that there is no absolute obligation upon the doctor who has the patient in his care to prolong his life, regardless of the circumstances. Indeed, it would be most startling, and could lead to the most adverse and cruel effects upon the patient if any such absolute rule were held to exist. . .'

(*iii*) '. . . But in the end, in a case such as the present, it is the futility of the treatment which justifies its termination. I do not consider that, in circumstances such as these, a doctor is required to initiate or to continue life-prolonging treatment or care in the best interests of his patient. It follows that no such duty rests upon the respondents, or upon Dr.Howe, in the case of X, whose condition is in reality no more than a living death, and for whom such treatment or care would, in medical terms, be futile.'

NOTE: 'Euthanasia is not lawful at common law': *per* Lord Goff.

14. The 'situation offences'

In these offences (or, as they are also known, 'state-of-affairs' cases) criminal liability is imposed even where the accused has performed *no voluntary act leading to an actus reus.* In these unusual cases, X finds himself involved in a situation which, *in itself*, is prohibited. X's responsibility for being in that situation is of no relevance and is not considered as part of the offence. Note the following cases.

(a) *R* v. *Larsonneur* (1933). X, a French national, landed in England with a French passport endorsed with words which prevented her working in the United Kingdom. She was required to leave England and went to Eire from where she was deported. Later, she was brought back to the United Kingdom by the Irish police and held in custody by the English police. She was charged that 'being an alien to whom leave to land in the United Kingdom had been refused, she was found in the United Kingdom'. Her appeal against conviction was dismissed. It was held that X had been 'found' in the United Kingdom (the *actus reus* of the offence) and the crime as charged had been proved correctly. The circumstances of X's re-entry to the United Kingdom were immaterial. 'She was found here and was, therefore, deemed to be in the class of persons whose landing had been prohibited by the Secretary of State, by reason of the fact that she had violated the condition on her passport': *per* Lord Hewart CJ.

(b) *Winzar* v. *Chief Constable of Kent* (1983). The police were called to remove X, who was drunk, from a hospital corridor. He was placed in a police car stationed in the hospital forecourt, and was then charged with being found drunk 'on a highway or public place', contrary to the Licensing Act 1872, s. 12. It was held that it sufficed to show that X had been present on the highway and was *perceived to be drunk.* It mattered not that his presence on the highway was momentary and not of his volition. The conditions of the relevant *actus reus* were satisfied.

Draft Criminal Code Bill

15. Acts and omissions
(Note that clause references relate to the Bill.) The following definitions should be noted.

(a) *Acts.* A reference in the Bill to an 'act' as an element of an offence refers also, where the context permits, to any result of the act, and any circumstances in which the act is done or the result occurs, that is an element of the offence, and references to a person's acting or doing an act shall be construed accordingly: cl. 15.
(b) *Omissions.* For the purpose of an offence which consists wholly or in part of an omission, state of affairs or occurrence, references in the Bill to an 'act' shall be read, where the context permits, as including references to the omission, etc., by reason of which a person may be guilty of the offence, and references to a person's acting or doing an act shall be construed accordingly: cl. 16.

16. Proof
'Unless otherwise provided – (*a*) the burden of proving every element of an offence and any other fact alleged or relied on by the prosecution is on the prosecution; (*b*) where evidence is given (whether by defendant or the prosecution) of a defence or any other fact alleged or relied on by the defendant the burden is on the prosecution to prove that an element of the defence or such other fact did not exist': cl. 13(1). 'The burden is on the defendant to prove any fact necessary to establish – (*a*) any plea made by him in bar to an indictment or any corresponding plea on summary trial; (*b*) the competence of any witness called by him; or (*c*) the admissibility of any evidence tendered by him': cl. 13(1), (3).

17. Causation
(1) 'Subject to subsecs 2 and 3 [intervening act or event and exception for accessories], a person causes a result which is an element of an offence when – (*a*) he does an act which makes a more than negligible contribution to its occurrence; or (*b*) he omits to do an act which might prevent its occurrence and which he is under a duty to do according to the law relating to the offence'.

(2) A person does not cause a result where, after he does such an act or makes such an omission, an act or event occurs – (a) which is the immediate and sufficient cause of the result; (b) which he did not foresee, and (c) which could not in the circumstances reasonably have been foreseen': c. 17.

Progress test 2

1. What, in general, must be proved by the prosecution 'beyond reasonable doubt' in a criminal trial? **(5)**

2. Comment on *R.* v. *Lebrun* (1992). **(5)**

3. Outline the nature of the 'proper standard of proof' in a criminal case. **(6)**

4. 'The crime is constituted by the event, and not by the activity which caused the event.' Comment. **(7)**

5. Comment on the decision in *R.* v. *Deller* (1952). **(9)**

6. Outline the significance of *R.* v. *Holland* (1841). **(10)**

7. Explain the decision in *R.* v. *Cheshire* (1991). **(11)**

8. 'An *actus reus* can result from a failure to act.' Explain. **(12)**

9. What is the importance of *R.* v. *Larsonneur* (1933)? **(14)**

3

Criminal responsibility (2): *mens rea*

Essence of *mens rea*

1. Meaning of the phrase

The loose translation of the phrase as 'guilty or wicked mind' is generally inadequate, since *mens rea* may exist even though a person acts in good faith. A more accurate meaning of the phrase might be 'criminal intention', i.e. an intention to do an act which is an offence by statute or common law, *or* recklessness as to the consequences of that act – in effect, *the essential mental element of a crime.*

'Criminal law is about the right of the state to punish persons for their conduct, generally where that conduct is undertaken *with a wicked intent or without justificatory excuse*': *per* Lord Diplock in *Treacy* v. *DPP* (1971) (unwarranted demand with menaces).

> NOTE: See *Peterssen* v. *RSPCA*(1993) in which the phrase *mens rea* was used in exceptional fashion to include the appellant's 'unreasonable conduct and act'.

2. Examples

Consider the following.

(a) The *mens rea* required for the crime of *rape* (*see* 13:4) is X's *intention* to have sexual intercourse with a female, Y, either *knowing* that Y is not consenting or *being reckless* as to whether she is consenting or not.

(b) The *mens rea* required for the crime of *theft* (*see* 15:2) is X's *dishonest* appropriation of Y's property, accompanied by the *intention* of permanently depriving Y of that property. *See* 3(b) below.

(c) The *mens rea* required for the crime of *handling stolen goods* (*see* 18:16) is X's *intending* to undertake the handling, acting *dishonestly* and *knowing or believing* the goods to be stolen.

In each of the offences mentioned above, *the external conduct* of X will be punished *only* where it has been shown beyond reasonable doubt to have been produced by the requisite form of *mens rea*. (Gross reminds us: 'Judgments sometimes are rendered about what a person *is* rather than about what a person *has done* . . . When determining criminal liability, the criminal law confines its concern with culpability to *specific conduct* that is alleged to constitute a crime, placing . . . other matters entirely out of bounds'.)

For the temporal coincidence of *mens rea* and *actus reus*, see 2:**5**.

3. *Mens rea,* motive and intention

These terms should not be confused; each has a separate meaning in the context of criminal law.

(a) 'The intention is the aim of the act, of which the motive is the spring': Austin *(The Province of Jurisprudence Determined,* 1832). *Motive is,* essentially, the 'source of power' for a given act; *intention* supplies purpose, design and direction; *mens rea* shapes the form of the *actus reus.* Thus, X has an overwhelming desire to take revenge on Y for a perceived wrong: this is X's *motive,* explaining *why* he wishes certain events to happen. X then determines that his revenge shall involve the physical punishment of Y: this is X's *intention.* X subsequently launches an attack on Y which is calculated to cause him serious bodily harm, and Y suffers severe injuries: this is *mens rea* culminating in an *actus reus,* leading to X's being charged under the Offences against the Person Act 1861, s. 47 *(see* 12:**12**). *See,* further, for 'intention', **8–10** below

(b) As a further example, consider X, who is cold and hungry, and wishes to change this condition. This motivates an intention to enjoy Y's food and clothes. (Motive generally precedes an intention.) X then acts deliberately and dishonestly, and appropriates food from Y's kitchen and clothes from his wardrobe, with the aim of depriving Y permanently of that property. This is the *mens rea* which culminates in an *actus reus,* leading to X's being charged under the Theft Act 1968, s. 1 *(see* 14:**1**).

(c) Motive is usually *irrelevant* to the question of the determination of criminal responsibility.

(i) 'The motive by which an offender was influenced, as distinguished from his intention, is never material to an offence. If the prohibited act be done, and be done with the intention by law essential to the offence, it is complete, without reference either to any ulterior intention or to the motive which gave birth to the intention': *Seventh Report of the Criminal Law Commissioners (1843).*

(ii) A laudable motive will not, in itself, negate criminal liability. X, in stealing money from the very rich Y, may wish to give it to the deserving poor. X, in killing his wife, Y, who is suffering from an incurable disease, may be inspired by motives of deep pity for Y. In both cases, however, criminal responsibility may attach to X.

(iii) In *Hills* v. *Ellis* (1983), X was convicted of obstructing the police who were making a lawful arrest of Y. X believed that Y was the innocent party, and had touched the police officer's arm so as to draw attention to this. It was held that his motive was irrelevant on a charge under the Police Act 1964, s. 51(3) (*see* 12:**22**).

(*iv*) Note the comment of Lord Herschell in *Allen* v. *Flood* (1898): 'It is certainly a general rule of our law that an act *prima facie* lawful is not unlawful and actionable on account of the motives which dictated it.'

(*v*) The mere existence of a wicked motive (and the absence of *mens rea* or *actus reus*) will not, *in itself*, suffice to constitute a crime. *See R.* v. *Smith* (1960).

(d) Note the comments of Lord Hailsham LC in *Hyam* v. *DPP* (*see* 9:**23**): 'Motive means an emotion prompting an act. . . . The motive for murder in this sense may be jealousy, fear, hatred. . . . In this sense motive is entirely distinct from intention or purpose. It is the emotion which gives rise to the intention and it is the latter and not the former which converts an *actus reus* into a criminal act.'

(e) Motive may be *relevant*, nevertheless, as circumstantial evidence, and in deciding punishment after conviction. *See R.* v. *Court* (1988) (at 13:**18(d)**), in which the House of Lords held that, in a case of indecent assault, evidence of motive *was admissible* as tending to prove the indecency of an otherwise equivocal assault. In *R.* v. *Rowley* (1991) X was charged under the Criminal Attempts Act 1981, ss. 1(1), 4(3) (*see* 8:**6**), with outraging public decency and attempting to incite a child to commit an act of gross indecency. He had left notes in public toilets inviting boys to act as his messengers in return for money and sweets. His appeal against conviction was *allowed*: evidence of *motive* was *not capable* of supplying the element of obscenity which was *missing* from the act complained of itself.

4. The significance of *mens rea*

In general, as noted above, where there is no *mens rea* there is no criminal offence (but *see* Chap. 4). This vital feature of English criminal law has been referred to, thus:

(a) 'It is a principle of natural justice, and of our law, that *actus non facit reum nisi mens sit rea*. The intent and the act must both concur to constitute the crime': *per* Lord Kenyon CJ, in *Fowler* v. *Padget* (1798).

(b) 'The full definition of every crime contains expressly or by implication a proposition as to a state of mind. Therefore if the mental element of any conduct alleged to be a crime is proved to have been absent in any given case, the crime so defined is not committed; or, again, if a crime is fully defined, nothing amounts to that crime which does not satisfy that definition. Crimes are in the present day much more accurately defined by statute or otherwise than they formerly were . . . but it is the general –

I might, I think, say the invariable – practice of the legislature to leave unexpressed some of the mental elements of crime': *per* Stephen J in *R*. v. *Tolson* (1889).

(c) 'It has frequently been affirmed and should unhesitatingly be recognised that it is a cardinal principle of our law that *mens rea*, an evil intention or a knowledge of the wrongfulness of the act, is in all ordinary cases an essential ingredient of guilt of a criminal offence. It follows from this that there will not be guilt of an offence created by statute unless there is *mens rea* or unless Parliament has by the statute enacted that guilt may be established in cases where there is no *mens rea*': *per* Lord Morris in *Sweet* v. *Parsley* (1970).

Three fundamental 'blameworthy' states of mind in relation to criminal activity, to be outlined below, are *negligence, intention* and *recklessness*.

Negligence

5. Definitions
The following should be considered carefully.

(a) 'A person is negligent if he fails to exercise such care, skill or foresight as a reasonable man in his situation would exercise': *Law Commission Report No. 89*.
(b) 'The absence of such care as it was the duty of the defendant to use': *per* Willes, J in *Grill* v. *General Iron Screw Colliery Ltd* (1886).
(c) 'The mental attitude of undue indifference with respect to one's conduct and its consequences': Salmond.
(d) 'The omission to do something which a reasonable man, guided upon those considerations which ordinarily regulate the conduct of human affairs, would do, or doing something which a prudent and reasonable man would not do': *per* Alderson B in *Blyth* v. *Birmingham Waterworks Co.* (1856). (Note Lord Diplock's doubts, however, as to the place in criminal law of the concept of the 'reasonable man': *see R*. v. *Sheppard* (1981).)
(e) 'Negligence implies inadvertence, ie, that the defendant was completely unaware of the dangerousness of his behaviour although actually it was unreasonably increasing the risk of the occurrence of an injury': Hall.

Negligence is viewed in these and many other definitions as, essentially, *culpable carelessness* (i.e. conduct, rather than a state of mind). It is a failure to exercise that degree of care which a reasonable, prudent and careful person in the same circumstances and with equal experience would not have omitted to take into account. A person is negligent, therefore, in relation to a situation when he fails to take those actions which a reasonable person in his position would have taken to prevent that situation arising or continuing: Glazebrook. Note that negligence should not be confused with 'neglect', i.e. a *state of affairs* resulting from negligence.

> NOTE: The American Model Penal Code (s. 2.02(2)(d)) refers to 'acting "negligently" ' in the following words: 'A person acts negligently with respect to a material element of an offence when he should be aware of a substantial and unjustifiable risk that the material element exists or will result from his conduct. The risk must be of such a nature and degree that the actor's failure to perceive it, considering the nature and purpose of his conduct, the circumstances known to him and the care that would be exercised by a reasonable person in his situation, involves substantial culpability.'

6. Degrees of negligence

Negligence may range from mere 'inadvertence' through 'rashness' (the state of mind of one who 'thinks of the probable mischief, but, in consequence of a missupposition begotten by insufficient inadvertence, he assumes that the mischief will not ensue in the given instance or cause': Austin) to 'gross negligence' (which is very near to 'recklessness' (*see* **14** below)).

(a) 'Gross negligence' has not been defined by statute. It has been held to arise when the negligence of the accused goes beyond a mere matter of compensation and shows such disregard for life and safety as to amount to a crime against the state and conduct deserving punishment: *R. v. Bateman* (1925).

(b) 'All crimes of negligence consist of conduct that is blameless in one aspect but quite blameworthy in another. If the acts of the accused are merely negligent, the activity in which he was engaged could not in itself be condemned as wrong . . . If we are heedless of the hazards in what we do, or even insufficiently attentive, our conduct merits blame according to how heedless or inattentive it is': Gross.

(c) For an example of gross negligence amounting to criminal negligence, *see R. v. Adomako* (1993), at 10:**11**.

(d) Some legal writers have suggested that within the range of degrees of negligence the determination of culpability should take into account: how manifest the danger was; how imminent was the injury of which there was a danger; how serious that injury was; the feasibility in all the circumstances of adequate precaution against the harm which produced the injury.

7. Negligence as the *mens rea* of criminal conduct

Negligence as the basis of liability for an offence *at common law* exists in the case of manslaughter (*see* Chap. 10). *See* e.g. *Andrews* v. *DPP* (1937). In such a case the prosecution will have to prove that the actions of the accused were of such a nature that in the circumstances death was a very high probability (i.e. that there was 'gross negligence'). Note the following statutory offences, for example.

(a) Dangerous driving, contrary to the Road Traffic Act 1988, s. 2A, as substituted by the Road Traffic Act 1991, s. 1, which provides that a person drives dangerously if the way he drives falls far below what would be expected of a competent and careful driver, and it would be obvious to a careful and competent driver that driving in that way would be dangerous. *See* 10:15.

(b) Selling firearms or ammunition to a person whom the accused 'knows or has reasonable cause for believing to be drunk or of unsound mind', contrary to the Firearms Act 1968, s. 25. In such a case the accused has acted negligently if he ought to have known that the person to whom he sold the gun was drunk or of unsound mind.

Intention

8. 'The most culpable form of blameworthiness'
If, as has been suggested by some jurists, negligence is the least culpable form of blameworthiness, the most serious and culpable is the *deliberate, intentional* performance of some prohibited act. Essentially, intention is a 'state of affairs which the party "intending" does more than merely contemplate. It connotes a state of affairs which, on the contrary, he decides, so far as in him lies, to bring about, and which, in point of possibility, he has a reasonable prospect of being able to bring about by his own act of volition': *Cunliffe* v. *Goodman* (1950). It has been suggested, further, that a man's intention is a question of fact. 'Actual intent may unquestionably be proved by direct evidence or may be inferred from surrounding circumstances. Intent may also be imputed on the basis that a man must be presumed to intend the natural consequences of his own act': *Lloyds Bank* v. *Marcan* (1973).

9. Intention in criminal conduct
'An intention to do the act forbidden by law is . . . normally the sufficient mental element for criminal responsibility and also is normally, although not always, necessary for responsibility': Hart. Consider the following situations.

(a) X, actively desiring Y's death, administers poison to him so that Y dies.

(b) X, wishing to deprive Y permanently of his purse and contents, removes them from Y's coat.

(c) X, having as his deliberate goal sexual intercourse with Y, and aware that she is not consenting, proceeds with that course of action.

In each of these cases X has an *intention* which will relate directly to the *mens rea* of the offence with which he may be charged (murder, theft, rape). He is acting 'intentionally' in that *his conscious goal is a (prohibited) consequence of his conduct.* In general, where the *actus reus* of the offence with which X is charged requires that his conduct shall produce particular consequences, his *intention that these consequences shall occur* is a sufficient mental state for the offence.

10. Definitions
The following should be noted.

(a) 'An intention is the purpose or design with which an act is done. This may consist of an intention to perform some further act, an intention to bring about certain consequences or perhaps merely an intention to do the act itself': Salmond.

(b) 'A decision to bring about, in so far as it lies within the accused's power, [a particular consequence], no matter whether the accused desired that consequence or not': *R. v. Mohan* (1976).

(c) 'The standard test of intention is: Did the person whose conduct is in issue either intend to produce the result or have no substantial doubt that his conduct would produce it?': *Law Commission Report No. 89.*

(d) 'A person acts "intentionally" with respect to a result when it is his purpose to cause it; or although it is not his purpose to cause that result, he is aware that it would occur in the ordinary course of events if he were to succeed in his purpose of causing some other result': *Law Commission Report No. 122 (1992).*

From these definitions 'intention' emerges as *a 'mental formulation', related to some end, and a desire to seek that end.* There is, however, no one authoritative definition. Indeed, in *R. v. Moloney* (1985) (*see* 9:**25**), Lord Bridge said that the judge, when directing a jury, should avoid any 'elaboration or paraphrase' of what is meant by 'intent' and should leave it to 'the jury's good sense to decide whether the accused acted with the necessary intent, unless the judge is convinced that, on the facts and having regard to the way the case has been presented to the jury in evidence and arguments, some further explanation or elaboration is strictly necessary to avoid misunderstanding.'

11. Intention and foresight
Intention *may be inferred* from foresight of consequences, but *must not be*

equated with foresight. The appropriate mental element in murder is now constituted by an intention to kill or cause really serious injury, rather than mere foresight that death or serious injury will be a probable consequence of the actions of the accused; *R.* v. *Moloney* (1985) (*see* 9:**25**). *See also R.* v. *Hancock and Shankland* (1986) at 9:**28**.

12. Crimes of specific/ulterior intent.

Crimes of specific/ulterior intent, as contrasted with those of basic/general intent (*see* **13** below), are those in which the requirement of *mens rea* is satisfied *only* by proof beyond reasonable doubt (*see* 2:**6**) that X had a special *intention* of committing the *actus reus*. In the case of a crime of ulterior intent, however, there must also be proof that X intended to perform a further (prohibited) act ulterior to the *actus reus*. Thus, on a charge of burglary with intent, contrary to the Theft Act 1968, s. 9(1)(a) (*see* 16:**9**), the prosecution must first show that X entered premises as a trespasser – the *actus reus* of the offence. It must then be shown that X had the *ulterior motive* of intending to steal or cause damage to the premises, etc.

(a) In *DPP* v. *Majewski* (1977) (*see* 6:**19**) Lord Simon cited with approval the description of 'specific intent' given by Fauteux J in *George* (1960): 'In considering the question of *mens rea*, a distinction is to be made between (i) intention as applied to acts considered in relation to their purposes and (ii) intention as applied to acts apart from their purpose. A general intent attending the commission of an act is, in some cases, the only intent required to constitute the crime while, in others, there must be, in addition to that general intent, a specific intent attending the purpose for the commission of the act.'

(b) Other examples of crimes of specific intent are stealing, robbery, handling stolen goods, wounding with intent, murder, attempt to commit an offence.

(c) Only *proof of intention* will be sufficient for a conviction. Proof of negligence or recklessness will *not* suffice.

13. Crimes of basic/general intent

In cases of this type proof of either or both *recklessness or intention* (but not negligence) will suffice as proof of the necessary *mens rea*. 'By "crimes of basic intent" I mean those crimes whose definition expresses (or, more often, implies) a *mens rea* which does not go beyond the *actus reus*': per Lord Simon in *DPP* v. *Morgan* (1976). See *DPP* v. *Majewski* (1977) at 6:**19**.

(a) Crimes of basic intent include manslaughter, rape (*see R.* v. *Eatch* (1980)), assault (common and indecent), offences under the Offences against the Person Act 1861, ss. 20, 47 (as amended by the Criminal Justice

Act 1988, Sch. 16), kidnapping, false imprisonment (*see R.* v. *Hutchins* (1988)).

(b) Voluntary intoxication is *not* accepted as a defence in relation to crimes of basic/general intent; it *may* be accepted in relation to crimes of specific/ ulterior intent.

> NOTE: (1) The classification of crimes in **12** and **13** above results from the decision of the courts, not from statute. (2) 'A court or jury in determining whether a person has committed an offence shall not be bound in law to infer that he intended or foresaw a result of his actions by reason only of its being a natural and probable consequence of those actions, but shall decide whether he did intend or foresee that result by reference to all the evidence, drawing such inferences from the evidence as appear proper in the circumstances': *see* the Criminal Justice Act 1967, s. 8.

Recklessness

14. The concept of recklessness in criminal law

The term 'recklessness' has not been defined by statute, but has been used to indicate, generally, the wanton indifference of an accused person to the consequences of his actions. Note, for example, the following comments. 'A man is *reckless* . . . when he carries out a deliberate act knowing that there is some risk of damage resulting from that act but nevertheless continues in the performance of that act': *R.* v. *Briggs* (1977). 'A person is *reckless* if, knowing there is a risk that an event may result from his conduct or that a circumstance may exist, he takes that risk, and it is unreasonable for him to take it, having regard to the degree and nature of the risk which he knows to be present': *Law Commission Working Party.* '[In recklessness] the actor is conscious of a forbidden harm [and] realises that his conduct increases the risk of its occurrence and he has decided to take that risk': Hall.

These, and similar descriptions of 'recklessness', must be read in the light of the apparent existence of *two types of recklessness* recognised in the criminal law (*see* **15** and **16** below). It is important to understand which type of 'recklessness' is being referred to when the term is used.

15. Subjective 'Cunningham recklessness'

The facts in *R.* v. *Cunningham* (1957) were as follows: X, in stealing from a gas meter, fractured a gas pipe so that gas escaped, with the result that Y, who was sleeping on the premises, inhaled it. X was convicted under the Offences against the Person Act 1861, s. 23 (*see* 12:**15**), of unlawfully and maliciously causing Y to take a noxious thing, thereby endangering her life (an offence of basic intent). X appealed.

(a) *Court of Appeal.* The Court held that the judge's direction to the jury ('. . . "Malicious" means wicked – something which [X] had no business to do and perfectly well knew it') was *incorrect*. The word 'malicious' required *either* that X intended to administer the gas *or*, without intending to administer it, he foresaw that he might cause gas to escape and thus injure Y (this being a crime of basic intent). The second limb of the statement involves a 'deliberate risk-taking'.

(b) *Consequences of the decision.* Recklessness involves *the accused being aware of a risk which is not justified and taking that risk deliberately*. This so-called 'Cunningham recklessness' will suffice for a crime which is defined by statute so as to require that it be committed 'maliciously'. *See also R. v. Stephenson* (1979). Note *Yugotours* v. *Wadsley* (1988); *R. v. Farrell* (1989) – importance of applying the 'subjective' Cunningham test when 'malicious' appeared in the indictment.

16. Objective 'Caldwell recklessness' (1)

The facts in *R.* v. *Caldwell* (1982) (*see* 19:**8**) were as follows. X, pursuing a grievance against Y, a hotel proprietor, set the hotel on fire, and was convicted of arson under the Criminal Damage Act 1971, ss. 1, 3 (*see* 19:**9**). X claimed that he had set fire to the premises, but had been so drunk that the thought that he might be endangering life (of the hotel guests) had never crossed his mind. The prosecution appealed from the Court of Appeal's quashing of X's conviction to the House of Lords.

(a) *House of Lords.* 'A person would be reckless within the meaning of s. 1(1) if (*i*) he does an act which in fact creates an *obvious risk* that property will be damaged or destroyed, *and* (*ii*) when he does the act had *either* not given any thought to the possibility of there being any such risk *or* he recognised that there was some risk involved and has nevertheless gone on to do it.'

(b) X's failure to consider an obvious risk sufficed as a form of recklessness; it constituted an alternative to an actual 'subjective' appreciation of the risk involved. Lord Diplock noted, in considering the two alternative states of mind, that neither state seemed less blameworthy than the other, but if the difference between the two constituted the distinction between what does and does not in legal theory amount to a 'guilty mind' in relation to the statutory offence concerning damage to property, it would be an impracticable distinction for use in jury trials.

(c) *Consequences of the judgment.* The concept of liability through recklessness has been extended, with the result that the prosecution may succeed by proving a type of recklessness which is something *less* than that contemplated in 'Cunningham recklessness'. *Caldwell* created, in effect, *a second type of recklessness*, which has general application to offences of basic intent only. (*See R.* v.*R.(S.M.)* (1984); *R.* v.*Sangha* (1988) at 19:**11**.)

17. Objective 'Caldwell recklessness' (2)

The *Caldwell* view of recklessness was intended to have application beyond offences under the Criminal Damage Act 1971. In *R.* v. *Lawrence* (1982), heard by the House of Lords on the same day as *Caldwell* was decided, Lord Diplock noted that his statement in *Caldwell* should apply to any modern statute containing the word 'recklessness'. *R.* v. *Lawrence* turned upon the concept of 'recklessness' in 'reckless driving' (under the Road Traffic Act 1972, which had not defined 'recklessness').

(a) *Per* Lord Diplock: 'In my view an appropriate instruction to the jury on what is meant by driving recklessly would be that they must be satisfied of two things: *first*, that the defendant was in fact driving the vehicle in such a manner as to create an obvious and serious risk of causing physical injury to some other person who might happen to be using the road or of doing substantial damage to property; and *second*, that in driving in that manner the defendant did so without having given any thought to the possibility of there being any such risk or, having recognised that there was some risk involved, had nonetheless gone on to take it.'

(b) 'It is for the jury to decide whether the risk created by the manner in which the vehicle being driven was both obvious and serious and, in deciding this, they may apply the standard of the ordinary prudent motorist as represented by themselves. If satisfied that an obvious and serious risk was created by the manner of the defendant's driving, the jury are entitled to infer that he was in one or other of the states of mind required to constitute the offence and will probably do so; but regard must be given to any explanation he gives as to his state of mind which may displace the inference.'

(c) This definition of recklessness is based on *Caldwell* save for its requirement that the risk be not only 'obvious' but also 'serious'.

(d) Critics of the *Lawrence* test suggested that it was too subjective, that it was much too wide in its scope and that defendants might attempt to excuse themselves by agreeing that their driving had created an 'obvious' risk, while arguing that they had applied their minds to the possibility of the existence of a risk but had concluded, perhaps imprudently, that there was no such risk.

18. Recklessness and *mens rea*: the situation summarised

Note the following.

(a) There are, at the present time, *two types of recklessness* for purposes of the criminal law:

   (i) '*Cunningham type*': X knows the risk, is willing to take it, and takes it deliberately (so-called '*subjective recklessness*').

(*ii*) '*Caldwell type*': X performs an act which creates an obvious risk, and, when performing the act, he has *either* given no thought to the possibility of such a risk arising, *or* he has recognised that some risk existed, but goes on to take it (so-called '*objective recklessness*').

(b) The risks referred to must be of an *unjustifiable nature*.

(c) 'Caldwell recklessness' will *not* apply to any crimes of specific/ ulterior intent, e.g. burglary or murder. Nor has it any application to some crimes of basic intent such as rape (*see R. v. Satnam and Kewal* (1984) at 13:**7**); a statutory offence involving the term 'maliciously' performing some prohibited act (*see W. v. Dolbey* (1989)); and, probably, common law assault and battery. *see R. v. Savage* (1992) at 12:**19**.

19. Recent consideration of the 'two types' of recklessness
The following cases should be examined carefully.

(a) In *Chief Constable of Avon* v. *Shimmen* (1987) (*see* 19:**8(e)**), X wished to demonstrate his prowess in the martial arts by aiming a controlled kick at a shop window: his intention was to show his skill in control by not breaking the window. His control was ineffective and he was charged with criminal damage, having broken the window. X argued that he was not reckless, having satisfied himself that he would not cause any damage to the window. The argument was accepted by the magistrates and the charge was dismissed. A Divisional Court allowed the prosecutor's appeal, stating that where a defendant who recognises the risk involved in some action of his, but thinks that, because of some expertise he possesses, he has minimised that risk, and goes on to perform the act, he may be considered 'reckless' if damage results. X had recognised the risk *and had been reckless* (within the *Caldwell* definition).

(b) In *R. v. Morrison* (1989), the Court of Appeal considered the trial judge's summing up in a case of wounding with intent to resist arrest, contrary to the Offences against the Person Act 1861, s. 18. The word 'maliciously' appears in s. 18 and in the indictment; hence the Cunningham ('subjective') definition was appropriate. But the summing up had failed to drive home to the jury that what was going on *in the defendant's mind*, not in the ordinary prudent observer's mind, was what they had to consider. They had been directed in terms of *Caldwell*, and should have been alerted to the necessity to consider *Cunningham* rather than *Caldwell*.

(c) In *R. v. Reid* (1992) the House of Lords considered, and dismissed, X's appeal against conviction of the offence of reckless driving. At X's trial, the judge had directed the jury on reckless driving by using Lord Diplock's instruction in *R. v. Lawrence* (1982). X argued that the test in *Lawrence* was incorrect and that the objective limb of that test ought to be removed.

(*i*) The House *rejected* X's appeal. *Lawrence* remained essentially good law. The exact-wording of the model direction could be adapted to suit the circumstances of individual cases.

(*ii*) In the context of 'reckless driving', the recklessness cannot be restricted to a subjective test; it includes an objective element, that is 'heedlessness of the presence of risk as well as disregard of a recognised risk'.

(*iii*) *Per* Lord Browne Wilkinson: 'In the absence of a general statutory definition of the word "reckless" I do not accept that the constituent elements of recklessness must be the same in *all* statutes'. (It may be, therefore, that the *Caldwell* test which is to be applied to *all* statutory offences including the terms 'reckless' or 'recklessly' could be modified.)

(*iv*) *Per* Lord Goff, referring to possible exceptions to the *Caldwell* test: 'Another example [might be] where a driver who, while driving, is afflicted by illness or shock which impairs his capacity to address his mind to the possibility of risk; it may well not be right to describe him as "driving recklessly" in such circumstances. '

Draft Criminal Code Bill

20. Proof of states of mind

'A court or jury, in determining whether a person had, or may have had, a particular state of mind, shall have regard to all the evidence including, where appropriate, the presence or absence of reasonable grounds for having that state of mind': cl. 14.

21. Fault

The Law Commission stresses (*see* Vol. 2, para 8.4) the necessity 'to encourage consistency in the language of the criminal law by providing a standard vocabulary of "key fault" terms, and to promote certainty as to the meaning of that language . . .' The meaning of 'fault' emerges from the definition of 'fault element' in cl. 6: '"Fault element" means an element of an offence consisting (*a*) of a state of mind with which a person acts; or (*b*) of a failure to comply with a standard of conduct; or (*c*) partly of such a state of mind and partly of such a failure . . .'

22. Fault terms

'. . . A person acts – (*a*) "knowingly" with respect to a circumstance not only when he is aware that it exists or will exist, but also when he avoids taking steps that might confirm his belief that it exists or will exist; (*b*) "intentionally" with respect to (*i*) a circumstance when he hopes or knows that it exists or will exist; (*ii*) a result when he acts either in order to bring it about or being aware that it will occur in the ordinary course of events; (c) "recklessly" with respect to – (*i*) a circumstance when he is aware of a risk that it exists or will exist; (*ii*) a result when he is aware of a risk that it will occur; and it is, in the circumstances known to him, unreasonable to take the risk; and these and related words (such as "knowledge", "intention", "recklessness") shall be construed accordingly unless the context otherwise requires': cl. 18.

23. Degrees of fault
'(1) An allegation in an indictment or information of knowledge or intention includes an allegation of recklessness. (2) A requirement of recklessness is satisfied by knowledge or intention': cl. 19.

Progress test 3

1. Comment on the meaning of the phrase '*actus reus*'. **(1, 2)**

2. What is the relevance of motive in the determination of criminal liability? **(3)**

3. 'Negligence is culpable carelessness. ' Discuss.   **(5)**

4. Define 'intention' in relation to criminal law. **(8–10)**

5. Explain the concept of crimes of 'specific' and 'general' intent. **(12, 13)**

6. Explain '*Cunningham* recklessness'. **(15)**

7. How did *R*. v. *Caldwell* (1982) modify the concept of recklessness? **(16, 17)**

8. Comment on *R*. v. *Reid* (1992). **(19)**

4

Criminal responsibility (3): strict and vicarious liability

Strict liability

1. The exclusion of the requirement of *mens rea* from certain offences

There are two categories of case from which the requirement of *mens rea*, in relation to *some* elements of the *actus reus*, may be said to be excluded.

(a) Certain statutory offences involving so-called *'strict liability'*. ('These are crimes where it is no defence to show that the accused, in spite of the exercise of proper care, was ignorant of the facts that made his act illegal. Here he is liable to punishment even though he *did not intend* to commit an act answering the definition of the crime': Hart.)

> 'By the general principles of the criminal law, if a matter is made a criminal offence, it is essential that there should be something in the nature of *mens rea*. . . . But there are exceptions to this rule . . . and the reason for this is, that the legislature has thought it so important to prevent the particular act from being committed that it *absolutely forbids it to be done*; and if it is done the offender is liable to a penalty whether he has any *mens rea* or not, and whether or not he intended to commit a breach of the law': *per* Channel J in *Pearks, Gunston & Tee, Ltd* v. *Ward* (1902).

In such cases a person may be convicted without any proof of intention, recklessness or negligence.

(b) Cases in which *vicarious liability* (*see* 10 below) attaches to a 'master' (i.e. an employer) for a statutory offence committed by his 'servant' (i.e. his employee) in the course of carrying out his duties and which was not authorised (or was even forbidden) by the master.

2. The construction of statutes

(Note that 'construction' means here the process of ascertaining the sense or meaning of a document, e.g. a statute.) The question whether *mens rea* is required for a given statutory offence often involves the construing of the provisions of the statute. The language of the statute as a whole may be considered and attention may be paid to its legislative history and to previous statutes of a similar nature, so that Parliament's intentions concerning the point at issue might be discovered. Reference to *Hansard* may be made in certain circumstances, i.e. where the legislation is obscure or ambiguous, or might lead to an absurdity: *Pepper* v. *Hart* (1992). The social reason for the statute's enactment may also be considered: see *Hobbs* v. *Winchester Corporation* (1910) – a civil action concerning the selling of unfit meat under the Public Health Act 1875.

A statute may contain terms, such as 'knowingly', or 'wilfully', which, in themselves, suggest some element of *mens rea. (See* e.g. *R.* v. *Sheppard* (1981), in which the House of Lords decided that, under the Children and Young Persons Act 1933, s. 1, the word 'wilful' (in the phrase 'wilful neglect' of a child) requires some mental element. But contrast this with 'wilfully' as used in the Police Act 1964, s. 51(3), and as interpreted in *Rice* v. *Connolly* (1966) and *Lewis* v. *Cox* (1984).) 'Malicious' seems to suggest the necessity of *mens rea: see R.* v. *Vickers* (1957). 'Permitting' appears to imply *mens rea: see James & Son Ltd* v. *Smee* (1955). *See Westminster CC* v. *Croyalgrange* (1986): in order to prove a charge of 'knowingly using' premises as a sex establishment (*see* Local Government (Misc. Provs.) Act 1982, Sch.3), it has to be shown that defendant had *actual knowledge* that they were being used in this manner. 'Cause' has been taken to indicate a requirement of *mens rea: see Alphacell* v. *Woodward* (1972). 'Uses' suggests strict liability: *see Green* v. *Burnett* (1955). But where a statute is silent concerning *mens rea,* a problem arises: does the statute impose strict liability?

3. The presumption that *mens rea* is required for a criminal offence

'There is a presumption that *mens rea,* or evil intention, or knowledge of the wrongfulness of the act, is an essential ingredient in every offence; but that presumption is liable to be displaced either by the words of the statute creating the offence or by the subject-matter with which it deals, and both must be considered': *per* Wright J in *Sherras* v. *de Rutzen* (1895).

(a) *Warner* v. *Metropolitan Police Commissioner* (1969). This was, according to Lord Reid, 'the first case in which [the House of Lords] has had to consider whether a statutory offence is an absolute offence in the sense that the belief, intention, or state of mind of the accused is immaterial and irrelevant.' X was charged with being in possession of tablets contrary to the Drugs (Prevention of Misuse) Act 1964. The tablets were in a parcel which X said that he believed contained scent. The House of Lords held that the offence was one of strict liability, that *mens rea* was unnecessary. It was also held that, nevertheless, where the drugs were contained in a parcel, the prosecution has to prove that X was 'in possession' of the contents of the parcel, i.e. that he was not entirely ignorant of the nature of the contents. (*See* now the Misuse of Drugs Act 1971, s. 28, at 23:**12**.)

(b) *Sweet* v. *Parsley* (1970). X was charged under the Dangerous Drugs Act 1965, s. 5, with being concerned in the management of premises used for the purpose of smoking cannabis. X had no knowledge whatsoever that her farmhouse, which she had let, was being used for that purpose. Her conviction was quashed by the House of Lords on the grounds (*inter alia*) that knowledge of the use of the premises was essential to the offence, and, since X had no such knowledge, she did not commit the offence. *Per* Lord Diplock:

> '[The importance of *mens rea*] stems from the principle that it is contrary to a rational and civilised criminal code, such as Parliament must be presumed to have intended, to penalise one who has performed his duty as a citizen to ascertain what acts are prohibited by law ... and has taken all proper care to inform himself of any facts which would make this conduct unlawful.'

Strict liability under statute

4. Strict liability and statute
Where a statute is silent as to *mens rea*, the presumption that it is required may be rebutted. The following decisions illustrate the problem:

(a) *R.* v. *Prince* (1875). The facts are set out in 2: **2(c)**. (*See* now the Sexual Offences Act 1956, s. 20.) It was held that Prince's honest belief that the girl was eighteen was not a defence, and his conviction was upheld. Although the statute made no reference to *mens rea*, its words were plain and it was not considered necessary to read into it phrases such as 'with knowledge that the girl was under sixteen'. 'The legislature has enacted that if anyone does this wrong he does it at the risk of [the girl] turning out to be under sixteen': *per* Bramwell B.

(b) *Cundy* v. *Le Cocq* (1884). X, a licensee, was charged and convicted under the Licensing Act 1872, s. 13, with selling liquor to a drunken person, Y. (*See* now the Licensing Act 1964, s. 172.) It was proved that X did not know that Y was drunk.

> 'I am of opinion that the words of the section amount to an absolute prohibition of the sale of liquor to a drunken person, and that the existence of a *bona fide* mistake as to the condition of the person served is not an answer to the charge. ... It is necessary to look at the object of each Act that is under consideration to see whether and how far knowledge is of the essence of the offence created': *per* Stephen J.

(c) *R. v. Duke of Leinster* (1924). X was charged and convicted under the Bankruptcy Act 1914, s. 155, with having obtained credit from Y without informing him that he (X) was an undischarged bankrupt. X had directed his agent to disclose the fact and believed on reasonable grounds that this had been done. (*See* now the Insolvency Act 1986, s. 360; *R. v. Brockley* (1993).)

> 'It is necessary to refer to the words of the statute and to see what its object is. . . . The words "wilfully", or "knowingly", or "fraudulently", could have been inserted. But they are not, and an absolute obligation is imposed by the section. . . . If it were otherwise, the section would be, to a great extent, nugatory. . . . If the information is not conveyed, then, in the opinion of the Court, whatever the state of mind of the bankrupt may be, the offence is committed': *per* Lord Hewart CJ.

(d) *Smedleys* v. *Breed* (1974). X, a large-scale manufacturer of tinned peas, producing over three million tins in a seven-week season, was convicted under the Food and Drugs Act 1955, s. 2(1) (*see* now the Food Safety Act 1990, s. 8), when one tin was found to contain a very small caterpillar. The House of Lords dismissed X's appeal, holding that it was not sufficient to show that X took all reasonable care to avoid the presence of extraneous matter in his food products. The offence was one of strict liability. (This is an example of the so-called 'regulatory offences': the enforcement of regulations is made easier as the result of the imposition of strict liability.) *Per* Lord Hailsham LC: 'To construe the Food and Drugs Act 1955 in a sense less strict than that which I have adopted would make a serious inroad on the legislation for consumer protection which Parliament has adopted and . . . extended.'

(e) *Pharmaceutical Society of Great Britain* v. *Storkwain* (1986). X, a pharmacist, supplied drugs for which a prescription was required, upon being handed a forged prescription. There was no evidence of any want of care or dishonesty on X's part. It was held by the House of Lords that on a true construction of the Medicines Act 1968, s. 58(2)(a), and having regard to its overall scheme, an offence of strict liability was created, and therefore no *mens rea* was required.

(f) *Kirkland* v. *Robinson*(1987). In an appeal by X against conviction of possessing live wild birds, contrary to the Wildlife and Countryside Act 1981, s. 1(2)(a), it was held that the offence was one of strict liability. It was not necessary to show that X knew that the birds were 'wild birds' within the meaning of the Act.

(g) *R. v.Bradish* (1990). The Court of Appeal held that the Firearms Act 1968, s. 5 (*see* 12:**30**) created offences of strict liability. Thus, in *R. v. Waller* (1991), X had looked after a bag for a friend. It contained cartridges and a gun, and X was convicted of possessing a firearm without a certificate, contrary to s. 1(1). His appeal against conviction was rejected; it was held that the offence was one of strict liability so that it was not necessary for the prosecution to prove that X was aware of what was in the bag.

(h) *R.* v. *Cheshire CC ex p Helliwell* (1991). It was held that the offence of subjecting animals to unnecessary suffering, under the Transit of Animals (Road and Rail) Order 1975, was one of strict liability.

(i) *R.* v. *Collett* (1993). Using land in contravention of an enforcement notice, contrary to the Town and Country Planning Act 1971, s. 89(5) (*see* now the Town and Country Planning Act 1990, s. 179, substituted by the Planning and Compensation Act 1991, s. 8), is an offence of strict liability. The penalties are intended, *per* Tuckey J, to further a policy of 'encouraging vigilance on the part of landowners and users'.

(j) *R.* v. *Bezzina* (1993). The Dangerous Dogs Act 1991, s. 3(1), imposes strict liability on the owners or handlers of dogs which were dangerously out of control in public places.

5. 'Imposing an impossible duty'

The construing of a statute by the courts so as to impose a duty which it is impossible or almost impossible to perform is rare. This is illustrated by the following cases.

(a) *Sherras* v. *de Rutzen* (1895). X was charged under the Licensing Act 1872, s. 16, with supplying liquor to Y, a constable on duty. Y had removed his armlet (which was worn when a constable was on duty) before entering X's premises, and X made no enquiry as to whether he was on duty. X's conviction was quashed. 'It is plain that if guilty knowledge is not necessary, no care on the part of the publican could save him from a conviction under s. 16': *per* Wright J.

(b) *Harding* v. *Price* (1948). X was charged under the Road Traffic Act 1930, s. 22, with failing to report to the police an accident to his motor vehicle. X's defence, which was accepted, was that he could not have known that a collision had occurred because of the noise made by his vehicle (a 'mechanical horse' with trailer attached). 'Unless a man knows that the event has happened, how can he carry out the duty imposed? If the duty be to report, he cannot report something of which he has no knowledge . . . Any other view would lead to calling on a man to do the impossible': *per* Lord Goddard CJ.

(c) *Lim Chin Aik* v. *R.* (1963). X was convicted under an ordinance of Singapore of entering and remaining in the territory as a prohibited person. There was no evidence that the prohibition order had been published or served on him. The Privy Council allowed X's appeal. *Per* Lord Evershed: 'It is not enough . . . merely to label the statute as one dealing with a grave social evil and from that to infer that strict liability was intended. It is pertinent also to inquire whether putting defendant under strict liability will assist in the enforcement of the regulations. . . . Unless this is so, there is no reason for penalising him, and it cannot be inferred that the legislature imposed strict liability merely in order to find a luckless victim.'

6. Statutory defences

In some cases a statute imposing strict liability may also provide a defence. (Note the use of 'strict', and not 'absolute', which would preclude the applicability of *any* defence.) The onus of proving the statutory defence is upon the accused. *See*, for example:

(a) Food Safety Act 1990, ss. 20, 21, under which X's liability for contravention of the Act may be escaped where he is able to show that such contravention resulted from the act or default of a third party, and that he (X) *acted with all due diligence* in complying with the Act.

(b) Trade Descriptions Act 1968, s. 24(1), under which it is a defence for X to prove that the commission of the offence under the Act resulted from a mistake or reliance on information supplied to him or from the act or default of another person, and that he (X) *exercised all due diligence* to avoid the commission of such an offence by himself or any other person under his control: *see Tesco Supermarkets* v. *Nattrass* (1972); *Texas Homecare* v. *Stockport* BC (1987); *Wings* v. *Ellis* (1985).

7. The case for strict liability

The case made *against* the concept of strict liability usually turns on the preceived 'unjustness' of convicting those whose behaviour has been 'correct', and on the consequences of any extension of the principle of excluding the requirement of *mens rea*. The case *for* strict liability is based on the following arguments:

(a) It is essential to ensure that certain important regulations necessary for the welfare of the community be obeyed. 'Such statutes are not meant to punish the vicious will, but to put pressure upon the thoughtless and inefficient to do their whole duty in the interest of public health or safety or morals' (Dean Pound (the American jurist), referred to in *Reynolds* v. *Austin & Sons* (1951)). Note the comments of Lord Diplock in *R.* v. *Lemon* (1979) (*see* 22:**6**): 'The usual justification for creating by statute a criminal offence of strict liability . . . is the threat that the *actus reus* of the offence poses to public health, public safety, public morals or public order'. Thus, in *Alphacell Ltd* v. *Woodward* (1972) the House of Lords held that to cause poisonous, noxious or polluting matter to enter a stream was an absolute offence under the Rivers (Prevention of Pollution) Act 1951, s. 2(1) (repealed under the Control of Pollution Act 1974), and that the prosecution need not establish, therefore, that the pollution was caused intentionally or negligently. *Per* Lord Wilberforce: 'In my opinion this is a clear case of causing the polluted water to enter the stream. The whole complex operation which might lead to this result was an operation deliberately conducted by [the accused] and I fail to see how a defect in one stage of it, even if we assume that this happened without their negligence, can enable them to say they did not cause the pollution. In my opinion, complication of this case by infusion of the concept of *mens rea*, and its exceptions, is unnecessary and undesirable. The section is clear, its application plain.'

(b) The existence of a high probability of 'social danger' arising from certain types of activity may justify the interpretation of an offence as one involving strict liability : hence the number of strict liability offences in relation to the sale of food, public health, etc.

(i) In *R. v. St. Margaret's Trust* (1958), a finance company was convicted for a breach of regulations under the Hire Purchase Order 1956 which was held to impose strict liability. *Per* Donovan J: 'The object of the order was to help to defend the currency against the peril of inflation which, if unchecked, would bring disaster on the country ... There would be little point in enacting that no one should breach the defences against a flood, and at the same time excusing anyone who did it innocently.'

(ii) *Per* Lord Diplock in *Sweet* v. *Parsley* (*see* 2:2): 'Where the subject matter of a statute is the regulation of a particular activity involving potential danger to public health, safety or morals, in which citizens have a choice whether they participate or not, the court may feel driven to infer an intention of Parliament to impose, by penal sanctions, a higher duty of care on those who choose to participate and to place on them an obligation to take whatever measures may be necessary to prevent the prohibited act, without regard to those considerations of cost or business practicability which play a part in the determination of what would be required of them in order to fulfil the ordinary common law duty of care.'

NOTE: For an example of the power of the courts to create offences of strict liability at common law, *see R. v. Lemon* (1979) (22:6) in which the court declared that blasphemy was a common law offence of strict liability. *See also R. v. Gibson* (1990) (common law offence of outraging public decency, by wearing 'foetus earrings'), in which it was held that there was *no requirement* that the prosecution should prove an intention to outrage or recklessness, or an appreciation that there was a risk of such outrage coupled with a determination nevertheless to run that risk.

8. A Canadian decision on strict liability

In *R. v. City of Sault Ste Marie* (1978), the Supreme Court of Canada considered the problem of strict liability. Dickson J, delivering the judg-ment of the Court, gave 'compelling grounds for the recognition of *three* categories of offences rather than the traditional two'. In the *first category* were offences in which *mens rea must be proved*. In the *second category* were offences in which there is *no need for the prosecution to prove the existence of mens rea*: 'the doing of the prohibited act *prima facie* imports the offence, leaving it open to the accused to avoid liability by proving that he took all reasonable care. This involves consideration of what a reasonable man would have done in the circumstances. ' In the *third category* are the offences of *absolute liability* where it is not open to the accused to exculpate himself by showing that he was free from fault.

The defence available to a defendant in the second category (strict liability offences) should be available 'if the accused reasonably believed in a mistaken set of facts which, if true, would render the act or omission innocent, or if he took all reasonable steps to avoid the particular event.'

9. A recent consideration of strict liability: *Gammon* v. *A.-G. of Hong Kong* (1985)

The Privy Council considered the case of a contractor and site agent for building works in Hong Kong who had been charged, following the collapse of a building, with deviating from approved plans in a manner likely to cause risk or injury to any person or damage to any property, contrary to a Hong Kong ordinance. The Privy Council held that:

(a) the presumption of law that *mens rea* was necessary could be dis-placed when the statute creating the offence was concerned with an issue of public concern (e.g. public safety);
(b) the presumption would still stand unless it could also be shown that the creation of strict liability would be effective to promote the objects of the statute by encouraging greater vigilance to prevent the commission of the prohibited act;
(c) it was consistent with the Hong Kong ordinance that some, at least, of the criminal offences it created should be of strict liability since this would promote greater vigilance, and since it would seriously weaken the effectiveness of local regulations if proof of knowledge of the materi-ality of deviations or the likelihood of risk was required, it followed that proof of knowledge was not required and the offences were of strict liability.

> NOTE: Comments by Gross are of interest: 'Perhaps the most prominent feature of most strict liability offences is that *conviction does not affect respectability*. Neither his conduct nor the punishment he receives for it stigmatises the offender. Not only is there an absence of wrongdoing, but the prohibited act might have been excused if only the law allowed the excuse to be heard.' He suggests that if there is to be 'strict liability',

certain conditions must be met: the risk of the harm for which liability may be imposed must be such that the person to be held liable must appreciate it; the individual to be held liable must have the capacity to prevent the harm; the measures necessary to prevent the harm must not be such as to prohibit the activity from which the risk of harm may arise.

Vicarious liability

10. Vicarious liability in general
Vicarious liability means the legal responsibility of one person for the wrongful acts of another, as, for example, when the acts are done within the scope of employment. The problem is: under what circumstances, if any, is a master or principal responsible for the wrongful acts committed by his servant or agent? (*See* e.g. *Portsea Island Co-op. Society* v. *Leyland* (1978).) The problem may be considered under two headings:

(a) the position at common law (*see* **11** below);
(b) the position under statute (*see* **12** below).

11. Vicarious liability at common law
The general rule at common law is that X is *not* vicariously liable for a crime committed by his servant, Y.

(a) In *R.* v. *Huggins* (1730), X, a prison warden, was charged with the murder of Z, a prisoner. Z's death had been caused by Y, a servant of X. It was held that Y was guilty, but that X was not, because the acts in question had been committed without X's knowledge.

> 'It is a point not to be disputed, but that in criminal cases the principal is not answerable for the act of the deputy as he is in civil cases: they must each answer for their own acts, and stand or fall by their own behaviour. All the authors that treat of criminal proceedings proceed on the foundation of this distinction; that to affect the superior by the act of his deputy, there must be the command of the superior, which is not found in this case': *per* Lord Raymond CJ.

(b) An *exception to this general rule* is found in the offence of *public nuisance* (i.e. the causing of substantial annoyance to the subjects of the Crown, by exposing to danger, or affecting injuriously in other ways, their lives, health or property). (*See* 21: **36**.) So, X will be criminally liable for such a nuisance created by Y, his servant, even though Y, in so acting, was disobeying X's orders. The reason for this exception is probably that the purpose of the prosecution is to prevent the nuisance from being continued, rather than to punish X: *see R.* v. *Stephens* (1866).

12. Vicarious liability under statute

Note e.g. the Transport Act 1982, s. 31: for the purpose of proceedings in relation to fixed penalty notices, it is conclusively presumed (notwithstanding that the person on whom a notice has been served may not be an individual) that he was the driver of the vehicle at the time of the alleged offence and, accordingly, that acts or omissions of the driver of the vehicle at the time were his acts or omissions. (But the presumption does *not* apply where it is proved that at the time of the alleged offence the vehicle was in the possession of some other person without the consent of the accused.)

13. Vicarious liability under statute following delegation

The general rule is stated in *Moussell Bros* v. *L & NW Railway Co.* (1917), in which X was convicted of the offence of having given a false account of goods to be carried by the railway, so as to avoid payment of the appropriate tolls. It was found that the false account had been given by a servant of X, on the instruction of X's manager, with the intention of avoiding payment of the tolls.

> '*Prima facie* a master is not to be made criminally responsible for the acts of his servant to which the master is not a party. But it may be the intention of the legislature, in order to guard against the happening of the forbidden thing, to impose a liability upon a principal even though he does not know of, and is not a party to, the forbidden act done by his servant . . . In those cases the legislature *absolutely forbids the act* and makes the principal liable without *mens rea*': *per* Viscount Reading CJ.

(a) Where there has been a general delegation of authority and responsibility by X to his servant Y, X will generally be liable for Y's infringement of a statute which concerns the running of the business; Y will be convicted (if at all) only as a secondary party.

(i) *Allen* v. *Whitehead* (1930). X, the proprietor of a refreshment house, was convicted, under the Metropolitan Police Act 1839, s. 44, of 'knowingly suffering prostitutes to meet together in his house and remain there'. X had forbidden his manager, Y, to allow prostitutes on the premises. 'Here the keeper of the house had delegated his duty to the manager. He had transferred to the manager the exercise of discretion in the conduct of the business and it seems to me that the only conclusion is, regard being had to the purpose of the Act, that the knowledge of the manager was the knowledge of the keeper of the house': *per* Lord Hewart CJ.

(ii) *Barker* v. *Levinson* (1951). X, an estate agent, responsible for a group of flats, gave Y authority to grant a lease to Z, if Z proved suitable. Y took a premium from Z, and X was charged under the Landlord and Tenant (Rent Control) Act 1949. It was held that X was not liable, since Y had been employed on one occasion only, and X had no knowledge of the premium.

(b) Where there has been a delegation of authority and responsibility it must be complete. In *Vane* v. *Yiannopoullos* (1965). X, a restaurant proprietor, told Y, a waitress, to sell liquor only to customers buying a meal. He then retired to a room underneath the restaurant. He was held not guilty of an infringement of the Licensing Act 1961, s. 22, since he had not delegated the complete control of the restaurant to Y.

Draft Criminal Code Bill

14. Vicarious liability
'Subject to subsec. 3 [delegation, related to pre-Code offences] an element of an offence (other than a fault element [*see* 3:**20**]) may be attributed to a person by reason of an act done by another only if that other is – *(a)* specified in the definition of the offence as a person whose act may be so attributed; or *(b)* acting within the scope of his employment or authority and the definition of the offence specifies the element in terms which apply to both persons': cl. 29(1).

15. Attribution of fault element to another
'Subject to subsec. 3, a fault element of an offence may be attributed to a person by reason of the fault of another only if the terms of the enactment creating the offence so provide': cl. 29(2).

Progress test 4

1. What is meant by 'strict liability' in the criminal law? **(1,2)**

2. Comment on *Warner* v. *Metropolitan Police Commissioner* (1969). **(3)**

3. Explain the decision in *R.* v. *Waller* (1991). **(4)**

4. Outline the fundamentals of the case for strict liability. **(7)**

5. What was the essence of the decision in *Gammon* v. *Attorney-General of Hong Kong* (1985)? **(9)**

6. Outline the principle of vicarious liability under statute following delegation. **(13)**

5

Criminal responsibility (4): parties to a crime

Participants in a crime

1. General considerations

In some circumstances, criminal liability may be imposed not only on D_1, the actual, direct perpetrator of the crime, but also upon D_2 and D_3, other persons who have aided, abetted, counselled or procured the commission of that crime. D_1 is known as the *principal*; D_2 and D_3 are the *secondary parties*, i.e. the *accomplices* or *accessories*.

(a) Consider the complicity and criminal liability, if any, of X_1 and X_2 in the specific circumstances outlined below.

(i) X_1 and X_2 agree that X_1 shall rob Y by pushing him to the ground and seizing his bag. X_2 is to wait nearby in a car in which X_1 will make his escape. X_1 beats Y and kills him in the process: *R. v. Betts and Ridley* (1930).

(ii) X_1 and X_2 unlawfully take Y's motor car and drive off in it. X_1 drives the car in a reckless manner, causing the death of Z: *R. v. Baldessare* (1930).

(b) Note the liability attached to the activities of X_1 and X_2 in the cases outlined above.

(i) In *R. v. Betts and Ridley* (1930), X_1 and X_2 were convicted of murder. 'It is clear law that it is not necessary that the party, to constitute him a principal in the second degree (*see* 5 below), should be actually present. He [X_2] is, in construction of law, present aiding and abetting if, with the intention of giving assistance, he is near enough to afford it, should the occasion arise, . . .': *per* Avory J.

(ii) In *R. v. Baldessare* (1930), X_1 was held guilty of manslaughter, and X_2 was also guilty of manslaughter as a principal in the second degree. It mattered not whose hand was actually controlling the car at the time of the offence; the jury was entitled to infer that X_1, as the driver, was the agent of the passenger, X_2.

2. Accomplices

The governing statutes concerning accomplices are now:

(a) the Accessories and Abettors Act 1861, s. 8; and
(b) the Magistrates' Courts Act 1980, s. 44.

The situation today, following the Criminal Law Act 1967, must be considered in relation to the pre-1967 situation; both are outlined below. (The pre-1967 cases remain, in general, authoritative: *see* **10** below.)

The pre-1967 situation

3. General
Four categories of participation in a felony existed:

(a) as a principal in the first degree (*see* **4**);
(b) as a principal in the second degree (or 'aider and abettor') (*see* **5**);
(c) as an accessory before the fact (*see* **6**);
(d) as an accessory after the fact (*see* **7**).

4. Principal in the first degree
This was the *actual of offender*, i.e. the 'criminal actor', the actual *perpetrator* of the offence. He had brought about the *actus reus*, with the requisite *mens rea*, by his own conduct.

(a) Where the *actus reus* is brought about directly by an innocent agent (Y), the principal (X) was the participant whose act was the most immediate cause of Y's act, i.e. X's was the *'last mens rea'* to have preceded the crime. In *R. v. Butt* (1884) X made a false statement to his employer's book-keeper, Y, knowing that Y would record the statement in his accounts. Y did so, and X was convicted, as a principal, of falsifying his employer's accounts. *See also R. v. Michael* (1840), at 2:**10**.
(b) There could be more than one principal in the first degree (i.e. joint principals), for example, where X_1 holds down a victim in order that X_2 may steal from him.

5. Principal in the second degree
This was the person who *aided and abetted* the commission of the felony at the very time it was being committed. He has assisted in bringing about the crime, but not as the actual perpetrator. So, in *R. v. Baldessare* (1930) (*see* **1** (*a*)), X_2 was convicted as a principal in the second degree.

(a) 'Aiding and abetting' involved giving help or encouragement during the commission of the crime, e.g. by keeping watch: *see R. v. Griffith* (1553). (In *R. v. Jones and Mirrless* (1977), the Court of Appeal held that to be guilty of aiding and abetting an assault there must be some actual encouragement given. Mere presence did *not* suffice. 'It is well known that the words "aid and abet" are apt to describe the action of a person who is present at the time of the commission of an offence and takes some part therein': *per* Lord Goddard in *Ferguson* v. *Weaving* (1951).)

(b) The encouragement must be *intentional*. Presence alone did not suffice. 'A man may unwittingly encourage another in fact by his presence, by misinterpreted words, or by his silence, or non-interference; or he may encourage intentionally by expression, gestures or actions intended to signify approval. In the latter case he aids and abets, in the former he does not': *per* Hawkins J in *R.* v. *Coney* (1882). *See also NCB* v *Gamble* (1959).

(c) Presence at the scene of the crime was not always necessary; 'constructive presence' might be sufficient, as where the aider and abettor was some distance away, but near enough to give whatever assistance is required: *see R.* v. *Betts and Ridley* (1930).

(d) A person would not be guilty as an aider and abettor merely because he was present at the scene of the crime and took no action to prevent its commission: *see R.* v. *Alkinson* (1869); *R.* v. *Gray* (1917). Where there was a legal duty to intervene in order to prevent the commission of an offence, failure to do so could be held to be aiding and abetting: *see R.* v. *Harris* (1964), in which X_1 who was supervising X_2, a learner-driver, failed to stop X_2 driving at a dangerous speed; X_1 was held to have aided and abetted X_2's offence of causing death by dangerous driving.

(e) 'Before a person can be convicted of aiding and abetting the commission of an offence, he must at least know the essential matters which constitute the offence. He need not actually know that an offence has been committed, because he may not know that the facts constitute an offence, and ignorance of the law is not a defence': *per* Lord Goddard CJ in *Johnson* v. *Youden* (1950). *See also Ferguson* v. *Weaving* (1951); *Stanton & Sons* v. *Webber* (1973).

(f) There had to be a common purpose (not necessarily prearranged) between the principals in the first and second degrees and such purpose must have existed at the time of the commission of the felony: *see R.* v. *Hilton* (1858). Aiding, abetting and counselling almost always required some kind of *mental link* between the secondary party and the principal offender: *A. -G.'s Reference (No. 1 of 1975) (see* **11***)*. 'A person who is present aiding and abetting the commission of an offence without any pre-arranged plan or plot is guilty of the offence as a principal in the second degree': *Mohan* v. *R.* (1967).

(g) A person may be liable as aider and abettor even though the principal is not aware of his assistance: *see R.* v. *Kupferberg* (1918).

(h) The offence of aiding and abetting, as a common law offence, is applicable to all statutes unless specifically excluded by statute. (Thus, offences created by the Public Order Act 1986 *(see* 21:**23***)* can be committed by aiders and abettors as well as principals. *See R.* v. *Jefferson and Skerritt* (1993).)

6. Accessory before the fact

This was the person who 'being absent at the time of the felony committed, doth yet procure, counsel, command, or abet to commit a felony' (*1 Hale, P.C. 615*), i.e. the person who, before the commission of the crime, gave intentional encouragement to its commission, as where X_1, a week before X_2 unlawfully broke open Y's safe, provided X_2 with metal-cutting equipment, knowing that X_2 intended to commit an offence of that nature: *R. v. Bainbridge* (1960).

(a) Active and intentional encouragement was essential. In *R. v. Taylor* (1875), X had agreed merely to act as stakeholder in a prize fight between Y and Z, as a result of which Y died. X, who did not encourage the fight and was not present, was held not to be an accessory to the manslaughter of Y.

(b) Knowledge of the kind of felony intended was necessary, but knowledge of the particular offence, or its precise details, was not necessary: *see R. v. Bainbridge* (1960). *Per* Lord Parker: 'There must not be merely suspicion but knowledge that a crime of the type in question was intended, and that the equipment was bought with that in view.'

(c) If the principal committed a felony which differed in its mode from that instigated, the instigator was not excused from liability; but if the felony committed was, in fact, a different crime to that instigated, the instigator was afforded a defence: *see R. v. Saunders and Archer* (1576); *R. v. Creamer* (1966).

   (*i*) X_1 procures X_2 to kill Y by stabbing him. X_2 then kills Y by administering poison. X_1 is not excused.
   (*ii*) X_1 procures X_2 to steal Y's purse. In order to do so, X_2 shoots and kills Y. X_1 is not an accessory to the murder of Y.

7. Accessory after the fact

This was one who, knowing that a felony had been committed, subsequently harboured or relieved the felons, or in any way secured or attempted to secure their escape.

(a) An intention to assist the felon to escape justice was essential: *see R. v. Jones* (1949).

(b) Active assistance was also essential: *see R. v. Chapple* (1840).

(c) Inactivity, e.g. mere failure to report the felon's presence to the police, did not suffice. (*See* now **13**.)

8. Parties to the commission of a misdemeanour

Principals in the first and second degrees, and accessories before the fact, could participate in a misdemeanour; the category of 'accessory after the fact' had no application.

The situation after 1967

9. The effect of the Criminal Law Act 1967 (*See* 1:24)

By s. 1(1) distinctions between felony and misdemeanour are abolished. By s. 1(2) the law and practice in relation to all offences is the law and practice applicable at the commencement of the Act in relation to misdemeanours. By s. 12(6) the law concerning treason is not affected. *The present situation is, therefore*:

(a) The Accessories and Abettors Act 1861, s. 8 (*see* **10**), applies to all offences which were formerly classed as felonies or misdemeanours.

(b) By the Magistrates' Courts Act 1980, s. 44: '(1) A person who *aids, abets, counsels or procures* the commission by another person of a summary offence shall be guilty of the like offence and may be tried (whether or not he is charged as a principal) either by a court having jurisdiction to try that other person or by a court having by virtue of his own offence jurisdiction to try him. (2) Any offence consisting in aiding, abetting, counselling or procuring the commission of an offence triable either way (other than an offence listed in Schedule 1 to this Act) shall by virtue of this subsection be triable either way.'

(c) The category of accessory after the fact (to a felony) has *disappeared* except in the case of treason.

(d) Apart from the case of treason (in which the pre-1967 categories remain), liability for participation in a crime now involves:

    (*i*) committing the *actus reus* itself (or through an innocent agent); *or*

    (*ii*) aiding and abetting the commission of the offence at the very time of its commission; *or*

    (*iii*) counselling or procuring its commission.

10. Accessories and Abettors Act 1861, s. 8

'Whosoever shall aid, abet, counsel or procure the commission of any indictable offence whether the same be an offence at common law or by virtue of any Act passed or to be passed, shall be liable to be tried, indicted and punished as a principal offender'.

(a) 'Aiding and abetting' corresponds to the activities formerly carried out by a principal in the second degree (*see* **5**).

(b) 'Counselling or procuring' corresponds to the activities formerly carried out by an accessory before the fact (*see* **6**).

(c) According to the new terminology, therefore, parties to an offence may include a principal offender, aider, abettor, counsellor or procurer.

(The pre-1967 cases as they affect *principals in the first and second degrees and accessories before the fact* remain authoritative.)

11. *A.-G.'s Reference (No. 1 of 1975)*

The Court of Appeal answered *in the negative* the following question: 'Whether an accused who surreptitiously laced a friend's drinks with double measures of spirits when he knew that his friend would shortly be driving his car home, and in consequence his friend drove with an excess quantity of alcohol in his body and was convicted of the offence under the Road Traffic Act 1972, s. 6(1), is entitled to a ruling of no case to answer on being later charged as an aider, abettor, counsellor and procurer, on the ground that there was no shared intention between the two, that the accused did not by accompanying him or otherwise positively encourage the friend to drive, or on any other ground.' Note the following extracts from Lord Widgery's statement.

(a) 'Aiding and abetting almost inevitably involves a situation in which the secondary party and the main offender are together at some stage discussing the plans which they may be making in respect of the alleged offence, and are in contact so that each knows what is passing through the mind of the other. . . .'

(b) '. . . We approach s. 8 of the 1861 Act on the basis that the words should be given their ordinary meaning, if possible. We approach the section on the basis also that if four words are employed here, "aid, abet, counsel or procure", the probability is that there is a difference between each of these four words and the other three . . . each word must be given its ordinary meaning . . .'

(c) 'To procure means to produce by endeavour. You procure a thing by setting out to see that it happens and taking the appropriate steps to produce that happening . . . You cannot procure an offence unless there is a causal link between what you do and the commission of the offence.'

(d) '. . . Giving the words their ordinary meaning in English, and asking oneself whether in those circumstances the offence has been procured, we are in no doubt that the answer is that it has. It has been procured because, unknown to the driver and without his collaboration, he has been put in a position in which in fact he has committed an offence which he never would have committed otherwise. We think there was a case to answer. . . .'

12. 'To counsel': a recent decision

In *R.* v. *Calhaem* (1985), X_1 was indicted for murder under the Accessories and Abettors Act 1861, s. 8, as amended. The prosecution alleged that X_1 had counselled X_2 to murder Y. X_2 pleaded guilty to murder and gave evidence for the Crown at X_1's trial that he had decided not to kill Y, but had gone berserk and killed her. The trial judge directed the jury that 'to counsel' meant to incite, solicit, instruct or otherwise, or to 'put somebody up to something', and that it was for the Crown to prove that X_1 in that sense had counselled X_2 to kill Y, that Y was killed by X_2 in circumstances amounting to murder, and that the killing was within the scope of the instruction or authorisation. X_1 was convicted.

In dismissing the appeal, the Court of Appeal held that on the true construction of s. 8 of the 1861 Act, *'counsel' had no implication of any causal connection between the counselling and the principal offence*; the natural meaning of 'counsel' did not imply the commission of the offence; the offence was established if there was counselling and the principal offence was committed by the person who had been counselled acting, not by accident, but within the scope of his authority.

13. Assisting offenders
The Criminal Law Act 1967, s. 4(1), created a new offence of 'assisting offenders': 'Where a person has committed an arrestable offence, any other person who, knowing or believing him to be guilty of the offence or of some other offence, does without lawful authority or reasonable excuse any act with intent to impede his apprehension or prosecution shall be guilty of an offence.' (This replaces the offence of being an accessory after the fact to felony.)

(a) For 'arrestable offence' *see* now the Police and Criminal Evidence Act 1984, s. 24(1), Sch. 6, para. 17. (*See* 1: **27**.)

(b) It is for the prosecution to show in a case involving the 1967 Act, s. 4(1), that:

(*i*) an arrestable offence has been committed; *and*

(*ii*) the accused knew (or believed) that the other person had committed this kind of offence; *and*

(*iii*) the accused has acted intending to impede the apprehension or prosecution of the other person; *and*

(*iv*) the accused had no lawful authority or reasonable excuse for his action.

(c) It is *not* necessary for the prosecution to show that the accused had knowledge of the *identity* of the person committing the arrestable offence: *R.* v. *Brindley* (1971).

Some problems of participation in offences

14. Importance of differentiating parties
In most cases it is of importance that the principal offender be differentiated from secondary participants. Thus, in the case of an offence of strict liability (*see* 4: **1**), such liability attaches to the principal offender only and

will not fall on secondary parties. *See* e.g. *Callow* v. *Tillstone* (1900). A secondary party generally requires full *mens rea* in relation to the consequences of his actions and the *actus reus* of the principal offence.

15. *Mens rea* of the secondary party

The *mens rea* of a secondary participant is constituted by an *intention*, direct or oblique, that his conduct will assist, encourage, incite the commission of an offence (i.e. *mens rea* as to *consequences*), and *awareness* of the general facts which comprise the *actus reus* of that offence (i.e. *mens rea* as to *circumstances*).

(a) 'The knowledge that is required to be proved in the mind of [the accused secondary participant] is not the knowledge of the precise crime . . . It is not enough to show that he either suspected or knew that some crime was intended and was going to be committed . . . It must be proved that he knew that the type of crime which was in fact committed was intended': *R.* v. *Bainbridge* (1960).

(b) 'It is clear that if an alleged accessory is perfectly well aware that he is participating in one of a limited number of crimes and one of these is in fact committed, he is liable under the general law at least as one who aids, abets, counsels or procures that crime even if he is not actually a principal': *per* Lord Hailsham in *DPP for Northern Ireland* v. *Maxwell* (1978). In this case the House of Lords held that knowledge of the actual offence committed need *not* be shown before a person could be convicted of aiding and abetting. It sufficed that he knew the *type of offence* to be committed or the *essential matters* constituting the offence. *Per* Lord Scarman: 'An accessory who leaves it to his principal to choose is liable, provided always the choice is made from the range of offences from which the accessory contemplates the choice will be made.' (The accused, a member of an illegal terrorist organisation, was instructed by another member to drive his car so as to lead another car to a public house, where persons in the other car threw a bomb into the public house. The accused was convicted, as a secondary party, of doing an act with intent to cause an explosion, and being in possession of a bomb. He appealed, stating that, although he was aware that a terrorist attack was planned, he had not known that a bombing was contemplated. It was held that he had been rightly convicted.)

(c) Where the principal had *less mens rea* than the secondary party, the situation was governed by the decision in *R.* v. *Richards* (1974), in which the Court of Appeal had held that unless an accomplice was actually present at the scene of the crime he could not be charged with an offence more serious than that brought against the principal. But in *R.* v. *Howe and Bannister* (1987) it was suggested that *R.* v. *Richards* ought not to be followed; the House of Lords held that it *was* possible to convict an accessory of murder where he had the necessary intent, while the principal was guilty of manslaughter only.

16. Liability of a secondary party for unforeseen consequences

The general principle applicable in these circumstances seems to be that enunciated by Lord Parker CJ in *R.* v. *Anderson and Morris* (1966): 'Where two persons embark on a joint enterprise, each is liable for the acts done in pursuance of that joint enterprise, and that includes liability for unusual consequences if they arise from the execution of the agreed joint enterprise but . . . if one of the adventurers goes beyond what has been tacitly agreed as part of the common enterprise, his co-adventurer is not liable for the consequences of that unauthorised act . . . It is for the jury in every case to decide whether what was done was part of the joint enterprise, or went beyond it and was in fact an act unauthorised by that joint enterprise.'

(a) It would seem that where X_1 moves *beyond* his agreement with X_2, then X_2 may escape criminal liability for any consequence resulting from X_1's 'unauthorised' act.

(*i*) Assume, for example, that X_1 and X_2 plan a joint burglary of Y's premises and, in pursuance of that plan, enter the premises. Suddenly and unexpectedly, X_1 turns on Y, attacks him and kills him while he (Y) is attempting to protect his property. On these facts alone, X_2 is *not* liable as a party to the murder of Y.

(*ii*) Assume, next, that, in other circumstances, in pursuit of a joint plan by X_1 and X_2 to kill Y by stabbing him, X_1 unexpectedly produces a gun and shoots Y, killing him. X_2 *will* be considered as a party to the killing of Y.

(*iii*) But note carefully the comment of Lord Parker in *R.* v. *Anderson and Morris* (1966), that, 'considered as a matter of causation, there may well be an overwhelming supervening event which is of such a character that it will relegate into history matters which would otherwise be looked upon as causative factors.'

(b) In *R.* v. *Jubb and Rigby* (1984), X_1 and X_2 blamed each other for the murder of Y which occurred during a planned robbery. Their appeals against conviction for murder were dismissed. The Court of Appeal pointed out that whilst, in directing the jury on the question of joint enterprise and whether what occurred was within the contemplation or agreement of X_1 and X_2, the judge referred to 'may well' involve killing; it was made clear to the jury that this meant 'probably' involve killing. In future, a constant phrase should be used, namely, 'probably'.

(c) Note *Chan Wing-Siu* v. *R.* (1985). X_1, X_2 and X_3 were convicted in Hong Kong of the murder of Y. It was alleged that they had gone to Y's flat intending to rob him. They argued that they had gone to the flat to collect a debt from Y and that he had attacked them. X_1 and X_2 admitted taking knives to Y's flat. The trial judge had directed the jury that each of the accused could be convicted if it could be proved that he had contemplated that a knife might be used by either of the others with the intention of inflicting serious bodily harm on any occupant of the flat. The Privy Council dismissed the subsequent appeals.

(*i*) *Per* Sir Robin Cooke: 'Where a man lends himself to a criminal enterprise knowing that potentially murderous weapons are to be carried, and in the event they are in fact used by his partner with an intent sufficient for murder, he should not escape the consequences by relying on a nuance of prior assessment, only too likely to have been optimistic. . . . What has to be brought home to the jury is that occasionally a risk may have occurred to an accused's mind, fleetingly or even causing him some deliberation, but may genuinely have been dismissed by him as altogether negligible. If they think there is a reasonable possibility that the case is in that class, taking the risk should not make the accused a party to such a crime of intention as murder or wounding with intent to cause grievous bodily harm.'

(*ii*) *Chan Wing-Siu* v. *R.* seems to suggest that where the infliction of serious bodily injury is a *possible incident* within the commission of an unlawful enterprise, all those who are proved to have participated *with the knowledge that such serious injury might result* may be guilty, as the case may be, of murder or causing grievous bodily harm with intent. (*See R.* v. *Slack* (1989) at 9:43.)

(d) In *R.* v. *Dunbar* (1988), the Court of Appeal held that it was *not* open to a trial judge to direct that an alleged party to a conspiracy to murder would be guilty of manslaughter (*see* Chap. 10) where the degree of violence or harm to the victim contemplated or intended by the party fell short of serious injury.

(e) In *R.* v. *Hyde* (1991) it was held by the Court of Appeal that in order to secure convictions for murder (*see* Chap.9), it must be established that the actual killer did intend to kill or do serious bodily harm, and that the secondary party involved did realise that the killer *might* kill or *might* inflict some serious injury, but yet that secondary party continued his participation in the joint enterprise.

(f) In *Hui Chi-ming* v. *R.* (1992), the Privy Council held that where X and Y join in an unlawful enterprise and X performs an act which causes death, Y will be considered as possessing the appropriate *mens rea* to be guilty as a secondary party to murder if he (Y) contemplated that X *might* kill or *might* intentionally cause some serious injury. In order to convict Y it is *not* necessary that X contemplated that he(X) might act in that way. (It was held also that the trial judge had *not* erred in excluding evidence that X – the principal offender – had been acquitted of murder but convicted of manslaughter.)

(g) In *R. v. Roberts* (1993), the Court of Appeal held that the principle that where X and Y were involved in a joint unlawful enterprise, X may be guilty of murder if he realised (but without agreeing to such conduct being employed) that Y *might* kill or intentionally inflict serious injury, but nevertheless continued to participate with Y in the enterprise, and Y, with requisite intent, killed in the course of the enterprise, is of general application whether or not weapons are carried and whether the object of the enterprise is to cause physical injury or to engage in some other unlawful act such as burglary or robbery.

    (*i*) The principle in *R. v. Hyde* (1991) was *approved*.

    (*ii*) *Per* Lord Taylor CJ: 'The appellant knew the plan was to rob an old man in his cottage. He consistently conceded in evidence that he knew the victim was unlikely to yield up his money or goods without resistance. The nub of the case was therefore not whether the appellant (X) realised that force might be used but whether he realised only that some physical harm might be done or that really serious injury might be inflicted'. X's appeal was *dismissed*.

17. Aiding by inactivity or omission

In general, since one person is not under a duty to prevent another committing a crime, X_2 may not be liable for an offence committed by X_1 because he (X_2) failed to stop it.

(a) In *R. v. Clarkson and Carroll* (1971), X_1 and X_2, soldiers, entered a barrack room in which Y was being raped by other soldiers. X_1 and X_2 were charged with aiding and abetting the rape of Y, but there was no evidence that they had done any act or spoken any word which involved encouragement or participation. They were convicted, and their appeals were allowed. *Per* Megaw LJ: 'It is not enough that the presence of the accused has, in fact, given encouragement. It must be proved that the accused intended to give encouragement, that he wilfully encouraged . . . There must be an intention to encourage; and there must also be an encouragement in fact, in cases such as the present case.'

(b) Note, however, *R. v. Russell* (1933), an Australian case, in which X_1, a husband who stood by inactively, watching X_2, his wife, drown Y, their child, was held guilty of abetting unlawful homicide. X_1's omission to act was considered to have encouraged X_2's conduct.

(c) *See R. v. Bland* (1988), in which the fact that X lived with Y in the same room was insufficient evidence from which an inference of assistance could be drawn. 'Assistance'required more than mere knowledge by X that Y was dealing in drugs. Evidence of encouragement was essential.

18. Where there is no principal offender

In *Thornton v. Mitchell* (1940), a bus conductor, X_1, negligently directed his driver, X_2, to reverse the bus. X_2, who could not see to the rear, reversed the bus and, in doing so, killed a pedestrian. X_2 was acquitted of careless driving and it was held that X_1 could not, therefore, be convicted of aiding and abetting X_2 in doing something he had not done.

Where, however, the prosecution shows that the *actus reus* of the offence was in fact the result of the conduct of some person, then, even though that person has not been produced or ascertained, or evidence of his guilt cannot be presented to a court, others may be convicted as secondary parties: *see* e.g. *R.* v. *Davis* (1977).

19. Repentance and withdrawal from a joint enterprise by secondary parties
Assume that X_1 counsels X_2 to commit a crime and that some time later, and *before* the crime is committed, X_1 voluntarily withdraws from the enterprise *and* communicates the withdrawal in express terms to X_2, then X_1 may escape liability for that crime: *see R.* v. *Croft* (1944).

(a) It was held, in *R.* v. *Becerra and Cooper* (1975), that for one member to withdraw from a joint criminal enterprise, a mere mental change of intention and physical change of place would *not* suffice, save in exceptional circumstances. Where practicable and reasonable, there must be a 'timely and unequivocal communication' of his intention to withdraw to the other participants. There was, therefore, no such appropriate communication of withdrawal where one party shouted, 'Someone is coming. Come on, let's go', and disappeared through a window during a burglary: *see R.* v. *Grundy* (1977); *R.* v. *Whitefield* (1984).

(b) In *R.* v. *Rook* (1993), the Court of Appeal restated the law: a person who changes his mind concerning his participating in the commission of an offence but who, nevertheless, fails to communicate that intention to others engaged in that offence has *not* effectively withdrawn from the commission of the offence, and *remains liable* as a secondary party.

(i) X, the appellant, and Y agreed to carry out the 'contract killing' of the wife of another person and recruited Z to participate. X did not turn up to participate in the killing, which was carried out by Y and Z. X argued that he had never intended the woman to be killed. His deliberate absence on the day chosen for the killing was a reflection of his belief that if he were not there, Y and Z would not carry on without him. He was convicted, and appealed.

(ii) *Per* Lloyd LJ: '. . . It is no defence to a secondary party to say that he did not intend the victim to be killed, or to suffer serious harm, if he contemplated or foresaw the event as a real or serious risk . . . In *R.* v. *Whitefield* (1984), Dunn LJ stated the law as follows: "If a person has counselled another to commit a crime, he may escape liability by withdrawal before the crime is committed, but it is not sufficient that he should merely repent or change his mind. If his participation is confined to advice or encouragement, he must at least communicate his change of mind to the other, and the communication must be such as will serve unequivocal notice upon the other party to the common unlawful cause that if he proceeds upon it he does so without the aid and assistance of those who withdraw" . . . In the present case the appellant never told the others that he was not going ahead with the crime. His absence on the day could not possibly amount to "unequivocal communication of his withdrawal" . . . The minimum necessary for withdrawal from the crime was *not* established on the facts.'

(*iii*) X's appeal was *dismissed*.

20. Victims as aiders and abettors

In relation to some sexual offences there seems to be a rule that where legislation has been designed for the protection of a specific group of persons, those persons cannot become accessories to offences committed against them where they have given their consent.

(a) In *R.* v. *Tyrrell* (1984), X_1, a girl under sixteen, was convicted of abetting X_2 to have unlawful sexual intercourse with her, under the Criminal Law Amendment Act 1885, s. 5. (*See* now the Sexual Offences Act 1956, s. 6.) X_1's conviction was quashed on appeal. It was held that she could *not* be convicted of abetting since the statute 'was passed for the purpose of protecting women and girls against themselves': *per* Lord Coleridge CJ. It could not have been intended that the girls for whose protection the Act had been passed should be punishable under it for offences committed upon themselves.

(b) Note that this rule relates to *victims only*. Hence it would seem possible for an under-age girl to be convicted of abetting a man to have sexual intercourse with another under-age girl.

(c) In *R.* v. *Whitehouse* (1977), the rule was applied in a charge of incest, under the Sexual Offences Act 1956, s. 11. X_1 had pleaded guilty to a charge of inciting X_2, his fifteen-year-old daughter, to commit incest with him. 'Clearly the relevant provisions of the 1956 Act are intended to protect women and girls. Most certainly s. 11 is intended to protect girls under the age of sixteen from criminal liability, and the Act as a whole exists, insofar as it deals with women and girls exposed to sexual threat, to protect them. The very fact that girls under the age of sixteen are protected from criminal liability for what would otherwise be incest demonstrates that this girl who is said to have been the subject of incitement was being incited to do something which, if she did it, could not be a crime by her': *per* Scarman LJ. (*See* now the Criminal Law Act 1977, s. 54.)

NOTE: (1) For *attempting* to aid, abet, counsel or procure, *see* the Criminal Attempts Act 1981, s. 1(4)(b), at 8:9, and *R. v. Dunnington* (1984), in which the Court of Appeal held that it is still an offence under the 1981 Act, ss. 1(1) and 4, to aid and abet an *attempt* to commit a crime. (2) The Law Commission Consultation Paper (1993, No. 131), '*Assisting and Encouraging Crime*', suggests a new scheme of statutory offences of 'assisting' and 'encouraging' the commission of a crime. The law in this area is criticised as unclear and inconsistent.

Draft Criminal Code Bill

21. Principals
'(1) A person is guilty of an offence as a principal if, with the fault required for the offence – (*a*) he does the act or acts specified for the offence, or (*b*) he does at least one such act and procures, assists or encourages any other such acts done by another; or (*c*) he procures, assists or encourages such act or acts done by another who is not himself guilty of the offence because (*i*) he is under ten years of age; or (*ii*) he does the act or acts without the fault required for the offence; or (*iii*) he has a defence. (2) A person guilty of an offence by virtue of the attribution to him of an element of the offence under cl. 29 (vicarious liability) is so guilty as a principal': cl. 26.

22. Accessories
'(1) A person is guilty of an offence as an accessory if – (*a*) he intentionally procures, assists or encourages the act which constitutes or results in the commission of the offence by the principal; and (*b*) he knows of, or (where recklessness suffices in the case of the principal) is reckless with respect to, any circumstance that is an element of the offence; and (*c*) he intends that the principal shall act, or is aware that he is or may be acting, or that he may act, with the fault (if any) required for the offence': cl. 27(1).

Progress test 5

1. Comment on *R. v. Betts and Ridley* (1930). **(1)**

2. What were the pre-1967 categories of participation in a felony? **(3)**

3. Outline the general effect of the Criminal Law Act 1976, s. 1. **(9)**

4. Explain *A-G.'s Reference (No. 1 of 1975)*. **(11)**

5. What is meant by 'counselling' a person to commit an offence? **(12)**

6. Outline the decision in *DPP for Northern Ireland* v. *Maxwell* (1978). **(15)**

7. Explain the decision in *Chan Wing-Siu* v. *R.* (1985). **(16)**

8. What was the essence of the decision in *R.* v. *Roberts* (1993)? **(16)**

9. Can one aid an offence by inactivity or omission? **(17)**

10. Comment on *R.* v. *Rook* (1993). **(19)**

Criminal responsibility (5): general defences

The nature of the defences

1. General and special defences

Persons charged with criminal offences may have defences of both a *general* and a *special* nature. A defence is, essentially, based upon evidence offered by the accused person in order to defeat a criminal charge. (Note that to allow a defence does not imply in any way the court's approval of the actions of the accused person: *per* Lord Edmund-Davies in *DPP for N. Ireland* v. *Lynch* (1975), at **9** below.)

(a) *A general defence* (of the type considered in this chapter) is one which can apply in the case of crimes *generally*; e.g. X, charged with murder, may plead that he was *insane* at the time when he performed the act: *see R.* v. *Windle* (1952) (*see* **30**).

(b) *A special defence* is one which applies in the case of certain *particular crimes*; e.g. the defence available in a charge under the Abortion Act 1967 (*see* **11:8**) that the act was *necessary* because of a substantial risk that the child if born would suffer from such abnormalities as to be seriously handicapped; the defence in a charge under the Obscene Publications Act 1959 (*see* **22:12**) that the publishing of the article was justified as being 'for the public good' because it was in the interest of science, literature, art, etc.

2. The general defences enumerated

The following *general defences* are considered below:

(a) mistake (*see* **3–6**);
(b) compulsion (*see* **7–13**);
(c) intoxication (*see* **14–19**);
(d) automatism (*see* **20–25**);
(e) insanity (*see* **26–35**);
(f) self-defence (*see* **36–40**).

Other variations in liability are considered under **41–49**.

Mistake

3. General rules

The following rules apply to the general defence of mistake. Note Black's comment: 'A mistake exists when a person, under some erroneous conviction of law or fact, does, or omits to do, some act which, but for the erroneous conviction, he would not have done or omitted.'

(a) Mistake is a defence where it has prevented the accused, X, from having the *mens rea* required by law for the offence for which he has been charged: *see DPP* v. *Morgan* (1976) (*see* **5**).

(b) Where a crime requires proof of a subjective *mens rea*, a mistake, reasonable or unreasonable, which negates intention or recklessness required in the *actus reus*, affords a defence: *DPP* v. *Morgan* (1976).

(c) Where the *actus reus* necessarily involves only *negligence*, a reasonable mistake may excuse, if honestly held.

(d) In the case of an offence based on strict liability, mistake will not generally excuse: *see R.* v. *Bishop* (1880); *Cundy* v. *Le Cocq* (1884). (*see* **4:4(b)**.)

(e) Ignorance of the law is in itself no excuse (*see* **6**).

(f) In the case of a statutory offence which is not one of strict liability (*see* Chap. 4) and where the statutory words do not require, expressly or by implication, *mens rea*, a mistaken belief will not succeed as a defence *unless* based on reasonable grounds: *R.* v. *Tolson* (1889).

(g) Mistaken belief suggests that defendant cannot have been reckless according to the *Caldwell* type of recklessness: *see* **3:16**.

4. 'Reasonable mistake'

Before *DPP* v. *Morgan* (1976), it appeared that *only a reasonable mistake* afforded a defence. Thus, in *R.* v. *Tolson* (1889), X had been deserted by her husband, Y. Following enquiries, X learned that Y had been drowned at sea. Five years later, in the belief that she was a widow, she married Z. Later, Y re-appeared. It was held that X was not guilty of bigamy; her defence of mistake was accepted because of her *honest belief on reasonable grounds* that Y was dead. Following *DPP* v. *Morgan* (1976), it would now seem that *the dictum according to which only a reasonable belief affords a defence is no longer valid. See* **5**. (The defence of mistake as to legal rights will not extend to a case where a court has made an order stating what these rights are: *R.* v. *Barrett* (1981).) *See R.* v. *Williams* (1984) – in a case of alleged assault by X, his mistaken belief that some other person was being unlawfully assaulted (which led to his (X's) intervention during an arrest) need not have been reasonable, provided it was *honestly held*.

5. *DPP* v. *Morgan* (1976)

This important case turned on the Sexual Offences Act 1956, s. 1 (*see* **13:3**).

(a) *The facts.* A invited B, C and D to his house to have intercourse with W (A's wife). A told them that if W should appear to resist, this would be pretence only. B, C and D had intercourse with W in spite of her struggles and protests. B, C and D were charged with rape and were convicted. The judge directed the jury that if they were satisfied that W did not consent, defendants' belief that W did consent was no defence *unless based on reasonable grounds*.

(b) *Court of Appeal.* The appeals of B, C and D were dismissed. A defendant *could be* properly convicted of rape where he *mistakenly but honestly believed* that the woman consented *unless* that belief was based *on reasonable grounds.* Leave to appeal to the House of Lords was granted and the Court certified the following to be a point of law of general public importance: '*Whether in rape the defendant can properly be convicted notwithstanding that he in fact believed that the woman consented if such belief was not based on reasonable grounds.*'

(c) *House of Lords.* It was held that there had been a *misdirection* by the trial judge. *So long as defendants honestly held the belief, it did not matter that there were no reasonable grounds for doing so*, though the reasonableness or otherwise of the alleged belief was important evidence as to whether it had been truly held. (The proviso to the Criminal Appeal Act 1968, s. 2(1), was applied and the appeals were dismissed.)

> NOTE: Suggestions that the decision in *DPP* v. *Morgan* (1976) was limited solely to the offence of rape (*see R. v. Phekoo* (1981)) do not now seem valid. Thus, in *Beckford* v. *R.* (1987) (*see* **39** below), the Privy Council referred to *DPP* v. *Morgan* as a 'landmark decision in the development of the common law.' *See* e.g. *R. v. Fisher* (1987).

6. *Ignorantia facti excusat; ignorantia juris non excusat* (ignorance of the fact excuses; ignorance of the law does not excuse)

The general rule is that when mistake is pleaded, the mistake must be *one of fact, not of law.* (A mistake of law occurs 'when a party having full knowledge of the facts, comes to an erroneous conclusion as to their legal effect': Black.)

(a) That it is impossible for a person to have known the law is *no defence.* In *R.* v. *Bailey* (1800), X was charged and convicted under a statute enacted when he was at sea, i.e. at a time when he could not have known that the Act in question existed.

(b) A reason for this apparently harsh rule has been stated thus: 'Every man must be taken to be cognisant of the law, otherwise there is no knowing of the extent to which the excuse of ignorance might be carried. It would be urged in almost every case': *per* Lord Ellenborough in *Bilbie* v. *Lumley* (1802). (Blackstone reasons thus: '. . . every man in England is, in judgment of law, party to the making of an Act of Parliament, being present thereat by his representatives.')

(c) For a statement of the fundamental importance of this rule, *see* the comments of Lord Bridge in the House of Lords in *Grant* v. *Borg* (1982) (an offence under the Immigration Act 1971, s. 24): 'The principle that ignorance of the law is no defence in crime is so fundamental that to construe the word "knowingly" in a criminal statute as requiring not merely knowledge of facts material to the offender's guilt, but also knowledge of the relevant law, would be revolutionary and, to my mind, wholly unacceptable'.

(d) Ignorance of the law will in itself excuse no person, either citizen or foreigner: *see R.* v. *Esop* (1836) (*see* 2:**2(d)**; *R.* v. *Arrowsmith* (1975) – defendant's belief that she will not be prosecuted is no defence.

(e) As an exceptional case, however, a mistake of law *may* be a defence where it establishes that the accused did not have the *mens rea* required for the offence charged. So, if X, charged with stealing under the Theft Act 1968, shows that he has appropriated Y's property in the belief that he had *in law* the right to deprive Y of it, on behalf of himself or a third person, X's appropriation is not to be regarded as dishonest: *see* the Theft Act 1968, s. 2(1) (a), at 15:**9**. X's belief may have resulted from his mistaken understanding of the law; he is, nevertheless, not guilty under the Act. *See also R.* v. *Smith* (1974) at 19:**6**; *Secretary of State for Trade* v. *Hart* (1982) (auditor acting when disqualified). *See also* the Statutory Instruments Act 1946, s. 3.

Compulsion

7. The general principle

By 'compulsion' is meant 'forcible inducement to the commission of some act' (Black). Where X_1 seizes X_2's hand, places a pistol in it and, applying further physical force, causes X_2 to shoot at and kill Y, liability for Y's death is not to be attributed to X_2, but to X_1. Where a person is charged with perjury, for example, he may raise the defence of having been under a threat of severe violence at the time he made the false statement (*see* **9 (f)**). In general, where a person raises the defence of compulsion he is seeking to establish that he performed an act *involuntarily as the result of another's actions*. 'All laws admit certain cases of just excuse when they are offended in the letter and where the offender is under necessity, either of compulsion or inconvenience': *per* Hobart J in *Moore* v. *Hussey* (1609). 'It is highly just and equitable that a man should be excused for those acts which are done through unavoidable force and compulsion': Blackstone.

8. Examples of compulsion

The following defences are considered here:

(a) duress *per minas* (*see* 9);
(b) necessity, and duress of circumstances (*see* 11);
(c) obedience to orders (*see* 12);
(d) marital coercion (*see* 13).

9. Duress *per minas* (by threats)

'The use of threats and menaces to compel a person, by the fear of death, or grievous bodily harm, . . . to do some unlawful act or commit a misdemeanour': Blackstone. 'Duress, whatever form it takes, is a coercion of will so as to vitiate consent': *per* Lord Scarman in *Pao On* v. *Lau Yiu Long* (1980). This defence is based on X's plea that his will-power had been decisively weakened as a direct consequence of Y's threats. 'Threats of immediate death or serious personal violence so great as to overbear the ordinary powers of human resistance should be accepted as a justification for acts which would otherwise be criminal': *A.-G.* v. *Whelan* (1934).

'[Duress] is something which is superimposed upon the other ingredients which by themselves would make up an offence, ie, upon act and intention . . . the victim completes the act and knows that he is doing so; but the addition of the element of duress prevents the law from treating what he has done as a crime': *per* Lord Wilberforce in *DPP for Northern Ireland* v. *Lynch* (1975).

(a) 'No man from a fear of consequences to himself has a right to make himself a party to committing a mischief on mankind': *per* Denman J in *R.* v. *Tyler* (1838). In *DPP for Northern Ireland* v. *Lynch* (1975), the House of Lords held that on a charge of murder it was open to a person accused as a *principal in the second degree* (i.e. as aider and abettor) to plead duress. In *Abbott* v. *R.* (1977), the Privy Council stated that the defence of duress is *not* available to a person charged with murder as a *principal in the first degree*. But in *R.* v. *Howe and Bannister* (1987) the House of Lords departed from its previous decision in *Lynch* and held that the defence of duress was *not* available to a person charged with murder, whether as a principal in the first *or* second degree.

(b) In *R.* v. *Gotts* (1992), the House of Lords (by three votes to two) ruled that the defence of duress is *not* available to a person charged with *attempted murder*.

(i) X, aged 16, had stabbed his mother with intent to kill her. He alleged that he had done so on his father's instructions and that his father had threatened to kill him if he disobeyed him. The trial judge had ruled that the defence of duress was *not* available on this charge.

X appealed against his conviction to the Court of Appeal which upheld it. He then appealed to the House of Lords.

(*ii*) The House of Lords *upheld* the conviction. *Per* Lord Jauncey: 'I would depart from the decision of this House in *Lynch* and declare the law to be that duress is *not* available as a defence to a charge of murder, or to attempted murder ... An attempt to kill must be proved in the case of attempted murder but not necessarily in the case of murder. Is there logic in affording the defence [of duress] to one who kills intending to kill but fails, and denying it to one who mistakenly kills intending only to injure? . . . I can see no justification in logic, morality or law in affording to an attempted murderer the defence which is withheld from a murderer. The intent required of an attempted murderer is more evil than that required of a murderer and the line which divides the two offences is seldom, if ever, of the deliberate making of the criminal'.

(c)   The threat must be of a serious nature, e.g. a threat of death or serious bodily harm. A threat to property will not suffice. *See R. v. Steane* (1947), in which a British subject, following beatings, and conscious of threats to his wife and children, made broadcasts in Germany during the war. His conviction on a charge of doing acts likely to assist the enemy with intent to assist the enemy was set aside by the Court of Appeal because of the failure to prove intent. The jury should have been instructed that they could have found lack of intent if it had been shown that the accused carried out his acts in subjection to an enemy. Duress may be raised as a defence, however, where it *negatives a specific intent* required for the commission of an offence. *See R. v. Ortiz* (1986). (The direction on duress should be: 'Has the prosecution made you sure that defendant was not acting under duress in the sense that he did not commit the crime charged because of threats being made, either of death or serious injury to himself or another?'. Defendant's wife and child had been threatened.)

(d)   Note *R. v. Willer* (1987), in which the Court of Appeal held that duress *was* capable of amounting to a defence to a charge of reckless driving when a motorist mounted a pavement so as to get away from a gang who were shouting 'We'll kill you', and one of whom entered the car and fought with a passenger when the motorist drove to a police station to make a complaint. *See DPP v. Bell* (1992), in which X had been drinking with others when trouble broke out. X drove off in his car, pursued by others, and in fear of serious personal injury. He reversed the car and accidentally injured a friend. His appeal against conviction for driving with excess alcohol in his body was allowed, on the basis of duress. The prosecutor's appeal was rejected: X had been in terror when he drove off, and that fear, inspired by threats, had caused him to lose control of his will.

(e)   The defence of duress will not be accepted if the accused had the opportunity to escape from the threat.

(f) Where the threat is one of violence it must be a 'present threat', suggesting immediate violence. In *R.* v. *Hudson and Taylor* (1971), X_1 and X_2 were convicted of perjury. Their defence was duress, in that Y had threatened them with violence before the trial of Z if they identified Z, and that Y had been present in the courtroom while they were giving evidence. The appeals of X_1 and X_2 against conviction were allowed. It was held that Y's threat was no less 'present' because he could not carry it out at the moment of the commission of the offence but only at some time later. 'The threats were likely to be no less compelling because their execution could not be effected in the court room, if they could be carried out in the streets of Salford on the same night'. Y's threat was a 'present threat' in the sense that it effectively 'neutralised the wills' of X_1 and X_2 at the time.

(g) Where X has raised evidence of duress it is for the prosecution to negative that defence and not for X to establish it: *see R.* v. *Gill* (1963); *R.* v. *Bone* (1968).

(h) Note *R.* v. *Fitzpatrick* (1971), in which X had shot and killed Y during the course of robbery. X, a member of the proscribed Irish Republican Army, was charged with murder and pleaded duress, stating that he had tried to leave the organisation, but was met with a threat that his parents would be shot unless he took part in the robbery. His appeal against conviction was *dismissed*. 'If a person voluntarily exposes and submits himself, as [X] did, to illegal compulsion, he cannot rely on the duress to which he has voluntarily exposed himself as an excuse either in respect of the crimes he commits against his will or in respect of his continued but unwilling association with those capable of exercising upon him the duress which he calls in aid': *per* Lowry LCJ.

(i) In *R.* v. *Sharp* (1987), the Court of Appeal held that duress is *not* available as a defence to X who joins a gang of robbers voluntarily, when he knows the nature of the gang and that he might be put under pressure to commit an offence. In *R.* v. *Shepherd* (1988), it was held that where X voluntarily participates in a criminal group, the defence of duress (threats of violence to himself and his family) *may* be available to him if, when he joined the criminal enterprise, he did not appreciate the risk of the use of violence.

(j) Where the defence of duress is raised, the jury should be directed to consider, first, whether X's will, subjectively considered, was overborne, and, secondly, if the answer is or might be affirmative, whether his action under duress was reasonable. The fact that X's will to resist had been eroded by the voluntary consumption of drink or drugs is irrelevant to the second question.

(k) *See also R.* v. *Howe and Bannister* (1987) – the test in duress is whether the threat was of such gravity that it might well have caused a reasonable man in the same situation to act in the same way, and whether a sober man of reasonable firmness sharing the defendant's characteristics would have responded to the threat as did the defendant.

10. Essence of the defence

Duress is a defence in its own right; it does not involve a mere denial of *mens rea*, and, where a plea of duress succeeds, the defendant is not guilty: *see*, for a full discussion, *R.* v. *Gotts* (1992), in which the House of Lords considered in detail problems arising from the defence of duress.

(a) The defence of duress should not be confused with that of automatism (*see* **20**). In a situation involving *duress*, the accused has exercised some choice (to assist or refuse to assist in a criminal enterprise); the defence of *automatism* suggests, however, that the accused had no choice; what he did involved no volition.

(b) Nor should duress be confused with the defence of *necessity* (*see* **11**). Involuntary conduct may indeed characterise both types of defence. But duress arises from pressures applied by one person on another, whereas the defence of necessity suggests the existence of *circumstances* (rather than persons) which have created the situation involving the accused. *See*, however, 'duress of circumstances' and necessity at **11(h)** below.

11. Necessity and duress of circumstances

'A power or impulse so great that it admits no choice of conduct': Black. The general defence of necessity may arise in the case of X, who, faced with committing a crime or allowing a greater evil to take place, chooses the first course of action. The scope of this defence is uncertain. In general, X's course of action must constitute a *lesser evil* than the evil averted by that action, and it ought not to have been possible for the evil to have been averted other than by X's action. More precise rules have not been formulated.

(a) In *Perka* v. *The Queen* (1984) (a Canadian case) Dickson J stated: 'At the heart of this defence [necessity] is the perceived injustice of punishing violations of the law in circumstances in which the person had no other viable or reasonable choice available; the act was wrong but it is excused because it was realistically unavoidable. Punishment of such acts, as Fletcher notes [in *Rethinking Criminal Law*], can be seen as purposeless as well as unjust: "...Involuntary conduct cannot be deterred and therefore it is pointless and wasteful to punish involuntary actors".'

(b) The defence was put forward in *R.* v. *Dudley and Stephens* (1884). Three men, X_1, X_2 and W, and a boy, Y, escaped from shipwreck in an open boat. After eighteen days without food Y was killed by X_1, with the agreement of X_2, and eaten by X_1, X_2 and W. Four days later they were rescued. X_1 and X_2 were indicted and convicted for the murder of Y. In defence, they raised the probability that, without having eaten Y, they would have died of starvation. The defence failed.

> 'The temptation to the act which existed here was not what the law has ever called necessity. Nor is this to be regretted. Though law and morality are not the same, . . . yet the absolute divorce of law from morality would be of fatal consequence; and such divorce would follow if the temptation to murder in this case were to be held by law an absolute defence of it. It is not so': *per* Lord Coleridge CJ.

(c) In *Southwark London Borough Council* v. *Williams* (1971), 'squatters' who had occupied the Council's empty houses raised the defence of necessity. It was held, in disallowing their appeal, that this was no defence, even though they were in desperate need of housing. 'If home-lessness were once admitted as a defence to trespassing no one's house would be safe. Necessity would open a door which no man could shut': *per* Lord Denning. 'Necessity can very easily become simply a mask for anarchy': *per* Edmund-Davies LJ.

(d) Necessity may be an element of certain recognised *specific* defences, e.g.:

(*i*) Where X, charged with murder, pleads that he acted in self-defence. *See*, in this context, the Criminal Law Act 1967, s. 3 (1) (at **37**).

(*ii*) Where a doctor has to kill a child in order to save the life of the mother giving birth to it.

(e) It was held in *Johnson* v. *Phillips* (1976) that a police officer may, in the execution of his duty, order a motorist to disobey traffic regulations, 'if it were reasonably necessary for the protection of life or property' (motorist refused to obey police order to drive the wrong way down a one-way street). *See* also *Buckoke* v. *GLC* (1971), in which the Court of Appeal held that a fire brigade order giving guidance to its drivers concerning the crossing of red traffic lights in an emergency was not unlawful.

(f) Evidence of necessity may be relevant in mitigation of sentence.

(g) *See* the Criminal Damage Act 1971, s. 5(2)(b) at **19:3**; Abortion Act 1967, s. 1(4) at **11:8**. Both are examples of statutory defences related closely to necessity.

(h) The defence of duress to a charge of dangerous driving (where X had driven dangerously so as to escape from persons he believed were threaten-ing him – they were, in fact, police officers) was *rejected* in *R.* v. *Jones* (1963).

(*i*) In *R.* v. *Conway* (1988), the Court of Appeal considered the question of *necessity as a defence to a charge of reckless driving*, contrary to the Road Traffic Act 1972, s.2. Y, a passenger in a car driven by the appellant, X, had previously been the target in a shooting incident, and was known to the police as the subject of a bench warrant. X had driven off because he feared that Y was about to be attacked by persons who were, in fact, plain clothes police officers. The Court held that necessity *could* be a defence to a charge of reckless driving when the facts established *duress of circumstances*, but the defence was available *only if*, from an objective standpoint, the driver could be said to have been acting reasonably and proportionately so as to avoid a threat of injury or death. *See R. v. Willer* (1987), at 9 above.

(*ii*) In *R. v. Martin* (1989), the Court of Appeal applied the decision in *R. v. Conway* in an appeal by X, who had driven while disqualified in response to the suicidal threats of his wife. *Per* Simon Brown J: '*English law does, in extreme circumstances, recognise a defence of necessity.* Most commonly this defence arises as duress, that is pressure on the accused's will from the wrongful threats or violence of another. Especially, however, it can arise from other objective dangers threatening the accused or others. Arising thus, it is conveniently called "*duress of circumstances*".' Further, 'the defence is available only if, from an objective standpoint, the accused can be said to be acting *reasonably and proportionately* in order to avoid a threat of death or serious injury.'

(i)   The Law Commission has recommended (*see Law Comm, No. 83, 1977*) that any general defence of necessity ought to be abolished.

12. Obedience to orders

'Obedience' means in this context compliance with an authoritative command. In some circumstances obedience to orders of a superior may be relevant in negativing *mens rea*, e.g as in *R. v. James* (1837), where X was charged with having maliciously and unlawfully obstructed an air-way in a mine. X had built the obstruction in accordance with the instructions of his master, Y, and it was held that, if, as a result of Y's orders, X believed he was acting lawfully, he could not be guilty of the offence. *See* also *Lewis v. Dickson* (1976), in which it was held that it was no defence for a person charged with obstructing the highway to claim that he was acting on his employer's instructions.

The position, in the case of orders given by a military superior, seems to be that 'an officer or soldier acting under the orders of his superior not being necessarily or manifestly illegal would be justified by his orders': *per* Willes J in *Keighley v. Bell* (1866). In *R. v. Thomas* (1816), X, a marine, acting under orders to keep all boats at a distance, fired on and killed Y. It was found that X had fired under the mistaken belief that he had a duty to do so. He was held guilty of murder. *See* also *R. v. Smith* (1900).

13. Marital coercion

'Coercion' involves compelling a person to act against his/her will by force or threat. At common law there was a *prima facie* presumption that where X, the wife of Y, had committed a felony in the presence of Y, she had acted under such coercion by Y as to entitle her to be acquitted. No proof of actual intimidation of X by Y was required. (The defence did *not* extend to treason, murder, or, possibly, manslaughter and robbery.)

(a) The presumption was *abolished* by the Criminal Justice Act 1925, s. 47: 'Any presumption of law that an offence committed by a wife in the presence of her husband is committed under the coercion of the husband is hereby abolished, but on a charge against a wife for an offence other than treason or murder, it shall be a good defence to prove that the offence was committed in the presence of, and under the coercion of, the husband.'

(b) Although the common law presumption is abolished, the defence remains (except in treason or murder) so that the burden of proof is on the accused, who must prove that the offence was committed as the result of the husband's coercion and in his presence. *See R. v. Richman* (1982), in which X claimed that her husband, Y, had coerced her into signing documents which would assist him in offences of deception. X had to prove the defence on a balance of probabilities, and had to show that Y's coercion (which differs from persuasion and can be either physical or moral) had resulted in her unwilling participation. *See R. v. Ditta* (1988) – X must show that she *is* a wife, if she wishes to bring herself within s. 47, and a reasonable belief that she is married is, on its own, insufficient. The Law Commission has recommended abolition of the defence.

Intoxication

14. General principles
'Intoxication' is a situation where, as a result of an intake of intoxicants (e.g. alcohol), a person loses the ordinary use of his mental or physical faculties. Prior to the early years of the nineteenth century, self-induced drunkenness was regarded, not as an excuse for the commission of an offence, but rather as aggravating guilt. 'By the laws of England [a person who was drunk] shall have no privilege by this voluntary acquired madness, but shall have the same judgment as if he were in his right senses': Hale (1609–76). The rule was relaxed, so that, today, drunkenness (which, in itself, is not a defence) may be pleaded where it is claimed to have negatived the *mens rea* required for the crime charged. 'If there is material suggesting intoxication, the jury should be directed to take it into account and to determine whether it is weighty enough to leave them with a reasonable doubt about the accused's guilt': *per* Lord Devlin in *Broadhurst v. R.* (1964). (Note that the term 'drunk', often used synonymously with 'intoxicated', has the specific meaning of 'deprived of

self-control through intoxicating liquor'; it does not refer, for example, to the effects of glue-sniffing: *see Neale* v. *R.M.J.E.* (1985).)

The following principles have been established:

(a) Voluntary drunkenness (which is not, in itself, insanity) may be a defence where it *produces insanity* within the *M'Naghten Rules* (*see* 28). 'Drunkenness is one thing and the diseases to which it leads are different things': *per* Stephen J in *R.* v. *Davis* (1881).

(b) It will also be a defence where it negatives the existence of any intent, or of some specific *mens rea* required for the crime charged. A jury should not be asked to decide whether a defendant was incapable, through drunkenness, of forming a specific intent. They should be warned that a drunken intention may nevertheless be an intention and, subject to that, having regard to all the evidence, they ought to be asked whether they are satisfied that, at the material time, the defendant had, in fact, the requisite intent: *see R.* v. *Sheehan* (1975).   BASIC INTENT

(c) A mistake of fact induced by voluntary intoxication cannot be relied on for a plea of self-defence: *R.* v. *O'Grady* (1987). In this case, X, while very drunk, had fought with Y, his drinking companion. Under the mistaken impression that Y was launching a deadly attack on him, X had inflicted serious injuries on Y, so that Y bled to death. X denied wanting to kill Y and pleaded that he had acted in order to prevent Y from killing him.

O'GRADY

(*i*) X was charged with murder and convicted of manslaughter. In the Court of Appeal Lord Lane explained that a sober man who mistakenly believes he is in danger of immediate death at the hands of an attacker is entitled to be acquitted of both murder and manslaughter if his reaction in killing his supposed assailant was a reasonable one. But where the type of mistake had resulted from self-intoxication, the public interest had to be taken into account. 'Reason recoils from the conclusion that in such circumstances a defendant is entitled to leave the Court without a stain on his character.'

(*ii*) *Per* Lord Lane: 'We come to the conclusion that, where the jury are satisfied that the defendant was mistaken in his belief that any force or the force which he in fact used was necessary to defend himself and are further satisfied that the mistake was caused by voluntarily induced intoxication, the defence *must fail*. We do not consider that any distinction should be drawn on this aspect of the matter between offences involving what is called specific intent and offences of so-called basic intent . . . the question of mistake can and ought to be considered separately from the question of intent.'

(d) No distinction is drawn between the effects of drunkenness voluntarily induced and of drugs taken voluntarily: *see R.* v. *Lipman* (1970).

15. Involuntary intoxication as a defence

The matter was considered by the Court of Appeal in *R. v. Kingston* (1993).

(a) *The facts.* In pursuit of a blackmail plan, X, the appellant, who had paedophiliac tendencies, was invited by Y to sexually abuse Z, a 15 year old boy, who had been lured to Y's flat. X and Y were indicated jointly for indecent assault on Z. X claimed that he had acted under the influence of drugs administered to him (in a laced drink) by Y.

(b) *The judge's decision.* The judge directed the jury that X should be acquitted if they found that he was so affected by the drugs that he did not intend or may not have intended to indecently assault Z; but if they were sure that despite the effect of any drugs he still intended to commit an indecent assault, the case was proved because a drugged intent was still an intent. X was convicted and appealed.

(c) *Court of Appeal.* The Court considered Hale's principle, which appeared in 1685, and which was restated in *Pearson's Case* (1835) by Park J: 'Voluntary drunkenness is no excuse for crime. *If a party be made drunk by stratagem or the fraud of another he is not responsible.*'

(*i*) The purpose of the criminal law was to inhibit by proscription and sanctions, anti-social acts which individuals might other wise commit. Having paedophiliac inclinations and desires was not proscribed; putting them into practice was. If the sole reason why the threshold between the two had been crossed was the clandestine act of a third party, the purposes of the criminal law were not served by nevertheless holding that the person performing the act was guilty of an offence. A man was not responsible for a condition produced by stratagem or the fraud of another.

(*ii*) 'If, therefore, drink or a drug, surreptitiously administered, causes a person to lose his self-control and for that reason to form an intent which he would not otherwise have formed, it is consistent with principle that the law should exculpate him because the operative fault is not his. The law permits a finding that the intent formed was not a criminal intent or, in other words, that the *involuntary intoxication negatives the mens rea*': *per* Lord Taylor C J.

(*iii*) There had to be evidence capable of giving rise to the defence of involuntary intoxication before a judge was obliged to leave the issue to the jury. But once there was an evidential foundation for the defence, the burden was on the Crown to prove that the relevant intent was formed and that, notwithstanding the evidence relied on by the defence, it was a criminal intent.

(*iv*) X's conviction was *quashed.*

Four cases illustrating the development of the law relating to intoxication, assault and homicide are set out at **16–19** below.

16. *R.* v. *Meade* (1909)

At the time this and the two following cases were heard, murder was unlawful homicide 'with malice aforethought' (*see* 9:**14**), and malice aforethought included an intention to commit any felony involving violence.

(a) *The facts.* X was charged with murdering Y, his wife. It was alleged that he had ill-treated Y in brutal fashion and killed her by a blow with his fist. X's defence was that he was drunk and did not intend to cause death or grievous bodily harm to Y. The verdict, he claimed, should be manslaughter.

(b) *The verdict.* X was convicted of murder. Lord Coleridge directed the jury in terms which were subsequently approved by the Court of Criminal Appeal:

> 'In the first place, everyone is presumed to know the consequences of his acts. If he be insane, that knowledge is not presumed. Insanity is not pleaded here, but where it is part of the essence of a crime that a motive, a particular motive, shall exist in the mind of the man who does the act, the law declares this – that if the mind at that time is so obscured by drink, if the reason is dethroned and the man is incapable of forming that intent, it justifies the reduction of the charge from murder to manslaughter.'

(c) *On appeal.* X's conviction was *affirmed*. Per Darling J: 'A man is taken to intend the natural consequences of his acts. This presumption may be rebutted . . . in the case of a man who is drunk by showing his mind to have been so affected by drink . . . that he was incapable of knowing that what he was doing was dangerous, i.e. likely to inflict serious injury.'

17. *DPP* v. *Beard* (1920)

This was a case of murder in the furtherance of rape. (As the law then stood, the intent to commit a violent felony was in itself sufficient *mens rea* for murder.)

(a) *The facts.* X, in furtherance of the rape of Y, caused her death by suffocation. His defence was that he was drunk and incapable of knowing that what he was doing was likely to cause injury.

(b) *The verdict.* X was convicted of murder, and appealed.

(c) *On appeal.* The Court of Criminal Appeal substituted a verdict of manslaughter on the ground that, on the authority of *R.* v. *Meade*, the jury ought to have been asked whether they considered that X knew that what he did was dangerous. The prosecution appealed to the House of Lords.

(d) *Judgment of the House of Lords.* The conviction of murder was *restored*.

> 'Where a specific intent is an essential element in the offence,

evidence of a state of drunkenness rendering the accused incapable of forming such an intent should be taken into consideration in order to determine whether he had in fact formed the intent necessary to constitute the particular crime. . . . Insanity whether produced by drunkenness or otherwise is a defence to the crime charged. . . . Evidence of drunkenness falling short of a proved incapacity in the accused to form the intent necessary to constitute the crime, and merely establishing that his mind was affected by drink so that he more readily gave way to some violent passion, does not rebut the presumption that a man intends the natural consequences of his acts': *per* Lord Birkenhead LC.

18. *A.-G for Northern Ireland* v. *Gallagher* (1963) DUTCH COURAGE

In this case the problem of drunkenness induced with intent to commit an offence was considered.

(a) *The facts.* X was charged with the murder of Y, his wife. Having decided to kill her, he bought a knife and a bottle of whisky. After drinking the whisky he killed Y. His defence was that he was either insane or so drunk as to be incapable of forming the intent necessary for murder.

(b) *The verdict.* X was convicted of murder, and appealed.

(c) *On appeal.* The Court of Criminal Appeal in Northern Ireland allowed X's appeal on the ground that the summing up was wrong, in that it suggested to the jury that the M'Naghten Rules (*see* 28) ought to be applied to X's state of mind at the time *before* he drank the whisky and not at the time of *committing the act*.

(d) *Judgment of the House of Lords.* The House of Lords *allowed* the appeal of the Attorney-General. *Per* Lord Denning:

> 'If a man while sane and sober forms an intention to kill and makes preparation for it, knowing it is the wrong thing to do, and then gets himself drunk so as to give himself Dutch courage to do the killing, and whilst drunk carries out his intention, he cannot rely on this self-induced drunkenness as a defence to a charge of murder, nor even as reducing it to manslaughter.'

19. *DPP* v. *Majewski* (1977)

This was a case of alleged assault.

(a) *The facts.* X was involved in a public house brawl. He was ejected and attempted to get back into the public house, injuring the landlord and another customer. When arrested, X kicked the police officer. He was charged under the Offences against the Person Act 1861, s. 47, and the Police Act 1964, s. 51(1), with assault occasioning actual bodily harm and assault on a constable in the execution of his duty. His defence was that for some time he had been taking a mixture of drugs and that the effect of alcohol had affected him adversely. The jury was directed that self-induced intoxication was no defence to the alleged assault.

(b) *The verdict.* X was convicted and appealed.

(c) *On appeal.* The Court of Appeal dismissed X's appeal, holding that, except for offences requiring a specific intent, self-induced intoxication is no defence to a criminal charge and the common law rule has not been altered by the Criminal Justice Act 1967, s. 8. X was given leave to appeal to the House of Lords by the Court of Appeal which certified as a point of law of general public importance the question: *'Whether a defendant may properly be convicted of assault notwithstanding that, by reason of his self-induced intoxication, he did not intend to do the act alleged to constitute the assault.'*

(d) *House of Lords.* The certified question was answered in the *affirmative* and X's appeal was *dismissed.* Self-induced intoxication is no defence to a charge of a crime of basic intent (that is, a crime whose definition expresses or implies a *mens rea* not going beyond the *actus reus*). It is a reckless course of conduct and recklessness suffices to constitute the necessary *mens rea* in a crime of basic intent. But self-induced intoxication could be a defence to a charge of a crime of special or specific intent, that is, a crime where the prosecution has to prove that the *purpose* for the commission of the act extends to the intent expressed or implied in the definition of that crime. Special intent cases were not restricted to crimes in which absence of special intent leaves available some lesser crime embodying no special intent, nor, perhaps, a crime of ulterior intent. Further, when death or physical injury to another person results from something done by the accused for which no legal justification can be found, and he has been charged with murder, manslaughter, common assault or assault occasioning actual bodily harm or unlawful wounding (*see* the Offences against the Person Act 1861, ss. 20, 47), a jury may properly be instructed, as in the case under consideration, that they can ignore the subject of drink or drugs as being in any way a defence.

> NOTE: (1) For a consideration of 'alcohol dependence syndrome' in relation to diminished responsibility (*see* 9:**34**), *see R. v. Inseal* (1992). (2) The Law Commission's consultation paper (*Intoxication and Criminal Liability*, No. 127, 1993) asks whether it is really necessary to have special rules so as to ensure that defendants do not escape conviction merely by reason of intoxication. (Research into some overseas criminal trials suggests that most intoxicated defendants were sufficiently aware of what they were doing, making possible their conviction under ordinary rules of law.) Further, it might be advisable to consider replacing the existing complex rules with a special offence aimed speci-

fically at a person who causes damage or injury while dangerously intoxicated.

Automatism

20. Meaning of the term
'An act done by the muscles without any control by the mind such as a spasm, a reflex action or a convulsion, or an act done by a person who is not conscious of what he is doing, such as an act done whilst suffering from concussion or whilst sleepwalking': *per* Lord Denning in *Bratty* v. *A.-G. for Northern Ireland* (1963) (*see* **25(a)** below). 'Behaviour performed in a state of mental consciousness or dissociation without full awareness': Black. (For defence that wounding with intent was committed while defendant was sleep walking, *see R.* v. *Burgess* (1991) at **25** below.)

21. Essence of the defence
Where an *actus reus* necessarily involves some act on the part of X, that act must have been willed by him. In a state of automatism X's actions are not voluntary and, as such, will not generally be punishable. 'In the case of *Woolmington* v. *DPP* (1935), Viscount Sankey LC said that "when dealing with a murder case, the Crown must prove death as a result of a voluntary act of the accused and malice of the accused." The requirement that it should be a voluntary act is essential, not only in a murder case, but also *in every criminal case*. No act is punishable if it is done involuntarily': *per* Lord Denning. The defence of automatism (in any type of crime) is, in effect, a denial that the prosecution has proved the voluntary nature of the *actus reus*. (Hence, an accused person who is shown to have acted in a state of automatism should be acquitted, save where the automatism has been self-induced.)

22. Insane and non-insane automatism
The courts have differentiated 'insane automatism', which derives from disease of the mind, and 'non-insane automatism', e.g. somnambulism, which is not based on any disease of the mind.

(a) *Insane automatism.* Where the court finds that X was acting in a state of automatism because of a disease of the mind, his plea will amount to a plea of insanity, so that the M'Naghten Rules (*see* **28**) apply. Whether a certain condition constitutes a disease of the mind involves a question of law, which is for the judge to decide. A ruling by the judge that X suffers from insane automatism should result in a verdict of 'not guilty by reason of insanity' (*see* **32**).

(b) *Non-insane automatism.* Where it is pleaded that automatism has arisen from a cause such as concussion, X's defence is known as 'non-insane automatism' and ought to lead to X's acquittal.

23. Burden of proof

Assume that X puts forward a defence of automatism. It is then *for him* to bring forward appropriate and sufficient evidence so that, in the minds of the jury, there is created a reasonable doubt concerning the voluntary nature of his conduct. Should he fail to discharge this burden, the judge will *not* leave the question of automatism to the jury. Where X has discharged the burden, the judge should direct the jury that the prosecution must show beyond reasonable doubt that X did not act in circumstances of automatism. (In the case of a defence of insane automatism, the burden of proof is on X; in a case of a plea of non-insane automatism, the burden of disproving it is on the prosecution.) Where issues of insanity and automatism arise, the judge must distinguish between them in his summing up, particularly with regard to burden of proof: *R. v. Burns* (1973).

In *Moses v. Winder* (1981), it was held that the defence of automatism would rarely succeed without medical evidence. Expert medical or other scientific evidence is admissible to assist the jury in distinguishing genuine and fraudulent automatism: *R. v. Smith* (1979). 'I do not doubt that there are genuine cases of automatism and the like, but I do not see how the layman can safely attempt without the help of some medical or scientific evidence to distinguish the genuine from the fraudulent': *per* Devlin J in *Hill v. Baxter* (1958). *See R. v. Toner* (1991), in which the Court of Appeal held that a jury should be allowed expert assistance on a medical question such as the effect of hypoglycaemia on intent. (On a charge of attempted murder, defendant had raised a defence of automatism, alternatively inability to form the specific intent required under the law due to hypoglycaemia which had been brought on, it was suggested, by a period of fasting followed by the consumption of carbohydrates.) *See also R. v. Pullen* (1991).

24. Self-induced automatism

Automatism arising from X's voluntary taking of drugs or alcohol will *not* generally be acceptable as a defence. But *see R. v. Bailey* (1983) at **25**.

25. Some decisions on automatism

The following should be noted.

(a) *Bratty v. A.-G. for N. Ireland* (1963). X was accused of the murder of Y, whom he admitted strangling. X stated that when he was with Y a 'feeling of blackness' had come over him. Some medical evidence was adduced at the trial suggesting that X may have been suffering from psychomotor epilepsy. He raised the defences of automatism, lack of intent for murder, and insanity. The judge refused to leave the first two defences to the jury and they rejected his third defence. The House of Lords held that where there was evidence of automatism arising other than from a disease of the mind, the accused was entitled to have the question of automatism left to the jury. But 'there was [in the present case] no evidence of automatism apart from insanity. There was no need for the judge to put it to the jury': *per* Lord Denning.

(b) *R. v. Quick and Paddison* (1973). X_1 and X_2, mental hospital nurses, were charged with assaulting a patient and causing grievous bodily harm. In pleading not guilty, X_1 raised the defence of automatism, saying that he had taken insulin on the morning in question, had then drunk spirits and eaten little food, and could not remember the assault. Medical evidence did suggest a hypoglycaemic state. It was held by the Court of Appeal that a malfunctioning of the mind of transitory effect caused by the application to the body of some external factor is *not* a 'disease of the mind' within the M'Naghten Rules (*see* **28**). Such malfunctioning, if self-induced or induced by failure to take appropriate precautions, will not relieve an accused person from criminal responsibility, but in other cases it may entitle him to an acquittal.

(c) *R. v. Isitt* (1978). After involvement in a traffic accident, X drove off in an erratic and dangerous fashion, avoiding a road block and escaping. He claimed to remember nothing of the incident. At his trial he produced medical evidence suggesting that the accident had induced a state of 'hysterical fugue', so that he did not know why he had driven away without conscious thought. The Court of Appeal, dismissing his appeal against a conviction for dangerous driving, stated that although insanity and automatism produced a defence against such a charge, at the time X was driving he was doing so purposefully although his mind may have been 'closed to moral inhibition'.

(d) *R. v. Bailey* (1983). X was charged with wounding Y with intent to cause grievous bodily harm. His defence was that he had been suffering from automatism caused by hypoglycaemia, resulting from a failure to take food after a dose of insulin for diabetes. The recorder directed the jury that the defence did not apply to a self-induced incapacity. The Court of Appeal held that self-induced automatism *is a defence to a crime of specific intent*, such as wounding with intent. (But, as it is not a matter of common knowledge, even among diabetics, that a sufferer could be a danger to others in those circumstances alleged by X, the prosecution would have to show recklessness by the defendant. On the facts of the case, no jury would have believed X's version of events, and his appeal was dismissed.)

(e) *R. v. T.* (1990). X was charged with robbery and causing bodily harm. There was evidence to support X's allegation that she had been raped three days before the incident and a psychiatrist diagnosed posttraumatic stress disorder causing X to be in a 'dissociative state' with the result that she had not been acting with a conscious mind or will. It was held that rape could be an external factor causing a malfunctioning of the mind, and that X was acting 'as though in a dream'. The defence of automatism should be left to the jury.

(f) *R.* v. *Burgess* (1991). X was charged on a count of wounding with intent to do grievous bodily harm. He claimed to have been sleepwalking when he wounded a woman sleeping in a flat above his own; he claimed also that he was suffering from non-insane automatism and lacked, therefore, the necessary *mens rea* to make him guilty of wounding with intent. He appealed against a finding of not guilty by reason of insanity and against a subsequent order of detention in hospital.

(*i*) The Court of Appeal *dismissed* the appeal. The trial judge had concluded that, assuming X was not conscious at the time of what he was doing, this amounted to *insanity within the M'Naghten Rules*, and not merely to evidence of non-insane automatism. There was a danger of recurrence of X's abnormal condition, according to expert medical evidence.

(*ii*) The Court cited with approval the statement of Lord Denning in *Bratty* v. *A.-G. for Northern Ireland* (*see* **25** above): 'Any mental disorder which has manifested itself in violence and is prone to recur is a disease of the mind. At any rate it is the sort of disease for which a person should be detained in hospital rather than be given an unqualified acquittal'.

(*iii*) The Court agreed with the trial judge's finding that X's state was an abnormality which was due to an internal disorder manifesting itself in violence which might recur. The judge's conclusions and decision were *correct*.

(g) See also *R.* v. *Smith* (1982) – defence of automatism based on effects of pre-menstrual tension was *rejected*; *R.* v. *Hennessy* (1989) – the M'Naghten Rules (see **28** below) remain relevant in relation to a defence of automatism, so that stress, anxiety and depression are *not* the type of external factor capable in law of causing or contributing to a state of automatism; *A.-G's Ref. (No.2 of 1992)* – driving without awareness (so-called 'automatic driving') did not involve *total loss* of voluntary control and was *not* a state capable of founding a defence of automatism.

Insanity

26. Insanity in the criminal law
It is important to note that the terms 'insanity' and 'insane' have highly specialised meanings in the criminal law; *they are not necessarily used in*

their medical sense. 'Insanity, from a medical point of view, is one thing; insanity from the point of view of the criminal law is a different thing': *per* McCardie J. The defence is available in *any* criminal charge.

27. Insanity and the trial

The issue of the sanity of an accused person, X, will be of relevance not only at the time of commission of the alleged offence, but also at the following stages:

(a) *Before the trial*, where X has been committed in custody for trial. If the Secretary of State for the Home Department is satisfied by reports from two doctors that X is suffering from mental disorder, he may order, under the Mental Health Act 1983, Part III, that X be detained in a hospital, if he considers this to be in the public interest.

(b) *Where X is put up for trial.* At this stage X may be found unfit to plead, i.e. too insane to stand his trial: *see* the Criminal Procedure (Insanity) Act 1964, s. 4 as amended by the Criminal Procedure (Insanity and Unfitness to Plead) Act 1991. (An accused person is considered unfit to plead if, as a result of some physical or mental condition, he is unable to follow the proceedings (i.e. he cannot understand the charge) and, therefore, is unable to make a proper defence to the charge: *see R. v. Podola* (1960).)

(*i*) The issue of X's fitness to plead may be raised at any time up to that at which the case for the defence is opened.

(*ii*) The issue may be raised by the prosecution, the defence, or the judge. Where *the defence* raises the issue, the burden of proving unfitness is on the accused and this must be proved *on a balance of probabilities.* Where *the prosecution* raises the issue the burden is on them and proof must be beyond reasonable doubt. Where *the judge* raises the issue, the burden of proof rests on the prosecution. (Note that the accused need not use the term 'insanity' to describe his defence; it suffices merely that he puts in issue his mental state.)

(*iii*) The judge may, if he wishes, *postpone* a decision on the fitness of the accused to plead until the opening of the case for the defence: 1964 Act, s. 4 (2), substituted by the 1991 Act, s. 2. Postponement should be in the interests of the accused.

(*iv*) Under the 1964 Act, s. 4A, inserted by the 1991 Act, a person cannot be found unfit to plead except on the oral or written evidence of two or more medical practitioners. The question of unfitness to plead is to be determined by *a jury*, and where the accused is found unfit to be tried, the trial shall not proceed, or proceed further. But on the basis of evidence already adduced by the prosecution or defence, the jury shall determine whether the accused did the act or made the omission charged against him as the offence. (The appropriate standard of proof is probably 'beyond reasonable doubt'.) If the jury is satisfied that the accused was responsible for the act or omission, a verdict to that effect is returned; if not satisfied, a verdict of acquittal is recorded. A person found unfit to plead but *not* to have performed the act or made the omission must be freed; a person found unfit to plead *and* to have *performed* the act or *made* the omission may be dealt with under the 1964 Act, s. 5, as amended.

(c) *At the trial.* Where X raises at the trial the issue of his sanity *at the time he performed the act,* his responsibility will be determined by reference to the criteria set out in the M'Naghten Rules (*see* **28**). X's insanity in the accepted medical sense will not, in itself, be sufficient to ground a defence; *it must be such as to affect his legal responsibility.*

(d) Powers to deal with persons not guilty by reason of insanity or unfit to plead are set out in the 1964 Act, s. 5, as substituted by the 1991 Act, s. 3. They include the admittance of accused to a hospital specified by the Secretary of State, the making of a guardianship order and supervision order (or an order for absolute discharge). In the case of an offence for which the sentence is fixed by law (i.e, murder), an admission order shall be made, together with a restriction direction unlimited in time.

(e) It should be noted that the trial judge himself may, exceptionally, of his own volition, raise the issue of insanity at a trial where 'there is relevant evidence which goes to all the factors involved in the M'Naghten test, and only where he gives the parties sufficient opportunity to deal with the issue': *R. v. Dickie* (1984), in which X adduced medical evidence that he had damaged property while in an uncontrolled state of hypomania (i.e. the manic phase of a manic-depressive psychosis).

28. Background to the M'Naghten Rules

Daniel M'Naghten, acting under an insane delusion that the statesman, Sir Robert Peel, was persecuting him, killed Sir Robert's secretary in mistake for him. He was found not guilty on the ground of insanity and was committed to Bethlem Hospital: *see R. v. M'Naghten* (1843). Subsequent dissatisfaction with the verdict was widespread, and the House of Lords (not the House in its judicial capacity), after debating the matter, put a hypothetical case to the judges in the form of five questions.

(a) The answers are known as the *M'Naghten Answers* or the *M'Naghten Rules;* the main Rules are summarised in **29–31**.

(b) The Rules have been treated by the courts as possessing the authority of a decision of the House of Lords.

(c) The Rules remain today the legal criteria which are considered when insanity is pleaded as a defence.

(d) The Rules are only a 'partial definition of the common law concept of insanity', designed to extend insanity to include certain situations where the accused is not totally deprived of understanding, but is suffering from delusions: *R* v. *Sullivan* (1984). (*See* **33**.)

29. Presumption of sanity
A 'presumption' is an assumption which must or may be made and maintained until evidence to the contrary is given. *Every person is presumed to be sane, and to possess a sufficient degree of reason to be responsible for his crimes until the contrary is proved to the satisfaction of a jury.* The onus of proof of insanity is on *the defence* – an exception to the general rule in the criminal law: *see Woolmington* v. *DPP* (1935) (*see* 9:**32**). The presumption of sanity may be rebutted by evidence which satisfies the jury on a balance of probabilities that the accused was insane at the time of his commission of the offence charged.

30. Defect of reason
To establish a defence on the ground of insanity, it must be clearly proved that, at the time of the committing of the act, the party accused was labouring under such a defect of reason, from disease of mind, as not to know the nature and quality of the act he was doing; or if he did know it, that he did not know what he was doing was wrong. If the accused was conscious that the act was one which he ought not to do and if that act was at the same time contrary to the law of the land, he is punishable. The following questions of interpretation arise:

(a) *'Defect of reason, from disease of mind.'* The words 'disease of mind' were included in the Rules, it has been said, so as to exclude 'defects of reason caused simply by brutish stupidity without rational power': *per* Devlin J in *R* v. *Kemp* (1957). In that case X was charged with causing grievous bodily harm to his wife with intent to murder her. It was argued that X's defect of reason arose from a physical cause (arteriosclerosis), and *not* from a mental disease. The argument was rejected; it was held that X was suffering from a disease of the mind.

> 'The law is not concerned with the brain but with the mind, in the sense that "mind" is ordinarily used, the mental faculties of reason, memory and understanding. . . .In my judgment the condition of the brain is irrelevant and so is the question of whether the condition of the mind is curable or incurable, transitory or permanent': *per* Devlin J.

> (*i*) Note that 'disease of the mind' has been used to include those conditions *directly affecting* the brain, e.g. brain tumours, epilepsy, arteriosclerosis.
> (*ii*) Whether a condition amounts to a 'disease of the mind' is essentially a *matter of law*, which the judge must decide. See *R.* v. *Hennessy* (1989) in which the Court of Appeal upheld the ruling of the trial

judge in relation to a claim that X was suffering from hyperglycaemia (caused by *high* blood sugar levels). *Hyperglycaemia* was an 'inherent defect', a disease of the mind, *within* the M'Naghten Rules. See also *R. v. Bingham* (1991) – consideration of *hypoglycaemia* (caused by *low* blood sugar levels) in relation to shoplifting charge.

(b) *'Nature and quality of the act.'* 'The court is of opinion that in using the language "nature and quality" the judges were only dealing with the physical character of the act, and were not intending to distinguish between the physical and moral aspects of the act': *per* Lord Reading CJ in *R. v. Codere* (1916).

(c) *'Did not know that what he was doing was wrong.'* The accused is held to have known that his act was 'wrong' if he knew it was contrary to the law, or wrong 'according to the ordinary standard adopted by reasonable men': *per* Lord Reading. So, where X knows that his act is contrary to the law (i.e. that it was 'wrong') it will be no defence that he believed that act to have been morally right.

(*i*) In *R. v. Windle* (1952), X killed Y, his wife, by administering an overdose of aspirins. Y was probably insane and had complained to X on many occasions of her unhappy life. On giving himself up to the police, X had said: 'I suppose they will hang me for this. ' Medical evidence suggested that X suffered from some kind of insanity, but that he knew he had done wrong according to the law. X's conviction was upheld. *Per* Lord Goddard: 'Courts of law can only distinguish between that which is in accordance with the law and that which is not. . . . In the opinion of the court there is no doubt that in the M'Naghten Rules "wrong" means contrary to law and not "wrong" according to the opinion of one man or of a number of people on the question whether a particular act might or might not be justified.'

(*ii*) *Per* Ackner J in *R. v. Clarke* (1972), in which the defence of insanity was raised in a case of shoplifting, and X adduced psychiatric evidence suggesting a state of absent-mindedness (as the result of depression):

'The M'Naghten Rules relate to accused persons who by reason of a disease of the mind are deprived of the power of reasoning. They do not apply and never have applied to those who retain the power of reasoning but who in moments of confusion or absent-mindedness fail to use their powers to the full.'

31. Insane delusion

Where a person under an insane delusion as to existing facts commits an offence in consequence thereof, and making the assumption that he labours under such partial delusion only, and is not in other respects insane, he must be considered in the same situation as to responsibility as if the facts with respect to which the delusion exists were real. If, therefore, X under the influence of an insane delusion that Y is attempting to kill him, kills Y, as he supposes, in self-defence, X would be exempt from punishment for unlawful homicide. If, however, X under an insane delusion that Y had insulted him, were to kill Y in revenge for the supposed insult, he would be liable to punishment.

32. The verdict
By the Criminal Procedure (Insanity) Act 1964, the verdict of 'guilty but insane' (under the Trial of Lunatics Act 1883) was replaced by one of *'not guilty by reason of insanity'*. Under the Criminal Procedure (Insanity and Unfitness to Plead) Act 1991, a jury *may not acquit on the ground of insanity* (under the Trial of Lunatics Act 1883, s. 2) *except in accordance with the 1991 Act, s. 1,* which requires written or oral evidence supporting that finding to be given by two or more registered medical practitioners, at least one of whom is duly approved by the Secretary of State as having special experience in the area of mental disorders. By the Criminal Appeal Act 1968, s. 12, there is an appeal against this 'special verdict'. Under that section, a person may appeal against the verdict to the Court of Appeal on any ground which involves a question of law alone and, with the leave of the Court of Appeal, on any ground which involves a question of fact alone, or a question of mixed law and fact, or on any other ground which appears to the Court of Appeal to be a sufficient ground of appeal. But if the judge of the court of trial grants a certificate that the case is fit for appeal on a ground which involves a question of fact, or a question of mixed law and fact, appeal lies under s. 12 without leave of the Court of Appeal.

33. 'Disease of the mind': a recent consideration
In *R. v. Sullivan* (1984), the House of Lords considered the meaning of 'disease of the mind'. X, who had suffered from motor epilepsy since childhood, was talking to a friend, Y, when a fit came on. He had kicked Y's head and body and was charged with causing grievous bodily harm with intent, under the Offences against the Person Act 1861, ss. 18, 20. X's defence was automatism (*see* **20**). The trial judge ruled that X's defence was one of 'automatism by reason of insanity, rather than automatism *simpliciter'*, so that if the jury accepted X's defence they would have to return the special verdict of not guilty by reason of insanity.

(a) *Court of Appeal.* X appealed against conviction on the ground that the judge ought to have left to the jury the defence of non-insane automatism, which, if accepted by them, would have entitled him to a verdict of not guilty. The Court upheld the judge's ruling and certified the following point of law as of general public importance: *Whether a person who is proved* *to have occasioned actual bodily harm to another, whilst recovering from a seizure due to psychomotor epilepsy and who did not know what he was doing when he caused such harm and has no memory of what he did, should be found 'not guilty by reason of insanity'.*

(b) *House of Lords.* The House held that the answer to the question was: 'Yes'; the case did *not* fall outside the M'Naghten Rules, because psychomotor epilepsy was a 'disease of the mind' and X's state of mind was covered by the phrase 'as not to know the nature and quality of the act he was doing', in the Rules (*see* **30**). Lord Diplock rejected the submission that the case could be distinguished from *Bratty* v. *A.-G. for Northern Ireland* (1963), in which psychomotor epilepsy was recognised by the House as a 'disease of the mind'. The meaning of the expression 'disease of the mind' as the cause of a 'defect of reason' remains unchanged for purposes of application of the M'Naghten Rules. He agreed with the statement in *R.* v. *Kemp* (1957), that 'mind' in the Rules is used in the ordinary sense of the mental faculties of *reason, memory and understanding*. 'If the effect of a disease is to impair these faculties so severely as to have either of the consequences referred to in the latter part of the Rules, it matters not whether the aetiology of the impairment is organic, as in epilepsy, or functional, or whether the impairment itself is permanent or is transient and intermittent, provided that it subsisted at the time of the commission of the act.'

34. The question of 'irresistible impulse'

Where X has known the nature and quality of the offence he has committed and understood that it is wrong, he may, nevertheless, have acted under an impulse which, he claims, he could not control. In *R.* v. *Kopsch* (1925), X admitted that he had killed Y, and was convicted. Evidence was given that X had acted under such an impulse. In argument before the Court of Criminal Appeal it was suggested that the jury ought to have been directed that a person acting under an irresistible impulse was not criminally liable. *Per* Lord Hewart CJ: 'It is a fantastic theory of irresistible impulse which, if it were to become part of our criminal law, would be merely subversive. It is not yet part of our criminal law, and is to be hoped that the time is far distant when it will be made so.'

The defence continues to be unacceptable within the M'Naghten Rules. But *see* the plea of 'diminished responsibility' under the Homicide Act 1957, s. 2, set out in 9:**34**. In *R.* v. *Byrne* (1960) (at 9:**35**), Lord Parker spoke of 'the step between "he did not resist his impulse" and "he could not resist his impulse"' as being 'incapable of scientific proof'. 'There is no scientific measurement of the degree of difficulty which an abnormal person finds in controlling his impulses. These problems . . . the jury can only approach in a broad, common-sense way.'

35. Criticism of the M'Naghten Rules

The Rules have been criticised from the very time they were propounded. It is suggested that they are founded on obsolete, misleading views of insanity, that they ignore modern studies of the mind, that they are much too narrow, and that they ignore the important matter of 'irresistible impulse'.

Self-defence

36. Essence of the common law defence

Where X has acted so as to prevent a crime, or, specifically, to defend himself, or, possibly, some other person, such as a spouse or child (*see R. v. Duffy* (1967)) or his property (*see R. v. Hussey* (1924)) against violence or a reasonable apprehension of it, or in effecting the lawful arrest of an offender, he may seek to answer a charge (such as one under the Offences against the Person Act 1861) by pleading self-defence. This involves showing that *he used no more force than was necessary and that he had an honest belief, based on reasonable grounds, that force was necessary in the circumstances as he perceived them.* Thus, X may claim that Y and Z were about to launch an attack on him, (i.e. that an attack was *imminent*) so that he was forced to defend himself by striking (and injuring) Y and Z. Where there is evidence of self-defence, the jury should be directed to acquit the accused unless satisfied that the prosecution has disproved that defence: *see Palmer v. R.* (1971). *See* also *R. v. Whyte* (1987); *R. v. O'Grady* (1987) at **14(c)** above.

> NOTE: See Dicey's comments in 'The Right of Self-Defence', in *The Law of the Constitution* (1885): 'Discourage self-help, and loyal subjects become the slaves of ruffians. Over-stimulate self-assertion, and for the arbitrament of the courts you substitute the decision of the sword or the revolver.'

37. Self-defence in the prevention of crime

'A person may use such force as is reasonable in the circumstances in the prevention of crime, or in effecting or assisting in the lawful arrest of offenders or suspected offenders or of persons unlawfully at large': Criminal Law Act 1967, s. 3(1). Note *R. v. Williams* (1984), in which the Court of Appeal held that a *mistaken belief* that someone is being unlawfully assaulted need not be reasonable, *provided that it was honestly held.* The Privy Council approved this decision in *Beckford v. R.* (*see* **39** below). (*See* also *DPP v. Morgan* (1976) at **5**.) Note that in *R. v. Cousins* (1982) it was accepted that the common law defence and the statutory defence in s. 3(1) could be claimed concurrently. *See R. v. Asbury* (1986), and 12:**10**.

38. Self-defence in relation to property

See the Criminal Law Act 1967, s. 3(1). Whether it would be held 'reason-able' if X were to attempt to protect his *property* by making a deliberate, deadly attack on Y, who was seeking to steal that property, is doubtful. *See R.* v. *Hussey* (1924), and the Offences against the Person Act 1861, s. 31.

39. Defending oneself and others

X will have a defence if he uses *reasonable force* to protect himself or members of his family or even some stranger who is under attack, and if he can show that the force was reasonable *in the circumstances* as he perceived them. Note that failure to demonstrate unwillingness to fight is *not* fatal to a plea of self-defence, but it is a factor to be taken into account: *R.* v. *Bird* (1985). In this case, the Court of Appeal stated that if an accused person was proved to have been attacking or retaliating or revenging himself, he was *not* truly acting in self-defence. Proof that he had tried to retreat or to call off the fight might be a cast-iron method of rebutting the suggestion that he was an attacker or retaliator, or trying to revenge himself. But it should be stressed that that was not the only way of doing so.

In *Beckford* v. *R.* (1987), X, a police officer, charged with murder, submitted that he believed the deceased, Y, to have been shooting at him, and he had fired on Y in self-defence. The judge, in his direction to the jury, referred to X having 'reasonably believed' that his life was in danger. X appealed against conviction and the Privy Council allowed the appeal. The correct test to be used was whether X *honestly believed* those facts which, if true, would entitle him to use force to defend himself or another. The reasonableness or otherwise of X's belief has relevance *only* to the question of whether X *honestly* held that belief. 'Where there are no reasonable grounds to hold a belief it will surely only be in exceptional circumstances that a jury will conclude that such a belief was or might have been held': *per* Lord Griffiths.

40. Excessive force

The use of excessive and unreasonable force will prevent the accused relying on *either* the common law *or* the statutory defence. 'Proportion-ality' is of significance in the doctrine of self-defence. What is 'excessive' will depend on a consideration of the circumstances in which the accused had to decide his course of action.

(a) *Palmer* v. *R.* (1971). When the defence of self-defence is raised on a charge of murder, it is not automatically necessary that the judge shall direct the jury that, if they consider excessive force has been used in self-defence, they should return a verdict of manslaughter; *all will depend on the particular facts and circumstances.* 'The defence of self-defence is one which can be and will be readily understood by any jury. It is a straight-forward conception . . . Only common sense is needed for its understanding . . . It requires no set words by way of explanation': *per* Lord Morris.

(b) *Priestnall* v. *Cornish* (1979). X was charged with assault occasioning actual bodily harm to Y and criminal damage. An appeal against a finding of no case to answer was allowed. X could not rely on self-defence if Y, having retreated, had ceased to be a threat.

(c) *R.* v. *Shannon* (1980). The Court of Appeal held that the real issue on self-defence is whether the act done is within the concept of *necessary* self-defence judged by the standards of common sense, considering the position of the accused, at the time in question. *See also R.* v. *Fisher* (1987).

(d) *A.-G.'s Reference (No. 2 of 1983)*. X, a person of good character, had made petrol bombs, intending to use them in the event of an attack on his shop by rioters in an area in which serious rioting had occurred. The Court of Appeal held, in answer to a point of law referred by the A.-G., that 'the defence of "lawful object" is available to a defendant against whom a charge under the Explosive Substances Act 1883, s. 4, has been preferred, if he can satisfy the jury on balance of probabilities that his object was to protect himself or his family or property against imminent apprehended attack and to do so by means which he believed were no more than reasonably necessary to meet the force used by the attackers.' (This would cease to apply if he remained in possession of the bombs after the threat had passed.)

(e) *R.* v. *Oatridge* (1991). The Court of Appeal considered the question of an honest but mistaken belief by defendant that she was under attack and whether her response was commensurate with the level of risk which she believed to have been created by the attack.

(f) Note that the question of 'reasonable' or 'excessive' force will be related to the question of whether it was possible to prevent the evil by some other means: *Allen* v. *MPC* (1980). In considering 'reasonable de-fensive action', note *Palmer* v. *R.* (1971): 'If a jury thought that in a moment of unexpected anguish a person attacked had only done what he honestly and instinctively thought was necessary, that would be most potent evidence that only reasonable defensive action had been taken.'

Other variations in liability

41. General
Certain variations in, and exemption from, criminal liability are discussed below under the following headings:

(a) the Sovereign, and diplomatic immunity (*see* **42**);
(b) corporations (*see* **43**);
(c) young persons (*see* **44–48**).

42. The Sovereign, and diplomatic immunity

The Sovereign and foreign reigning monarchs are immune from criminal proceedings. In the case of the Queen, this is probably explained by the absence of a court with jurisdiction to try her.

(a) Foreign sovereigns may waive their immunity.
(b) Foreign ambassadors and High Commissioners are also immune from criminal proceedings. Their immunity may be waived, however, by the Sovereign they represent. *See* the Diplomatic Privileges Acts 1964 and 1971 (under which members of the service staffs of diplomatic representatives may be liable for acts performed outside the course of their duties); the International Organisations Act 1968 (under which immunity is accorded to certain members of organisations of which the UK is a member); and the State Immunity Act 1978, giving certain States, their governments and departments, general immunity from the jurisdiction of UK courts. *See R.* v. *Jiminez-Paez* (1993).

43. Corporations

A corporation is, in general terms, a body of persons associated for some purpose and considered as having in law an existence, rights and duties distinct from those of its members.

(a) At one time a corporation was held to be outside the criminal law. Since it had no actual existence, it could have no *mens rea* in relation to an alleged offence, nor could it be punished.
(b) As the country's economic structure developed in the nineteenth and twentieth centuries, so the power of corporations grew, and the theory summarised under (a) above came to be rejected. *See* e.g. *R.* v. *Birmingham & Gloucester Railway Co.* (1842) – conviction of corporation for failure to fulfil a statutory duty. Following the Criminal Justice Act 1925, s. 33, corporations could be indicted. Today, in general, a corporation has virtually the same criminal responsibility as a human being (but much will depend on the extent of authority enjoyed by the person who committed the offence, the nature of the offence, etc.). *See R* v. *ICR Haulage Co Ltd* (1944). Note the Theft Act 1968, s. 18(1)(2) (at 17:**39**); Trade Descriptions Act 1968, s. 20; Interpretation Act 1978, Sch.1; Road Traffic Act 1988, s. 138.
(c) In the case of the accused corporation, there must be persons, 'who represent the direct mind and will of the company and control what it does. The state of mind of these managers is the state of mind of the

company and is treated by the law as such. . . . In the criminal law, in cases where the law requires a guilty mind as a condition of a criminal offence, the guilty mind of the directors or the managers will render the company itself guilty': *per* Denning LJ in *Bolton Engineering Co.* v. *Graham & Sons* (1957).

So, in *R.* v. *I.C.R. Haulage Co. Ltd* (1944) the acts of the company's managing director rendered the company liable for a conspiracy to defraud. In *Henshall Quarries Ltd* v. *Harvey* (1965) it was held that a weighbridge attendant employed by a company occupied too subordinate a position for his knowledge to be attributed to the company.

(d) *See Tesco Supermarkets Ltd* v. *Nattrass* (1972), in which the House of Lords considered the question of *criminal liability* of a company. It was held that a company may be criminally liable for the acts of the board of directors, the managing director and perhaps other superior officers who carry out management functions and speak and act as the company. Lord Reid spoke of a person in these categories as one who 'is acting as the company, and his mind which directs his acts is the mind of the company . . . If it is a guilty mind then that guilt is the guilt of the company.' *See Bolton Engineering Co.* v. *Graham and Sons Ltd* (1957).

(e) In *R.* v. *Andrews-Weatherfoil Ltd* (1972), the Court of Appeal considered a charge under the Public Bodies Corrupt Practices Act 1889, s. 1, and held that a company is only criminally responsible for the acts of persons whose status and authority make their acts those of the company itself – the so-called *doctrine of identification*.

(f) In *Essendon Engineering Company* v. *Maile* (1982), it was held that in order for the agent of a company to make the company guilty of a crime requiring *mens rea* (insuing a false test certificate), he must have been given complete discretion to act independently of instructions from the company and must have had the necessary knowledge.

(g) Note *Ex p. Spooner* (1987) – a corporate body can be guilty of manslaughter (*see* 10:1) but only where the *actus reus* and *mens rea* can be established against those persons who are identified as the embodiment of that corporate body. *See also R.* v. *P. & O. European Ferries Ltd* (1991).

(h) In *Richmond BC* v. *Pinn* (1989), it was held that a limited company cannot be convicted of 'driving' a vehicle without a permit. Note *Redhead Freight* v. *Shulman* (1989) (whether a firm merely 'shutting its eyes' to an employee's failure to fill in record sheets can be said to be 'causing' that offence).

(i) Note e.g. the Human Organ Transplants Act 1989, s. 4(1), relating to offences under the Act by bodies corporate, and a comparable provision in e.g. the Companies Act 1989, s. 42: 'Where an offence under this Act committed by a body corporate is proved to have been committed with the consent or connivance of, or to be attributable to any neglect on the part of, any director, manager, secretary or other similar officer of the body corporate or any person who was purporting to act in any such capacity, he as well as the body corporate is guilty of the offence and is liable to be proceeded against and punished accordingly.'

NOTE: For the question of *unincorporated bodies*, see, e.g. the Banking Act 1987, s. 98 (1).

44. Young persons

For the purposes of the criminal law, the following classification applies:

(a) those under ten years of age (*see* 45);
(b) those of ten and under fourteen years of age (*see* 46);
(c) those over fourteen years of age (*see* 47).

45. Under ten years

There is a conclusive presumption that a child under ten years (at date of commission of the alleged offence) is *doli incapax* (incapable of criminal intention or malice); he cannot, therefore, be guilty of any offence: *see* the Children and Young Persons Act 1963, s. 16. *See Walters* v. *Lunt* (1951). (Note: the 'care and supervision orders' made by the court on the application of a local authority or authorised person, placing a child (under seventeen) in the care of a designated local authority or under the supervision of such authority or a probation officer: Children Act 1989, s. 31.)

46. Ten and under fourteen years

There is a presumption that children in this age group are *doli incapax*, but the presumption may be rebutted by proof of the *actus reus* and *mens rea*, including a 'mischievous discretion', i.e. that the child knew that what he was doing was wrong. 'Malitia supplet aetatem' (malice supplies [the want of] age). The burden of rebutting the presumption of *doli incapax* was held by the Court of Appeal, in *R*. v. *B*. (1979), to be on the prosecution, and evidence of previous convictions and character was admissible to show this. (Failure of a trial judge to direct a jury on the presumption is normally fatal to a conviction where defendant is under fourteen: *R*. v. *Coulborn* (1988).) *See* the Sexual Offences Act 1993.

(a) Proof of the 'mischievous discretion' required to rebut the presumption was considered in *R*. v. *Gorrie* (1918) where X, a thirteen-year-old boy, lightly wounded Y with a penknife. Y died and X was charged with manslaughter. *Per* Salter J: '[The jury must be satisfied] that when the boy did this he knew what he was doing was wrong – not merely what was wrong, but what was gravely wrong, seriously wrong.' It would seem that mere knowledge by the infant of the act's being against the law is insufficient. *See T*. v. *DPP* (1989).
(b) In *McC*. v. *Runeckles* (1984), X, aged thirteen, had stabbed another girl,

Y, using a broken milk bottle. The magistrates held that X's actions, including her running off after the stabbing and attempting to evade the police, rebutted the presumption of *doli incapax*. In dismissing X's appeal against conviction, the Court of Appeal held that the prosecution had to prove that X knew that what she was doing was seriously wrong; what was 'morally wrong' was a species of what was 'seriously wrong'. *See I.* v. *DPP* (1989).

(c) In *A.* v. *DPP* (1991), A was convicted of an offence under the Public Order Act 1986, s. 5(1) (a). He was aged 11 and was observed by the police throwing a brick at one of their vehicles. He appealed against conviction on the ground that the presumption of *doli incapax* had not been rebutted. It was held by a Divisional Court that the test was whether A knew that what he was doing was seriously wrong and went beyond 'childish mischief'. A's running away from the scene of the offence *was not in itself sufficient* to rebut the presumption of *doli incapax*; a naughty child might run away from a teacher or parent even if what he had done was not a criminal act. A's appeal was *allowed*.

47. Above fourteen years
A person of this age is presumed to be fully responsible for his actions 'as if he were forty': *per* Erle J in *R.* v. *Smith* (1845).

48. Children and Young Persons Act 1969
Under s. 4 (when and if this section is brought into force) criminal proceedings will be brought, against a child under fourteen years of age *for homicide only*. In all other cases he will only be brought before the court in care proceedings (designed to show whether or not he is in need of control), which may result in a 'care order' or 'supervision order'. See also the Children Act 1989, Part IV.

> NOTE: Under the Criminal Justice and Public Order Bill, published in December 1993, the categories of offences for which 10–13 year olds can be detained for long periods (and which are currently restricted to murder and manslaughter) would be extended so as to cover all offences carrying a maximum sentence of 14 years for adults, and offences involving indecent assaults on females. Detention would be in local authority secure accommodation. Persistent offenders, aged 12–14, who have committed three or more offences for which adults can be imprisoned and who have breached a supervision order, would be held in 'secure training centres'.

49. Entrapment no defence
The enticing of a person into the commission of a crime so that he may be prosecuted – the process of entrapment – constitutes no defence in English

law: *R. v. McEvilly* (1975). In *R. v. Sang* (1979), the House of Lords stated that it would be wrong in principle to import into the law a defence of entrapment. 'The true relevance of official entrapment into the commission of crime is on the question of sentence when its mitigating value may be high (*see R. v. Birtles* (1969))': *per* Lord Scarman. For entrapment as a mitigating factor, *see R. v. Beaumont* (1987). (Consider, however, the possible effects of the Police and Criminal Evidence Act 1984, s. 78, which allows the court a discretion to exclude evidence likely to have an adverse effect on the fairness of a trial.) *See R. v. Christou* (1992); *Williams v. DPP* (1993); *R. v. Smurthwaite* (1993).

Draft Criminal Code Bill

50. Belief in circumstances affording a defence
'(1) Unless otherwise provided, a person who acts in the belief that a circumstance exists has any defence that he would have if the circumstance existed . . . (3) Any requirement as to proof or disproof of a defence applies to proof or disproof of a belief mentioned in subsec.(1)': cl. 41.

51. Mental disorder
'A mental disorder verdict shall be returned if the defendant is proved to have committed an offence but it is proved on a balance of probabilities (whether by the prosecution or by the defendant) that he was at the time suffering from severe mental illness or severe mental handicap': cl. 35(1). But subsection (1) is not to apply if the court or jury is satisfied beyond reasonable doubt that the offence was not attributable to the severe mental illness or severe mental handicap: cl. 35(2).

'A mental disorder verdict shall be returned if – (*a*) the defendant is acquitted of an offence only because, by reason of evidence of mental disorder or a combination of mental disorder and intoxication, it is found that he acted or may have acted in a state of automatism, or without the fault required for the offence, or believing that an exempting circumstance existed; and (*b*) it is proved on the balance of probabilities (whether by the prosecution or defendant) that he was suffering from mental disorder at the time of the act': cl. 36.

A defendant may plead 'not guilty by reason of mental disorder'; and (*a*) if the court directs that the plea be entered the direction shall have the same effect as a mental disorder verdict; and (*b*) if the court does not so direct the defendant shall be treated as having pleaded not guilty': cl. 37.

Note carefully: '"Mental disorder" means – (*a*) severe mental illness; or (*b*) a state of arrested or incomplete development of mind; or (*c*) a state of automatism (not resulting only from intoxication) which is a feature of a disorder, whether organic or functional and whether continuing or recurring, that may cause a similar state on another occasion': cl. 34.

52. Acts justified or excused by law

'A person does not commit an offence by using such force as, in the circumstances which exist or which he believes to exist, is immediately necessary and reasonable': to prevent crime and effect an arrest; to prevent or terminate a breach of the peace; to protect himself or another from unlawful force or unlawful personal harm; to prevent or terminate unlawful detention; to protect property from unlawful appropriation, destruction or damage; to prevent or terminate a trespass to his person or property: cl. 44.

'A person does not commit an offence by doing an act which is justified or excused by (*a*) any enactment; or (*b*) any "enforceable Community right" as defined in the European Communities Act 1972; or (*c*) any rule of the common law continuing to apply by virtue of s. 4(4)': cl. 45.

53. Corporations

'(1) A corporation may be guilty as a principal of an offence not involving a fault element [*see* 3:20] by reason of (*a*) an act done by its employee or agent, as provided by s. 29; or (*b*) an omission, state of affairs or occurrence that is an element of the offence. (2) A corporation may be guilty – (*a*) as a principal, of an offence involving a fault element; or (*b*) as an accessory, of any offence, only if one of its controlling officers, acting within the scope of his office and with the fault required, is concerned in the offence. (3) "Controlling officer" of a corporation means a person participating in the control of the corporation in the capacity of a director, manager, secretary or other similar officer (whether or not he was, or was validly, appointed to any such office) . . . (7) A corporation cannot be guilty of an offence that is not punishable with a fine or other pecuniary penalty': cl. 30.

Progress test 6

1. When, in general, may mistake be accepted as an excuse? **(3–5)**

2. '*Ignorantia juris non excusat.*' Explain. **(6)**

3. What are the differences between duress *per minas* and duress of circumstances? **(9–11)**

4. Is obedience to orders ever acceptable as a defence? **(12)**

5. Outline the decision in *R.* v. *Kingston* (1993).   **(15)**

6. Outline the significance of *DPP* v. *Majewski* (1977).   **(19)**

7. Explain the decision in *R.* v. *Burgess* (1991).   **(25)**

8. Summarise the M'Naghten Rules.   **(28–31)**

9. Outline the decision in *Beckford* v. *R.* (1987).   **(39)**

10. In what sense may criminal liability be attributed to a corporation? **(43)**

11. *'Malitia supplet aetatem.'* Explain.   **(46)**

The inchoate offences (1): incitement and conspiracy

Preliminary crimes

1. Activities preceding the commission of a crime
The actual commission of a crime often involves a series of prior, related activities. Consider, for example, the following events:

(a) X writes a letter to Y, which Y reads, suggesting that Y should steal Z's goods.
(b) A_1 and A_2 agree to waylay and rob B.
(c) D decides, with no lawful excuse, to burn down E's house. In pursuance of his objective D stacks inflammable material against the door of the house and prepares to throw a lighted match into that material. At that point D is arrested.

These examples illustrate the nature of the 'preliminary offences' which are discussed in this and the following chapter.

2. The three preliminary offences
The examples in **1** above illustrate, respectively, the 'inchoate' (or 'anticipatory') offences of *incitement, conspiracy* and *attempt*. Although each of these offences may be considered as part of some wider offence (which may, or may not, be committed), *each is an independent offence, complete in itself*. Each is an *offence of specific intent (see* 3:**12**); recklessness will *not* constitute the appropriate *mens rea*.

Incitement

3. The basis of the offence
It is a *common law offence* for X to instigate intentionally, i.e. incite or solicit, Y to commit a criminal offence, whether the incitement is successful or not.

In *R.* v. *Higgins* (1801), X was convicted on a count 'that he did falsely, wickedly, and unlawfully solicit and incite' Y to steal the property of Y's master. It was argued that the count contained no indictable offence. *Per*

Lord Kenyon CJ: 'It is argued that a mere intent to commit evil is not indictable without an act done; but is there not an act done when it is charged that the defendant solicited another to commit a felony? The solicitation is an act . . .' *Per* Lawrence J: 'All such acts or attempts as tend to the prejudice of the community are indictable . . . A solicitation is an act. The offence does not rest in mere intention; for in soliciting [Y] to commit the felony, the defendant did an act towards carrying his intention into execution.'

4. Statutory offences of inciting

Separate offences of inciting are created by some Acts, e.g.:

(a) Official Secrets Act 1920, s. 7. It is an offence for a person to incite another person to commit an offence under the Act. *See* 21:**17**.
(b) Criminal Law Act 1977, s. 54. 'It is an offence for a man to incite to have sexual intercourse with him a girl under the age of sixteen whom he knows to be his grand-daughter, daughter or sister.' *See* 13:**11**.
(c) *See* Offences against the Person Act 1861, s. 4 (*see* 9:**42**); Incitement to Disaffection Act 1934, s. 1 (*see* 21:**12**).

5. Form of the incitement

The following points should be noted.

(a) An inciter 'is one who reaches and seeks to influence the mind of another to the commission of a crime': *per* Holmes J.
(b) Incitement may be constituted by the *written or spoken word* and may be in the form of a suggestion, persuasion, or even a threat. 'A person may "incite" another to do an act by threatening or by pressure, as well as by persuasion': *per* Lord Denning in *Race Relations Board* v. *Applin* (1973). An element of encouragement, pressure or persuasion seems to be essential in the offence: *see R.* v. *Hendricksen and Tichner* (1977).
(c) Incitement may be *express or implied,* and directed to a specific individual or people in general: *see Invicta Plastics* v. *Clare* (1976), in which an advertisement to the public for the sale of a police radar-trap warning system was held to constitute an incitement to an offence under the Wireless Telegraphy Act 1949. *See* also *R.* v. *Most* (1881), in which an article published in a London newspaper, urging foreigners to assassinate their heads of state, was held to constitute an incitement to murder.

6. Communication of the incitement

The incitement must be communicated. 'There can be no incitement of anyone unless the incitement, whether by words or written matter, reaches the man whom it is said is being incited': *per* Lord Parker CJ in

Wilson v. *Danny Quastel Ltd* (1966). In the case of a failure of communication, the inciter could be charged with attempted incitement: *R.* v. *Ransford* (1874). (For a statutory offence of attempt to incite another person to commit an offence under the Act, see the Misuse of Drugs Act 1971, s. 19.)

(a) Where X incites Y to commit a crime which Y then commits, X will be considered as a principal offender (*see* 5:4) in relation to that crime.

(b) Note *R.* v. *Leahey* (1985). X had encouraged Y to wound Z_1, whereupon Y wounded Z_2. No evidence was given as to why Y wounded Z_2 rather than Z_1. It was held that there was no case for X to answer on a charge of inciting Y to wound Z_2, since the offence committed by Y was not the offence X had incited Y to commit.

(c) In *R.* v. *Rowley* (1991), X was charged with outraging public decency: *see* 3:3. The Court of Appeal held that sending notes to arrange meetings where persons would have been incited to acts of indecency could *not* constitute attempts to incite; sending the notes was merely preparatory to the incitement.

7. Effect of the incitement

Where X moves Y to commit a crime, no act is required from Y in order that the offence of incitement might be constituted. 'It matters not that no steps have been taken towards the commission of the attempt or the substantive offence. It matters not, in other words, whether the incitement had any effect at all. It is merely the incitement or the attempting to incite which constitutes the offence': *per* Lord Widgery in *R.* v. *Assistant Recorder of Kingston-upon-Hull* (1969). (The appropriate *actus reus* is simply X's encouragement of Y to commit an act which is, in fact, a crime, whether X knows it is a crime, or not.)

8. Further problems

The following matters should be noted.

(a) The fact that the crime incited cannot, in the circumstances, be committed is of no relevance. In *R.* v. *McDonough* (1963), X was convicted on counts including inciting Y to receive lamb carcases, knowing them to have been stolen; but, in fact, no such carcases existed at the material time. It was held that this was no impediment to X's conviction. *See R.* v. *Fitzmaurice* (1983), where it was held that where an offence is capable of being committed at the time X incites Y, then although later circumstances render the offence impossible to commit, X may nevertheless be convicted of inciting Y.

(b) An 'incitement to incite' seems possible: *see R.* v. *Cromack* (1978) – inciting another to incite perjury. An 'attempt to incite' is also an offence: *see R.* v. *Banks* (1873). *See* also *R.* v. *Sirat* (1986).

Conspiracy

9. The basis of the offence at common law

Conspiracy was a common law misdemeanour which consisted 'not merely in the intention of two or more, but in the *agreement* of two or more, to do an unlawful act by unlawful means. So long as such a design rests in intention only it is not indictable. When two agree to carry it into effect, the very plot is an act in itself': *per* Willes J in *Mulcahy* v. *R.* (1868). *See R.* v. *Bolton* (1992) (in a case of conspiracy as opposed to the substantive offence, it is what was agreed to be done and not what was in fact done which is all-important).

(a) For examples of the offence at common law, *see R.* v. *Gill* (1818); *R.* v. *Meyrick* (1929); *Churchill* v. *Walton* (1967).

(b) The view of common law conspiracy as including *any* agreement to effect a public mischief was *rejected* in *DPP* v. *Withers* (1975).

10. *Mens rea* of common law conspiracy

Mens rea in relation to this offence is the intention to carry out the agreement *and* knowledge of those facts which make the agreement unlawful: *Churchill* v. *Walton* (1967). The House of Lords stated: 'In cases of this kind, it is desirable to avoid the use of the phrase *mens rea*, which is capable of different meanings, and to concentrate on the terms or effect of the agreement made by the alleged conspirators. The question is, "What did they agree to do?" If what they agreed to do was, on the facts known to them, an unlawful act, they are guilty of conspiracy and cannot excuse themselves by saying that, owing to their ignorance of the law, they did not realise that such an act was a crime. If, on the facts known to them, what they agreed to do was lawful, they are not rendered artificially guilty by the existence of other facts, not known to them, giving a different and criminal quality to the act agreed upon.'

(a) *See R.* v. *Blake* (1844) – existence of agreement may be inferred from detached acts done in pursuance of a purpose held in common between the accused persons.

(b) *See R.* v. *Thomson* (1965) – persons were not guilty of conspiracy unless they genuinely intended to carry out the purpose of the agreement.

The statutory offence

11. Law Commission Report No. 76

'The crime of conspiracy should be limited to agreements to commit criminal offences: an agreement should not be criminal where that which it was agreed to be done would not amount to a criminal offence if committed by one person.' This aim of the Report was attained in part by the Criminal Law Act 1977.

12 Criminal Law Act 1977, s. 1(1): a radical amendment of the law

'Subject to the following provisions of this part of the Act, if a person agrees with any other person or persons that a course of conduct shall be pursued, which, if the agreement is carried out in accordance with their intentions, either –

(a) will necessarily amount to or involve the commission of any offence or offences by one or more of the parties to the agreement, or
(b) would do so but for the existence of facts which render the commission of the offence or any of the offences impossible, he is guilty of conspiracy to commit the offence or offences in question': s. 1(1) (as substituted by the Criminal Attempts Act 1981, s. 5(1)).

Note that conspiracy is an offence of *specific intent* (*see* 3:**12**); direct intention to carry out the agreed crime must be proved and recklessness will not suffice for the appropriate *mens rea*.
See also the Criminal Justice Act 1993, s. 5.

13. Criminal Law Act 1977, s. 5

'Subject to the following provisions of this section, the offence of conspiracy at common law is hereby abolished': s. 5(1). 'Subsection (1) above shall not affect the offence of conspiracy at common law so far as relates to conspiracy to defraud, [and s. 1 above shall not apply in any case where the agreement in question amounts to a conspiracy to defraud at common law']: s. 5(2). 'Subsection (1) above shall not affect the offence of conspiracy at common law if and in so far as it may be committed by entering into an agreement to engage in conduct which (*a*) tends to corrupt morals or outrages public decency; but (*b*) would not amount to or involve the commission of an offence if carried out by a single person otherwise than in pursuance of an agreement . . . .':s. 5(3).

NOTE: The Criminal Justice Act 1987, s. 12(2), repealed the words placed within square brackets in s. 5(2) above, following 'and'. *See* **15** below.

14. Conspiracy to defraud.

For a definition of 'conspiracy to defraud', *see* the statement by the House of Lords in *Scott* v. *MPC* (1975): 'It is clearly the law that an agreement by two or more by dishonesty to deprive a person of something which is his or to which he is or would be or might be entitled and an agreement by two or more by dishonesty to injure some proprietary right of his, suffices to constitute the offence of conspiracy to defraud.'

(a) In this type of conspiracy to defraud, the element of deception is *not* essential. Note, however, the offence of dishonestly deceiving an individual into acting contrary to his public duty: see *Welham* v. *DPP* (1961); *DPP* v. *Withers* (1975).

(b) In *R.v. Moses* (1991), X and Y were convicted of conspiracy to defraud by facilitating applications for immigrants' work permits; this involved the withholding of important information from departmental supervisors. X and Y appealed against conviction, on the ground that the department, having suffered no economic loss, had not been defrauded. The appeal was dismissed: economic loss is *not* an essential element of the offence charged, and the supervisors had been induced to act in a way which was contrary to their public duty.

(c) In *Wai Yu-Tsang* v. *R.* (1992), a bank's chief accountant had agreed dishonestly with other persons to conceal in the bank's accounts dishonoured cheques purchased by the bank. He was charged with conspiracy; his defence was that he had acted on instructions and his basic motive was to prevent a run on the bank. The Privy Council dismissed his appeal against conviction. To be guilty of conspiracy, it was not necessary for the accused person to have intended any economic loss to the victims; motive and underlying purpose were irrelevant.

(d) The *mens rea* necessary for conspiracy to defraud is *intent*. See *R.* v. *Cooke* (1986). Dishonesty, as set out in *R.* v. *Ghosh* (1982) (*see* 15:6) is a necessary element of the requisite *mens rea* in a conspiracy to defraud.

15. Overlap of statutory conspiracy and conspiracy to defraud
The following points should be noted.

(a) Under the Criminal Justice Act 1987, s. 12(1), if a person agrees with any other person or persons that a course of conduct shall be pursued, and that course of conduct will necessarily amount to or involve the commission of any offence or offences by one or more of the parties to the agreement if the agreement is carried out in accordance with their intentions, the fact that it will do so shall *not* preclude a charge of conspiracy to defraud being brought against any of them in respect of the agreement.

(b) The 1987 Act, s. 12 amends the Criminal Law Act 1977, s. 5(2) (*see* **13** above).

(c) As a result, the prosecution has a *choice* in relation to the charge to be preferred. Defendant may be charged, therefore, with conspiracy to defraud notwithstanding that conspiracy to commit another, statutory offence could also be charged. *See R.* v. *Boyle* (1991).

16 Other matters arising from s. 1, 1977 Act
Note the following.

(a) The essence of a conspiracy remains *the agreement*, so that a conspiracy to import a certain drug can be established only by proof of an agreement to import that particular drug: *R.v. Siracusa* (1989).

(b) 'Where liability for any offence may be incurred without knowledge on the part of the person committing it of any particular fact or circumstances necessary for the commission of the offence, a person shall nevertheless not be guilty of conspiracy to commit that offence by virtue of s. 1(1) unless he and at least one other party to the agreement intend or know that that fact or circumstance shall or will exist at the time when the conduct constituting the offence is to take place': s. 1(2). This subsection removes the concept of strict liability (*see* 4:1) from conspiracy. Further, at least two of the parties to the agreement constituting the alleged conspiracy must have the appropriate *mens rea*.

(c) Where in pursuance of any agreement as is mentioned in s. 1(1) the acts in question in relation to an offence are to be done in contemplation or furtherance of a trade dispute, the offence shall be disregarded for the purpose of s. 1(1) if it is a summary offence which is not punishable with imprisonment: s. 1(3), amended by the Trade Union and Labour Relations (Consolidation) Act 1992, s. 242.

17. Exemptions from liability under the 1977 Act
Note the following points.

(a) 'A person shall not by virtue of s. 1 be guilty of conspiracy to commit any offence if he is an intended victim of that offence': s. 2(1). (The term 'victim' is not defined in the Act.)

(b) 'A person shall not by virtue of s. 1 be guilty of conspiracy to commit any offence or offences if the only other person or persons with whom he agrees are (both initially and at all other times during the currency of the agreement) persons of any of the following descriptions . . . his spouse, a person under the age of criminal responsibility, and an intended victim of that offence or each of those offences': s. 2(2).

> (*i*) In *R. v. Chrastny (No. 1)* (1992), Mrs X had participated in a conspiracy with several persons, including her husband, Mr X, who was one of the chief conspirators. She was convicted of a conspiracy to supply controlled drugs and appealed on the ground that she had conspired *only* with her husband and, therefore, was not liable because of s. 2(2).
>
> (*ii*) Mrs X's appeal was *dismissed*. The Court of Appeal held that a wife who joins her husband in a conspiracy, when she is aware that he was involved with other participants in it to commit an unlawful act, is equally guilty of conspiracy.
>
> (*iii*) *See R. v. Lovick* (1993).

(c) A person is under the age of criminal responsibility for purposes of

s. 2(2) so long as it is conclusively presumed, by virtue of the Children and Young Persons Act 1933, s. 50, that he cannot be guilty of any offence: s. 2(3). Hence, a conspiracy could exist with a young person of at least ten but under fourteen if it could be shown that he had a 'mischievous discretion' (*see* 6:**46**).

Further aspects of conspiracy

18. Incitement to commit conspiracy
'Incitement and attempt to commit the offence of conspiracy (whether the conspiracy incited or attempted would be an offence at common law or under s. 1 . . . or any other enactment) shall cease to be offences': 1977 Act, s. 5(7). *See R.* v. *Sirat* (1986). (Where A incites B to agree with C that C will wound D, A's incitement of B does *not* constitute an offence under s. 5(7).) Note that an uncommunicated intention to participate in a criminal enterprise will not amount *per se* to an *indictable conspiracy: R.* v. *Scott* (1978).

19. Two or more conspirators
A man cannot conspire with himself: at least two minds must meet in order that the *actus reus* of conspiracy might exist. *See Mawji* v. *R.* (1957); and *R.* v. *McDonnell* (1966) – a person responsible for the affairs of a limited company cannot 'conspire' with that company.

20. Different verdicts for the conspirators
In *DPP* v. *Shannon* (1975), the House of Lords held that where one of two alleged conspirators has been fairly and properly tried, and, on the evidence, rightly convicted, there is no reason why his conviction should be invalidated if for any reason the other is acquitted at the subsequent trial. This rule has been preserved.

(a) Note the 1977 Act, s. 5(8): 'The fact that the person or persons who, so far as appears from the indictment on which any person has been convicted of conspiracy, were the only parties to the agreement on which his conviction was based have been acquitted of conspiracy by reference to that agreement (whether after being tried with the person convicted or separately) shall not be a ground for quashing his conviction unless under all the circumstances of the case his conviction is inconsistent with the acquittal of the other person or persons in question.' (Any rule of law or practice inconsistent with s. 5(8) is abolished: s. 5(9). *See R.* v. *Ashton* (1992).

(b) Where the strength of the evidence against each conspirator is markedly different, the jury should be directed that they may convict one and acquit the other: *R.* v. *Longman and Cribben* (1980). But it is for the judge, and not for the jury, to decide whether there is a marked difference between the cases against the conspirators: *R.* v. *Roberts* (1984).

21. Conspiracy to do the impossible
See the Criminal Law Act 1977, s. 1(1), as substituted by the Criminal Attempts Act 1981, s. 5(1), at **12**. Where X and Y agree on a course of conduct which would involve the commission of an offence by any one party, or both, or would do so but for the existence of facts rendering commission of the offence impossible, that agreement amounts nevertheless to a conspiracy. (*See DPP* v. *Nock* (1978) at 8:**3**.)

22. Lack of intention to carry out an agreement
In *R.* v. *Anderson* (1985), the House of Lords considered, and dismissed, an appeal by X against the decision of the Court of Appeal, dismissing his appeal against conviction of conspiracy to effect the escape of a prisoner, contrary to the 1977 Act, s. 1. X had agreed with others to purchase and supply cutting material to be smuggled to the prisoner. X maintained that he had intended only to provide that material and to take no further part in the scheme which he believed to be doomed to failure. The House held that he was *guilty of statutory conspiracy*. It was no defence to the charge that X did not intend that the conspiracy be carried out and that he did not believe it could succeed. It sufficed for the prosecution to show that X knew that the course of conduct to be pursued would amount to or involve the commission of an offence and that he intended to play *some part* in the agreed course of conduct in furtherance of the criminal purpose that it was intended to achieve. 'Nothing less will suffice; nothing more is required': *per* Lord Bridge.

23. Other matters
Note the following.

(a) For conspiracy to pervert the course of justice, *see R.* v. *Jackson* (1985) – it was no defence that the offence referred to in a conspiracy count depended on a contingency which may not have taken place. For conspiracy to corrupt public morals, *see Shaw* v. *DPP* (1962) at 1:**22**.
(b) A person may *not* be held liable for *attempting to conspire*: Criminal Attempts Act 1981, s. 1(4)(*a*). *See* 8:**9**.
(c) A person may be held liable for *conspiracy to conspire* in the case of a common law conspiracy, but not in the case of a statutory conspiracy.
(d) Conspiracy at common law is *not* an arrestable offence (*see* 1:**27**): *see R.* v. *Spicer* (1970). A statutory conspiracy is an arrestable offence if the offence which the parties conspire to commit is punishable with a sentence of five years or more: *see* Police and Criminal Evidence Act 1984, s. 24(3).

no attempt to. conspire.

(e) A conspiracy entered into overseas which was intended to result in criminal acts in this country is justiciable in this country: *R.* v. *Sansom* (1991). *See also* the Criminal Justice Act 1993, s. 5.

Draft Criminal Code Bill

24. Incitement
'A person is guilty of incitement to commit an offence or offences if – (*a*) he incites another to do or cause to be done an act or acts which, if done, will involve the commission of the offence or offences by the other; and (*b*) he intends or believes that the other, if he acts as incited, shall or will do so with the fault required for the offence or offences': cl. 47(1).

25. Conspiracy
'A person is guilty of conspiracy to commit an offence or offences if – (a) he agrees with another or others that an act or acts shall be done which, if done, will involve the commission of the offence or offences by one or more of the parties to the agreement; and (b) he and at least one other party to the agreement intend that the offence or offences shall be committed': cl. 48(1).

Progress test 7

1. What is the general nature of the 'inchoate offences'? **(1,2)**

2. Give examples of statutory offences of incitement. **(4)**

3. 'Incitement must be communicated.' Explain. **(6)**

4. What was the effect of the Criminal Law Act 1977, s. 1(1)? **(12)**

5. Explain the nature of conspiracy to defraud. **(14)**

6. What are the exemptions from liability under the 1977 Act? **(17)**

7. Is it possible to incite a person to commit the offence of conspiracy? **(18)**

8

The inchoate offences (2): attempt

Attempt at common law

1. Basis of criminal attempt at common law

At common law it was a misdemeanour to attempt to commit an offence, whether that offence was a crime at common law or under statute: *see R. v. Hensler* (1870).

(a) *Actus reus.* 'The mere intention to commit a misdemeanour is not criminal. *Some act is required,* and we do not think that all acts towards committing a misdemeanour are indictable. Acts remotely leading towards the commission of the offence are not to be considered as attempts to commit it, but acts immediately connected with it are . . .': *per* Parke B in *R. v. Eagleton* (1855). Note, too, Stephen's definition, quoted with approval by Lord Parker CJ in *Davey* v. *Lee* (1968): 'An attempt to commit a crime is an act done with intent to commit that crime, and forming part of a series of acts which would constitute its actual commission if it were not interrupted.'

(b) *Mens rea.* 'It is implicit in the concept of an attempt that the person acting intends to do the act attempted, so that the *mens rea* of an attempt is essentially that of the complete crime': *per* Edmund-Davies LJ in *R. v. Easom* (1971).

2. Problems of the common law approach: proximity and unequivocalness

At what precise point does an act become highly proximate to, and, therefore, sufficiently connected unequivocally with, a crime, so as to constitute an 'attempt'? At what precise point does a person's action move him towards 'striking distance' of committing an offence? When may it be said of an offender that he 'must have crossed the Rubicon and burnt his boats'? (*See DPP* v. *Stonehouse* (1978).) The cases decided under *common law* seem to establish that the *actus reus* of attempt to commit an offence existed when the accused performed some act which could be regarded as a movement to the commission of that offence, *and* the performance of that act could not be reasonably interpreted as having any other objective than the commission of the offence. ('The act speaks for itself.') Consider the following cases.

(a) *R. v. Robinson* (1915). X, a jeweller, after insuring his stock against theft, tied himself up and called for assistance, telling the police that he had been attacked by thieves, who had robbed his safe. Later he admitted that he had hoped to make a claim on the insurers. He was convicted, but the conviction was *quashed* on appeal. *Per* Lord Reading CJ: 'We think that the appellant's act was only remotely connected with the commission of the full offence, and not immediately connected with it. . . . We think that the conviction must be quashed . . . upon the broad ground that no communication of any kind of the false pretence was made to the underwriters. '

(b) *Comer* v. *Bloomfield* (1971). X crashed his van, but told the police that it had been stolen. Although he was unsure as to whether it was insured against theft, he wrote to Y, his insurer, saying that the van had been stolen and enquiring whether he could make a claim. The van was found and X admitted that he had intended to obtain money from Y. The prosecution appealed against X's acquittal of attempting to obtain the value of the van by deception. The appeal was *disallowed*: it was held that a mere preliminary enquiry concerning insurance cover, although made with fraudulent intent, did not constitute an act sufficiently proximate to the obtaining of the insurance money to constitute an attempt to obtain money by deception.

(c) *Davey* v. *Lee* (1968). X_1 and X_2 were charged with attempting to steal copper from a compound, and convicted. They had been observed climbing a fence which they had cut. There were other stores in the compound and they argued that the acts proved against them were not sufficiently proximate to the stealing of copper. Their appeal was *dismissed*. The following extract from *Archbold* (37th edition) was approved: 'It is submitted that the *actus reus* necessary to constitute an attempt is complete if the prisoner does an act which is a step towards the commission of the specific crime, which is immediately and not merely remotely connected with the commission of it, and the doing of which cannot reasonably be regarded as having any other purpose than the commission of the specific crime.'

3. Problems of the common law approach: impossibility
Could X be convicted of attempting to perform an act which was impossible?

(a) *R.* v. *Ring, Atkins and Jackson* (1892). X and his confederates were shown to have tried to pick pockets, but there was no evidence that the pockets in question contained anything. A conviction of attempted larceny was *upheld*. *See* also *R.* v. *Osborn* (1919): 'It is well known that the impossibility of the thing does not prevent an attempt being made': *per* Rowlatt J.

(b) *Haughton* v. *Smith* (1975). A van, stopped by the police, was found to contain stolen goods. To trap X, with whom the van driver had a rendezvous, the van was allowed to proceed, with police concealed inside. X met the van and proceeded to dispose of the contents. He was arrested and convicted of handling stolen goods, the conviction being quashed by the Court of Appeal. The House of Lords *dismissed the prosecution's appeal*, holding that a person who carries out certain acts in the mistaken belief that they constitute an offence *cannot* be convicted of an attempt to commit that offence, because he has taken no steps to the commission of the offence. The goods, which had fallen into the hands of the police, were not stolen goods at the time of X's alleged handling and it was irrelevant that X believed them to be stolen.

(c) *DPP* v. *Nock and Alsford* (1978). The accused and others agreed to produce cocaine (a controlled drug: *see* Chap. 23) from a powder they had obtained, believing that it was a mixture of cocaine and lignocaine. In fact, it was impossible to produce cocaine from it. The House of Lords, following its decision in *Haughton* v. *Smith* (1975), held that the accused could *not* be convicted of conspiring to produce cocaine, since it was absolutely impossible to produce it from the powder.

4. Law Commission Report 1980
The Report of the Law Commission (*Attempt, and Impossibility in relation to Attempt, Conspiracy and Incitement*) was followed by the Criminal Attempts Act 1981 which created *a new, statutory, offence of attempting to commit an offence*, appeared likely to end the controversy concerning 'impossible attempts', and abolished the offence at common law.

The statutory offence

5. Common law attempt abolished
By s. 6(1) of the Criminal Attempts Act 1981, the offence of *attempt at common law was abolished*.

(a) Additionally, s. 6(1) *abolished* the common law offence of 'procuring materials for crimes'. (But note the Theft Act 1968, s. 25: *see* 16:**21**.)

(b) By s. 6(2) existing statutory references to the common law offence were converted into references to the offence under s. 1.

6. The statutory offence of attempt
'If, with intent to commit an offence to which this section applies, a person

does an act which is *more than merely preparatory* to the commission of the offence, he is guilty of attempting to commit the offence': 1981 Act, s. 1(1).

7. 'With intent'
Section 1(1) requires an *intent* to commit the complete offence. (This is, therefore, the *mens rea* of attempt, a crime of *specific intent: see* 3:**12**.)

(a) Note the words of James LJ in *R.* v. *Mohan* (1976): '. . . proof of specific intent, a decision to bring about, in so far as it lies within the accused's power, the commission of the offence which it is alleged the accused attempted to commit, no matter whether the accused desired that consequence of his act or not.'

(b) In *R.* v. *Pearman* (1985), the Court of Appeal allowed the appeal of X, convicted under the Offences against the Person Act 1861, s. 18, and the Criminal Attempts Act 1981, s. 1(1). X had been driving and was signalled to stop by an unmarked police car following him. On being told that the unmarked car contained police, X reversed his car at high speed, collided with the police car, and drove forward, injuring a police officer. The judge directed the jury that X had the necessary intent within s. 1(1) if he did a voluntary act foreseeing that really serious bodily harm would result from it. The Court of Appeal held that although foresight of consequences could be something from which a jury *could infer* an intent to cause those consequences, foresight of consequences of an act must *not* be equated with intent to do it, so that the judge's direction was *wrong*. 'Intent' in s. 1 has the meaning which it possesses in common law attempt.

(c) *See R.* v. *Millard and Vernon* (1987). In this case, which turned on an alleged attempt to damage a wall, recklessness was held to be *incompatible* with the intent required by s. 1(1) for the offence of attempt.

8. 'More than merely preparatory'
The phrase in s. 1 contemplates conduct which is a *substantial step* towards the commission of the ultimate offence, and *not* conduct constituted by an act of mere preparation.

(a) Examples of such acts might be: X's aiming a pistol at Y, intending to kill him unlawfully; X's taking matches from his pocket with the intention of igniting petrol poured over Y's property so as to destroy it without lawful justification.

(b) Whether an act would be so regarded is *a question of fact for the jury*. Note s. 4(3): 'Where, in proceedings against a person for an offence under s. 1 above, there is evidence sufficient in law to support a finding that he did an act falling within subsection (1) of that section, the question whether or not his act fell within that subsection is a question of fact.'

(c) In *R.* v. *Ilyas* (1984), X was charged with dishonestly attempting to obtain property by deception (*see* Chap. 17). He had made a false report to the police and his insurance company that his car had been stolen. He had obtained, but not completed, an insurance claim form. He was convicted and appealed, arguing that his actions were not sufficiently proximate, and, therefore, incapable in law of constituting an attempt. X's conviction was *quashed*. He had *not done every act necessary* to achieve the result intended. The act of obtaining a claim form was *preparatory only* and *remote* from the contemplated offence.

(d) In *R. v. Gullefer* (1990), X had backed a greyhound at the races. When it appeared to be losing he jumped on the track, hoping that a 'no race' would be declared and that his stake would be returned to him. X's appeal against his conviction of attempted theft was allowed by the Court of Appeal because there was insufficient evidence to demonstrate that his acts had gone *beyond* mere preparations within s. 1.

(e) In *R. v. Jones* (1990), the Court of Appeal held that s. 1(1) should be construed according to its natural meaning and *not* by seeking to fit to the words of the section a test derived from the old case law. In *R. v. Campbell* (1991), the Court of Appeal stated that the law of attempt was 'fully contained' within the 1981 Act. A judge need tell the jury only that the accused must have performed an act which was more than merely preparatory to committing the offence with the intention of committing it. The trial judge should *not* have made reference to the law prior to 1981.

9. Scope of s. 1

By s. 1(4), section 1 has application to any offence which, if completed, would be triable on indictment in England and Wales, *except*:

(a) conspiracy (whether common law or statutory – *see* the Criminal Law Act 1977, s. 1, at 7:**12**);

(b) aiding, abetting, counselling, procuring or suborning the commission of an offence;

(c) assisting offenders or accepting or agreeing to accept consideration for not disclosing information about an arrestable offence (*see* the Criminal Law Act 1967, ss. 4(1), 5(1), as amended by the Police and Criminal Evidence Act 1984, Sch.6). (The section will not apply, of course, where 'attempt' is impossible, e.g. in a case of involuntary manslaughter (*see* 10:**2**).) Note *R. v. Dunnington* (1984): it is still an offence to aid and abet *an attempt* to commit a crime. (An 'attempt to attempt' is not an offence: *see* s. 1(1).)

> NOTE: See Criminal Justice Act 1993, s. 5, for the extension of jurisdiction over certain conspiracies and certain attempts.

10. Specific offences of attempt

Section 3 applies to certain offences of attempt created by enactments other than s. 1 of the 1981 Act and which are expressed as offences of attempting to commit another offence, the same definitions and other principles provided by s. 1(1)–(3). For an example of the type of specific offence contemplated by s. 3, *see* e.g. the Official Secrets Act 1920, s. 7, creating the offence of attempting to commit an offence (summary or indictable) under the Official Secrets Acts 1911 and 1920.

> NOTE: No defence is provided by the 1981 Act (or, indeed, common law) for the case of one who voluntarily 'withdraws' after an attempt. This is a matter of mitigation only.

Attempting the impossible

11. 1981 Act, s. 1(2)
'A person may be guilty of attempting to commit an offence to which this section applies even though the facts are such that the commission of the offence is *impossible.*'

12. Effect of s. 1(2)
'. . . It is plainly intended to reverse the law. . . .reaffirmed in *Haughton* v. *Smith* (1975), that the pickpocket who puts his hand in an empty pocket commits no offence. Putting the hand in the pocket is the guilty act, the intent to steal is the guilty mind, the offence is appropriately dealt with as an attempt, and the impossibility of committing the full offence for want of anything in the pocket to steal is declared by the subsection to be *no obstacle to conviction*': *per* Lord Bridge.

13. 1981 Act, s. 1(3)
'In any case where –

(a) apart from this subsection a person's intention would not be regarded as having amounted to an intent to commit an offence; but
(b) if the facts of the case had been as he believed them to be, his intention would be so regarded, then, for the purpose of subsection (1) above, he shall be regarded as having had an intent to commit that offence.'

14. Effect of s. 1(3)
It was thought with some confidence that this subsection, together with s. 1(2), would put to rest the controversy on 'attempting the impossible'; the question of 'impossibility' had now become – so it was thought – an irrelevance. Thus, X receives goods he believes to be stolen, but, in fact, they never had been stolen. In such a case, X, under the terms of s. 1, would

clearly be guilty of an attempt to commit an offence. Controversy, however, was not put to rest: *see* **15–16**.

Recent controversy on 'attempting the impossible'

15. *Anderton* v. *Ryan* (1985)

In this case, the House of Lords re-opened the controversy. X bought a video recorder (from a person she refused to name), believing it to have been stolen, and was charged subsequently with dishonestly attempting to handle the recorder knowing or believing it to be stolen, contrary to the 1981 Act, s. 1(1). No evidence was given by the prosecution to show that the recorder was in fact stolen. The charge was dismissed by the magistrates on the ground that X's mere belief that it was stolen was insufficient for a conviction under s. 1(1). The prosecution appealed and a Divisional Court held that X *was guilty* of attempt notwithstanding that the full offence was either uncompleted or impossible. X then appealed to the House of Lords.

(a) *House of Lords.* X's appeal was *allowed*. The House held that where a person's actions are *objectively innocent*, although he mistakenly believes facts which if true would make his actions a complete crime, then, on the true construction of s. 1(3) of the 1981 Act, he *cannot be guilty* of the offence of attempting to commit that crime, since the crime itself is impossible and he has throughout not acted in a criminal way despite his belief that he was committing a crime.

(b) *Per Lord Bridge:* 'It seems to me that subsections (2) and (3) are in a sense complementary to each other. Subsection (2) covers the case of a person acting in a criminal way with a general intent to commit a crime in circumstances where no crime is possible. Subsection (3) covers the case of a person acting in a criminal way with a specific intent to commit a particular crime which he erroneously believes to be, but which is not in fact, possible. Given the criminal action, the appropriate subsection allows the actor's guilty intention to be supplied by his subjective but mistaken state of mind, notwithstanding that on the true facts that intention is incapable of fulfilment. But if the action is throughout innocent and the actor has done everything he intended to do, I can find nothing in either subsection, which requires me to hold that his erroneous belief in facts which, if true, would have made the action a crime makes him guilty of attempt to commit that crime.'

(c) *The decision criticised.* The decision drew considerable criticism from some legal writers. Prof. Glanville Williams, for example, wrote, in *The Lords Achieve the Logically Impossible* (1985) 135 NLJ 502–5, that subsection (3) had been included in the 1981 Act for the precise purpose of preventing judges from saying, in cases of mistake of fact, that the accused had done everything he intended to do when he has not done everything he intended to do because a fact that he believed to be present was missing. The decision in *Anderton* v. *Ryan* had resurrected the old law in part, and the result was, once again, to distinguish between punishable and non-punishable attempts to do the impossible, with practically no guidance on how the distinction was to be worked.

16. *R.* v. *Shivpuri* (1986)

In this case the House of Lords took the unusual step of departing from one of its previous decisions (*see* (b) below), and declared that *Anderton* v. *Ryan was wrongly decided.* X, the appellant, had been arrested carrying a package he had brought from India which he believed to contain either cannabis or heroin. In fact, the package was found to contain snuff, or some similar harmless vegetable matter. X was convicted on counts of attempting to be knowingly concerned in dealing with and harbouring a controlled drug contrary to the 1981 Act, s. 1(1), and the Customs and Excise Management Act 1979, s. 170(1)(*b*). X's appeal against conviction was dismissed by the Court of Appeal.

(a) *House of Lords.* The House considered the 'true construction' of the 1981 Act.

(*i*) Did X intend to receive, store, and pass smuggled drugs? The answer was: Yes. Did he, in relation to such an offence, do an act which was more than merely preparatory to the commission of the offence? His acts were clearly more than preparatory to the commission of the *intended* offence; they were not and could not be more than merely preparatory to the commission of the *actual* offence, because the facts were such that it was impossible.

(*ii*) Did the act which is 'more than merely preparatory to the commission of the offence' in s. 1(1) require any more than an act which was more than merely preparatory to the commission of the offence which X intended to commit? Section 1(2) indicated a negative answer; if it were otherwise, whenever the facts were such that the commission of the actual offence was impossible, it would be impossible to prove an act more than merely preparatory to the commission of that offence, and subs. (1) and (2) would contradict each other.

(*iii*) X was, therefore, *rightly convicted.*

(b) *Anderton* v. *Ryan wrongly decided.* The House used its *Practice Statement (Judicial Precedent)* [1966] 1 WLR 1234, in which Lord Gardiner LC set out the circumstances in which the House would depart from a previous decision, to declare that the decision in *Anderton* v. *Ryan* was *wrong.*

(*i*) The distinction between acts which were 'objectively innocent' and those which were not was an essential element in the reasoning in *Anderton* v. *Ryan*, and the decision, unless it could be supported on some other ground, had to stand or fall by the validity of that distinction. Any attempt to commit an offence which involved 'an act which was more than merely preparatory to the commission of the offence' but for any reason failed, so that in the event no offence was committed, had to be *ex hypothesi*, from the point of view of the criminal law, 'objectively innocent'.

(*ii*) What turned what would otherwise be an innocent act into a crime was the *intent* of the actor to commit an offence.

(*iii*) The distinction sought to be drawn in *Anderton* v. *Ryan* between innocent and guilty acts considered objectively and independently of the state of mind of the actor could *not* be sensibly maintained.

(c) *The situation following R. v. Shivpuri.* A person commits an offence under s. 1 of the 1981 Act where, if the facts had been as he had believed them to be, the full offence would have been committed by him, even though on the true facts, the offence which he set out to commit was impossible. *See R. v. Tulloch* (1986) – X had sold pieces of paper that he believed had been impregnated with LSD. In fact they were not so impregnated. The Court of Appeal held that X's conviction for attempting to supply drugs *should stand*.

> NOTE: Note that under the Criminal Law Act 1967, s. 6, where the allegations in an indictment for an offence (except treason or murder) amount to or include, expressly or by implication, an allegation of another indictable offence, the jury may find the accused not guilty of the offence charged, but guilty of some other offence: s. 6(3). The allegation of a completed offence usually includes an allegation of an attempt to commit it, so that on a count for a completed offence, the jury may convict of an *attempt to commit* that offence, and notwithstanding that the evidence proves that the accused did commit the completed offence: s. 6(4). (*See also Webley* v. *Buxton* (1977).)

Suspected persons

17. Abolition of the offence of loitering, etc., with intent

Section 8 of the 1981 Act states that the provisions of the Vagrancy Act 1824, s. 4, which applied to suspected persons and reputed thieves frequenting or loitering about the places described in that section with the intent there specified, shall cease to have effect.

(a) Not all s. 4 was repealed. Thus, the offence under that section relating to indecent exposure (*see* 13:**27**) remains.

(b) The offence of being a suspected person loitering with intent to commit an arrestable offence (*see* the 1824 Act, s. 4) has now effectively disappeared.

18.   Interference with vehicles

By s. 9(1) of the 1981 Act a new summary offence was created, whereby a person is guilty of the offence of *vehicle interference* if he interferes with a motor vehicle or trailer or with anything carried in or on a motor vehicle or trailer with the intention that an offence specified in subs. (2) shall be committed by himself or another person. *See Reynolds and Warren* v. *Metropolitan Police* (1982): more than looking into vehicles and touching them is necessary for the offence. (*See also R.* v. *Liverpool Stipendiary Magistrate ex p Ellison* (1990).)

(a)   The offences under subs. (2) are: theft of the motor vehicle or trailer or part of it; theft of anything carried in or on the motor vehicle or trailer; and an offence under the Theft Act 1968, s. 12(1) (taking a vehicle without consent).

(b)   If it is shown that a person accused of an offence under s. 9 intended that one of the offences mentioned should be committed, it is immaterial that it cannot be shown which it was: s. 9(2).

(c)   In s. 9, 'motor vehicle' means 'a mechanically propelled vehicle intended or adapted for use on roads', and 'trailer' means 'a vehicle drawn by a motor vehicle': *see* the 1981 Act, s. 9(5), and the Road Traffic Act 1988, s. 185(1).

Draft Criminal Code Bill

19.   Issues of law and fact

'Where there is evidence to support a finding that an act was more than merely preparatory to the commission of the offence intended, the question whether that act was more than merely preparatory is a question of fact': cl. 49(4).

20.   Impossibility and preparatory offences

'A person may be guilty of incitement, conspiracy or attempt to commit an offence although the commission of the offence is impossible, if it would be possible in the circumstances which he believes or hopes exist or will exist at the relevant time': cl. 50(1).

Progress test 8

1. What was the basis of criminal attempt at common law? **(1)**

2. Comment on *R. v. Robinson* (1915). **(2)**

3. What was the common law approach to 'attempting the impossible'? **(3)**

4. Comment on 'intent' in the Criminal Attempts Act 1981, s. 1(1). **(7)**

5. Explain the decision in *R. v. Gullefer* (1990). **(8)**

6. What is the significance of *Anderton* v. *Ryan* (1985) and *R.* v. *Shivpuri* (1986)? **(15,16)**

Part two
Offences against the person

9
Murder

The nature of homicide

1. Categories of homicide
Homicide is the killing of a human being by the act or omission of another human being. It may be categorised as:

(a) *lawful* homicide (*see* **2**); *and*
(b) *unlawful* homicide, e.g. murder, manslaughter, child destruction and infanticide (*see* **3** and Chaps. 10, 11).

2. Lawful homicide
Homicide is *not generally unlawful* in the following circumstances:

(a) *Where death is caused in the execution of the lawful death sentence of a competent court* by the person on whom rests the duty to carry out that sentence, e.g. the executioner who executes a condemned person.
(b) *Where death is caused in the interests of the advancement of justice*, as where force is used in effecting a lawful arrest. 'A person may use such force as is reasonable in the circumstances in the prevention of crime, or in effecting or assisting in the lawful arrest of offenders or suspected offenders or of persons unlawfully at large': Criminal Law Act 1967, s. 3(1).
(c) *Where a person acts in self-defence*. This usually involves the use of force to prevent the commission of some crime. (*See* 6:**36**.)
(d) *Where death is caused by misadventure*, e.g. by a lawful act performed without any negligence, or even by an unlawful, non-dangerous act: *see R.* v. *Bruce* (1847).
  In the circumstances outlined above, there is no *actus reus*.

Unlawful homicide: the *actus reus*

3. The *actus reus* of unlawful homicide

The traditional description is in the words of Coke (in defining *murder*) in 1640: '. . . when any man of sound memory, and of the age of discretion, unlawfully killeth within any county of the realm any reasonable creature *in rerum natura* under the king's peace, with malice aforethought, either expressed by the party or implied by law, so as the party wounded, or hurt, etc., die of the wound or hurt, etc., within a year and a day after the same' (*3 Inst. 47*).

The definition applies to unlawful homicide *in general*. In essence, it involves X causing, unlawfully (i.e. without legal justification or excuse) and voluntarily, the death of Y by some act or omission.

4. 'Any man of sound memory and of the age of discretion'

This is taken to mean a person to whom criminal responsibility may be attached. It *excludes*, for example: persons under ten years of age and those aged ten to fourteen who lack a 'mischievous discretion' (*see* 6:**45, 46**); and persons who are insane within the M'Naghten Rules (*see* 6:**28**).

5. 'Within any county of the realm'

The limitations in this phrase have now disappeared. Murder and manslaughter committed by a citizen of the UK and colonies in territory *outside* the UK may be tried *in England*: *see* the Offences against the Person Act 1861, ss. 9, 10, and the British Nationality Act 1948, s. 3. Murder committed on a British aircraft or ship may be tried in England: *see* the Civil Aviation Act 1982, s. 92. Note the War Crimes Act 1991 which provides for the conferring of jurisdiction on UK courts over offences of murder and manslaughter committed as war crimes in Germany or German-occupied territory during the war of 1939-45.

6. 'Reasonable creature *in rerum natura*'

This is taken to mean 'any human being'.

(a) An infant is considered as 'in being' when extruded totally from the mother's body and alive, i.e. when it has an existence independent of its mother. The umbilical cord need not have been cut: *see R.* v. *Reeves* (1839).
(b) Where the infant is born alive, but dies from injuries inflicted in the womb, this will be unlawful homicide.
(c) Where a person inflicts injuries which prevent an infant from being born alive, he may be guilty of child destruction: *see* 11:**3**.

7. 'Under the king's peace'

This phrase referred to a right of the community to freedom from violence. (Today, all persons in the realm are 'under the Queen's peace'.) The killing of the Sovereign's enemies during the conduct of war does not ordinarily constitute the *actus reus* of unlawful homicide. *See R. v. Page* (1954).

8. 'Malice aforethought'

A highly specialised meaning now attaches to this phrase, which is considered in its place as the *mens rea* of murder: *see* **14** below.

9. 'Within a year and a day'

The death must occur within a year and a day of the injury inflicted by the accused person on the deceased. This old common law rule may have grown out of difficulties experienced in identifying the precise cause of death when there was a considerable interval between the act causing the injury and the subsequent death. *See R. v. Dyson* (1908). The Criminal Law Revision Committee, in its Fourteenth Report (1980), recommended retention of the rule because a person ought not to be left indefinitely in a state of risk for prosecution on a charge of murder.

NOTE: Murder is triable only on indictment.

Causation and homicide

10. Causation

This matter was considered briefly in 2:**10–11**. Where X, intending to kill Y unlawfully, stabs Y so that he dies, there is no obvious problem of causation. Such a problem, arises, however, in other circumstances, such as the following: Y drowns after jumping into a river so as to avoid further violent attacks by X: *see R. v. Pitts* (1842). X_1 and X_2 strike Y with the intention of killing him. Y dies, but it is shown that the blow delivered by X_1 could not on its own have killed him: *see R. v. Garforth* (1954).

(a) Some general principles are set out in 2:**11**. See, in particular: *R. v. Jordan* (1956); *R. v. Smith* (1959); *R. v. Blaue* (1975), the facts of which are set out in 2:**11**(b)(*iv*); *R. v. Cheshire* (1991) at 2:**11**.

(b) The act of the accused person need not be the sole cause of death: *see R. v. Swindall and Osborne* (1846).

(c) Killing by shock can be an unlawful homicide: *see R. v. Hayward* (1908) (death from fright alone, resulting from an illegal act, would suffice).

11. R. v. Malcherek (1981)

In this case X stabbed his wife, Y. She was taken to hospital where her condition suddenly deteriorated. Y was placed on a life-support system, but after brain death was diagnosed, treatment was discontinued and doctors disconnected Y from the life-support system.

(a) X was charged with murder, and was convicted after the judge withdrew the issue of causation from the jury.

(b) X appealed against the trial judge's ruling that there was no evidence on which the jury could conclude that X did not cause Y's death.

(c) X's appeal was *dismissed* by the Court of Appeal. *Per* Lord Lane LCJ: In this case it was clear that the initial assault was the cause of the grave injury and was the reason for the medical treatment being necessary. There was no evidence that the original wound was other than a continuing, operating and substantial cause of Y's death. Nothing which any of the doctors could say would alter the fact that X's *action continued to be an operating cause of the death*. Nothing they could say would provide any grounds for a jury concluding that the assailant might not have caused the death. Discontinuance of the treatment did *not* break the chain of causation between the initial injury and the death.

12. *R. v. Pagett* (1983)

In this case X, armed with a gun, shot at police officers attempting to arrest him for various offences. He used Y, a 16-year old girl, as a body shield. Y was killed when the police returned X's shots. X was acquitted of murder but convicted of manslaughter. He appealed on the ground that the judge should have left it to the jury to determine whether his firing at the police was a substantial or operative or imputable cause of Y's death.

X's appeal was *dismissed* by the Court of Appeal. In homicide cases it is rarely necessary for the judge to give the jury any direction on causation as such. Even where necessary, it would suffice that the jury were directed as to the general principles of law relating to causation and it could be left to them to decide whether or not a relevant causal link had been established. In such a case it would be enough to direct them that *the accused's act need not be the sole or even the main cause of the victim's death, it would suffice that the act contributed significantly to the result*. A reasonable act performed for the purpose of self-preservation, including a reasonable act of self-defence, does not operate as a *novus actus interveniens* ('new act intervening'), nor does an act done in the execution of a legal duty. The jury must have found that X's unlawful and dangerous acts (firing at the police, using the girl as a shield) *resulted in Y's death*, thus constituting the *actus reus* of manslaughter. (See Chap. 10).

The *mens rea* of murder: malice aforethought

13. The essence of the crime
There is no *statutory* definition of murder. It is often described as *unlawful homicide with malice aforethought, and is a crime of specific intent: see* 3:**12**.

14. The meaning of the phrase
'Malice aforethought' is a term of art when used in the context of the crime of murder, and its meaning cannot be determined by reference to the everyday use of the words 'malice' and 'aforethought'. It may be considered as consisting of an *intention on the part of the accused person to kill or to cause really serious injury to another person. See R.* v. *Moloney* (1985) at **25**.

15. 'Grievous bodily harm'
At one time this phrase was used, rather than 'really serious injury', and was interpreted as 'some harm which is sufficiently serious to interfere with the victim's health or comfort': *per* Willes J *R.* v. *Ashman* (1858). More recently, in *DPP* v. *Smith* (1961) (*see* **19**), it was stated that there existed 'no warrant for giving the words "grievous bodily harm" a meaning other than that which the words convey in their ordinary and natural meaning. "Bodily harm" needs no explanation, and "grievous" means no more and no less than "really serious"': *per* Viscount Kilmuir. *See* 12:**17**.

16. Categories of malice
Note the following.

(a) *Express and implied malice. Express malice* has been said to consist of an intention to kill; *implied malice*, of an intention to do grievous bodily harm.
(b) *Universal malice.* X fires a pistol in a random fashion into a crowd of people. He intends to kill some person, but does not care who is killed. He kills Y.
(c) *Transferred malice.* The doctrine is related to the situation in which an injury intended to be done to one person falls on some other accidentally. X, intending to murder Y, shoots at him, misses, and kills Z, who, unknown to X, was standing near Y. The malice directed by X against Y, i.e. X's *mens rea* in relation to the person of Y, is considered as having been 'transferred to' the person of Z. (It should be noted that there is no requirement in the definition of murder (*see* 3 above) that the actual person killed shall be the same person as the intended victim; the definition speaks of 'any reasonable creature . . .'; *see* also **14** above – 'to another person'.) *See R.* v. *Salisbury* (1553); *R.* v. *Monger* (1973).

(d) *Constructive malice.* The word 'constructive' means 'inferred'. 'Constructive malice aforethought' was abolished by the Homicide Act 1957, s. 1 (*see* (iii) below).

(*i*) Before 1957, where X caused death in the course or furtherance of committing a felony, he had committed murder. Only the *mens rea* of the felony had to be proved. Proof of foresight of grievous bodily harm or death was not necessary: *see DPP* v. *Beard* (1920) (*see* 6:**17**).

(*ii*) Where X caused death in the course of resisting arrest by a police officer, he could be convicted of murder on proof of his intention to resist arrest by force: *see R.* v. *Porter* (1873).

(*iii*) The Homicide Act 1957, s. 1, *abolished* this category of constructive malice aforethought. 'Where a person kills another in the course or furtherance of some other offence, the killing shall not amount to murder unless done with the same malice aforethought (express or implied) as is required for a killing to amount to murder when not done in the course or furtherance of another offence ... A killing done in the course or for the purpose of resisting an officer of justice, or of resisting or avoiding or preventing a lawful arrest, or of effecting or assisting an escape or rescue from legal custody, shall be treated as a killing in the course or furtherance of an offence.'

Where, today, X is charged with the murder of Y, and he is shown to have killed him in furtherance of another offence or in resisting lawful arrest by Y, the vital question is whether X had the kind of malice described in **(a)** above.

Recent interpretations of malice aforethought

17. The mental element in the offence of murder

It is for the prosecution in a trial for murder today to prove that X killed Y *and* that X's act was accompanied by the state of mind known as 'malice aforethought'. (Thus, there is no offence known to the common law of 'murder by recklessness': *Leung Kam-Kwok* v. *R.* (1985). (Accused had fired a shot 'as a warning' but it had killed Y who was standing near the doorway in the next room.)) Perceptions of this mental element have changed fundamentally and in recent years the House of Lords has considered on a number of occasions the nature and significance of malice aforethought. Five leading cases are touched on below. Reference is made also to the Criminal Justice Act 1967, s. 8.

> NOTE: For *attempted murder* the prosecution has to prove that the accused intended to cause death; an intention to cause really serious harm will *not* suffice: *see R.* v. *Whybrow* (1951). *Per* Lord Goddard: 'If the charge is one of attempted murder, the intent becomes the principal ingredient of

the crime ... If one attacks a person intending to do grievous bodily harm and death results, that is murder, but ... if one attacks a person and only intends to do grievous bodily harm and death does not result, it is *not* attempted murder, but wounding with intent to do grievous bodily harm'.

18. *R. v. Vickers* (1957)

X broke into a shop, intending to steal, and was seen by an old lady, Y, who lived on the premises. X struck Y several blows and kicked her in the face, killing her. Although it was not suggested that X intended to kill Y, X was convicted of murder after the judge had directed that he was guilty *if he intended grievous bodily harm*, which the judge considered sufficient *mens rea*.

(a) X appealed, arguing that intent to cause grievous bodily harm was no longer malice aforethought in murder, and the causing of grievous bodily harm was 'another offence' within the meaning of the Homicide Act 1957, s. 1.

(b) The Court of Criminal Appeal *rejected* X's appeal, holding that the 1957 Act left unchanged the common law principles of express and implied malice; it sought only to abolish the doctrine of constructive malice. X had attacked Y so as to escape recognition; that was murder because *an intention to do grievous bodily harm is and always was implied malice aforethought*. (But it would not have been murder *merely* because it was killing in the course of burglary – the 'another offence' mentioned in s. 1.) *Per* Lord Goddard CJ: 'If a person does an act which amounts to the infliction of grievous bodily harm he cannot say that he only intended to cause a certain degree of harm. It is called *malum in se* in the old cases and he must take the consequences. If he intends to inflict grievous bodily harm and that person dies, that has always been held in English law, and was at the time [the Homicide Act 1957] was passed, sufficient to imply the malice aforethought which is a necessary constituent of murder.'

(c) *R. v. Vickers* was considered further by the House of Lords in *Hyam v. DPP* (1975) (*see* 23). Two members, in dissenting from the majority decision, stated that *R. v. Vickers* was wrongly decided and that the intention to cause grievous bodily harm was *not* sufficient for the *mens rea* of murder. But in *R. v. Cunningham* (1982) (*see* 24) the House of Lords held unanimously that *R. v. Vickers* was 'a *correct statement* of the law as it was after amendment by the Homicide Act 1957.'

19. *DPP v. Smith* (1961)

This decision of the House of Lords (which was very widely criticised) seemed to have revived the doctrine of constructive malice.

(a) *The facts.* X was ordered by Y, a police officer, to halt the car he was driving, which was loaded with stolen goods. In an attempt to stop the car Y jumped on to it and was shaken off as a result of X's driving. Y fell under another car, and received injuries from which he subsequently died.

(b) *Verdict and appeal.* X was found guilty of capital murder. The Court of Criminal Appeal altered this to manslaughter, but the House of Lords later *restored* the original conviction.

20. Judgment of the House of Lords in *DPP* v. *Smith*

Per Viscount Kilmuir:

'. . . It matters not what the accused in fact contemplated as the probable result or whether he ever contemplated at all, provided he was in law responsible and accountable for his actions, that is, was a man capable of forming an intent, not insane within the M'Naghten Rules and not suffering from diminished responsibility. On the assumption that he is so accountable for his actions, the sole question is whether the lawful and voluntary act was of such a kind that grievous bodily harm was the natural and probable result. The only test available for this is *what the ordinary responsible man would, in all the circumstances of the case, have contemplated as the natural and probable result.* That, indeed, has always been the law . . .'

This judgment was interpreted as laying down that, for X to be found guilty of murder, it was not necessary to prove *either* an intention to kill *or* to cause grievous bodily harm, but that X could be convicted *if the prosecution could show that death or grievous bodily harm was, through an objective assessment, the natural and probable consequence of X's acts.*

21. Criminal Justice Act 1967, s. 8

The Law Commission proposed in 1967 a statutory reversal of *DPP* v. *Smith*. The Criminal Justice Act, s. 8, provided that: 'A court or jury, in determining whether a person has committed an offence:

(a) shall not be bound in law to infer that he intended or foresaw a result of his actions by reason only of its being a natural and probable consequence of those actions; but

(b) shall decide whether he did intend or foresee that result by reference to all the evidence, drawing such inferences from the evidence as appear proper in the circumstances. ' *See Frankland* v. *R.* (1987) at 30 below.

22. Effect of the 1967 Act, s. 8

Juries should be directed, in cases of murder, in the terms of the 1967 Act. Thus, in *R.* v. *Wallett* (1968) the Court of Appeal *allowed* an appeal against a conviction of murder where the judge had used words which suggested an objective test: 'The position is if you did find this man intended either to kill . . . or as the prosecution suggest really to do serious bodily harm, knowing quite well at the time that he was doing something any ordinary person like himself would know was doing [the person killed] really serious bodily harm . . .' The Court of Appeal held that this direction was *contrary to s. 8;* it left within the contemplation of the jury the test of what an 'ordinary person' would or was likely to foresee (the 'objective' *DPP* v. *Smith* test), instead of the 'subjective test' required by s. 8. A conviction of manslaughter was substituted. (The decision in *DPP* v. *Smith* was *disapproved* in 1987 by the Privy Council: *see* **30** below.)

23. *Hyam* v. *DPP* (1975)
In this case the problem of *malice aforethought* in the crime of murder was again considered by the House of Lords.

(a) *The facts.* X set fire to a house by pouring petrol through the door and igniting it. Of four persons asleep in the house, two escaped and two died of asphyxia by fumes generated by the fire. X's defence was that she had intended only to frighten Y (who escaped) into leaving the neighbourhood and that she did not intend to cause death or grievous bodily harm.

(b) *The verdict.* The judge directed the jury thus: 'The prosecution must prove, beyond all reasonable doubt, that the accused intended to (kill or) do serious bodily harm to Y. . .. If you are satisfied that when the accused set fire to the house she knew that it was highly probable that this would cause (death or) serious bodily harm then the prosecution will have established the necessary intent. It matters not if her motive was, as she says, to frighten Y.' The judge put 'kill or' and 'death or' in brackets because he advised the jury to concentrate on the intent to do serious bodily harm rather than the intent to kill. X was convicted of murder and appealed.

(c) *On appeal.* X's appeal was *dismissed.* The Court of Appeal put the following question, certified as of general importance: '*Is malice aforethought in the crime of murder established by proof beyond reasonable doubt that when doing the act which led to the death of another the accused knew that it was highly probable that the act would result in death or serious bodily harm?*'

(d) *Judgment of the House of Lords.* X's appeal was *dismissed.* Lord Hailsham gave as the answer to the question the following propositions:

(*i*) Before an act could be murder it must be 'aimed at someone' as explained in *DPP* v. *Smith* and must be, *in addition*, an act committed with one of the following intentions, the test of which was always subjective to the actual defendant: the intention to cause death; the intention to cause grievous bodily harm in the sense of that term as explained in *DPP* v. *Smith*, namely, serious injury; where the defendant knew that there was a serious risk that death or grievous bodily harm would ensue from his acts, and committed those acts deliberately and without lawful excuse, the intention to expose a potential victim to that risk as a result of those acts. It did not matter in such circumstances whether the defendant desired those consequences to ensue or not and in none of those cases did it matter that the act and the intention were aimed at a potential victim other than the one who succumbed. (*ii*) Without an intention of one of those types, the mere fact that the defendant's conduct was done in the knowledge that grievous bodily harm was likely or highly likely to ensue from his conduct *was not by itself enough* to convert a homicide into the crime of murder.

24. *R. v. Cunningham* (1982)

X made an unprovoked attack on Y, motivated by jealousy, fracturing Y's skull so that he died one month later. X was accused of murder. He pleaded guilty to manslaughter, but not to murder, since he had not intended to kill Y. He was convicted of murder.

(a) *Court of Appeal.* X's appeal was *dismissed*. The trial judge had directed the jury to ask whether the prosecution had proved an intent to do really serious bodily harm, and that direction was correct. An intention to endanger life or do such really serious harm as would do so was unnecessary. The Court certified as a point of law of general public importance the question: '*Whether a person is guilty of murder by reason of his unlawful killing of another intending to do grievous bodily harm.*'

(b) *House of Lords.* X's appeal was *dismissed*. The House of Lords, in answer to the question, stated that *a person who unlawfully kills another, intending only to do him grievous bodily harm, is guilty of murder.*

(*i*) *R. v. Vickers* (1957) (*see* **18**) was upheld as a correct statement of the law as to murderous intention.

(*ii*) The House declined an invitation to substitute the minority opinion expressed in *Hyam* v. *DPP* (*see* **23**) by Lord Diplock, that to kill with the intention of causing grievous bodily harm is murder *only* if the accused knew that such injury was likely to cause death.

(*iii*) *Per* Lord Hailsham: The way was now clear to accept as decisive the law prior to 1957, as stated by Lord Goddard CJ in *R. v. Vickers* (1957): 'Murder is, of course, killing with malice aforethought but "malice aforethought" is a term of art. It has always been defined in English law as either an express intention to kill, as could be inferred when a person, having uttered threats against another, produced a lethal weapon and used it on a victim, or implied where, by a voluntary act, the accused intended to cause grievous bodily harm to the victim, and the victim died as the result.'

(*iv*) The suggestion of a reformulation of murder to confine the *mens rea* to an intention to endanger life instead of an intention to do really serious harm was *not acceptable*.

(c) *R.* v. *Cunningham* was *approved* by the House of Lords in *R.* v. *Moloney* (1985) (*see* **25**).

Intention, foresight and *mens rea*

25. *R.* v. *Moloney* (1985)
During a drunken argument between X, a soldier on leave, and Y, his stepfather, both competed to see who could load and shoot a gun with greater speed. When X showed that he was the fastest, Y challenged him to pull the trigger. X's gun then went off and Y, who was six feet away, was killed. X and Y had been on good terms, and X, in his statement to the police, said: 'I didn't aim the gun. I just pulled the trigger and he was dead.' X's appeal against conviction of murder was *dismissed* by the Court of Appeal which certified the following question as of general importance: '*Is malice aforethought in the crime of murder established by proof that when doing the act which causes the death of another the accused either (a) intends to kill or do serious harm; or (b) forsees that death or serious harm will probably occur, whether or not he desires either of those consequences.* '

26. House of Lords
'The golden rule should be that, when directing a jury on the mental element necessary in a crime of specific intent, the judge should avoid any elaboration or paraphrase of what is meant by intent, and leave it to the jury's good sense to decide whether the accused acted with the necessary intent, unless the judge is convinced that, on the facts and having regard to the way the case has been presented to the jury in evidence and argument, some further explanation or elaboration is strictly necessary to avoid misunderstanding . . . I cannot accept that the suggested criterion that the act of the accused, to amount to murder must be "aimed at someone" as explained in *DPP* v. *Smith* is one which would be generally helpful to juries . . . I believe that Lord Hailsham's inclusion in *Hyam* v. *DPP* in the mental element necessary to a conviction of murder of the "intention to expose a potential victim", *inter alia*, to "a serious risk that . . . grievous bodily harm will ensue from his acts" comes dangerously near to causing confusion': *per* Lord Bridge.

(a) Lord Bridge continued: 'Starting from the proposition established in *R.* v. *Vickers* as modified by *DPP* v. *Smith* that the mental element in murder requires proof of an intention to kill or cause really serious injury, the first fundamental question to be answered is whether there is any rule of substantive law that foresight by the accused of one of those eventualities as a probable consequence of his voluntary act, where the probability can be defined as exceeding a certain degree, is equivalent or alternative to the necessary intention. I would answer this question in the *negative*.'

(b) 'I am firmly of opinion that foresight of consequences, as an element bearing on the issue of intention in murder, or indeed any other crime of specific intent, belongs, not to the substantive law but to the law of evidence': *per* Lord Bridge.

(c) 'I know of no clearer exposition of the law than that . . . delivered by Lord Goddard CJ in *R.* v. *Steane* (1947) [*see* 6:**9c**)]. . . "No doubt, if the prosecution prove an act the natural consequence of which would be a certain result and no evidence or explanation is given, then a jury may, on a proper direction, find that the prisoner is guilty of doing the act with the intent alleged, but if on the totality of the evidence there is room for more than one view as to the intent of the prisoner, the jury should be directed that it is for the prosecution to prove the intent to the jury's satisfaction, and if, on a review of the whole evidence, they either think that the intent did not exist or they are left in doubt as to the intent, the prisoner is entitled to be acquitted"': *per* Lord Bridge. (X's appeal was *allowed*, and a verdict of manslaughter substituted.)

27. The 'two-questions' guidelines

Lord Bridge added that in the rare cases in which it is necessary to direct a jury by reference to foresight of consequences, the jury should be invited to consider two questions:

(a) First, was death or really serious injury a *natural consequence* of the defendant's voluntary act?

(b) Secondly, did the defendant *foresee* that consequence as being a natural consequence of his act?

The jury should then be told that if they answer 'yes' to *both* questions it is a proper inference for them to draw that defendant intended that consequence.

28. The 'two-questions' guidelines rejected

Lord Bridge's guidelines (which were *not* part of the *ratio decidendi* in *R.* v. *Moloney*) were *rejected as 'defective'* by the House of Lords in *R.* v. *Hancock and Shankland*(1986). The case concerned two miners, X and Y, who were on strike. They pushed two large concrete objects off a bridge onto a road so that a taxi carrying another miner to work was struck and the taxi driver killed. X and Y claimed that they had no intention of injuring or killing any person; their intention was to block the road. The jury were directed in accordance with the *Moloney* guidelines, thus: 'You may or may not, for the purpose of considering what inferences to draw, find it helpful to ask: Was death or serious injury a natural consequence of what was done? Did a defendant foresee that consequence as a natural consequence?

If you find yourselves not satisfied so as to be sure that there was an intent to kill or to cause really serious injury, then it is open to you to return a verdict of not guilty of murder, but guilty of manslaughter': *per* Mann J. X and Y were convicted of murder and appealed.

(a) *Court of Appeal.* The appeals of X and Y were *allowed.* The Court held that the case was indeed one of those rare cases in which it was necessary to give an explanation of intent when directing the jury. An explanation of this nature was required when the defendant's motive or purpose was not primarily to injure or kill but the method adopted by the defendant to achieve his purpose was so very dangerous that the jury might arrive at the conclusion that death or injury was highly likely. The trial judge's direction was *ambiguous* in that it did not explain adequately the require-ment that death or injury be *highly likely.* The phrase 'a natural consequence' did not properly convey the degree of likelihood required, in that an event might be the natural consequence of some act, yet be improbable. The Crown appealed.

(b) *House of Lords.* The House *dismissed the Crown's appeal.* 'The *Moloney* guidelines are *defective* and should not be used as they stand without further explanation. . . .Guidelines are not rules of law; judges should not think that they must use them. A judge's duty is to direct the jury in law and to help them upon the particular facts of the case': *per* Lord Scarman.

(*i*) Where, in a murder case, it is necessary to direct the jury on the issue of intent by reference to foresight of circumstances, the direction should not refer merely to 'the natural consequences' of the accused's voluntary act, but should also refer to the 'probable consequences' of that act, since the probability of death or serious injury resulting from the accused's act may be critically important, depending on the degree of probability.

(*ii*) In such a case the judge should explain that the greater the probability of a consequence, the more likely it is that the conse-quence was foreseen and that if the consequence was foreseen the greater probability is that that consequence was also intended.

(*iii*) The judge could well emphasise that the probability, however high, of a consequence is only a factor, though it may be a very significant factor, to be considered along with all the other evidence, in determining whether the accused intended to bring it about.

29. The mental element in murder after *R. v. Moloney* (1985)

The situation today concerning the interpretation to be placed on 'malice aforethought' as the *mens rea* of murder seems to be as follows. *First,* the prosecution must prove malice aforethought in murder *solely* by proof that X *either* intended to kill another person *or* that he intended to cause that person really serious harm. (It seems not necessary for the prosecution to prove that X's act was aimed at the victim.) *Secondly,* 'foresight' is *not* to be equated with 'intention'. Intention *cannot* be proved *merely* by showing *either* that X desired a certain consequence to happen, whether or not he foresaw that it would probably happen, *or* that X foresaw that it would probably happen, whether he desired it or not. *See* also *R.* v. *Walker* (1990).

In *R.* v. *Nedrick* (1986), X was tried for murder. He had poured paraffin through a house letter box and set it alight; as a result a child had died. X claimed that he wished only to frighten the occupant, but had not wanted anyone to die, nor had he any intention to inflict grievous bodily harm. His appeal was *allowed* and a conviction for manslaughter substituted. Lord Lane LCJ attempted to summarise the effects of decisions of the House of Lords in *R.* v. *Moloney* and *R.* v. *Hancock and Shankland:*

(a) It might be advisable, first of all, to explain to the jury that a man might intend to achieve a certain result while at the same time *not* desiring it to come about. (*See* also *R.* v. *Barr* (1989).)

(b) When determining whether X (the defendant) had the necessary intent, it might be helpful for a jury to ask themselves:

(*i*) How *probable* was the consequence which resulted from X's voluntary act?

(*ii*) Did X foresee that consequence?

(c) If X did not appreciate that death or really serious harm was likely to result from his act, he could not have intended to bring it about. If he did, but thought that the risk to which he was exposing the person killed was only slight, then it might be easy for the jury to conclude that he did *not* intend to bring about that result.

(d) On the other hand, if the jury were satisfied that at the material time X recognised that death or serious harm would be virtually certain – barring some unforeseen intervention – to result from his voluntary act, then that was a fact from which they might find it easy to infer that he intended to kill or do serious bodily harm, even though he might not have had any desire to achieve that result.

(e) Where the charge was murder and in the rare cases where the simple direction was not enough, the jury should be directed that they were *not* entitled to infer the necessary intention *unless* they felt sure that death or serious bodily harm was a virtual certainty – barring an unforeseen intervention – as a result of X's actions and that X appreciated that such was the case.

(f) *Where a man realised that it was for all practical purposes inevitable that his actions would result in death or serious harm the inference might be irresistible that he intended that result, however little he might have desired or wished it to happen.*

(g) The decision was one for the jury, to be reached on a consideration of *all* the evidence.

30. *Frankland and Moore* v. R. (1987)

The Judicial Committee of the Privy Council considered the decision of a Manx court concerning intent in murder. *DPP* v. *Smith was disapproved.*

(a) *The facts.* X had bound and gagged Y so as to prevent him from giving information to Z, X's girlfriend, that was intended to break up the relationship between X and Z. Y suffered from chronic bronchitis and died 48 hours later before X returned to free him. X stated that he thought Y was healthy, that no serious harm would result from his action and that he intended merely to keep Y away from Z, not to kill him. The trial judge directed the jury in accordance with *DPP* v. *Smith* on the matter of intent, stating that relevant intent would be established if the jury were satisfied that X intended to do something unlawful to Y, knowing the circumstances, whether he realised them or not, which would render his act likely to cause serious injury or death. X appealed against his conviction of murder.

(b) *The JCPC.* The judge had erred. *The test of intent in murder at common law was not of an objective but a subjective nature.* At common law there was a rebuttable presumption of fact that a man intended the natural and probable consequences of his acts; the direction to the jury, in so far as it had invited them to ignore X's state of mind, improperly elevated the presumption to an irrebuttable rule of law. *DPP* v. *Smith did not represent the common law of England and should not be followed.*

31. R. v. *Ward* (1987)

The Court of Appeal considered the direction of a trial judge who had stated that 'intention' means a desire to bring about a particular consequence or foresight that killing or harm would result, and, if such foresight were proved, defendant could be taken to have intended the killing or harm. The Court of Appeal held that the direction on foresight was *wrong* because it failed to make clear that *foresight was merely evidence of intent.* The jury must feel sure that defendant intended to kill or to do serious harm.

Proof of guilt, and the penalty for murder

32. Establishing guilt

The burden of proving the *actus reus* of murder and the requisite *mens rea* rests *on the prosecution.*

'Throughout the web of the English criminal law one golden

thread is always to be seen, that it is the duty of the prosecution to prove the prisoner's guilt subject to . . . the defence of insanity and subject also to any statutory exception. . . . No matter what the charge or where the trial, *the principle that the prosecution must prove the guilt of the prisoner is part of the common law of England* and no attempt to whittle it down can be entertained': *per* Viscount Sankey LC in *Woolmington* v. *DPP* (1935).

33. Penalty for murder

The Murder (Abolition of Death Penalty) Act 1965 abolished the offence of capital murder. By s. 1, an accused person found guilty of murder *must* be sentenced to imprisonment for life. The court is empowered, by s. 1(2), at the time of sentencing, to recommend a minimum period of imprisonment which is to be served before the convicted person is released on licence. (The recommended period should not be less than 12 years.) A person under eighteen at the time of committing the murder must be detained during the Sovereign's pleasure: Children and Young Persons Act 1933, s. 53.

> NOTE: (1) For alternative verdicts where, on an indictment for murder, a person is found not guilty, *see* the Criminal Law Act 1967, s. 6. (2) For a criticism of the mandatory penalty for murder, by Lord Lane (Lord Chief Justice, 1980–92), see *The Times*, 7 December 1993.

The plea of diminished responsibility

34. Essence of the plea

As a special defence to a charge of murder only, an accused person, X, may plead 'diminished responsibility', i.e. that *at the time of the killing he was suffering from some mental abnormality or disease of the mind*. Unlike the plea of insanity (*see* 6:**26–35**) it is immaterial whether or not X appreciated what he was doing and appreciated that it was wrong. If X succeeds in his defence he will be found not guilty of murder, but *guilty of manslaughter* (*see* Chap. 10). (Note that a person may be charged directly with manslaughter where he has killed unlawfully, but with diminished responsibility.) The plea is regulated by the Homicide Act 1957, s. 2.

> '(1) Where a person kills or is party to the killing of another, he shall not be convicted of murder if he was suffering from such abnormality of mind (whether arising from a condition of arrested or retarded development of mind or any inherent causes or induced by disease or injury) as substantially impaired his mental
> ·   responsibility for his acts and omissions in doing or being a party

to the killing.

(2) On a charge of murder, it shall be for the defence to prove that the person charged is by virtue of this section not liable to be convicted of murder.

(3) A person who but for this section would be liable, whether as principal or accessory, to be convicted of murder shall be liable instead to be convicted of manslaughter.

(4) The fact that one party to a killing is by virtue of this section not liable to be convicted of murder shall not affect the question whether the killing amounted to murder in the case of any other party to it.'

35. Aspects of the plea of diminished responsibility

In *R. v. Byrne* (1960), X, a violent sexual psychopath who suggested that he was unable to control his perverted desires, strangled Y and mutilated her body. On being charged with murder X pleaded diminished responsibility. On appeal against conviction for murder, the Court of Criminal Appeal substituted a verdict of *manslaughter* on the ground of diminished responsibility. It was held that the phrase 'abnormality of mind' (*see* the Homicide Act 1957, s. 2(1)) covered the mind's activities in all its aspects.

(a) 'Abnormality of mind, which has to be contrasted with the time-honoured expression in the M'Naghten Rules, "defect of reason", means a state of mind so different from that of ordinary human beings that the reasonable man would term it abnormal. It appears to us to be wide enough to cover the mind's activities in all its aspects, not only the perception of physical acts and matters, and the ability to form a rational judgment as to whether an act is right or wrong, but also the ability to exercise will power to control physical acts in accordance with that rational judgment. The expression "mental responsibility for his acts" points to a consideration of the extent to which the accused's mind is answerable for his physical acts which must include a consideration of the extent of his ability to exercise will power to control his physical acts': *per* Lord Parker CJ in *R. v. Byrne*.

(b) The phrase 'substantially impaired' should be left as a question of fact to the jury who ought to approach it in a broad, commonsense way: *per* Lord Parker. The impairment need not be total, but it should be *more than trivial* in its nature: *R. v. Lloyd* (1967).

(c) In *R. v. Di Duca* (1959), it was doubted whether the transient effect of alcohol, even if it produces a toxic effect on the brain, would bring the accused within the 1957 Act, s. 2. In *R. v. Fenton* (1975), X shot and killed four persons. At his trial his evidence was that he had been suffering from an abnormality of mind because of four causes: general medical state; reactive depression; a car chase by the police after the first shooting;

drinking alcohol excessively. His appeal against conviction for murder was *dismissed*, the Court of Appeal holding that self-induced intoxication could not of itself produce an abnormality of mind due to inherent causes, and the jury had been correctly advised to ignore the effects of alcohol on him.

(d) In R. v. *Kiszko* (1978), the Court of Appeal emphasised that in considering a defence of diminished responsibility, the jury must have regard to *all* the circumstances of the case and not merely to the medical history adduced by one side. Defendant's personal history, the circumstances of the killing, defendant's conduct before and after it, are all relevant.

(e) In R. v. *Dix* (1982), the Court of Appeal held as correct the trial judge's ruling that the defence of diminished responsibility necessarily required medical or other scientific evidence in support – it is a 'practical necessity'.

(f) In R. v. *Gittens* (1984), the Court of Appeal held that where the defence of diminished responsibility is raised, and the effect of drink or drugs on the mind of the accused is a factor to be considered, together with other 'inherent causes' or any abnormality in his mind, the jury should be directed to disregard what was, in their view, the effect of the drink or drugs, and to concentrate instead, and to decide, on whether there are other 'inherent abnormalities' which, taken together, substantially impaired the mental responsibility of the accused. *See* also R. v. *Atkinson* (1985).

(g) In R. v. *Tandy* (1989), the Court of Appeal held that the defence of diminished responsibility arising from alcoholism exists only where there was an abnormality of mind induced by the disease of alcoholism that impaired mental responsibility *substantially*. An alcoholic state induced by *voluntary* drinking does *not* amount to a defence.

(h) In R. v. *Egan* (1992), X had been drinking heavily, and had attacked and killed an elderly person. He was charged with murder and pleaded guilty to manslaughter on grounds of diminished responsibility arising from an abnormality of mind which 'substantially impaired' his mental responsibility. He appealed against conviction.

(i) His appeal was *dismissed*. The questions for the jury were whether, disregarding intoxication, X would have killed had he not been drunk, and whether he would have been affected by diminished responsibility when he did so. The trial judge had directed the jury to X's abnormality of mind regardless of intoxication. There was, therefore, no misdirection.

(ii) The jury should approach the word 'substantial' in relation to 'substantial impairment' in a common-sense way. They should be told that 'substantial' does mean more than a trivial degree of impairment (which makes no appreciable difference to a person's ability to control himself), but less than 'total impairment'. *See (b) above.*

(i) In *R.* v. *Sanderson* (1993), the Court of Appeal did *not* accept the view that the phrase 'induced by disease or injury' necessarily referred to an organic or physical injury or disease of the body including the brain. (Appellant's defence was based on medical evidence that at the time of the killing he was suffering from a paranoid psychosis which caused him to form abnormal beliefs about persons.)

36. Where the plea is raised

Where the plea of diminished responsibility is raised, the burden of proof is on the defence; it will be sufficient for the defence to show a balance of probabilities in favour of the accused: *R.* v. *Byrne* (1960).

(a) It is for the judge to explain to the jury *the meaning* of s. 2: *R.* v. *Byrne* (1960); *R.* v. *Terry* (1961). It is rarely helpful to read s. 2(1) in its entirely to the jury: *R.* v. *Sanderson* (1993).

(b) Where the accused raises the issue of diminished responsibility, the prosecution may adduce evidence to prove insanity: *see* the Criminal Procedure (Insanity) Act 1964, s. 6.

(c) If the plea succeeds in the case of one accused person this does not affect liability of others charged with him: *see* the Homicide Act 1957, s. 2(4).

(d) In *Walton* v. *R.* (1977), the Privy Council stated that a jury is not bound to accept the plea even where medical evidence adduced by the defence is not contradicted by the prosecution. See *R.* v. *Sanders* (1991): Where the defence of diminished responsibility to a charge of murder is raised, and the medical evidence in support is unequivocal and has not been contradicted, the judge should direct the jury to accept it *if there are no other circumstances which should have been considered*.

(e) In *R.* v. *Vinagre* (1979), the Court of Appeal held (after consideration of the so-called 'Othello syndrome') that the plea of manslaughter on grounds of diminished responsibility should be accepted only where there is clear evidence of mental *imbalance*.

(f) In *R.* v. *Chambers* (1983), the principles of sentencing relating to diminished responsibility were discussed. In this case X had killed his wife after she had ceased to live with him, his manslaughter plea being accepted on the basis that he was suffering from an 'anxiety-depressive state', substantially impairing his mental responsibility. *See* also *R.* v. *Yeomans* (1988) – X suffered from acute reactive depression brought on by marriage breakdown.

(g) In *R.* v. *Seers* (1985), the Court of Appeal held that the test to be applied in directing the jury on diminished responsibility must be tailored to the particular circumstances of each case. Further, it was not appropriate to direct a jury that only 'partial or borderline insanity' amounted to diminished responsibility. *R.* v. *Byrne* was not to be taken to have laid down that in *every* case the jury must necessarily be directed that the test was always to be the 'borderline of insanity'.

Occasionally the defence is not specifically raised even though the evidence seems to justify it being put forward. Since s. 2(2) leaves it to the *defence* to decide whether the issue should be raised, the judge must not mention the possibility of the plea to the jury unless he has first obtained the agreement of the defence; an adjournment of the jury may be needed to allow this to be done. *See R. v. Campbell* (1987).

The plea of provocation

37. Effect of the plea

Provocation may be pleaded *only* on a charge of murder, so as to reduce the charge to manslaughter (see Chap. 10). Its acceptance as a defence does not make the killing lawful, and it is not equivalent to a plea of self-defence. (It may *not* be raised as a plea on a charge of attempted murder: *see R. v. Bruzas* (1972).) Where evidence is adduced which supports the claim that the accused was provoked, the burden falls upon *the prosecution* to show *beyond reasonable doubt* that the case does not involve provocation.

38. The position arising from common law

'Provocation is some act, or series of acts, done by the dead man to the accused, which would cause in any reasonable person, and actually causes in the accused, a sudden and temporary loss of self-control, rendering the accused so subject to passion as to make him or her for the moment not master of his mind': *per* Devlin J in *R. v. Duffy* (1949). (See, however, **39**.)

The following *common law principles* have been formulated.

(a) *The provocation should have come from the person at whom the retaliatory act had been aimed by the accused.*
(b) *The provocation should have been directed against the accused person* (or even, for example, his daughter): *see R. v. Harrington* (1866); *R. v. Porritt* (1961). Note, however the extension of this rule: *see*, e.g. *R.v.Pearson* (1992), in which two brothers, X and Y, were charged with the murder of their father, described as 'violent and tyrannical'. X and Y who had struck their father with hammer blows, pleaded provocation. The trial judge distinguished between X, who had endured his father's violence for eight years, and Y, who was visiting X. X was convicted of manslaughter due to provocation. Y was convicted of murder and appealed; his appeal was *allowed* and a verdict of manslaughter substituted. The jury should have been directed to take into account, in deciding whether Y had reasonably lost self-control, the father's abusive conduct not only to Y, but also to X,

particularly as it was shown that one of the reasons for Y's return home was a wish to protect his brother, X.

(c) *The provocation should have been such as to cause a reasonable man to lose control of himself.*

(i) 'Reasonable man' meant in this context a normal person. No allowance was made for the fact that the accused was highly excitable or pugnacious, or more liable than most other men to be provoked by particular types of taunt: *see Bedder* v. *DPP* (1954), in which it was held to be *not relevant* that the accused, X, was sexually impotent and, therefore, highly susceptible to taunts from Y, the prostitute he killed. The jury were directed to consider the effect of Y's taunts on an ordinary person, not necessarily on X. (Note, however, that *this case was not followed by the House of Lords in DPP* v. *Camplin* (1978) (see 39). See also *R.* v. *Raven* (1982), in which it was held that, in considering the defence of provocation raised by X, who was 22, but had a mental age of 9, in applying the 'reasonable man' test, the jury should be directed to consider the reasonable man as having lived the same type of life as X for 22 years, but with his retarded development and mental age.

(ii) No special allowance will be made where X had been drinking at the time of the killing and, as a result, had lost control over his actions more easily than he might have done had he been sober: *see R.* v. *McCarthy* (1954).

(d) The killing should have been done in the heat of the moment: 'It is of particular importance to consider whether a sufficient interval has elapsed since the provocation to allow a reasonable man time to cool': per Lord Simon LC in *Mancini* v. *DPP* (1942). So, in *R.* v. *Hayward* (1833), X, ejected by Y from the house of Y's mother, went to his (X's) house and took a knife with which he then killed Y. The jury were directed to consider 'whether there had been time for the blood to cool, and for reason to resume its seat, before the mortal wound was given; in which case the crime would amount to murder.' X was convicted of murder. *See R.* v. *Ibrams* (1982) – provocation could *not* provide a defence to a charge of murder where there was a delay of seven days between an act of provocation and the subsequent killing.

(i) In *R.* v. *Thornton* (1992), X, who had experienced continuous and serious domestic violence at the hands of her husband, Y, was subjected to an incident involving intense verbal abuse, following which she went to the kitchen 'to calm down'. There she picked up and sharpened a knife to defend herself against possible attack from Y, and then returned to the room in which he was sitting. He threatened to kill her as soon as she fell asleep. Intending to frighten him, she moved the knife towards him and the blade entered his stomach. X's defence of provocation was *rejected* and she appealed against conviction of murder. The Court of Appeal *affirmed* the conviction. Provocative acts during the course of domestic violence that do not result in a sudden and temporary loss of control do not amount in law to provocation. X's actions had not resulted from any sudden loss of control. Beldam LJ stressed that the phrase 'sudden and temporary loss of self-control' is to be regarded as appropriate to convey to a jury the legal concept of provocation 'first expressed by Tindal CJ in *R. v. Hayward* (1833) in mitigation of the rigour of the law for acts committed "while smarting under a provocation so recent and so strong, that the prisoner might not be considered at the moment the master of his own understanding"'.

(*ii*) In *R. v. Ahluwalia* (1993), X had suffered continuous domestic violence from her husband, Y. She threw petrol into Y's room and set fire to it, causing Y's death. Her defence of lack of malice aforethought (*see* **14**) and provocation were *rejected*. X's appeal against conviction of murder was *dismissed*. So as to satisfy the *subjective limb* of the test (*see* **39**), the complete history of X's marriage should be considered. But while delay between the final provocative behaviour and X's reaction to it was not necessarily fatal to the defence, X's lack of self-control must be shown to have been sudden and temporary. In relation to the *objective limb* of the test (*see* **39**), it was possible to include purely mental factors in the characteristics of X which could be attributed to 'the reasonable person'; yet there was a lack of evidence which would have necessitated the trial judge drawing those factors to the attention of the jury. (In the event, the Court of Appeal allowed a retrial so that X might raise the defence of diminished responsibility (*see* **34**). This plea was accepted and the period of her sentence for voluntary manslaughter allowed her immediate release.)

(e) *The mode of resentment must bear a reasonable relationship to the provocation': per* Viscount Simon LC in *Mancini v. DPP* (1942). 'Fists might be answered with fists, but not with a deadly weapon': *per* Devlin J in *R. v. Duffy* (1949). (But this rule is now modified by the Homicide Act 1957, s. 3. It must be made clear to the jury that the 'reasonable relationship rule' was merely *one matter to be considered* when deciding whether a reasonable man, if provoked, would have acted as did the accused: *R. v. Brown* (1972).)

(f) Words alone were an insufficient provocation (e.g. a confession of adultery: *see Holmes v. DPP* (1946)). (*See*, however, **39**.)

Note that these principles no longer operate as *rules* today; they have, however, *evidential significance*.

39. The position under statute

Note the following:

> 'Where on a charge of murder there is evidence on which the jury
> can find that the person charged was provoked (whether by things
> done or by things said or by both together) to lose his self-control,
> the question whether the provocation was enough to make a
> reasonable man do as he did shall be left to be determined by the
> jury; and in determining that question the jury shall take into
> account everything both done and said according to the effect
> which, in their opinion, it would have on a reasonable man':
> Homicide Act 1957, s. 3.

(a) Following s. 3, *two conditions* must be satisfied in order that the
defence of provocation shall be made out:

(i) the *subjective condition* that the accused person was *actually provoked so that he lost his self-control*; and

(ii) the *objective condition* that 'the reasonable man' would have done
as the accused did. (*See Phillips* v. *R.* (1969): 'The question is not merely
whether in their opinion the provocation would have made a reasonable man lose his self-control but also whether, having lost his
self-control, he would have retaliated in the same way as the person
charged did.')

(b) The House of Lords considered the effect of s. 3 in *DPP* v. *Camplin*
(1978).

(i) *The facts.* X, aged fifteen, had killed Y, a middle-aged man, with a
heavy kitchen pan. X alleged that Y had committed a sexual offence
against him against his (X's) will, that Y had later laughed at him so
that he (X) was overcome with shame, lost his self-control and
attacked Y.

(ii) *The trial.* X's counsel invited the trial judge to instruct the jury to
take into consideration the effect of provocation on a boy of fifteen.
The judge rejected this argument and directed that the appropriate
test was the effect of provocation on a reasonable man, not on a
reasonable boy. X was convicted of murder.

(iii) *Court of Appeal.* The Court of Appeal allowed X's appeal and
substituted a verdict of manslaughter. It was bound by the principle
in *Bedder* v. *DPP* (1954) (*see* **38(c)**(i)) so that a jury should be directed
in terms of a reasonable man 'of tender years'.

(iv) *House of Lords.* The House of Lords *did not follow Bedder* v. *DPP*
(1954). The DPP's appeal was *dismissed* and it was held that the trial
judge was *wrong* in instructing the jury to disregard X's age. 'The
judge should state what the question is, using the very terms of the
section. He should then explain to them that the reasonable man

referred to in the question is a person having the power of self-control to be expected of an ordinary person of the sex and age of the accused, but in other respects sharing such of the accused's characteristics as they think would affect the gravity of the provocation to him; and that the question is not merely whether such a person would in like circumstances be provoked to lose his self-control, but also would react to the provocation as the accused did': *per* Lord Diplock.

(c) Words alone, as well as deeds, may now constitute a provocation (*see* s. 3 above), so that the decision in *Holmes* v. *DPP* (1946) no longer stands. Acts or words emanating from some person other than the victim are capable of amounting to provocation as a defence to a charge of murder: *see R.* v. *Davies* (1975).

(d) A characteristic necessary to uphold a defence of provocation must be sufficiently permanent as to form *part of the character or personality of the accused*: *R.* v. *Newell* (1980) (the accused's chronic alcoholism was unconnected with the nature of the provocation, i.e. derogatory remarks made about his girlfriend). 'The characteristic must be something definite and of sufficient significance to make the offender a different person from the ordinary run of mankind, and have also a sufficient degree of permanence to warrant its being regarded as something constituting part of the individual's character or personality . . . It would not be sufficient, for instance, for the offender to claim merely that he belongs to an excitable race, or that members of his nationality are accustomed to resort readily to the use of some lethal weapon': *R.* v. *McGregor* (1962), cited in *R.* v. *Newell* (1980).

(e) In *R.* v. *Morhall* (1993), the Court of Appeal considered whether appellant's addiction to glue-sniffing should have been left to the jury as a characteristic which they could take into account as affecting the gravity of the provocation to the appellant.

(*i*) *Per* Lord Taylor CJ: 'In our judgment, it must be a matter for the judge as to whether any suggested characteristic is capable of being considered by the jury consistent with the concept of a reasonable man and capable of affecting the gravity of the provocation to the defendant. If he decides the characteristic is so capable he should leave it to the jury to decide whether it is in fact consistent with the reasonable man and whether, if so, it might have affected the gravity of the provocation to a reasonable man invested with it so as to cause him to lose his self-control and do as this defendant did . . .'

(*ii*) 'In our judgment, however, a self-induced addiction to glue-sniffing brought on by voluntary and persistent abuse of solvents is wholly inconsistent with the concept of a reasonable man . . .'

(*iii*) The appeal against conviction for murder was *dismissed*.

40. 'Self-induced provocation'

See Edwards v. *R.* (1973). X, who had been associating with Y's wife, stabbed Y during a struggle, causing his death. X pleaded self-defence, contending that his intention was to blackmail, not murder, Y, and that when he attempted blackmail, Y had attacked him with a knife, which he (X) had pulled away from him, stabbing him 'in a white-hot passion'. The Privy Council stated that a blackmailer cannot rely on the predictable results of his blackmailing as constituting provocation sufficient to reduce his killing from murder to manslaughter, and that the 'predictable results' may include a considerable degree of hostile reaction by the person sought to be blackmailed, for instance vituperative words and even some hostile action such as blows with the fist; but if the hostile reaction by the person sought to be blackmailed goes to extreme lengths it might constitute sufficient provocation even for the blackmailer. In many cases there would be a question of degree to be decided by the jury. In this case the issue should have been left to the jury, and the Privy Council substituted a verdict of manslaughter for the verdict of murder.

See R. v. *Johnson* (1989), in which the Court of Appeal held that self-induced provocation was a jury issue. *Per* Lord Watkins: The jury should consider *all* the circumstances of the incident, including *all* the relevant behaviour of the defendant, and decide whether he was in fact provoked *and* whether the provocation was enough to make a reasonable man do what the defendant did. The fact that a defendant caused a reaction in others which in turn led him to lose his self-control should not result in the issue of provocation being kept outside the jury's consideration.

41. Judge and jury on a plea of provocation: a summary

Initially, the judge will consider the following questions:

(a) Is there evidence of provocation of X?

(b) Is there any evidence that the provocation caused X to lose self-control? If the answer is affirmative, the judge must leave the issue of provocation to the jury, even though he believes that no reasonable jury would possibly arrive at a conclusion of provocation sufficient to cause a loss of self-control (*see R.* v. *Gilbert* (1977)), or even if the defence has not been raised by X (*see R.* v. *Cascoe* (1970)). *See R.* v. *Rossiter* (1992); *R.* v. *Wellington* (1993); *R.* v. *Cambridge* (1994).

The jury must be asked to consider whether X was provoked and whether the provocation would have sufficed to make a reasonable person act as did X. The jury should then be asked to take into account, when considering how a reasonable man might have reacted to that provocation, any characteristics of X which would have an effect on the seriousness of the provocation to him.

Note *R.* v. *Doughty* (1986), in which the Court of Appeal emphasised the importance of leaving to the jury the issue of the objective test, under s. 3. (X's defence to a charge of murdering his 17-day old baby was that the baby's crying had provoked him, so that he lost self-control.) *See R. v. Crocker* (1989); *R. v. Richens* (1993).

Soliciting, conspiracy and threats to murder

42. Soliciting and conspiracy to murder

Under the Offences against the Person Act 1861, s. 4, it is an offence punishable with life imprisonment to solicit, encourage, persuade, or endeavour to persuade or propose to any person to murder another person. *See R. v. Krause* (1902). Conspiracy to murder is now covered by the Criminal Law Act 1977, s. 1 (*see* Chap. 7).

43. Threats to murder

Under the Offences against the Person Act 1861, s. 16: 'A person who without lawful excuse makes to another a threat, intending that that other would fear it would be carried out, to kill that other or a third person shall be guilty of an offence. . . .' It is immaterial that the accused had no real intention to carry out the threat. It is for the jury to say whether or not a letter amounts to a threat to kill or murder.

(a) In *R. v. Cousins* (1982) the Court of Appeal held that a lawful excuse may exist within s. 16 if a threat to kill was made for the prevention of crime or for self-defence, provided that it is reasonable in the circumstances to make such a threat. Further, what is 'reasonable' is always a question for the jury, never a 'point of law' for the judge. The prosecution had to show that there was no lawful excuse.

(b) *See R. v. Tait* (1989), in which the Court of Appeal held that a *foetus in utero* was *not* 'another person' distinct from its mother, for purposes of the Offences against the Person Act 1861, s. 16. (A threat made by a burglar to a woman five months pregnant, 'If you tell the police, I will come back for you . . . and I am going to kill your baby', was no offence under s. 16.)

> NOTE: On a charge of murder against a co-accused who did not carry out the actual killing *and was not present at the scene of the crime*, the Court of Appeal held that the precise form of words used in directing the jury is not important, provided that it is made clear to the jury that, for co-accused to be guilty, he must have lent himself to a criminal joint enterprise involving the infliction, if necessary, of serious harm or death, or to have had an express or tacit understanding with the killer that such harm or death should, if necessary, be inflicted: *R. v. Slack* (1989).

Draft Criminal Code Bill

44. Murder
'A person is guilty of murder if he causes the death of another – (*a*) intending to cause death; or (*b*) intending to cause serious personal harm and being aware that he may cause death, unless cl. 56 [diminished responsibility], 58 [provocation], 59 [use of excessive force], 62 [suicide pact killing], or 64 [infanticide] applies': cl. 54(1).

45. Diminished responsibility
'(1) A person who, but for this section, would be guilty of murder is not guilty of murder if, at the time of his act, he is suffering from such mental abnormality as is a substantial enough reason to reduce his offence to manslaughter. (2) In this section "mental abnormality" means mental illness, arrested or incomplete development of mind, psychopathic disorder, and any other disorder or disability of mind, except intoxication. (3) Where a person suffering from mental abnormality is also intoxicated, this section applies only where it would apply if he were not intoxicated': cl. 56.

46. Provocation
'A person who, but for this section, would be guilty of murder is not guilty of murder if – (*a*) he acts when provoked (whether) by things done or by things said or by both and whether by the deceased person or by another) to lose his self-control; and (*b*) the provocation is, in all the circumstances (including any of his personal characteristics that affect its gravity), sufficient ground for the loss of self-control': cl. 58.

Progress test 9

1. Outline Coke's definition of murder. **(3)**

2. Comment on the decision in *R*. v. *Pagett* (1983). **(12)**

3. What is meant by 'malice aforethought'? **(13, 14)**

4. Explain the decision in *R*. v. *Vickers* (1957). **(18)**

5. What was the basis of the criticism of *DPP* v. *Smith* (1961)? **(19, 20)**

6. Outline the Criminal Justice Act 1967, s. 8. **(21)**

7. Discuss *R*. v. *Moloney* (1985). **(25, 26)**

8. What is the essence of the plea of diminished responsibility? **(34)**

9. Comment on *R.* v. *Thornton* (1992). **(38)**

10. Explain the Homicide Act 1957, s. 3. **(39)**

11. Outline the Offences against the Person Act 1861, s. 16. **(43)**

10

Manslaughter, offences related to driving, and suicide

The nature of manslaughter

1. Manslaughter described

Manslaughter (an offence which is triable only on indictment) may be described, in general terms, as *unlawful homicide which cannot be classified as murder*. X may be guilty of manslaughter where, for example:

(a) as a result of grossly negligent conduct he kills Y; *or*
(b) suffering from diminished responsibility or acting under provocation, he deliberately kills Y; *or*
(c) by an unlawful act, likely to cause bodily harm of a non-grievous nature, he kills Y; *or*
(d) in pursuance of a suicide pact (*see* **20**), he kills Y.

Note the comment of Lord Atkin in *Andrews* v. *DPP* (1937): 'Of all crimes, manslaughter appears to afford most difficulties of definition, for it concerns homicide in so many and so varying conditions . . . The law recognises murder on the one hand, based mainly, though not exclusively, on an intention to kill, and manslaughter on the other hand, based mainly, though not exclusively, on the absence of intention to kill but with the presence of an element of "unlawfulness" which is the elusive factor.'

Note, also, that *a company* may be convicted of manslaughter. Manslaughter is the unlawful killing of one human being by another, and the person that is the embodiment of a corporation, acting for the purposes of that corporation, could be guilty of the crime: *see R.* v. *HM Coroner for East Kent, ex p Spooner* (1987); *R.* v. *P&O European Ferries* (1991).

2. Classification of manslaughter

Manslaughter may be classified as voluntary or involuntary.

(a) *Voluntary manslaughter*. This expression originally referred to a homicide which was *reduced from murder to manslaughter* because of provocation. As a result of the Homicide Act 1957, voluntary manslaughter now refers to a killing which would have been murder (because the accused had the necessary mental intent), but is now considered as manslaughter, because the accused, X:

(*i*) successfully pleads *provocation* (*see* 9:**39**); *or*

(*ii*) successfully pleads *diminished responsibility* (*see* 9:**34**); *or*

(*iii*) shows that he acted in pursuance of a *suicide pact* with the deceased person (*see* **20**).

In essence, X has the malice aforethought appropriate to murder; there is an *actus reus* appropriate to that offence, but also a *partial defence* because of certain specifically recognised extenuating circumstances applicable to X. Note that a person may not be indicted for 'voluntary manslaughter'; it is, rather, a verdict (known merely as 'manslaughter') emerging from a trial based upon an indictment for murder. There is, apparently, no verdict of 'attempted manslaughter'.

(b) *Involuntary manslaughter.* 'Involuntary' does *not* refer to circumstances in which X has caused the death of Y while he, X, was in a state of 'involuntariness', ie, automatism (*see* 6:**20**). The term is used to *exclude* killings in which X may have the necessary mental intent for murder, but in which the offence is reduced to manslaughter because of any of the circumstances mentioned at (*a*) above.

(*i*) The phrase 'involuntary manslaughter' may be taken as referring to the *actus reus* of unlawful homicide, unaccompanied by malice aforethought (*see* 9:**14**) (ie, the accused did not evince the mental state required for a conviction of murder) *and* resulting from: an intention to do an unlawful dangerous act; *or* gross negligence in relation to likely death or grievous bodily harm; *or* recklessness in relation to bodily harm. Involuntary manslaughter may be considered, therefore, as 'unlawful act manslaughter', and 'manslaughter by gross negligence or recklessness'.

(*ii*) Note R. v. *Goodfellow* (1986), in which the Court of Appeal, considering involuntary manslaughter, suggested that the important questions for the jury should be: Was the act intentional? Was it unlawful? Was it an act which any reasonable person would realise was bound to subject some other person to the risk of physical harm, albeit not necessarily serious harm? Was the act the cause of death?

An unlawful dangerous act causing death, i.e., constructive manslaughter

3. The general rule

If Y's death results from the performance by X of a dangerous act unlawful in itself and *likely to cause bodily harm which is not grievous* (i.e. lacking in some element of the *mens rea* necessary for murder: *see* 9:**14**), X may be found guilty of manslaughter (known also in such a case as 'constructive manslaughter'). This is a crime of *basic intent* (see 3:**13**).

(a) In *R. v. Larkin* (1943), X flourished an open razor, intending only to frighten Z, who had been associating with Y, X's mistress. (The flourishing of the razor was, in itself, unlawful, since it constituted an assault: see 12:**3, 4**.) Y, who had been drinking, swayed against X and her throat was cut by the razor. X was found guilty of manslaughter, and his appeal was dismissed. *Per* Humphreys J: 'Where the act which a person is engaged in performing is *unlawful*, then if at the same time it is a *dangerous act*, that is, an act which is likely to injure another person, and quite inadvertently he causes the death of that other person by the act, then he is guilty of manslaughter.'

(b) In *R. v. Hall* (1961), X followed his wife, Y, and Z, with whom she was associating, carrying an unsheathed knife and intending, as he claimed, merely to frighten Y and Z. Z walked towards X and received a fatal wound from the knife. X was convicted of manslaughter, and his conviction was upheld by the Court of Criminal Appeal. *Per* Sachs J, in directing the jury: 'If when [X] went into the car park and produced that knife the intention in his mind was to use it for the unlawful purpose of terrifying his wife and [Z], that alone might well amount to an assault. And if in consequence of his having produced this knife he accidentally stabbed [Z] then I direct you as a matter of law that that is manslaughter.'

(c) In *R. v. Arobieke* (1988), Y was electrocuted while attempting to run across electrified railway lines. There was evidence of hostility between X and Y; further evidence showed that X had been walking along a platform peering into a train which Y had boarded and that Y had then run towards the railway lines. The Court of Appeal quashed X's conviction of manslaughter: for X merely to look into a train without knowing whether Y was on it could *not* constitute an unlawful act.

4. 'An unlawful act': some modern decisions

'The unlawful act must be such as all sober and reasonable people would inevitably recognise must subject the other person to, at least, *the risk of some harm resulting therefrom*, albeit not serious harm': *per* Edmund-Davies J in *R. v. Church* (1966). This appeared to have narrowed, in some measure, the old rule that manslaughter was committed where death was caused as the result of *any* unlawful act.

(For the act to be considered 'unlawful' it must amount at least to a *technical assault*. In *R. v. Lamb* (1967), X, in jest, pointed a loaded gun at his friend, Y. Neither X nor Y knew that there was any danger, because they misunderstood the gun's mechanism. When X pressed the trigger he shot and killed Y. X's conviction for manslaughter was quashed, since Y apprehended no injury and X did not intend to cause him any apprehension. Without the element of intent or recklessness there can be no assault (*see* 12:2).)

(a) *A reconsideration of the question of an unlawful act inadvertently causing death: DPP v. Newbury and Jones* (1977). X and Y, fifteen-year-old youths, pushed a paving stone over the parapet of a railway bridge. It fell onto an approaching train, killing the guard. X and Y were found guilty of manslaughter. The Court of Appeal dismissed their appeals against conviction and certified to be of general public importance the point of law contained within the question: '*Can a defendant be properly convicted of manslaughter when his mind is* not *affected by drink or drugs, if he did* not *foresee that his act might cause harm to another?'*

(b) *House of Lords.* The House of Lords *upheld* the convictions. It was stated that the trial judge, rightly, had *not* directed the jury that they should acquit unless they were satisfied beyond a reasonable doubt that X and Y had foreseen that they might cause harm to someone by pushing the stone off the parapet into the path of the approaching train. The direction he gave had been completely in accord with established law as set out in *R.* v. *Larkin* (*see* 3(*a*)). In that case it had been made plain that an accused *was* guilty of manslaughter if it was proved that he intentionally did an act which was unlawful and dangerous and that that act inadvertently caused death, and that it was *unnecessary* to prove that the accused knew that the act was dangerous or unlawful. *R.* v. *Church* (1966) (*see* above) *restated the objective test.* In judging whether the act was dangerous, the test was not, did the accused recognise that it was dangerous, but, *would all sober and reasonable people recognise its danger?* In *Gray* v. *Barr* (1971) Lord Denning had referred to *R.* v. *Lamb* for the proposition that in manslaughter there must always be a guilty mind. That was true of every crime except those of absolute liability. The guilty mind usually depended on the accused's intention. Some crimes, e.g. murder, required a *specific intention* – killing with intent to inflict grievous bodily harm. Others, including manslaughter, needed only a *basic intention* – to do the acts which constituted the crime. *R.* v. *Lamb* was no authority to the contrary. *See also R.* v. *Jennings* (1990).

5. Excessive force used against the victim

In *R.*v. *Scarlett* (1993), the Court of Appeal considered a case in which the deceased, Y, had entered a public house ten minutes after closing time, clearly the worse for drink, and had approached the bar. X, (the licensee) the appellant, told Y to get out or he would be put out. Y refused to leave and X took hold of him, pinning his arms to his side and pushing him out of the door into the lobby. Y fell backwards down a flight of five steps, striking his head fatally. X was charged with manslaughter.

(a) *The judge's decision*. The jury was directed that if they concluded that X had used more force than was necessary in the circumstances and were satisfied that that caused Y to fall and strike his head, then X was guilty of manslaughter. X was convicted and later appealed.

(b) *Court of Appeal*. X's conviction was *quashed*, the Court holding that in the circumstances the direction to the jury was inadequate to support a verdict of guilty of manslaughter.

(c) *Per* Beldam LJ: 'Where, as in the present case, an accused is justified in using some force and can only be guilty of an assault if the force used is excessive, the jury ought to be directed that he cannot be guilty of an assault unless the prosecution prove that he acted with the mental element necessary to constitute his action an assault, that is: ". . . that the defendant intentionally or recklessly applied force to the person of another", *per* James LJ in *R. v. Venna* (1975). Further, they should be directed that the accused is not to be found guilty merely because he intentionally or recklessly used force which they consider to have been excessive. They ought not to convict him unless they are satisfied that the degree of force used was plainly more than was called for by the circumstances as he believed them to be and, provided he believed the circumstances called for the degree of force used, he was not to be convicted even if his belief was unreasonable . . .'

6. Nexus required between an unlawful and dangerous act and death

In *R. v. Mitchell* (1983), X argued with, and struck, Y, who fell against Z, a woman aged 89. Z suffered a broken femur and died in hospital from a pulmonary embolism (following an operation) caused by a thrombosis due to the fractured femur. X's conviction of manslaughter was upheld on appeal. The Court of Appeal could see no reason of policy for holding that an act calculated to harm Y could not be manslaughter if, in the event, it killed Z. The criminality of the doer of the act was the same whether it was Y or Z who died. A person who threw a stone at P was just as guilty if, instead of hitting and killing P, it hit and killed Q. It was *not* necessary that the act of the accused should have been aimed at Z. (*See R. v. Dalby* (1982).) The only question was one of *causation* – whether Z's death was caused by X's act. *See also R. v. Armstrong* (1989); *R. v. Lebrun* (1991), at 2:5.

(a) In *R. v. Watson* (1989), X and another person broke into Y's house, confronted Y as he woke up, abused him verbally and made off without stealing anything. X did not know that Y, elderly and frail, suffered from a heart condition. Y died ninety minutes later following a heart attack. X argued that he was not responsible for Y's death. The Court of Appeal considered X's conviction of manslaughter. Two matters of particular importance were discussed.

(*i*) The trial judge had made the following statement: 'Manslaughter is the offence committed when one person causes the death of another by an act which is unlawful and which is also dangerous, dangerous in the sense that it is an act which all sober and reasonable people would inevitably realise, must subject the victim to the risk of some harm resulting whether the defendant realised that or not.'

(*ii*) When one was deciding whether the 'sober and reasonable person' (the 'bystander') would realise the risk of some harm resulting to the victim, how much knowledge of the circumstances did one attribute to the bystander?

(*iii*) The judge's definition of manslaughter, as it applied to the circumstances, was held by the Court of Appeal to be *correct*. Further, the judge had clearly taken the view that the jury were entitled to ascribe to the bystander the knowledge which X gained during the whole of his stay in Y's house, and so directed them. The Court held that this was *not* a misdirection. (*See* further 17:**13(g)**.) (X's appeal was allowed on other grounds.)

(b) In *R.v.Williams* (1992), the Court of Appeal considered causation in relation to involuntary manslaughter. The appellants were the driver and passengers in a car which had picked up a hitchhiker, H. Although direct evidence was lacking, it appeared that threats had been made by the appellants to H, following which he had jumped from the car while it was travelling at 30 mph. H had died from the injuries sustained, and the appellants had been convicted of robbery and manslaughter. The Court of Appeal held that when a victim is killed while he is attempting to escape from threats, a jury may convict of manslaughter *only if* the threats were a cause of death. The jury had to consider whether H's actions were so unreasonable and disproportionate to the threats that they constituted an *unforeseeable intervening cause* which effectively broke the chain of causation. The convictions for manslaughter were *quashed* (as were, for other reasons, the convictions for robbery).

7. Wilful omission to perform a duty
In some circumstances a person owes a duty to others, and where his wilful failure to perform that duty results in death, he may be charged with manslaughter.

(a) *R. v. Instan* (1893). X lived with her aged aunt, Y, a helpless invalid. Y's death was accelerated by X's failure to supply her with food or medical assistance. 'X was under a moral obligation to the deceased from which arose a legal duty towards her; that legal duty X has wilfully and deliberately left unperformed, with the consequence that there has been an acceleration of the death of the deceased owing to the non-performance of that legal duty': *per* Lord Coleridge CJ.

(b) *R.* v. *Bonnyman* (1942). X, a doctor, was convicted of the manslaughter of his wife, Y, a drug addict. X had neglected to treat Y and had refused to allow her to be moved elsewhere for treatment. His appeal was *dismissed*, the Court of Criminal Appeal holding that X's plain duty was to give Y, a helpless person, aid and treatment, and this he had failed to do.

8. Duty owed to others
See 2:**12**, where this matter was considered.

(a) The duty must be one recognised by the criminal law.

(b) It must be owed by the accused person because of his custody of, or control over, the deceased person, who must have been helpless.

(c) Breach of the duty must have *unintentionally* resulted in death. But where the death has been caused *intentionally* in circumstances in which the accused person must have contemplated its occurrence as a probable result of his omitting to act, it may constitute *murder*.

9. What the prosecution must prove
It is for the prosecution to show, in a case of alleged *constructive manslaughter*:

(a) that X has unlawfully committed the *actus reus* of some criminal offence, i.e. X has performed an unlawful act of a criminal and intentional nature, e.g. battery (*see R.* v. *Lamb* (1967)) which has been directed at some person;

(b) that the unlawful act caused Y's death;

(c) that the unlawful act was objectively dangerous and was such as was likely to involve the victim, Y, in some kind of physical harm.

(*i*) Note *R.* v. *Dawson* (1985), in which the Court of Appeal considered the case of X who had attempted to rob Y (who had a history of heart trouble). Y collapsed and died shortly after the attempt. X was convicted on charges including attempted robbery and manslaughter.

(*ii*) The trial judge had directed the jury that 'if an act puts a person in such terror that he or she may suffer emotional *or* physical disturbance which is detrimental, then that disturbance is harm within the meaning of what you have to consider.'

(*iii*) The Court *quashed* the conviction of X as unsafe and unsatisfactory. *Per* Watkins LJ: It was unfortunate that the judge used the disjunctive 'or'. The jury were left with a choice, and if they acted upon the basis that emotional disturbance was enough to constitute harm, that would have been acting upon a misdirection. Emotional disturbance did not occur to the court as sensibly descriptive of injury or harm to the person through the operation of shock produced by terror or fright, and the word 'detrimental' did not assist to clarify the expression 'emotional disturbance'. A proper direction would have been that *the requisite harm was caused if the unlawful act so shocked the victim as to cause him physical injury.*

Act performed with gross negligence causing death

10. The general rule

In a case of manslaughter by gross negligence, the degree of negligence must be *much higher* than that which might ground liability in tort. *Per* Lord Hewart CJ in *R.* v. *Bateman* (1925) (in which the conviction of a doctor of the manslaughter of a woman at whose confinement he had attended was quashed):

> 'To support an indictment for manslaughter the prosecution must prove the matters necessary to establish civil liability (except pecuniary loss) and, in addition, must satisfy the jury that the negligence or incompetence of the accused went beyond a mere matter of compensation and showed such disregard for the life and safety of others as to amount to a crime against the state and conduct deserving punishment.'

11. Examples

In the following cases X was held guilty of manslaughter.

(a) *Andrews* v. *DPP* (1937). X was driving by night on the wrong side of the road and ran over and killed Y. The House of Lords stated that 'there is an obvious difference in the law of manslaughter between doing an unlawful act and doing a lawful act with a degree of carelessness which the legislature makes criminal.' *Per* Lord Atkin:

> 'Simple lack of care such as will constitute civil liability is *not enough*: for purposes of the criminal law there are degrees of negligence; and a very high degree of negligence is required to be proved before the [offence] is established. Probably of all the epithets that can be applied, "reckless" most nearly covers the case . . . but it is probably not all-embracing, for "reckless" suggests indifference to risk whereas the accused may have appreciated the risk and intended to avoid it, and yet shown such a high degree of negligence in the means adopted to avoid the risk as would justify a conviction.'

(b) *R.* v. *Adomako (1993).* A patient died as the result of hypoxia which resulted from cardiac arrest during an operation on a detached retina. X, a locum anaesthetist, was charged with manslaughter and expert evidence was given to demonstrate that the patient had become disconnected from the oxygen apparatus for five minutes and that a competent anaesthetist would have been aware of this within a few seconds. D was convicted; the patient had died from hypoxia for which X was responsible and X's conduct in these circumstances constituted gross negligence which amounted to *criminal negligence*. X's appeal was dismissed (*see* 12).

12. A recent reconsideration of the ingredients which have to be proved in involuntary manslaughter: *R. v. Sulman* (1993); *R. v. Prentice* (1993); *R. v. Adomako* (1993); *R. v. Holloway* (1993).

The Court of Appeal reconsidered in 1993 the essential legal basis of involuntary manslaughter and restated the ingredients which had to be proved.

(a) Four appeals were heard. In *R. v. Sulman* and *R. v. Prentice*, a junior houseman, Dr. X, mistakenly injected a lethal drug (vincristine) into the spine, instead of the arm of a leukaemia patient while under the supervision of Dr. Y, the house officer. The convictions of X and Y for manslaughter were quashed. The third appeal was on behalf of Dr. Adomako (*see* 11 (**b**) above). In *R. v. Holloway*, X, an electrician, made a faulty live-to-earth connection while wiring a heating programmer, resulting in Y's death. X's conviction for manslaughter was quashed.

(b) Lord Taylor stated that there was no reason to doubt that *Andrews* (*see* 11) was still good law, and *Stone* (*see* 13(a)) had been referred to in argument and not disapproved in *Seymour* (*see* 13(b)). Leaving motor manslaughter aside, in the opinion of the Court *the proper test in manslaughter cases based on breach of duty was the gross negligence test established in Andrews and Stone.*

(c) Except in motor manslaughter, therefore, the ingredients of involuntary manslaughter *by breach of duty* which needed to be proved were:
  (*i*) the existence of a duty;
  (*ii*) a breach of the duty causing death;
  (*iii*) gross negligence which the jury considered to justify a criminal conviction.

(d) The Court considered proof of any of the following states of mind in the defendant might properly lead a jury to make a finding of *gross negligence*:
  (*i*) indifference to an obvious risk of injury to health;
  (*ii*) actual foresight of the risk coupled with the determination nevertheless to run it;
  (*iii*) an appreciation of the risk coupled with an intention to avoid it but also coupled with such a high degree of negligence in the attempted avoidance as the jury considered justified the conviction;
  (*iv*) inattention or failure to advert to a serious risk which went

beyond 'mere inadvertence' in respect of an obvious and important matter which the defendant's duty demanded he should address.

NOTE: For a critical review of these decisions, *see* 'Misadventures of Manslaughter' by Glanville Williams in *New Law Journal* (1993) pp. 1413–1415.

13. Recklessness in manslaughter by breach of duty
The following cases should be noted.

(a) R. v. *Stone* (1977)
X, an elderly widower, who was almost blind and deaf, looked after Y, an eccentric acquaintance who suffered from anorexia nervosa. Y, having come to lodge with X, became increasingly infirm, but X made no more than a half-hearted attempt to secure medical attention for her. Y died from toxaemia, brought on as the result of prolonged immobilisation. X's conviction of manslaughter was *upheld*.

Per Geoffrey Lane LJ: 'Indifference to an obvious risk and appreciation of such risk, coupled with a determination, nevertheless, to run it, are both examples of recklessness. The duty which a defendant has undertaken is a duty of caring for the health and welfare of the infirm person. What the prosecution have to prove is a breach of that duty in such circumstances that the defendant's conduct can properly be described as reckless, that is to say a reckless disregard of danger to the health and welfare of the infirm person. *Mere inadvertence is not enough.* The defendant must be proved to have been indifferent to an obvious risk of injury to health, or actually to have foreseen the risk but to have determined nevertheless to run it.'

(b) R. v. *Seymour* (1983)
The House of Lords considered in this case whether manslaughter and causing death by reckless driving under the Road Traffic Act 1972, s. 1 (but *see* now the Road Traffic Act 1991), were co-extensive. X had quarrelled with Y, with whom he had been living, and had met her later while he was driving his lorry and she was driving her car. Following a collision between the two, X drove his lorry at Y's car, allegedly only so as to move it. Y was crushed between the vehicles and died. The judge directed the jury on the question of recklessness according to *R. v. Lawrence* (1982). The jury were told that they had to be satisfied that X was driving the lorry in such a manner as to create an obvious and serious risk of causing physical injury to some other person using the road, and in driving in that manner X did so 'without having given any thought to the possibility of there being any such risk, or having recognised that there was some risk involved, had nonetheless gone on to take it.'

X appealed against conviction, arguing that the direction was inadequate and that, in a case of manslaughter, the prosecution had to prove that he had recognised and ignored the risk. The Court of Appeal dismissed X's appeal on the ground of the two offences being co-extensive. The House of Lords held that the elements of the two offences were the same (and where the prosecution charge both, the judge must put them to their election upon which charge to proceed). The direction in *R. v. Lawrence was appropriate*, except that it should be pointed out to a jury that the risk of death being caused by the manner of driving must be very high. Further, *per* Lord Roskill: '"Reckless" should today be given the same meaning in relation to all offences which involve "recklessness" as one of the elements unless Parliament has otherwise ordained.'

(c)   *Kong Cheuk Kwan* v. *R.* (1985)

Two hydrofoils had collided in fine weather at high speed and two passengers were killed. X, in charge of one of the hydrofoils, was convicted of manslaughter and his conviction was upheld by the Hong Kong Court of Appeal. The Privy Council *quashed* X's conviction, stating that the trial judge had failed to distinguish recklessness (as set out in *R. v. Caldwell* (1982) and *R. v. Lawrence* (1982)) and gross negligence (as referred to in *R. v. Bateman* (1925)). *Per* Lord Roskill: 'Their Lordships are of the view that the present state of the relevant law . . . is clear. The model direction suggested in *R. v. Lawrence*, and held in *R. v. Seymour* to be equally applicable to cases of motor manslaughter, requires, first, proof that the vehicle was in fact being driven in such a manner as to create an obvious and serious risk of causing physical injury to another, and, second, that defendant so drove either without having given any thought to the possibility of there being such a risk or, having recognised that there was such a risk, nevertheless took it. Once that direction is given, it is for the jury to decide whether or not on their view of the evidence the relevant charge has been proved.' The direction had *not* been given in this case.

14.   *R. v. Sulman* (1993)

Lord Taylor made the following comments in relation to recklessness and manslaughter.

(a)   The wide meaning given by Lord Diplock to recklessness in *Caldwell* and *Lawrence* had survived all attacks on it (most recently in *R. v. Reid* (1992)).

(b)   It was beyond doubt that, at least since 1982, the word 'reckless' had caused the courts problems in regard to voluntary manslaughter which would not have occurred had the focus been on gross negligence rather than recklessness.

(c)   The Court of Appeal accepted that Lord Roskill's sentence in *Seymour*, that 'reckless' was to be given the same meaning in relation to all offences which involved recklessness as one of the elements unless Parliament had otherwise ordained, was *obiter* and should *not* be followed in regard to the class of manslaughter involved in the cases under appeal (*see* **12** above).

(d) The *Lawrence/Caldwell* recklessness approach was *inappropriate* in the present class of case under consideration.

(e) The Court of Appeal had borne in mind dicta in *Seymour* and in *Kong Cheuk Kwan* to the effect that the word 'reckless' was to be preferred to the word 'negligence' with whatever epithet. However, in view of the different tests and meanings which had in various contexts been attached to reckless and recklessness, the Court thought it preferable to avoid those words when directing juries as to involuntary manslaughter by breach of duty.

> NOTE: (1) The House of Lords held in *R.* v. *Saunders* (1988) that on an indictment charging murder, if the jury cannot agree that the murder has been proved, and has been discharged from returning a verdict on the charge of murder, but are agreed that all the elements other than intent have been proved, they can validly return a verdict of manslaughter. (2) For sentencing principles relating to manslaughter, *see*, eg, *R.* v.*Coleman* (1991).

Unlawful homicide in relation to driving

15. Causing death by dangerous driving

'A person who causes the death of another person by driving a mechanically propelled vehicle dangerously on a road or other public place is guilty of an offence': Road Traffic Act 1988, s. 1, substituted by RTA 1991, s. 1.

(a) A person is to be regarded as driving 'dangerously' if the way he drives falls far below what would be expected of a competent and careful driver, and it would be obvious to a competent and careful driver that driving in that way would be dangerous. Further, a person is to be regarded as driving dangerously if it would be obvious to a competent and careful driver that driving the vehicle in its current state would be dangerous: RTA 1988, s. 2A, substituted by RTA 1991, s. 1.

(b) In determining what is to be expected of or obvious to 'a competent and careful driver', regard is to be had to those circumstances of which he could be expected to be aware and of circumstances 'shown to have been within the knowledge of the accused': s. 2A(3). Concerning the 'state of a vehicle' for purposes of s. 2A, 'regard may be had to anything attached to or carried on or in it and to the manner in which it is attached or carried': s. 2A(4).

16. Causing death by careless driving when under the influence of drink or drugs

'If a person causes the death of another person by driving a mechanically propelled vehicle on a road or other public place without due care and attention, or without reasonable consideration for other persons using the road or place, and (a) he is, at the time when he is driving, unfit to drive through drink or drugs, or (b) he has consumed so much alcohol that the proportion of it in his breath, blood or urine at the time exceeds the prescribed limit, or (c) he is, within 18 hours after that time, required to provide a specimen in pursuance of s. 7 of this Act, but without reasonable excuse fails to provide it, he is guilty of an offence': RTA 1988, s. 3A, as substituted by RTA 1991.s. 3. For the purposes of s. 3A, a person is taken to be 'unfit to drive' at any time when his ability to drive properly is impaired: s. 3A(2). For the interpretation of 'public place', see, eg, *DPP* v. *Coulman* (1993).

> NOTE: For penalties for causing death by dangerous driving or careless driving when under the influence of drink or drugs, see the Criminal Justice Act 1993, s. 67(1), and *A.-G.'s References (Nos. 14 and 24 of 1993)*.

Offences related to suicide

17. Background
Self-slaughter was at one time a felony (*felonia de se*) attended by harsh consequences, e.g. the goods of the *felo de se* were forfeited, and his corpse was buried in a degrading manner. It was not until the Forfeiture Act 1870 and the Interments Act 1882 that these practices ended.

Because suicide was a felony, the consequence of X's attempting suicide, and failing, was that X was guilty of the misdemeanour of attempted suicide. Further, if X, in attempting suicide, killed Y, the doctrine of transferred malice (*see* 9:**16**(*c*)) would operate, so that X was held guilty of murder.

18. Suicide no longer a crime
Under the Suicide Act 1961, s. 1: 'The rule of law whereby it is a crime for a person to commit suicide is hereby abrogated.'

This implies that *attempted suicide* is no longer a criminal offence, and that the effect of the doctrine of transferred malice (as where X, in the course of attempting to kill himself, kills Y) no longer applies.

19. Complicity in another's suicide
By the Suicide Act 1961, s. 2, it is an offence to aid, abet, counsel or procure the suicide of another, or an attempt by another to commit suicide. *See R. v. McShane* (1977); *R. v. Reed* (1982), in which X was convicted of conspiring to aid and abet suicide; the Court of Appeal held that the judge's direction that X was guilty of counselling or procuring suicide if he put

another in touch with a potential suicide, 'knowing and intending that he should help suicide if circumstances permitted,' was wholly appropriate; and *R.* v. *McGranaghan* (1988). *See also A.-G.* v. *Able* (1984) – X and others published a booklet on suicide and the A.-G. applied for a declaration that its distribution could constitute an offence under s. 2; but the declaration was *refused*, the court holding that there could well be circumstances in which distribution might not amount to a crime, as where it was required for genuine research. The offence is triable only on indictment.

20. Suicide pacts

A suicide pact is defined as 'a common agreement between two or more persons having for its object the death of all of them, whether or not each is to take his own life, but nothing done by a person who enters into a suicide pact shall be treated as done by him in pursuance of the pact unless it is done while he has the settled intention of dying in pursuance of the pact': Homicide Act 1957, s. 4(3).

(a) If the survivor of the pact has killed the deceased, the case falls within the Homicide Act 1957, s. 4(1): 'It shall be *manslaughter* and shall not be murder for a person acting in pursuance of a suicide pact between him and another to kill the other or be party to the other being killed by a third person.' *See R.* v. *Sweeney* (1968); *R.* v. *Osborne* (1992).
(b) If the deceased has killed himself, the survivor of the pact is guilty of the offence under the 1961 Act, s. 2 (*see* **19**).

21. Onus of proof

'Where it is shown that a person charged with the murder of another killed the other or was a party to his killing himself or being killed, it shall be for *the defence* to prove that the person charged was acting in pursuance of a suicide pact between himself and the other': Homicide Act 1957, s. 4(2). Proof would be on a balance of probabilities.

> NOTE: For the effect of the year-and-a-day rule (*see* 9:**9**) on a suicide verdict, *see R.* v. *Inner London Coroner ex p. De Luca* (1988).

Draft Criminal Code Bill

22. Manslaughter

'A person is guilty of manslaughter if – (*a*) he is not guilty of murder by reason only of the fact that a defence provided by cl. 56 (diminished responsibility), 58 (provocation) or 59 (use of excessive force) applies; or (*b*) he is not guilty of murder by reason only of the fact that, because of voluntary intoxication, he is not aware that death may be caused or believes that an exempting circumstance exists; or (*c*) he causes the death of another – (*i*) intending to cause serious personal harm; or (*ii*) being reckless whether death or serious personal harm will be caused': cl. 55.

23. Attempted manslaughter
'A person who attempts to cause the death of another, where ss. 56, 58 or 59 would apply if death were caused, is not guilty of attempted murder but is guilty of attempted manslaughter': cl. 61.

Progress test 10

1. What is meant by 'involuntary manslaughter'? **(2)**

2. Comment on *R. v. Larkin* (1943). **(3)**

3. Explain the decision in *R. v. Scarlett* (1993). **(5)**

4. What must the prosecution prove in a case of alleged constructive manslaughter? **(9)**

5. Outline the decision of the Court of Appeal in *R. v. Sulman* (1993). **(12, 14)**

6. Comment on *Kong Cheuk Kwan* v. *R.* (1985). **(13)**

7. Outline the offence of causing death by dangerous driving. **(15)**

8. What is the criminal liability of the survivor of a suicide pact who has killed the deceased? **(20)**

11

Infanticide, child destruction, abortion, and concealment of birth

The Infanticide Act 1938

1. The main provisions of the Act
By s. 1(1):

'Where a woman by any wilful act or omission causes the death of her child being a child under the age of twelve months, but at the time of the act or omission the balance of her mind was disturbed by reason of her not having fully recovered from the effect of giving birth to the child or by reason of the effect of lactation consequent upon the birth of the child, then, notwithstanding that the circumstances were such that but for this Act the offence would have amounted to murder, she shall be guilty of ... *infanticide*, and may for such offence be dealt with and punished as if she had been guilty of the offence of *manslaughter* of the child.'

The offence is triable only on indictment.

2. Aspects of the Act
It is important to note the following points.

(a) A woman may put forward as a defence to a charge of murder a plea of disturbance of the balance of her mind of a degree which would not constitute insanity under the M'Naghten Rules (*see* 6:28).
(b) Evidence of mental disturbance is essential; it will not suffice merely that the dead child was under the age of twelve months; *see R. v. Soanes* (1948).
(c) The crime of infanticide does not apply in the case of unborn children; it has application only in the case of a child who had an existence independent of its mother.
(d) The crime has application only in the case of the killing of an infant by *its mother*. The killing of an infant by any other person, or by its mother whose balance of mind is not disturbed, may amount to murder.
(e) By the 1938 Act, s. 1(2), a mother indicted for the murder of her child under the age of twelve months may be acquitted of murder and, if the conditions set out in s. 1(1) of the Act (*see* 1) are fulfilled, may be convicted

of infanticide. *See R.* v. *Scott* (1973). For attempted infanticide, *see R.* v. *Smith* (1983).

(f) For consideration of the appropriateness of custodial sentences in cases of infanticide, *see R.* v. *Lewis* (1989), *R.* v. *Sainsbury* (1990).

Child destruction

3. Infant Life (Preservation) Act 1929
By s. 1(1) of the Act:

> 'Any person who, with intent to destroy the life of a child capable of being born alive, by any wilful act causes a child to die before it has an existence independent of its mother, shall be guilty of an offence, to wit, of child destruction. ... . Provided that no person shall be found guilty of an offence under this section unless it is proved that the act which caused the death of the child was not done in good faith for the purpose only of preserving the life of the mother.'

By s. 1(2): '. . . evidence that a woman had at any material time been pregnant for a period of twenty-eight weeks or more shall be *prima facie* proof that she was at that time pregnant of a child capable of being born alive.'

(a) The offence is not, strictly speaking, one of homicide, since it does not involve the killing of a person 'in being' (*see* 9:6). It is triable only on indictment.

(b) The offence cannot be committed during the first stages of pregnancy; it involves the child's being 'capable of being born alive'.

(c) Because the *mens rea* for the offence is an intent 'to destroy the life of a child. . . .' the offence is not committed if the accused intended only to inflict injury on the woman and had no intention of injuring the child of which she was pregnant.

(d) Child destruction, unlike infanticide, can be charged against *any person*, not merely the mother.

(e) Note the special defence in the final words of s. 1(1) above. It is for the prosecution to show that the act of the accused was *not* undertaken in good faith so as to preserve the mother's life.

(f) A foetus of 18–21 weeks was *not* a 'child capable of being born alive', because it could not breathe naturally or with the aid of a ventilator. Termination of a pregnancy of that length was not an offence under the 1929 Act, s. 1: *C.* v. *S.* (1987). In *Rance* v. *Mid-Downs Health Authority* (1991), it was held that a child is 'born alive', if, after birth, 'it exists as a live child, that is to say, breathing and living by reason of its breathing through its own lungs alone, without deriving any of its living or power of living by or through any connection with its mother'.

4. Indictment for child destruction

On indictment for child destruction the accused person may be convicted of administering poison or other noxious thing with intent to procure an abortion (*see* 5): *see* the Infant Life (Preservation) Act 1929, s. 1(3).

> NOTE: 'No offence under the Infant Life (Preservation) Act 1929 shall be committed by a registered medical practitioner who terminates a pregnancy in accordance with the provisions of this Act': Abortion Act 1967, s. 5(1), substituted by the Human Fertilisation and Embryology Act 1990, s. 37.

Abortion

5. Offences against the Person Act 1861, s. 58

The current relevant statutes are the Offences Against the Person Act 1861, and the Abortion Act 1967 as amended by the Human Fertilisation and Embryology Act (1990). (*See* 7). By s. 58 of the 1861 Act:

> 'Every woman being with child who, with intent to procure her own miscarriage, shall unlawfully administer to herself any poison or other noxious thing, or shall unlawfully use an instrument or other means whatsoever with the like intent, and whosoever, with intent to procure the miscarriage of any woman, whether she be or be not with child, shall unlawfully administer to her or cause to be taken by her any poison or other noxious thing, or shall unlawfully use any instrument or other means whatsoever with the like intent, shall be guilty of an offence. . . .' *See R*. v. *Bourne* (1939); *R*. v. *Newton and Stungo* (1958).

(a) '*Poison or other noxious thing*'. The phrase is not limited to abortifacients, but a harmless substance will not satisfy s. 58: *see R*. v. *Marlow* (1964). Where something other than a recognised poison is administered it must be in a quantity which is, in fact, harmful: *see R*. v. *Cramp* (1880); *R*. v. *Marcus* (1981) – the question whether a substance was potentially harmful extended to whether it was capable of causing bodily injury directly or indirectly. The administering of a recognised poison, even in a quantity so small as to be harmless, is an offence: *see R*. v. *Weatherall* (1968).

(b) '*Other means*'. In *R*. v. *Spicer* (1955) the expression was held to include the fingers of the hand.

(c) Under the section, a woman who administers any poison or other noxious substance *to herself* can be guilty of the offence only if, in fact, she is pregnant, and not, therefore, if she merely believes that she is. But should another person administer poison or other noxious thing to her with intent to procure a miscarriage, whether or not the woman is pregnant is of no relevance. (In this latter event, the woman, if a consenting party, may be guilty of aiding and abetting the offence: *see R. v. Sockett* (1908).)

6. Offences against the Person Act 1861, s. 59

'Whosoever shall unlawfully supply or procure any poison or other noxious thing, or any instrument or thing whatsoever, knowing that the same is intended to be unlawfully used or employed with intent to procure the miscarriage of any woman, whether she be or be not with child, shall be guilty of a misdemeanour. . . .'

(a) *'Procure'*. It was held in *R. v. Mills* (1963) that the word is used, the first time it occurs in s. 59, in the ordinary meaning of 'getting possession from another person'.

(b) *'Knowing that the same is intended to be unlawfully used'*. It has been held to suffice for the purposes of the section that the accused has 'believed' that the poison, etc. is to be used in this way; it is, therefore, no defence for him to plead that the person to whom he supplied the poison, etc. did not intend to use it: *see R. v. Hillman* (1863).

> NOTE: 'If a person intending to procure abortion does an act which causes a child to be born so much earlier than the natural time that it is born in a state much less capable of living and afterwards dies as a consequence of its exposure to the external world, the person who by her misconduct so brings a child into the world and puts it merely into a situation in which it cannot live *is guilty of murder*': *per* Maule J in *R. v. West* (1848).

The Abortion Act 1967

7. Purpose of the Act

The 1967 Act amends and clarifies the law relating to the termination of pregnancy by registered medical practitioners. In the Act 'the law relating to abortion' includes the Offences against the Person Act 1861, ss. 58, 59 (*see* 5–6) and any rule of law relating to the procurement of abortion. Sections 58 and 59 must be read, therefore, in the light of the 1967 legislation as amended by HFEA 1990, set out below.

8. Medical termination of pregnancy

The situation is governed by the Abortion Act 1967, as amended by HFEA

1990. Under s. 1(1): 'Subject to the provisions of this section, a person shall not be guilty of an offence under the law relating to abortion when a pregnancy is terminated by a registered medical practitioner if two registered medical practitioners are of the opinion formed in good faith –

(a) that the pregnancy has not exceeded its 24th week and that the continuance of the pregnancy would involve risk, greater than if the pregnancy were terminated, of injury to the physical or mental health of the pregnant woman or any existing children of her family; *or*
(b) that the termination is necessary to prevent grave permanent injury to the physical or mental health of the pregnant woman; *or*
(c) that the continuance of the pregnancy would involve risk to the life of the pregnant woman, greater than if the pregnancy were terminated; *or*
(d) that there is a substantial risk that if the child were born it would suffer from such physical or mental abnormalities as to be seriously handicapped.'

> NOTE: In considering 'risk of injury to health', account may be taken of the pregnant woman's actual or reasonably foreseeable environment: s. 1(2).

9. Other relevant matters
The following points are of importance.

(a) Treatment for termination of the pregnancy must be carried out in a hospital vested in the Minister of Health or the Secretary of State under the NHS Acts: s. 1(3)(b).
(b) In the case of an emergency in which termination is immediately necessary so as to save the life or to prevent grave and permanent injury to the physical health of the pregnant woman, subsection (3) and that part of subsection (1), relating to the opinion of two medical practitioners, shall not apply: s. 1(4).
(c) In the case of a woman carrying more than one foetus, anything done with intent to procure her miscarriage of any foetus is authorised by s. 1 if the ground for termination of the pregnancy specified in subsection 1(d) applies in relation to any foetus and the thing is done for the purpose of procuring the miscarriage of the foetus, or any of the other grounds for termination of the pregnancy specified in s. 1 applies: s. 5(2).
(d) The question of whether a medical practitioner has acted 'in good faith' in deciding to terminate a pregnancy is for the jury to decide on the totality of the evidence: *R.v. Smith* (1973).
(e) Under the 1967 Act, s. 4, no person shall be under a duty to participate in any treatment under the Act to which he has a conscientious objection, but this must not affect his duty to participate in any treatment considered necessary to save life or prevent grave permanent injury to the physical

or mental health of a pregnant woman. *See R. v. Salford Health Authority ex p Janaway* (1988).

(f) In *Royal College of Nursing* v. *DHSS* (1981), the House of Lords held that a pregnancy is 'terminated by a registered medical practitioner' within s. 1(1) when the termination is prescribed and initiated by him and he remains in charge while qualified nursing staff carry out his instructions as a team effort.

(g) It should be noted that there is now a fixed time limit for abortions under the 1967 Act, s. 1(1)(a) of *24 weeks*. In the case of abortions under s. 1(b), (c), (d), there is no time limit.

Concealment of birth

10. Offences against the Person Act 1861, s. 60
'If any woman shall be delivered of a child, every person who shall, by any secret disposition of the dead body of the said child, whether such child died before, at, or after its birth, endeavour, to conceal the birth thereof, shall be guilty of misdemeanour. . . .'

(a) The offence may be committed by any person; and any person who assists in concealing the body is a principal in the offence.

(b) Mere concealment of the fact of birth does not suffice for s. 60.

(c) In *R. v. Berriman* (1854) (disposal of a foetus which was only a few months old), it was held that there was no offence of concealment of birth unless a child 'had arrived at that stage of maturity at the time of birth that it might have been a living child'; *per* Erle J.

(d) Mere concealment of birth from a particular person, e.g. a parent of the accused, does not constitute an offence: *R. v. Morris* (1848).

> NOTE: (1) Under the Magistrates' Courts Act 1980, Sch. 1, the offence of concealment of birth is triable either way. (2) *See* the Still-Birth (Definition) Act 1992.

11. 'Secret disposition'
Mere abandonment of the body will not suffice; there must have been an effort by the accused person to prevent the body being found. *See R. v. Opie* (1860); *R. v. Brown* (1870) (total concealment is not necessary).

Draft Criminal Code Bill

12. Infanticide
(1) 'A woman who, but for this section, would be guilty of murder or

manslaughter of her child is not guilty of murder or manslaughter, but is guilty of infanticide, if her act is done when the child is under the age of 12 months and when the balance of her mind is disturbed by reason of the effect of giving birth or of circumstances consequent upon the birth . . . (3) A woman may be convicted of infanticide (or attempted infanticide) although the jury is uncertain whether the child had been born or whether it had an existence independent of her when its death occurred (or, in the case of an attempt, when the act was done)': cl. 64.

13. Abortion
'A person is guilty of an offence if he intentionally causes the miscarriage of a woman otherwise than in accordance with the provisions of the Abortion Act 1967': cl. 66. '(1) A pregnant woman is guilty of an offence if she intentionally causes her own miscarriage otherwise than in accordance with the provisions of the Abortion Act 1967. (2) Notwithstanding cl. 50 (impossibility) a woman who is not pregnant cannot be guilty of an attempt to commit an offence under this Act': cl. 67.

14. Child destruction
'(1) A person is guilty of child destruction if he intentionally causes the death of a child capable of being born alive before the child has an existence independent of his mother, unless the act which causes death is done in good faith for the purpose only of preserving the life of the mother. (2) The fact that a woman had at any material time been pregnant for 28 weeks or more is *prima facie* proof that she was at that time pregnant of a child capable of being born alive': cl. 69.

Progress test 11

1. Outline the Infanticide Act 1938, s. 1 (1). **(1)**

2. What is the significance of the Infant Life Preservation Act 1929, s. 1 (1)? **(3)**

3. Outline the Offences against the Person Act 1861, s. 9. **(6)**

4. How is the medical termination of pregnancy governed by law? **(8)**

5. Comment on *Royal College of Nursing* v. *DHSS* (1981). **(9)**

6. Outline the Offences against the Person Act 1861, s. 60. **(10)**

Assault, battery, wounding, kidnapping and allied offences

Elements of assault

1. General
In common usage the terms 'assault' and 'battery' are often synonymous; in particular, 'assault' is widely used to refer to the unlawful application of physical force. (Assault and battery are torts *and* crimes.)

(a) Although for practical purposes the terms are generally synonymous, nevertheless assault and battery remain *distinct offences at common law*. A conviction, therefore, for 'assault or battery' will be quashed: *see Jones* v. *Sherwood* (1942).

(b) Common assault and battery are separate statutory offences triable summarily: Criminal Justice Act 1988, s. 39. *See* also *DPP* v. *Taylor* (1992) – where there is actual, as well as apprehended, unlawful force, the charge should be 'assault by beating', *not* 'assault and battery'.

2. Meaning of 'assault'
An assault is an *act by which any person, intentionally, or, possibly, recklessly, causes another person to fear the immediate application to himself of unlawful physical violence: see Fagan* v. *Metropolitan Police Commissioner* (1969); *R.* v. *Williams* (1984). ('Recklessly' has reference in this context to *Cunningham* recklessness: *see* 3:**15**.)

There is an assault, therefore, in the following circumstances:

(a) X points at Y a gun he (X) knows to be unloaded and threatens to shoot him. Y fears that he is to be shot: *see R.* v. *St George* (1840). *See* also *Logdon* v. *DPP* (1976), in which it was held that an assault was committed when the accused intentionally or recklessly caused another to believe that force was to be inflicted on her (when a toy pistol was pointed at her after she had been told it was a real, loaded weapon).

(b) X advances towards Y, shakes his fist and threatens to beat him there and then. Y is put in fear of immediate violence.

3. *Actus reus* of assault

The *actus reus* of assault is constituted by the creation in the mind of a person the belief that unlawful force is to be used *immediately*, against him. (*See* **4**.) Creation of a fear of future violence is insufficient.

(a) The old proposition that mere words in themselves cannot *constitute* an assault (*see R.* v. *Meade and Belt* (1823) is now doubtful. Note, for example, the dictum of Lord Goddard in *R.* v. *Wilson* (1955): '[Accused] called out "get out the knives", which itself would be an assault, in addition to kicking the gamekeeper.' Words, however, can in themselves *negative* an assault: see the old case of *Tuberville* v. *Savage* (1669) in which X laid his hand on his sword as if to draw it, but said to Y, at the same time: 'If it were not assize time I would not take such language from you.' Since it *was* assize time, the words cited unmade the assault. *See* also *Blake* v. *Barnard* (1840).

(b) There is no assault by X on Y when it is obvious to Y that X is unable to carry out his threat. *See Stephens* v. *Myers* (1830).

(c) For the possibility of an assault 'by omission', *see Fagan* v. *Metropolitan Police Commissioner* (1969), at **2:5**.

4. *Mens rea*

Common law assault is a crime of *basic intent* (*see* **3:13**). The *mens rea* is the intention to create in a person's mind belief in the *immediate application* of unlawful physical force or recklessness as to whether the belief is created or not. *Cunningham* recklessness (*see* **3:15**) is involved: *see R.* v. *Venna* (1975) at **7** below. Thus, if X strikes out in Y's direction, intending no physical contact with Y, but hoping merely to frighten him, this could, nevertheless, constitute an assault. 'The *actus reus* of assault is an act which causes another person to apprehend immediate and unlawful violence. The *mens rea* corresponds exactly. The prosecution must prove that the accused foresaw that his act would probably cause another person to have apprehension of immediate and unlawful violence or would possibly have had that consequence, such being the purpose of the act, or that he was reckless as to whether or not his act caused such apprehension. This foresight (the term of art is 'intention') or recklessness is the *mens rea* in assault. . . .': *per* Lord Simon in *DPP* v. *Morgan* (1976). *See Smith* v. *Chief Constable of Woking* (1983) – X's staring at Y through a window induced fear in Y and, although Y did not know what X was going to do next, it sufficed for the purposes of the offence that it was believed to be something of a violent nature, so that she (Y) was very frightened.

Battery

5. Meaning of 'battery'
'*The actual intended use of unlawful force on another person without his consent*': see *Fagan* v. *Metropolitan Police Commissioner* (1969). There is a battery, therefore, in the case of any unlawful contact with another, as where, for example:

(a) X, without lawful excuse, deliberately or recklessly pushes against Y, forcing him off the pavement; *or*

(b) X, without lawful excuse, deliberately strikes Y's face. (*See A.-G's Ref. (No. 6 of 1980).*)

6. *Actus reus* of battery
The *actus reus* is constituted by the actual application of unlawful personal violence by X to Y. 'The fundamental principle, plain and incontestable, is that every person's body is inviolate': *per* Goff LJ in *Collins* v. *Wilcock* (1984).

(a) 'Violence' includes the slightest force; no actual harm need result. Thus, to touch Y without his consent and without lawful excuse may suffice. *See Cole* v. *Turner* (1705).

(b) Those degrees of personal contact which are necessary or customary in the ordinary affairs of life, e.g. touching a person so as to draw his attention, will not constitute a battery. 'Nobody can complain of the jostling which is inevitable from his presence in a supermarket or busy street, nor can a person who attends a party complain if his hand is seized in friendship': *Collins* v. *Wilcock* (1984).

(c) It may suffice for X to strike at Y's clothing without touching Y's body: *see R.* v. *Day* (1845).

(d) The violence need not be applied directly by X to Y; it can be applied indirectly, as where X struck Y's horse so that Y was thrown: *see Dodwell* v. *Burford* (1670); *R.* v. *Martin* (1881) (*see* **18** (a).

(e) A battery does not always include an assault, as when it is committed on some person who does not expect it, e.g. because he is asleep.

(f) Battery is a continuing offence: *Fagan* v. *M.P.C.* (1969).

7. *Mens rea*
Mens rea is generally constituted by X's *intention* to apply unlawful personal force to Y. In *R.* v. *Venna* (1975) it was held that the mental element of *recklessness* was enough, when coupled with the *actus reus* of

physical contact, to constitute the battery involved in an assault occasioning actual bodily harm. (Battery is, therefore, a crime of *basic intent: see* 3:**13**.)

> NOTE: See Consultation paper No. 122, published by the Law Commission in 1992, *Legislating the Criminal Code: Offences against the Person.*

Defences

8. Nature of the defences

Assume that X adopts a posture which Y takes to be threatening, and strikes an intentional blow at Y, so that Y is struck on some part of his body. Superficially, there seems to exist the *actus reus* of assault and of battery. Consider, next, the following surrounding circumstances:

(a) Y has consented to the act, because X and Y are taking part in a (legal) boxing contest; *or*

(b) X is acting to defend himself against unlawful violence offered by Y.

The above circumstances illustrate some possible defences to charges of assault and battery: *consent (see* **9**); *self-defence (see* **10**). (Since assault and battery are crimes of basic intent – *see* 3:**13** – the defence of self-induced intoxication does not apply.)

9. Consent

Since assault and battery are effected against the will of the victim, it follows that they will usually be negatived by his consent.

(a) In games, for example, where the use of force might occur, the position is as stated in *R. v. Coney* (1882), *per* Cave J: '. . . a blow struck in anger, or which is likely or is intended to do corporal hurt, is an assault, but . . . a blow struck in sport, and not likely, nor intended, to cause bodily harm, is not an assault.' In *R. v. Billingshurst* (1978), X, in the course of a rugby match, during an 'off-the-ball' incident, punched Y's face, causing a fracture of Y's jaw. X was convicted of assault. *See R. v. Jones* (1986) – a genuinely-held belief that the victims had consented to rough, undisciplined games may be a defence to assault and is a matter which ought to be left to the jury.

(b) The consent must be given *freely*, i.e. without fear, fraud or force. *Per* Coleridge J in *R. v. Day* (1841): 'There is a difference between *consent* and *submission*: every consent involves a submission but it by no means follows that a mere submission involves consent. The mere submission of a child when in the power of a strong man, and most probably acted upon by fear, can by no means be taken to be such a consent as will justify the prisoner in point of law.'

(c) Fraud will negative consent if the victim is deceived as to a *fundamental fact*, e.g. the nature of the act, or the identity of the person performing that act. In *R. v. Clarence* (1888), X infected his wife, Y, with a venereal disease. X was aware of his condition; Y was not. X's conviction on a charge of assault was quashed. No assault had occurred. Stephen J stated that the only cases where fraud indisputably vitiates consent are cases of fraud as to *the nature of the act done*. Therefore, even if X's conduct did amount to a fraud, it would not vitiate Y's consent since *she understood the nature of the act*. Y's ignorance of X's disease was not, in itself, enough.

(d) Absence of consent must be proved by *the prosecution*.

(e) A person's consent to an act likely to result in serious injury to him is no defence. In *R. v. Donovan* (1934), X was charged with assaulting Y, whom he had beaten for purposes of sexual gratification. X's defence was that Y had consented.

> 'If an act is unlawful in the sense of being itself a criminal act, it is plain that it cannot be rendered lawful because the person to whose detriment it is done consents to it. No person can license another to commit a crime. So far as the criminal law is concerned, therefore, where the act charged is in itself unlawful, it can never be necessary to prove absence of consent on the part of the person wronged in order to obtain the conviction of the wrongdoer': *per* Swift J.

(f) In *R. v. Brown and Others* (1993), the House of Lords held that the consent of the willing recipients of sado-masochistic acts of violence did *not* constitute a defence to charges of assault occasioning actual bodily harm contrary to the Offences against the Person Act 1861, s. 47, and of wounding contrary to s. 20.

> (*i*) *Per* Lord Templeman: 'The authorities did not establish that consent was a defence to a charge under the 1861 Act; they established that the courts had accepted that consent was a defence to the infliction of bodily harm in the course of some lawful activities . . . Counsel for the appellants argued that consent should provide a defence to charges under ss. 20 and 47 because, it was said, every person has a right to deal with his body as he pleases. I do not consider that this slogan provides a sufficient guide to the policy decision which must now be made. It is an offence for a person to abuse his own body and mind by taking drugs. Although the law is often broken, the criminal law restrains a practice which is regarded as dangerous and injurious to individuals and which if allowed and extended is harmful to society generally.'
>
> (*ii*) Lord Templeman stated that in principle there is a difference between violence which is incidental and violence which is inflicted

for the indulgence of cruelty. 'I am not prepared to invent a defence of consent for sado-masochistic encounters which breed and glorify cruelty and result in offences under ss. 47 and 20.'

10. Self-defence

By the Criminal Law Act 1967, s. 3, a person may use *reasonable force* in preventing crime. This applies also, presumably, to an unlawful attack on that person. But where a person uses *unreasonable force* he may be liable for common assault. Where the defendant claims to have acted in self-defence, the jury must be directed that the onus is on *the prosecution* to disprove that defence: *see R. v. Abraham* (1973). *See* 6:37.

11. Other matters

It should be noted that *provocation* is generally no defence to charges of assault and battery: *see O'Connor* v. *Hewitson* (1979). On the matter of *corporal punishment in schools*, see the Education (No. 2) Act 1986, as amended by the Education Act 1993, s. 293, limiting teachers' rights to inflict corporal punishment and forbidding 'inhuman or degrading' punishment of pupils. *See Costello-Roberts* v. *UK* (1993).

Assaults occasioning actual bodily harm

12. Offences Against the Person Act 1861, s. 47

This section refers to 'any assault occasioning actual bodily harm'. The crime is one of *basic intent* (*see* 3:13).

(a) The prosecution must show that the assault produced the 'bodily harm'; but the harm may arise indirectly. *See R. v. Roberts* (1972), where X threatened Y, who then jumped out of X's car to save herself and was injured. X was convicted under s. 47. 'The test is: Was it the natural result of what the alleged assailant said and did, in the sense that it was something that could reasonably have been foreseen as the consequence of what he was saying or doing?': *per* Stephenson LJ.

(b) The offence is 'arrestable' (*see* the Police and Criminal Evidence Act 1984, s. 24, at 1:27) and is triable either way (*see* the Magistrates' Courts Act 1980, Sch. 1).

13. 'Bodily harm'

This phrase refers to hurt or injury calculated to interfere with a person's health or comfort. In *R. v. Miller* (1954) it was held to include a hysterical and nervous condition resulting from the actions of the accused person, as where he repeatedly threw his wife to the floor. Where there is evidence that an assault has caused psychiatric injury, the jury is to be directed that such an injury was capable of amounting to 'actual bodily harm': *R v. Chan-Fook* (1993).

(a) Note *R. v. Reigate Justices ex p. Counsell* (1984) – if the victim of an assault consequently suffers much pain immediately, and thereafter suffers tenderness and soreness, this is sufficient for the inference of 'actual bodily harm', even if there is no physically discernible injury.

(b) In *R. v. Wilson* (1983), the House of Lords held that when a person is charged with inflicting grievous bodily harm under s. 20 of the 1861 Act, or under s. 9(1)(*b*) of the Theft Act 1968 (*see* 16:9), it is open to the jury to find him guilty of the alternative offence of occasioning actual bodily harm contrary to s. 47. See *R. v. Savage* (1992) at **19** below.

(c) Neither foresight nor foreseeability of consequences of an act is necessary to establish the requisite *mens rea*.

Wounding with intent and malicious wounding

14. The essence of the offences
Under the Offences against the Person Act 1861, ss. 18 and 20, the following offences were created:

(a) 'Whosoever shall unlawfully and maliciously by any means whatsoever wound or cause any grievous bodily harm to any person, . . . with intent . . . to do some grievous bodily harm to any person, or with intent to resist or prevent the lawful apprehension or detainer of any person . . . shall be liable to imprisonment . . .': s. 18. This offence is commonly known as 'wounding with intent'. It is a crime of *specific intent* (*see* 3:**12**), i.e. proof that the accused was malicious *and* that there was an intent to do grievous bodily harm is required. *see R. v. Belfon* (1976); *R. v. Pearman* (1985); *R. v. Morrison* (1989).

(b) 'Whosoever shall unlawfully and maliciously wound or inflict any grievous bodily harm upon any other person, either with or without any weapon or instrument, . . . shall be liable . . . to imprisonment . . .': s. 20. This offence is commonly known as 'unlawful' or 'malicious' wounding. The essence of the appropriate *mens rea* rests in the term 'malicious'; it must be shown that the accused acted maliciously. *See R. v. Aitken* (1992).

(c) *See A. -G.'s Ref. (No.23 of 1990).*

15. 'Maliciously'
The meaning of the term was considered in *R. v. Cunningham* (1957). *See* 3:**15**.

(a) *The facts*. X was charged with larceny and with unlawfully and maliciously causing Y to take coal gas, thereby endangering her life, contrary to the Offences against the Person Act 1861, s. 23 (*see* **39**). X had torn a gas meter from a wall and stolen its contents. As a result, gas escaped into the adjoining house in which Y was sleeping, causing her bodily harm. X was convicted.

(b) *On appeal. X appealed successfully* on the ground that the jury had been misdirected concerning the meaning of the term 'maliciously'. The following principle was accepted as embodying an accurate statement of the law: 'In any statutory definition of a crime, "malice" must be taken *not* in the old vague sense of "wickedness" in general, but as requiring either (1) *an actual intention* to do the particular *kind* of harm that was done; or (2) *recklessness* as to whether such harm would occur or not (i.e. the accused has *foreseen* that the particular kind of harm might be done and yet has gone on to take the risk of it). It is neither limited to, nor does it indeed require, any ill will towards the person injured' (Kenny).

16. 'Wound'

The term is used in a very special sense and refers to *a break in the continuity of the whole skin*; a scratch or burn is not, therefore, necessarily a wound. It does not suffice that the outer skin alone be broken. In *R.* v. *Wood* (1830), X assaulted Y violently so that Y's collar-bone was broken. It was held to be no wounding, since Y's skin had not been breached. *See C.* v. *Eisenhower* (1984) – broken blood vessels in the eye did not constitute wounding within s. 20.

17. 'Grievous bodily harm'

This phrase means 'any really serious' bodily harm: *see DPP* v. *Smith* (1961) (*see* **9:19**); *R.* v. *Metharam* (1961). (For the relationship of 'assault occasioning actual bodily harm' and 'common assault' to 'grievous bodily harm' *see R.* v. *Salisbury* (1983).) In *R.* v. *Miller* (1954), 'bodily harm' was held to include a nervous or hysterical condition. (*See* also *R.* v. *Dawson* (1985) at **10:9**.) Note that in *R.* v. *Saunders* (1985), the Court of Appeal doubted whether there was any difference between 'serious' and 'really serious' injury. Note *R.* v. *Grundy* (1989), in which the Court of Appeal held that a jury should look at *all* the injuries together in order to decide whether they amounted to grievous bodily harm; *R.* v. *Lloyd* (1989). *See A.-G.'s Reference (No. 11 of 1992)*.

18. 'Inflict' (s. 20)

The injury which is held to constitute an assault under s. 20 (*see* **14**(*b*)) need not necessarily be inflicted directly. (Note that s. 18 refers to 'causing' grievous bodily harm, not 'inflicting'.) Releasing a (fierce) dog against the victim may be enough: *see R.* v. *Dume* (1986).

(a) In *R.* v. *Martin* (1881), X was convicted of inflicting grievous bodily harm, contrary to s. 20. He had turned off the lights in a theatre before the end of the performance and had barred the exit to a doorway. In the ensuing panic some members of the audience were injured. X's conviction was affirmed. *Per* Lord Coleridge CJ: 'The prisoner must be taken to have intended the natural consequences of that which he did. He acted "unlawfully and maliciously", not that he had any personal malice against the particular individuals injured, but in the sense of doing an unlawful act calculated to injure, and by which others were in fact injured.'

(b) In *R.* v. *Halliday* (1889), it was held that grievous bodily harm had been inflicted where X had so frightened Y that Y had jumped from a window and sustained injuries. 'If a man creates in another man's mind an immediate sense of danger which causes such a person to try to escape, and in so doing he injures himself, the person who creates such a state of mind is responsible for the injuries which result': *per* Lord Coleridge CJ.

(c) 'In the absence of any evidence that the accused did not realise that it was a possible consequence of his act that some physical harm might be caused to the victim, the prosecution must satisfy the relevant onus by proving the commission by the accused of an act which any ordinary person would realise was likely to have that consequence. There is no issue here to which the jury need direct their minds and there is no need to give to them any specific directions about it. In such a case, and these are the commonest of cases under s. 18, the real issues of fact on which the jury have to make up their minds are: (*i*) Are they satisfied that the accused did the act? (*ii*) If so, are they satisfied that the act caused a wound or other serious physical injury? (*iii*) If the defence of self-defence is raised or there is any evidence to support it, do they think that accused may have done the act in self-defence? (*iv*) If the answer to (*i*) and (*ii*) is *Yes* and to (*iii*), if raised, is *No*, are they satisfied that when he did the act he intended to cause a wound or other really serious physical injury? If (*iii*), (if raised), is answered *No* and (*i*) and (*ii*) are answered *Yes*, the lesser offence under s. 20 is made out; and if (*iv*) is also answered *Yes*, the graver offence under s. 18 is made out': *per* Diplock LJ in *R.* v. *Mowatt* (1968). (Note *R.* v. *Stubbs* (1989) – where drunkenness is pleaded it should be 'very extreme' before it justified a reduction of a s. 18 charge to a s. 20.)

(d) *See* also *R.* v. *Clarence* (1888) (*see* **9**(*c*)); *R.* v. *Sullivan* (1981) (judge's direction that an intention to frighten the victim and resultant injury sufficed to establish an offence under s. 20 was *incorrect*, since it had to be shown that the defendant *was aware* that the *probable consequences* of his voluntary act would be to cause injury to the victim).

19. The role of foreseeability and intent in assault offences: a reconsideration by the House of Lords.

In *R.* v. *Savage* and *R.* v. *Parmenter* (1992), the House of Lords considered appeals, in two unconnected cases, from the Court of Appeal. The following matters emerged.

(a) In order to establish an offence of wounding or causing grievous bodily harm under s. 20, it was necessary to prove that defendant actually foresaw that his unlawful act would cause some physical harm to the victim. It was not enough to show that defendant *ought* to have foreseen some harm.

(b) It was not necessary for defendant actually to foresee the gravity of harm that would be caused by his act, provided that he foresaw some physical harm, even if of a minor degree. *See R. v. Rushworth* (1992).

(c) In order to establish an offence of assault occasioning actual bodily harm, contrary to s. 47, it was sufficient for the prosecution to prove that defendant committed an assault and that actual bodily harm resulted from that assault. It was not necessary for the prosecution to show that defendant *intended* to cause some actual bodily harm.

(d) A verdict of guilty of assault occasioning actual bodily harm under s. 47 was a permissible alternative verdict to a count alleging unlawful wounding contrary to s. 20.

> NOTE: The Criminal Justice Act 1988, s. 134(1), created the offence of *torture*, which is committed where a public official or person acting in a public capacity, intentionally inflicts severe pain or suffering on another person in the performance or purported performance of his official duties. It is immaterial whether the pain or suffering be physical or mental or whether it be caused by an act or omission: s. 134(3). For the specific defence of 'lawful authority, justification or excuse for that conduct', *see* s. 134(4).

Assaults on the police

20. Assault on a constable

By the Police Act 1964, s. 51(1), it is an offence for any person to assault a constable in the execution of his duty or a person assisting a constable in the execution of his duty. *See* e.g. *Riley* v. *DPP* (1989) – it is essential that the constable's actions be *lawful*. The offence is triable summarily only.

(a) The *mens rea* required is an intention to assault (used in its broad sense). Knowledge that the person assaulted is a constable or acting in the course of his duty is not necessary: *see R. v. Forbes and Webb* (1865).

(b) The term 'constable' includes a prison officer: *see* the Prison Act 1952, s. 8. *See also* the Prison Security Act 1992.

> NOTE: For the offence of assaulting an officer of the court while in the execution of his duty, *see* County Courts Act 1984, s. 14; *Blackburn* v.

Bowering (1993) (defence of honest factual mistake as to identity of court officer).

21. 'Acting in the execution of his duty'

The problem of deciding exactly *when* a constable is acting in the execution of his duty was discussed in R. v. *Prebble* (1858), in which a constable was requested by a publican to turn certain persons out of licensed premises. The constable was assaulted by one of those persons. It was held that he was not acting in the execution of his duty. 'It would have been otherwise had there been a nuisance or disturbance of the public peace, or any danger of a breach of the peace': *per* Bramwell B. *See Sanders* v. *DPP* (1988); *Plowden* v. *DPP* (1991).

(a) In *McArdle* v. *Wallace* (1964), a constable had entered a café to enquire about stolen property. He was assaulted after being told to leave and refusing to do so (at which point he became a trespasser). At the time of the assault, therefore, he was not acting in the execution of his duty. *See Jones and Jones* v. *Lloyd* (1981).

(b) In R. v. *Waterfield* (1964), the Court of Criminal Appeal stated: 'It would be difficult . . . to reduce within specific limits the general terms in which the duties of police constables have been expressed. In most cases it is probably more convenient to consider what the police constable was actually doing and in particular whether such conduct was *prima facie* an unlawful interference with a person's liberty or property.' *See also Weight* v. *Long* (1986) – provided that a police officer's intention in attempting to speak to a person was in the pursuit of the preservation of peace or the prevention of crime, he was acting in the execution of his duty.

(c) Because a police constable has, generally, no power to detain for questioning, it is no assault to use reasonable force to attempt to escape from such detention: *see Kenlin* v. *Gardiner* (1967). In *Donnelly* v. *Jackman* (1970), Y, a constable, put his hand on X's shoulder, intending to stop and question him about an offence. X struck Y and was convicted under s. 51. His appeal was dismissed; it was held that such a trivial interference with X's liberty by Y did not constitute conduct placing Y outside the execution of his duty.

(d) In R. v. *Fennell* (1971), X struck Y, a constable, after Y had refused to release X's son, arrested after a street fight. X, in defence, stated that he believed the arrest of his son was unlawful, but it was held, on appeal, that such a belief provided *no defence*. *See* also R. v. *Ball* (1989), in which the Court of Appeal held that honest belief on reasonable grounds in the unlawfulness of arrest by the police, or that they were using excessive force in effecting a lawful arrest did *not* constitute a defence to assault.

22. Obstruction of the police

It is an offence under the Police Act 1964, s. 51(3), for any person to resist or wilfully obstruct a constable in the execution of his duty, or a person assisting a constable in the execution of his duty. 'Obstruct' has been interpreted to include 'making it more difficult for the police to carry out their duties': *per* Lord Goddard in *Hinchcliffe* v. *Sheldon* (1955) (*see* **26:13(c)**). 'Obstruction' in s. 51(3) does not necessarily involve a 'physical act' (as does 'resisting'); it may include warning someone so that he may postpone commission of a crime: *Moore* v. *Greene* (1983). A mere refusal to answer a question from the police is not, as such, an 'obstruction': *Rice* v. *Connolly* (1966). *See Lewis* v. *Cox* (1984) – X wilfully obstructs a police constable in the execution of his duty within s. 51(3) if he deliberately does an act which, although not necessarily aimed at or hostile to the police, in fact made it more difficult for him to carry out his duty, and X knew that his conduct would have that effect; *see* also *Bennett* v. *Bale* (1986).

In *Ingleton* v. *Dibble* (1972), it was held that where the alleged obstruction consists of a refusal to act it must be shown that the law imposes an obligation to act in accordance with a request of the constable. But where the alleged obstruction consists of a positive act it suffices that it is deliberate, and it need not be shown to be unlawful independently of the law concerning obstruction.

False Imprisonment

23. Essence of the offence

False imprisonment is a common law offence (and a tort). It is committed where X, intentionally or recklessly (in the *Cunningham* sense), and without lawful reason or excuse, *inflicts bodily restraint* on Y. Where, therefore, X unlawfully and forcibly detains Y anywhere, for any period of time, no matter how short, the offence has been committed, *see R.* v. *Smith* (1990). Note, however, that although every arrest involves a deprivation of liberty, not every deprivation of liberty will amount to an arrest: *R.* v. *Brown* (1977). *See R.* v. *Hutchins* (1988) – false imprisonment and kidnapping can be committed either intentionally or recklessly as to the victim's consent. The offence is triable only on indictment.

24. Bodily restraint

Restraint must be complete, i.e. Y's motion must be restrained in every direction so that it involves a total deprivation of liberty. There is no false imprisonment, therefore, where Y is left free to move away in certain directions: *see Bird* v. *Jones* (1845). This would not be so, however, if Y could move away only by taking actions which involve an unreasonable risk.

(a) It is not necessarily relevant that Y is unaware of his imprisonment. 'It appears to me that a person could be imprisoned without his knowing it. I think a person can be imprisoned while he is asleep, while he is in a state of drunkenness, while he is unconscious, and while he is a lunatic . . . though the imprisonment began and ceased while he was in that state': *per* Atkin LJ in *Meering* v. *Grahame-White Aviation Co.* (1919).

(b) It is not necessary to show assault to prove bodily restraint. In *R.* v. *Linsberg* (1905) it was held that an accoucheur had been falsely imprisoned by the accused, who had locked him in a room so as to prevent him leaving his patient. A person may, nevertheless, be falsely imprisoned even though he submits to the restraint without being touched.

(c) The restraint constituting false imprisonment may be effected through an innocent agent. If, therefore, Z, a police officer, arrests Y at the direction or request of X, there is an imprisonment by X. There is no imprisonment by X if he gives information to a police officer, Z, who then, *on his own initiative*, arrests Y; nor if X makes a charge against Y to a magistrate, who then issues a warrant for Y's arrest. *See Davidson* v. *Chief Constable of N. Wales Police* (1993) (liability for arrest).

25. 'False', i.e. 'unlawful', imprisonment

There will be *no* false imprisonment of Y, for example:

(a) where X, a constable, arrests Y under a valid warrant; *or*

(b) where X, a constable (or another person), arrests Y without a warrant under the Police and Criminal Evidence Act 1984, s. 24. *See Ward* v. *Chief Constable of Avon* (1986).

> NOTE: (1) The prosecution need prove only imprisonment by the accused, X; X must then show that it was justified. (2) Where a private person makes an arrest, he must take the arrested person before a magistrate or to a police station as soon as he reasonably can: *John Lewis & Co.* v. *Tims* (1952). (3) For limitations on police detention, *see* the Police and Criminal Evidence Act 1984, Part IV.

Kidnapping and child abduction

26. Essence of kidnapping under common law

'The stealing and carrying away, or secreting of some person, sometimes called kidnapping, which is an offence at common law': East (cited and approved in *R.* v. *Reid* (1973)).

(a) The offence may be committed in relation to a person *of any age* who is stolen and carried away against his will, or, if the person is a minor, against the will of his lawful guardian or friends.

(b) The use of force or fraud is an essential element of the offence: *see R. v. Hale* (1974).

(c) The offence is established if there is a carrying away of the victim even for a relatively short distance and time, and not necessarily to the kidnapper's destination: *R. v. Wellard* (1978). *See* e.g. *R. v. Brown* (1985), in which Y, forced into a car by X and driven away, escaped after twenty minutes; X's conviction for kidnapping was upheld.

(d) Self-help, which took the form of kidnapping, as an impatient response to dissatisfaction with the progress of a police investigation is inexcusable: *R. v. Chapman and Bond* (1993).

27. Elements of the common law offence

The House of Lords set out, in *R. v. D.* (1984), the elements of the common law offence of kidnapping.

(a) 'The taking or carrying away of one person by another'.

(b) 'By force or by fraud'.

(c) 'Without the consent of the person so taken or carried away'. Absence of consent is a necessary inference from the age of the child. 'I should not expect a jury to find at all frequently that a child under fourteen had sufficient understanding and intelligence to give its consent': *per* Lord Brandon.

(d) 'Without lawful excuse'. Note that *R. v. D.* established explicitly that a father could not plead his so-called 'rights as a father' so as to remove his child.

> NOTE: In *R. v. Henman* (1987), X's appeal against conviction for attempted kidnapping was dismissed by the Court of Appeal. X claimed to have attempted to take by force a friend, Y, whom he believed to be in moral danger from a religious sect she had joined. The Court held that X had no lawful excuse; the law recognised no necessity for his act in the circumstances.

28. Child Abduction Act 1984

The 1984 Act created the offence of *child abduction*, which is committed under s. 1 by 'a person connected with a child under the age of sixteen' who takes or sends the child out of the United Kingdom 'without the appropriate consent'. (Separate offences are created for England and Wales and for Scotland: *see* ss. 6–10.) 'A person connected with a child' includes its parent or guardian or one who has custody of the child under a custody order, or in the case of an illegitimate child, the person reasonably believed to be its father: s. 1(2). 'Custody' includes legal custody and care and control: s. 1(7)(*b*). *See R. v. C.* (1990).

Firearms, offensive weapons, etc.

29. General nature of the Acts

It is an offence: to produce, acquire or possess, firearms or ammunition without a certificate (Firearms Act 1968, s. 1); to manufacture, sell or transfer firearms, unless under certificate of registration as a firearms dealer (s. 3); to sell firearms, save under certain restricted circumstances, to young persons (s. 22); to sell firearms to persons who are prohibited from possessing them, e.g. certain ex-prisoners (s. 21). *See R. v. Harrington* (1984). *See* the Firearms (Amendment) Act 1992 (period of grant of certificate); European Weapons Directive (SI 1992/2823).

> NOTE: A person may be 'in possession' of firearms within the meaning of the 1968 Act, even though they are not actually in his physical custody, if they are under his control: *see Sullivan* v. *Earl of Caithness* (1976). *See* also *R.* v. *Howells* (1977); *Hall* v. *Cotton* (1987). In relation to the offence under s. 1, the fact that the accused did not know the nature of the article in his possession is immaterial: *R.* v. *Hussain* (1981).

30. Manufacturing, selling or possessing prohibited weapons

It is an offence to manufacture, sell or possess a prohibited weapon, without official consent. Such a weapon is an automatic gun (e.g. a machine pistol) or one designed to discharge gas: *see* the 1968 Act, s. 5(1). *See R.* v. *Pannell* (1982) (possession of component parts of three stripped-down weapons held to be an offence under the 1968 Act). When a weapon is a prohibited weapon within s. 5, it remains so even though an essential component may be missing: *R.* v. *Clarke* (1986). *See R.* v. *Formosa* (1991); *Brown* v. *DPP* (1992).

31. Carrying firearms and trespassing with them
Under the 1968 Act:

(a) It is an offence for a person to have with him a firearm or imitation with intent to commit an indictable offence, or to resist arrest or prevent another's arrest while in possession of that firearm: *see* s. 18. Mere possession with ultimate control is insufficient for the section: *R.* v. *Kelt* (1977).
(b) It is an offence to have in a public place without authority or reasonable excuse a loaded shot gun or loaded air weapon or other firearm together with ammunition: s. 19. 'Ammunition' was construed as consisting of 'a combination of components which when used with a compatible firearm could produce an explosive effect': *per* Taylor LJ in *R.* v. *Stubbings* (1990).
(c) It is an offence to enter a building or land as a trespasser while carrying a firearm: *see* s. 20.

32. Possessing firearms with intent

By s. 16 it is an offence for a person to have in his possession firearms or ammunition with intent to endanger life. 'Firearm' includes any component part of a lethal or prohibited weapon or any accessory to such a weapon. On a charge under this section of possessing a firearm with intent to endanger life, it is sufficient to show possession of the firearm with a view to using it if and when the occasion might arise. In *R. v. Bentham and Baillie* (1973), the accused were convicted of possession of firearms with intent to endanger life, under the 1968 Act. They contended, on appeal, that the prosecution had to show a present and unconditional intention to endanger life. The appeals were dismissed. It was held that the section was concerned with the possession of a firearm ready for use if and when an occasion arose in a manner which would endanger life.

33. Using firearms or imitations in resisting arrest

By s. 17(1) it is an offence for a person to make or attempt to make any use of a firearm or imitation firearm to resist or prevent the lawful arrest of that or any other person. 'Firearm' is defined by s. 57 as a lethal barrelled weapon or any prohibited weapon. See *R. v. Thorpe* (1987) – a 'lethal weapon' was held to be one which was capable of causing an injury from which deaths might result; *Grace v. DPP* (1989). 'Imitation' is defined as 'any thing which has the appearance of being a firearm'.

By s. 17(2) it is an offence for a person, at the time of his committing, or being arrested for, an offence specified in Schedule I to the Act, to have in his possession a firearm or imitation firearm, other than for a lawful object.

34. The Firearms Act 1982

Under this Act the provisions of the 1968 Act generally apply to imitation firearms which are readily convertible into firearms. Section 1(6)(*a*)(*b*) defines such firearms as being those which can be so converted without any special skill on the part of the person converting them in the construction or adaptation of firearms of any description, and the work involved in converting does not require equipment or tools other than such as are in common use by persons carrying out works of construction and maintenance in their own homes.

35. Firearms (Amendment) Act 1988

Under this Act, which extends the class of prohibited weapons and ammunition (which require a firearms certificate in relation to their possession, purchase, acquisition, manufacture, sale or transfer), the 1968 Act is amended so as to include specified types of weapon, e.g. burst-firing, self-loading, pump action, guns: 1988 Act, s. 1(1).

36. Prevention of Crime Act 1953

Any person who without lawful authority or reasonable excuse has with him in any public place any offensive weapon is guilty of an offence: *see* s. 1(1).

(a) *'Has with him'*. Possession, once established, continues until defendant does something to end it. Merely forgetting is not enough to end possession; nor does it constitute a reasonable excuse under s. 1(1): *R. v. McCalla* (1988).

(b) An *'offensive weapon'* is 'any article made or adapted for use for causing injury to the person, or intended by the person having it with him for such use by him or by some other person': s. 1(4) as amended. Such weapons may include: articles made for the purpose of causing an injury, e.g. a dagger; articles adapted for that purpose, e.g. a belt studded with rivets; articles neither adapted nor made, but carried by the accused for that purpose, e.g. a bicycle chain, flick-knife. *See Gibson* v. *Wales* (1983); *R. v. Simpson* (1983); *R. v. Fleming* (1989)–s. 1(4) should be so construed as to necessitate intention to cause injury *to another*, so that an intention to harm oneself is insufficient.

(c) *'Lawful authority or reasonable excuse'*. The reference to 'lawful authority' is a reference to 'those people who from time to time carry an offensive weapon as a matter of duty, such as the soldier and his rifle, the police officer and his truncheon': *Bryan* v. *Mott* (1975). *See Evans* v. *Wright* (1964), in which a defence of carrying a truncheon to guard against possible robbery of wages collected for employees was rejected; *Evans* v. *Hughes* (1972), in which it was held that a weapon carried for self-defence may still be an 'offensive weapon', and for the defence of reasonable excuse to succeed there must be at least some imminent threat to the accused, affecting the circumstances in which the weapon was carried. (In *Ohlson* v. *Hylton* (1975) it was stated that the prosecution has to show that the accused 'was carrying or was otherwise equipped with the weapon and had the intention to use it offensively before any occasion for its actual use had arisen.') *See* also *Malnick* v. *DPP* (1989) (individuals may not arm themselves to repel violence which they have deliberately brought about).

(d) ' *"Public place"* includes any highway and any other premises or place to which at the material time the public are permitted to have access whether on payment or otherwise': s. 1(4).

(e) If a weapon is offensive *per se*, the burden is on *the accused* to show he had lawful excuse for possession; but if it is not offensive, *per se*, the burden is on *the prosecution* to prove that the accused had the article in his possession for an offensive purpose: *per* Griffiths LJ in *Gibson* v. *Wales* (1983).

37. Criminal Justice Act 1988

Under s. 139(1) it is an offence to have in a public place an article with a blade or which is sharply pointed (except a folding pocket knife, the cutting blade of which does not exceed three inches). *See Harris* v. *DPP* (1993)(a lock-knife is not a 'folding pocket knife'). It is a defence to show good reason or lawful authority (s. 139(4)) or that the person charged had the article with him for use at work, for religious reasons or as part of a national costume (s. 139(5)). It is an offence to possess, sell, hire, lend, give or import a weapon proscribed by order of the Secretary of State and not covered by other statutes: s. 141. (For specification of weapons to which s. 141 applies, *see* Criminal Justice Act 1988 (Offensive Weapons) Order 1988 (No. 2019). The weapons include knuckledusters, push daggers, swordsticks, death stars.) *See Godwin* v *DPP* (1993) (defence of 'good reason'); *DPP* v *Gregson* (1993).

38. Public Order Act 1986

See the various provisions of the Public Order Act 1986 (Chap. 24) in relation to violence and disorder. Note also the Police and Criminal Evidence Act 1984, s. 17(1)(*c*), as amended.

The administering of poisons

39. Offences against the Person Act 1861, s. 23

By this section it is an offence to unlawfully and maliciously administer to, or cause to be administered to or taken by, any person, any poison or other destructive or noxious things so as to endanger life or inflict grievous bodily harm. The offence is triable only on indictment. The appropriate *mens rea* necessitates acting maliciously.

(a) Where X left poison for Y, who later took it up and consumed it, X was held to have 'administered' it: *see R.* v. *Harley* (1830). *See* also *R.* v. *Weatherall* (1968).

(b) In *R.* v. *Cato* (1976) X injected Y with heroin and Y died as a result of respiratory failure due to intoxication from drugs. X's conviction of manslaughter and of administering a noxious thing was upheld by the Court of Appeal. The use of heroin was potentially harmful and was, therefore, a noxious thing for purposes of s. 23. Consent by Y to its injection was no defence.

(c) 'If an article is liable to injure in common use, not when an overdose in the sense of an accidental excess is used but is liable to cause injury in common use, should it not then be regarded as a noxious thing for present purposes?': *per* Lord Widgery CJ.

40. Offences against the Person Act 1861, s. 24

By this section it is an offence unlawfully and maliciously to administer poison, a noxious thing, etc., with intent to injure, aggrieve or annoy. *See R. v. Wood* (1975). For a consideration of 'administer', *see R. v. Dones* (1987); *R. v. Gillard* (1988), in which the Court of Appeal held that the word included conduct which brought the noxious thing into contact with the victim's body although not applying direct physical force to the victim (e.g. spraying with a noxious fluid). For purposes of s. 24, the concept of 'noxious thing' involves not only the quality or nature of the substances, but also the quantity administered or sought to be administered: *R. v. Marcus* (1981) (sleeping tablets in bottle of milk). Note that the appropriate *mens rea* necessitates acting maliciously *and* having an intent to injure, etc. (For sentencing principles, *see R. v. Jones* (1990).)

(a) In *R. v. Hill* (1986), the House of Lords considered a case in which X had been charged and convicted under s. 24, having unlawfully administered tablets of tenuate despan to two boys, presumably with the motive of keeping them awake and rendering them susceptible to homosexual advances. The jury had been directed that they should convict *only* if they were sure that X intended to injure the boys in the sense of causing them physical harm by the administration of the drugs.
(b) The Court of Appeal allowed X's appeal against conviction, holding that the trial judge had erred in his direction that an intention on X's part to keep the boys awake sufficed to constitute an intention to injure.
(c) The House of Lords *restored X's conviction*. The only issue for the jury to determine was whether X administered the drugs with intent to injure. The only reasonable inference to draw from X's conduct was an intention that the drugs should injure the boys in the sense of overstimulation of their metabolism. The jury had been directed correctly.

Draft Criminal Code Bill

41. Assault

'A person is guilty of assault if he intentionally or recklessly –

(a) applies force to or causes an impact on the body of another; or
(b) causes another to believe that any such force or impact is imminent, without the consent of the other or, where the act is likely or intended to cause personal harm, with or without his consent': cl. 75.

42. Intentional serious personal harm

'(1)A person is guilty of an offence if he intentionally causes serious personal harm to another. (2) A person may be guilty of an offence under subsec. (1) if either – (*a*) the act causing serious personal harm is done; or (*b*) the serious personal harm occurs, within the ordinary limits of criminal jurisdiction': cl. 70.

43. Reckless serious personal harm
'A person is guilty of an offence if he recklessly causes serious personal harm to another': cl. 71.

44. Intentional or reckless personal harm
'A person is guilty of an offence if he intentionally or recklessly causes personal harm to another': cl. 72.

45. Unlawful detention
'A person is guilty of unlawful detention if he intentionally or recklessly takes or detains another without that other's consent': cl. 80.

46. Kidnapping
'A person is guilty of kidnapping if he intentionally or recklessly takes or detains another without that other's consent, intending (*a*) to hold him to ransom or as a hostage; or (*b*) to send him out of the UK; or (*c*) to commit an arrestable offence': cl. 82.

Progress test 12

1. Can words ever constitute an assault? **(3)**

2. Outline the *mens rea* of assault. **(4)**

3. What is the *actus reus* of battery? **(6)**

4. 'A person's consent to an act likely to result in serious injury to him is no defence.' Comment. **(9)**

5. Outline the Offences against the Person Act 1861, s. 47. **(12)**

6. Outline the Offences against the Person Act 1861, ss. 18, 20. **(14)**

7. Outline the Police Act 1964, s. 54(1). **(20)**

8. What is the essence of false imprisonment? **(23)**

9. Outline the Prevention of Crime Act 1953, s. 1(1). **(36)**

10. Comment on the Offences against the Person Act 1861, s. 23. **(39)**

13

Sexual offences

General matters

1. Sexual morality and the law

The close historical relationship between acceptable concepts of morality, based largely on church doctrine, and the law, was noted in **1:20**. The bending of the law to the moral winds of the time, which partially reflects changes in public attitudes towards aspects of private behaviour, is clearly evident in that part of the criminal law dealing with sexual offences. Adultery is no crime; prostitution is, in itself, not a crime, although (*see* **28–32**) certain related activities constitute offences; certain types of homosexual conduct (*see* **24**) no longer invariably constitute offences. 'What is striking in one age is normal in another; the perversions of yesterday may be the routine or the fashion of tomorrow': *per* Lord Wilberforce in *DPP* v. *Boardman* (1975).

Most of the offences dealt with here are covered by the Sexual Offences Act 1956, a consolidating statute.

For a definition of 'sexual offence' with reference to the Criminal Justice Act 1991, *see* s. 31(1); *R.* v. *Robinson* (1993).

2. Offences covered

The following offences are discussed in this chapter:

(a) rape (*see* **3–9**);
(b) incest (*see* **10–12**);
(c) other offences involving unlawful sexual intercourse (*see* **13–16**);
(d) indecent assault and indecency with children (*see* **17–21**);
(e) buggery, etc (*see* **22–25**);
(f) indecent exposure (*see* **26–27**);
(g) offences involving prostitution (*see* **28–32**);
(h) abduction (*see* **33–35**).

Rape

3. *Actus reus*

By the Sexual Offences Act 1956, s. 1(1): 'It is an offence for a man to rape a woman.' The offence was defined in common law as *unlawful sexual intercourse with a woman without her consent by force, fear or fraud*. By the Sexual Offences (Amendment) Act 1976 'a man commits rape if (*a*) he has unlawful sexual intercourse with a woman who at the time of the intercourse does not consent to it; and (*b*) at that time he knows that she does not consent to the intercourse or he is reckless as to whether she consents to it': s. 1(1). Rape is an offence of *basic intent* (*see* 3:**13**). Note that *Caldwell*-type recklessness (*see* 3:**16**) does *not* apply to rape: *see R. v. Satnam and Kewal* (1984) at **7** below.

Rape is a 'serious arrestable offence' under the Police and Criminal Evidence Act 1984, Sch. 5; it is triable only on indictment. For principles of sentencing *see R. v. Billam* (1986); *A.-G's References (Nos. 1 and 15 of 1991, No. 35 of 1992)* (undue leniency in sentences for rape and attempted rape); *A.-G's Reference (No. 25 of 1990)* (rape with grave aggravating features).

4. Mens rea

The appropriate *mens rea* is derived from an intention by a male (aged 14 or over) to have sexual intercourse with a female, *either* knowing that she does not consent to that act, *or* being reckless as to whether she consents or not. *See R. v. Breckenridge* (1984) – a defendant should be found guilty if his attitude to consent was that he 'could not care less'. (For a rejection of self-induced intoxication as a defence to a charge of rape, *see R. v. Fotheringham* (1989).)

(a) In *R. v. Khan and Others* (1990), the Court of Appeal examined *intent in attempted rape*. The trial judge had informed the jury that the principles relevant to consent in rape (*see* **6** below) applied in exactly the same way to attempted rape. The Court considered a submission that this amounted to a material misdirection, because, it was argued, recklessness as a state of mind (*see* **3** above) on the part of the offender had no place in the offence of attempted rape.

(b) The Court of Appeal *upheld* the judge's direction. The only difference between the two offences was that in rape intercourse took place, whereas in attempted rape it did not, although there had to be some act which was *more than preparatory* to intercourse. Considered in that way, the intent of defendant was precisely the same in rape and in attempted rape and the *mens rea* was identical, namely an intention to have intercourse *plus* a knowledge of or recklessness as to the woman's absence of consent.

(c) The Court considered that the words 'with intent to commit an offence' in the Criminal Attempts Act 1981, s. 1 (*see* 8:**6, 7**), mean, when applied to rape, 'with intent to have sexual intercourse with a woman in circumstances where she does not consent and defendant knows or could not care less about her absence of consent'. The attempt does not require any different intention on the part of defendant from that for the full offence of rape.

(d) On a charge of attempted rape it is *not* incumbent on the prosecution, as a matter of law, to prove that the defendant, with the requisite intent, had physically attempted penetration. It sufficed that there was evidence from which the intent could be inferred and there were proved acts which a jury could properly infer were more than merely preparatory to the commission of the offence (see the 1981 Act, s. 1 (1)): *A.-G.'s Reference (No. 1 of 1992)*.

5. 'Sexual intercourse'

'Where on the trial of any offence under this Act, it is necessary to prove sexual intercourse (whether natural or unnatural), it shall not be necessary to prove the completion of the intercourse by the emission of seed, but the intercourse shall be deemed complete upon proof of penetration only': 1956 Act, s. 44.

(a) The slightest degree of penetration will suffice for s. 44. If no penetration is proved, the accused person may be charged with attempt.

(b) There is no need to prove that the hymen was ruptured: *see R. v. Russen* (1777).

(c) Note *Kaitamaki v. R.* (1985). The Privy Council advised, concerning the nature of sexual intercourse for purposes of rape under New Zealand law, that intercourse is a continuing act which ends only with withdrawal, so that, under New Zealand law, a man is guilty of rape if he continues intercourse *after* he realises that the woman is no longer consenting, *even though she consented to the penetration*. (But note the dissenting judgment of Woodhouse J, in the New Zealand Court of Appeal: '. . . the crime has always been concerned with the criminal invasion of a woman's body by a male; and for my part I cannot understand how any woman could reasonably complain that she had been violated in the gross sense of being raped if she had agreed that her partner could enter her.')

6. 'Without her consent'

Consent of the woman is a complete defence. 'In every charge of rape the fact of non-consent must be proved to the satisfaction of the jury': *per* Humphreys J in *R. v. Harling* (1938). Absence of consent must be proved by the prosecution.

(a) Consent given as the result of a fundamental error induced by the fraud of the accused person is no real consent. 'A man who induces a woman to have sexual intercourse with him by impersonating her husband commits rape': Sexual Offences Act 1956, s. 1(2).

(b) Consent given following the woman's being deceived as to the nature of the transaction, as the result of the fraud of the accused person, is no real consent: *see R. v. Williams* (1923).

(c) Consent obtained by force or fear is no true consent. *See R. v. Camplin* (1845), in which a woman was ravished while in a state of complete intoxication, and this was held to be rape; *R. v. Jones* (1861), in which a woman submitted because of her fear of bodily injury or death, and this was held to be rape. *See* also *R. v. Lang* (1975) (drink vitiating consent).

(d) It is rape to ravish a woman while she is asleep: *see R. v. Mayers* (1872).

(e) There is no true consent where the victim is too young to understand the nature of the act: *see R. v. Howard* (1965), in which the accused was convicted of the attempted rape of a six-year-old girl. (It was stated that, in the case of a girl under sixteen, the prosecution, in order to prove rape, must prove *either* that the girl resisted physically, *or*, if she did not, that her understanding and knowledge were such that she was not in a position to decide to consent or resist.)

(f) In *DPP* v. *Morgan* (1976) (*see* 6:**5**), the House of Lords held that a defendant could not be convicted of rape if he believed, albeit mistakenly, that the complainant consented, *even though he had no reasonable ground for that belief.* Parliamentary and public concerns as to the implications of that decision were reflected in the passing of the Sexual Offences (Amendment) Act 1976 which declares: 'If at a trial for a rape offence the jury has to consider whether a man believed that a woman was consenting to sexual intercourse, the presence or absence of reasonable grounds for such a belief is a matter to which the jury is to have regard, in conjunction with any other relevant matters, in considering whether he so believed': s. 1(2). ('A "rape offence" means any of the following, namely, rape, attempted rape, aiding, abetting, counselling and procuring rape or attempted rape, incitement to rape, conspiracy to rape, and burglary with intent to rape': s. 7(2), as amended by Criminal Justice Act 1988, s. 158(6).) *See R.* v. *C.* (1992).

(g) Consent in rape was discussed in *R.* v. *Olugboja* (1982). The issue of consent should not be left to a jury without some further direction. They should be directed that 'consent' or the absence of it should be given its ordinary meaning; every consent involves a submission, but it by no means follows that a mere submission involves consent.

(h) The 1976 Act restricts evidence at trials for a rape offence. 'If at a trial any person is for the time being charged with a rape offence to which he pleads not guilty, then, except with the leave of the judge, no evidence and no question in cross-examination shall be addressed or asked at the trial, by or on behalf of any defendant at the trial, about any sexual experience of a complainant with a person other than that defendant': s. 2(1). *See R.* v. *Brown* (1989); *R.* v. *S.M.S.* (1992). There is also a general restriction on the publishing of matter likely to lead to the identification of complainants in rape offence cases: s. 4(1). Under the Criminal Justice

Act 1988, s. 158, the 1976 Act is amended so that the complainant is given anonymity from the time the complaint of rape is made. Anonymity for defendant charged with rape, given under the 1976 Act, s. 6, is *removed* under the 1988 Act, s. 158(5).

(i) The Sexual Offences (Amendment) Act 1992 extends to complainants of other sexual offences the statutory anonymity which applies to rape complainants under the Sexual Offences (Amendment) Act 1976.

(*i*) Section 1 gives anonymity to the alleged victim of any of the offences specified in s. 2.

(*ii*) The first level of protection (s. 1(1)) runs from the time an allegation is made. It prohibits publication or broadcasting of a complainant's name, address, picture, during that person's lifetime.

(*iii*) A second level of protection (s. 1(2)) commences at the time a person is accused of the offence. 'Accused' (*see* s. 6(3)) means that the person has appeared before a court charged with the offence, or an information is laid against him, or a bill of indictment is preferred. The publication or broadcast in England or Wales of any matter which might lead members of the public to identify a person as the complainant is prohibited throughout the complainant's lifetime.

(*iv*) A judge is empowered to displace s. 1, eg, to encourage witnesses to come forward: s. 3(1).

(*v*) There are special rules for cases of incest or buggery: *see* s. 4.

(j) For restriction of publicity in cases involving sexual misconduct heard by industrial tribunals, *see* Trade Union Reform and Employment Rights Act 1993, s. 40.

7. The plea of 'consent': a recent consideration

In *R.* v. *Satnam and Kewal* (1984), the appellants were accused of the rape of Y, aged thirteen, and with aiding and abetting each other to commit that rape. Their defence was that Y had consented. The judge, in considering the aspect of recklessness, referred to a risk 'obvious to an ordinary observer' that Y was not consenting. He gave no further consideration to the elements to be proved in 'reckless rape'. The accused were convicted and appealed on the grounds, *inter alia*, that the judge should have directed the jury that a genuine, albeit mistaken, belief that Y was consenting offered a defence to a charge of reckless rape, and that the direction as to recklessness was wrong.

(a) The Court of Appeal held that in the absence of a direction to the jury as to belief, they had been left without any guidance on the matter, so that the appeals would be allowed. Directions as to recklessness should be based on the 1976 Act, s. 1, and *DPP* v. *Morgan* (1976), without regard to *R.* v. *Caldwell* (1982) (*see* 3:16) or *R.* v. *Lawrence* (1982) which related to recklessness in a different context. On the matter of consent, the judge should direct the jury that the prosecution should prove *either* that the accused knew that Y did not want intercourse *or* was reckless as to whether she wanted it or not. Should the jury be unsure whether the accused knew that Y did not want intercourse, they should consider, next, reckless rape. If the accused might *genuinely* have believed that Y wanted intercourse, even though this was mistaken, the accused should not be found guilty. In considering whether the belief of the accused was genuine, they should take into account *all the circumstances* and ask whether the accused had *reasonable grounds* for that belief. If, after considering these circumstances, they were sure that the accused had no genuine belief that Y wanted intercourse, the accused should be found guilty. If they concluded that the accused 'could not have cared less' whether Y wanted intercourse or not, but that they continued 'regardless', then the accused would have been reckless and guilty of reckless rape.

(b) Note that where there are no possible grounds for 'mistaken belief', no general direction on that topic is required: *R. v. Taylor* (1985); *R. v. Haughian (1985).*

(c) Where consent is in issue on a charge of rape, the jury must be directed about the necessity of corroboration of the complainant's evidence: *see* e.g. *R. v. Birchall* (1986).

8. Rape by a husband upon a wife

In *R. v. R.* (1992), the House of Lords held that a husband *can* be guilty of raping his wife. Hale's proposition, stated in 1736, that a husband cannot be guilty of rape of his wife, 'for by their mutual matrimonial consent and contract the wife hath given herself up in this kind unto her husband which she cannot retract', was examined and found *unacceptable*. The status of women, and particularly married women, had changed out of all recognition since Hale's time. The supposed 'marital exemption in rape' formed no part of the law of England. *See R. v. W.* (1992) (appropriate sentence).

9. Liability of women, and boys under fourteen

A *woman* may be indicted for rape as an aider and abettor, as in *R. v. Ram and Ram* (1893), in which X's wife took a young girl by force to X's bedroom where he had intercourse with her.

A *boy under fourteen years of age* was presumed to be incapable of committing rape or any other offence involving sexual intercourse; but this presumption was abolished by the Sexual Offences Act 1993, s. 1.

NOTE: (1) On a charge of rape, conviction for indecent assault is possible: *see R. v. Hodgson and Marshall* (1973). (2) Where rape is alleged, a person may be guilty of aiding and abetting that alleged rape even though the principal is found innocent of the offence: *see R. v. Cogan and Leak* (1976).

Incest

10. Nature of the offence

Incest is *sexual intercourse between persons who are within certain specified degrees of consanguinity*. It was not a crime at common law, although punishable by the ecclesiastical courts; it became a statutory crime under the Punishment of Incest Act 1908.

11. Sexual Offences Act 1956

'It is an offence for a man to have sexual intercourse with a woman whom he knows to be his granddaughter, daughter, sister or mother': s. 10(1). 'It is an offence for a woman of the age of sixteen or over to permit a man whom she knows to be her grandfather, father, brother or son to have sexual intercourse with her by her consent': s. 11(1). For the offence of *incitement to incestuous intercourse, see* the Criminal Law Act 1977, s. 54; *see* 7:4(*b*). Incest with a girl under thirteen is a 'serious arrestable offence' under the Police and Criminal Evidence Act 1984, Sch. 5.

12. Consent

Consent of the female is no defence to a charge of incest. (In the absence of consent, the male will, of course, be guilty of rape.) If the female is aged sixteen or over and consents, in full knowledge of the relationship, she, too, will be guilty.

> NOTE: (1) It must be proved that the accused had knowledge of the relationship. X, accused of incest with Z, may have a defence, therefore, if he honestly believes that Z, the daughter of his wife, Y, is the offspring of an adulterous relationship between Y and another: *see R. v. Carmichael* (1940). (2) For sentencing guidelines and mitigating features in incest cases, *see A.-G.'s References (No. 1 of 1989* and *No. 4 of 1989); R. v. Coreless* (1989).

Other unlawful sexual intercourse

13. Intercourse with girls under thirteen years of age

'It is an offence for a man to have unlawful sexual intercourse with a girl under the age of thirteen': Sexual Offences Act 1956, s. 5. *See* .e.g. *R. v. Oakley* (1990); *A.-G.'s References (No. 4 of 1991), (No. 13 of 1993).*

(a) Belief, even though it is reasonable, that the girl is not under thirteen, is no defence: *see R. v. Maughan* (1934). The offence seems, therefore, to be one of strict liability (*see* Chap. 4).

(b) Whether the act was done with or without the consent of the girl is immaterial for purposes of s. 5, but if, in fact, it was without her consent, an indictment for rape may lie.

14. Intercourse with girls aged between thirteen and sixteen years

'It is an offence subject to certain exceptions for a man to have unlawful sexual intercourse with a girl . . . under the age of sixteen': Sexual Offences Act 1956, s. 6(1). *See* e.g. *R. v. Forrest* (1984).

(a) Consent is immaterial (*see* **13(b)**). *See R. v. O'Grady* (1978).
(b) It is not an offence for a girl under sixteen years of age to aid and abet a man, or to incite him, to have sexual intercourse with her: *see R. v. Tyrell* (1894), at 5:**20 (a)**.
(c) 'Where a marriage is invalid . . . (the wife being a girl under the age of sixteen), the invalidity does not make the husband guilty of an offence under [s. 6] because he has sexual intercourse with her, *if* he believes her to be his wife *and* has reasonable cause for the belief': s. 6(2). *See Mohamed v. Knott* (1969).
(d) 'A man is not guilty of an offence under this section because he has unlawful sexual intercourse with a girl under the age of sixteen, *if* he is under the age of twenty-four *and* has not previously been charged with a like offence, *and* he believes her to be of the age of sixteen or over *and* has reasonable cause for the belief': s. 6(3). 'Like offence' refers to unlawful sexual intercourse, or an attempt to commit such an offence, with a girl under sixteen: *see R. v. Rider* (1954).

15. Intercourse with defectives

It is an offence for a man to have unlawful sexual intercourse with a woman who is a defective, i.e. suffering from severe subnormality: *see* s. 7(1). *See* **20** (c). (Note that the term 'severe subnormality' was replaced, under the Mental Health Act 1983, s. 1(1), by 'severe mental impairment'.) *See R. v. Cleaver* (1992).

16. Procurement

It is an offence for a person to procure a woman by threats, intimidation, false pretences or false representations, to have unlawful sexual intercourse in any part of the world: *see* the Sexual Offences Act 1956, ss. 2(1), 3(1).

(a) The offence is not committed unless sexual intercourse takes place.
(b) The offence can be committed by a male or female person.
(c) For attempt to procure sexual intercourse by threats, *see R. v. Harold* (1984).

> NOTE: It is an offence to administer a drug, etc. to a woman with intent to stupefy or overpower her so as to enable any man to have unlawful sexual intercourse with her: *see* the Sexual Offences Act 1956, s. 4(1).

Indecent assault and Indecency with children

17. Sexual Offences Act 1956, ss. 14 and 15

It is an offence for any person (male or female) to make an indecent assault upon a male or female. ('Assault' is used both in its strict and broad senses: *see* 12:1.)

(a) There is no statutory definition of 'indecent assault'. The *actus reus* seems to be an intentional or reckless assault accompanied with circumstances of indecency on the part of the accused. *See R. v. Pratt* (1984) at **19**. (In *R. v. Kowalski* (1988), it was stated that the offence is concerned with 'contravention of standards of decent behaviour in regard to sexual modesty or privacy'.)

(b) A boy of under fourteen years of age *can* be charged with committing an indecent assault: *see R. v. Waite* (1892).

(c) Unequivocal indecent assault is a crime of *basic intent*: *R. v. C.* (1992).

18. The assault

There is no assault *unless* the accused, X, has moved towards committing a hostile act against, *or* has threatened, Y; physical contact with Y is not necessary.

(a) In *Fairclough v. Whipp* (1951), X invited Y, a young child, to touch his exposed body and Y did so. It was held that there was no hostile act by X and, therefore, no assault (but *see* **20**). 'I cannot hold that an invitation to somebody to touch the invitor can amount to an assault upon the invitee': *per* Lord Goddard CJ. (But *see* now **21**.)

(b) In *R. v. Rolfe* (1952), X exposed himself to Y and admitted moving towards her, inviting her to have intercourse with him. He denied touching Y. Held, the acts admitted by X constituted an indecent assault, since his approach to Y could be regarded as a threat.

(c) Hostility is *not* required in an indecent assault on a girl under sixteen; it is an indecent assault no matter how cooperative she is: *see R. v. McCormack* (1969). In *R. v. Thomas* (1985), the Court of Appeal held that the two requirements for an indecent assault on a child *under the age of sixteen* are: the act complained of must be *indecent*; and it must be one which would, without the victim's consent, be an *assault*. Further, it is *incorrect* to say that the act must be *either* inherently indecent *or* one that is hostile or threatening *or* an act which the child is demonstrably reluctant to accept.

(d) In *R. v. Court* (1988), the House of Lords held that on a charge of indecent assault, the prosecution must prove: (*i*) that the accused intentionally assaulted the victim; (*ii*) that the assault, or the assault under the circumstances accompanying it, are capable of being considered by right-minded persons as indecent; (*iii*) that the accused intended to commit such an assault as is referred to in (*ii*). *Per* Lord Ackner: 'I would add that evidence, if any, of the accused's explanation for assaulting the victim, whether or not it reveals an indecent motive, is admissible both to support or negative that the assault was an indecent one and was so intended by the accused.' *See* 3: **3(e)**.

(e) The necessary intention to found an indecent assault is only the intention to assault, not that the assault be of an indecent nature: *R. v. Culyer* (1992).

19. Indecent surrounding circumstances

In *Beal* v. *Kelley* (1951), X exposed himself to Y, a boy of fourteen, and pulled Y towards him. It was held to be a hostile act by X, against Y's will, *in circumstances of indecency*, which together constituted an indecent assault. Note *R.* v. *Pratt* (1984): in order to prove indecent assault, an indecent intention, an assault, *and* circumstances of indecency have to be proved. (But *see* also *R.* v. *Court* (1988).)

20. Consent as a defence

See R. v. *Hall* (1988) – the purpose of the 1956 Act is to protect those (e.g. defectives) who are incapable of giving consent. Consent is a complete defence, *except*:

(a) Where the consent has been obtained by fraud: *see R.* v. *Case* (1850).

(b) Where the assault is likely to cause the consenting party bodily harm: *see R.* v. *Donovan* (1934). The Court of Appeal held, in *R.* v. *Boyes* (1991), that an assault which was intended, or likely, to cause bodily harm, accompanied by indecency, is an offence irrespective of consent, provided that the harm was neither transient nor trifling.

(c) Where the consenting party is under sixteen, or a defective (except where the accused does not know, and has no reason to suspect, that she is, in fact, a defective) (*see Faulkner* v. *Talbot* (1981)):

(*i*) If X believes that Y, who is really under sixteen, is his wife, and has reasonable cause for that belief, this may be a defence: *see* **14**(*c*).

(*ii*) The defence available to a man under twenty-four charged with unlawful intercourse (*see* **14(d)**) is *not* available on a charge of indecent assault.

(d) *See R.* v. *Kimber* (1983), in which the Court of Appeal held that on a charge under the 1956 Act, s. 14, the prosecution must show that the accused *either* knew that his victim was not consenting *or* was reckless as to whether consent had been given. *Per* Lawton LJ: 'The evidence of the accused showed that his attitude had been one of indifference aptly described in the expression "couldn't care less" which in law was recklessness.'

(e) *See R*. v. *Kowalski* (1988), in which the Court of Appeal held that the state of marriage did *not* imply consent to an act which, if carried out without consent, would amount to indecent assault.

21. Indecency with Children Act 1960
By s. 1 it is an offence for any person to commit an act of gross indecency with or towards a child under the age of fourteen or to incite such a child to do such an act with him or with any other person. *See R*. v. *Speck* (1977) – passive inactivity may amount to an invitation. (Note that the act alleged in *Fairclough* v. *Whipp* (1951) (*see* 18) would be an offence today under the 1960 Act.) *See R*. v. *Francis* (1989), in which the Court of Appeal held that an offence of indecency 'with or towards' a child, contrary to s. 1, has to be directed towards the child with defendant deriving satisfaction from that fact. *See* also *R*. v. *May* (1989), in which the facts fitted both the statutory offence, under the 1960 Act, s. 1, *and* the common law offence of 'committing an act of a lewd, obscene and disgusting nature and outraging public decency.' (In that case, the Court of Appeal stated that it is not necessary that an act alleged to be lewd, obscene and disgusting should actually produce disgust in those in whose presence it was committed; it would suffice if it were calculated to do so.)

NOTE: *See* the Protection of Children Act 1978 (at 22:**16**).

Buggery, etc.

22. Buggery
'It is an offence for a person to commit buggery with another person or with an animal': Sexual Offences Act 1956, s. 12(1). (*See,* however, **24**.) (Note the decision of the House of Lords in *R*. v. *Courtie* (1984): s. 12(1) of the 1956 Act contains more than one offence of buggery, by reason of the provisions of ss. 1, 3, of the Sexual Offences Act 1967. For s. 1, see **24**; s. 3 deals with the penalties for buggery and attempted buggery.) The offence is triable only on indictment.

(a) The act consists in sexual intercourse *per anum* by a man with a man or woman, or sexual intercourse *per anum* or *per vaginam* by a man or woman with an animal: *see R*. v. *Bourne* (1952); *R*. v. *Higson* (1984); *R*. v. *Tierney* (1990). (There is no such offence as 'rape *per anum*': *R*. v. *Gaston* (1981).)
(b) The offence can be committed by husband with wife: *see R*. v. *Jellyman* (1838).
(c) Consent is no defence; the consenting party may be guilty as a principal offender.

(d) It is an offence, under the Sexual Offences Act 1956, s. 16(1), for one person to assault another with intent to commit buggery.

23. Indecency between males
'It is an offence for a man to commit an act of gross indecency with another man, whether in public or private, or to be a party to the commission of an act of gross indecency with another man, or to procure the commission by a man of an act of gross indecency with another man': Sexual Offences Act 1956, s. 13. (*See*, however, **24**.)

(a) 'Gross indecency' has not been defined by statute. (*See*, however, *Wolfenden Committee Report* 1957, p. 38. The term is used generally to refer to a sexual act, other than buggery, between males. *See R. v. Windle* (1985).)
(b) Consent is no defence; both parties to the act may be guilty.
(c) Attempting to procure an act of gross indecency is an offence: *Chief Constable of Hampshire* v. *Mace* (1986).

24. Sexual Offences Act 1967
The 1967 Act was passed as the result of the recommendations of the *Report of the Committee on Homosexual Offences and Prostitution* (1957) (the 'Wolfenden Report'). By s. 1 it is *not* an offence for a man to commit buggery or gross indecency with another man, *provided that* the parties consent, that they have attained the age of twenty-one years, and that the act was done in private. *See R. v. Reakes* (1974).

(a) An act will not be regarded as having taken place 'in private' if done when more than two persons took part or were present, or if that act took place in a lavatory to which the public had access.
(b) A man suffering from severe mental impairment, within the Mental Health Act 1983, cannot in law give consent.
(c) The Act does not legalise homosexual acts punishable under the Naval Discipline Act 1957, the Air Force Act 1955 or the Army Act 1955.
(d) A consenting partner who is under twenty-one is guilty of an offence; proceedings against him require the consent of the DPP: *see R. v. Angel* (1968).
(e) The 1967 Act does not affect the 1956 Act, s. 12(1), under which buggery committed by a man with a woman is an offence, although both consent, whether in private or not.

> NOTE: 'Lesbianism' (i.e. homosexual activity between females) is not a criminal offence.

25. Solicitation by men
Under the Sexual Offences Act 1956, s. 32, it is an offence for a man 'persistently to solicit or importune in a public place for immoral

purposes'. (For the meaning attached to 'solicit' and 'public', *see* **29(b)** and **(c)**.) In *Dale* v. *Smith* (1968), it was held that a solicitation implied repetition of an invitation. In *R.* v. *Grey* (1982), it was held that the question whether the purposes of homosexual activity were 'immoral purposes' within s. 32 was for the jury to decide; where a judge directs the jury that such purposes are immoral and refuses to leave the question to them, this amounts to misdirection. *See also R.* v. *Goddard* (1991); *R.* v. *Kirkup* (1993).

Indecent exposure

26. The common law offence
It is an offence at common law to commit an act injurious to public morals or to outrage public decency in public, e.g. by indecently exposing one's body: *see R.* v. *Rowed* (1842).

(a) 'In public' had been interpreted as referring to a place to which the public have access: *see R.* v. *Webb* (1848).
(b) It has been held that the act is no offence if visible only to one person: *see R.* v. *Webb* (1848).
(c) No intention to cause disgust or annoyance need be proved, and actual disgust or annoyance need not be proved: *see R.* v. *Mayling* (1963).

27. The Vagrancy Act 1824
By s. 4 it is an offence for a person wilfully, openly, lewdly and obscenely, to expose his person with intent to insult any female.

(a) The offence is confined to exposure of his penis by a male to a female person, and intent to insult is necessary.
(b) *See Ford* v. *Falcone* (1971); *Hunt* v. *DPP* (1990).

Offences involving prostitution

28. General
Prostitution is not *in itself* a criminal offence. The offences dealt with under **29–32** arise out of activities connected with prostitution.

(a) Prostitution was defined in *R.* v. *De Munck* (1918) as *the offering by a woman of her body 'for purposes amounting to common lewdness for payment in return'*: *per* Darling J. It is not confined to cases involving ordinary sexual intercourse: *see R.* v. *Webb* (1964).
(b) In *R.* v. *McFarlane* (1993), the Court of Appeal noted that the dictionary definitions and the cases appeared to show that the crucial feature in

defining prostitution was *the making of an offer of sexual services for reward.* (*See,* further, **31(d)** below.)

29. Loitering and soliciting by prostitutes

Under the Street Offences Act 1959, s. 1, it is an offence 'for a common prostitute to loiter or solicit in a street or public place for the purpose of prostitution'. *See* also the Criminal Justice Act 1982, s. 70.

(a) *'Common prostitute'.* This term is not defined by statute. In practice, however, proof that an accused person is a common prostitute is given by evidence of a recent similar conviction, or of two official cautions by a constable on occasions of suspected soliciting.

(b) *'Loitering and soliciting'.* One or other of these acts, but not both, has to be charged. 'Soliciting' involves the act of importuning prospective clients. *See Knight* v. *Fryer* (1976).

    (*i*) Soliciting may be by actions unaccompanied by words: *see Horton* v. *Mead* (1913). Tapping at a balcony window has been held to constitute soliciting. *See* also *Behrendt* v. *Burridge* (1976).

    (*ii*) There is no soliciting where the prostitute offers her services by advertisement on a notice board in the street: *see Weisz* v. *Monahan* (1962).

(c) *'Street or public place'.* Under the 1959 Act, s. 1(4), 'street' includes any road, lane, footway, etc., and doorways and entrances of premises abutting on a street. 'Public place' is not defined, but has been held to refer to a place to which there is public access, whether by right or not, and on payment or not.

30. Soliciting of women by men: 'kerb-crawling'

Under the Sexual Offences Act 1985, ss. 1(4), 4(1), it is an offence for a man to solicit a woman (for the purpose of obtaining her services as a prostitute) from a motor vehicle while it is in a street or public place, or in a street or public place while in the immediate vicinity of a motor vehicle that he has just got out of or off, persistently or in such a manner or circumstances as to be likely to cause annoyance to the woman solicited, or nuisance to other persons in the neighbourhood. Under s. 2, persistent soliciting is an offence. *See Darroch* v. *DPP* (1990) in which it was held that 'persistent' involved more than one act of soliciting. *See Paul* v. *DPP* (1990).

31. Living on the earnings of prostitution

By the Sexual Offences Act 1956, s. 30(1), it is an offence for a man 'knowingly to live wholly or in part on the earnings of prostitution'. *See R.* v. *Howard* (1991). (Note that it is irrelevant under s. 30 to consider the nature and quality of the 'living on': *R.* v. *Wilson* (1984).)

(a) The offence is committed where the accused person provides, in return for money, and in the knowledge that his acts will help the activities of prostitutes, goods or services or premises which refer exclusively to those activities. *See Shaw* v. *DPP* (1962) (*see* 1:22); *Calvert* v. *Mayes* (1954), where the accused allowed his car to be used by prostitutes and their clients; *R.* v. *Ansell* (1975). A landlord taking excessive rent from a tenant known to him to use the premises for purposes of prostitution may be convicted under s. 30(1): *R.* v. *Calderhead* (1978).

(b) Proof that a man lives with or is habitually in the company of a prostitute will suffice to raise the *presumption* that he is living on the earnings of prostitution and once it is presumed that he is living on the earnings of prostitution it is presumed also that he is doing so knowingly: *see R.* v. *Clarke* (1976); *R.* v. *Bell* (1978).

(c) By the Sexual Offences Act 1967, s. 5, it is an offence for a man or woman knowingly to live wholly or partly on the earnings of prostitution of another man. *See R.* v. *Puckerin* (1990).

(d) For a man to live on the earnings of a woman who habitually offered sexual services, took the money *and then reneged on the offer*, is to live off the earnings of prostitution: *R.* v. *McFarlane* (1993) (in which the Court of Appeal considered, in relation to s. 30, the definition of 'prostitution').

32. Other related offences
Other offences include:

(a) *Brothel keeping*: see the Sexual Offences Act 1956, s. 33, and the Sexual Offences Act 1967, s. 6; *R.* v. *Payne* (1980); *Kelly* v. *Purvis* (1983) (for consideration of what constitutes a brothel); *Stevens* v. *Christy* (1987); *Jones* v. *DPP* (1993) (assisting in management).

(b) *Procuring a woman* to become, in any part of the world, a common prostitute: *see* the Sexual Offences Act 1956, s. 22(1). In *R.* v. *Broadfoot* (1976), it was held that 'procure' means 'to recruit'. The word 'common' is not mere surplusage: it means procuring a woman to act as a prostitute on more than one occasion: *R.* v. *Morris-Lowe* (1984). Note *R.* v. *Brown* (1984), in which the Court of Appeal held that a man is not guilty of procuring a woman to be a common prostitute, or attempting to do so, if he genuinely believes on reasonable grounds that she already is a prostitute.

(c) *Exercising control over a prostitute*: *see* the Sexual Offences Act 1956, s. 31, under which it is an offence for a woman for purposes of gain to exercise control, direction or influence over a prostitute's movements in a way which shows she is aiding, abetting or compelling her prostitution.

Abduction of females

33. Sexual Offences Act 1956, ss. 17–21
The Act deals with the following offences concerning abduction:

(a) abduction, i.e. taking away or detaining, of a woman by force or for the sake of her property (s. 17);
(b) fraudulent abduction of an heiress under twenty-one from parent or guardian (s. 18);
(c) abduction of an unmarried girl under eighteen from parent or guardian (s. 19), amended by the Children Act 1989, Sch. 12;
(d) abduction of an unmarried girl under sixteen from parent or guardian (s. 20), amended by the 1989 Act, Sch 12; (*see R.* v. *Jones* (1973));
(e) abduction of a defective from her parent or guardian (s. 21), amended by the 1989 Act, Sch 12 (*see R.* v. *Tegerdine* (1982)).

34. 'Taking'
The term does not, in itself, imply the use of force: *see R.* v. *Henkers* (1886). The fact that the woman consents to go with the accused is of no relevance. 'Taking' with the intention that the woman or girl shall have unlawful sexual intercourse is essential to the offence (except in **33 (d)**). Note in **33 (a)** above 'taking or detaining'.

No permanent deprivation is necessary to constitute 'taking'. (In *R.* v. *Timmins* (1860), X was convicted, having taken away a girl for three days.)

35. Defences
There may be a defence to a charge under s. 19 (*see* **33(c)**) where the accused can prove, on a balance of probabilities, that he believed the girl to be over eighteen and had reasonable cause for that belief. As a defence to a charge under s. 21 (*see* **33(e)**), the accused may show that he did not know, and had no reason to suspect, that the woman was a defective.

See also *R.* v. *Prince* (1875) (*see* **2:2(c)** and **4:4**), a case decided under the Offences against the Person Act 1861, s. 55 (which was substantially re-enacted by the Sexual Offences Act 1956, s. 20).

Draft Criminal Code Bill

36. Rape
'(1) A man is guilty of rape if he has sexual intercourse with a woman without her consent and – (*a*) he knows that she is not consenting; or (*b*) he is aware that she may not be, or does not believe that she is, consenting.
(2) For the purposes of this section a woman shall be treated as not

consenting to sexual intercourse if she consents to it – (*a*) because a threat, express or implied, has been made to use force against her or another if she does not consent and she believes that, if she does not consent, the threat will be carried out immediately or before she can free herself from it; or (*b*) because she has been deceived as to – (*i*) the nature of the act; or (*ii*) the identity of the man': cl. 89.

37. Indecent assault
'A person is guilty of an indecent assault if he assaults another in such a manner, of which he is aware, or in such circumstances, of which he is aware, as are – (*a*) indecent, whatever the purpose with which the act is done; or (*b*) indecent only if the act is done with an indecent purpose and he acts with such a purpose': cl. 111.

> NOTE: With reference to **24** above (age of consent in homosexual activity), a reduction of that age seems likely, following a vote in Parliament in February, 1994.

Progress test 13

1. What is the *actus reus* of rape? **(3)**

2. Outline the Sexual Offences (Amendment) Act 1992. **(6)**

3. Comment on *R. v. Satnam and Kewal* (1984). **(7)**.

4. What was the effect of the decision in *R. v. R.* (1992)? **(8)**

5. Is consent ever a defence to a charge of incest? **(11,12)**

6. Outline the Sexual Offences Act 1956, s. 6(1). **(14)**

7. Outline the decision of the House of Lords in *R. v. Court* (1988). **(18)**

8. What is the essence of the Sexual Offences Act 1967? **(24)**

9. Comment on the term 'taking' as used in the Sexual Offences Act 1956, in relation to abduction. **(34)**

Part Three
Offences against property

14

The essence of theft (1): *actus reus*

Definition of theft

1. Theft Act 1968, s. 1(1)

'A person is guilty of theft if he dishonestly appropriates property belonging to another with the intention of permanently depriving the other of it; and "thief" and "steal" shall be construed accordingly.'

Theft is a crime of *specific intent* (*see* 3:**12**) and is triable either way. For punishment, *see* 1968 Act, s. 7; Criminal Justice Act 1991, s. 26.

2. *Actus reus* and *mens rea*

The *actus reus* of theft is, simply, an appropriation of property belonging to another (*see* **6**). The *mens rea* is the appropriation of property belonging to another done dishonestly *and* with the intention of permanently depriving the other of that property (*see* Chap. 15).

Essence of the *actus reus*

3. 'Appropriation'

This involves, for the purposes of s. 1, the dishonest assumption by X of any of the *rights* of Y, the owner of the property in question. *See R.* v. *Morris* (1984), approved on this point by the House of Lords in *R.* v. *Gomez* (1993) (*see* **9** below).

4. 'Property'

For the purposes of theft under s. 1, which is essentially a criminal interference with property rights, 'property' is defined comprehensively so as to include almost all types, except land, wild animals and wild flowers. *See* **11** below.

5. 'Belonging to another'

It is for the prosecution, in establishing the *actus reus* of theft, to show that at the time specific property was appropriated by X, it belonged to some other person who had possession or control of it or who had in it some proprietary right or interest. *See* **18**.

Appropriation

6. The assumption of another's rights

'*Any assumption by a person of the rights of the owner amounts to an appropriation*, and this includes, where he has come by the property (innocently or not) without stealing it, any later assumption of a right to it by keeping or dealing with it as owner': s. 3(1). There is an 'appropriation', therefore, where X dishonestly removes money from Y's purse and puts it in his own pocket, spending it later; or where X makes an unauthorised and dishonest pledge of Y's property. *See, e.g. R.* v. *Rader* (1992).

(a) There is *no one way* of appropriating for the purposes of theft: the act constituting appropriation can be carried out in many ways. Note that s. 3(1) refers to '*any* assumption'.

(b) There is no exhaustive list of 'the rights of an owner'. They arise, in general, from an owner's right to 'use and enjoy' his property. Appropriation, for the purposes of the 1968 Act, would be constituted, therefore, when X 'takes' Y's property by dishonestly assuming control of it, or when X 'uses' Y's property in some dishonest, unauthorised way, or when X makes, dishonestly, an unauthorised sale of Y's property (*see R.* v. *Pitham* (1976).

(c) In *R.* v. *Stringer* (1992), the Court of Appeal considered appropriation involving innocent agents. It was held that the signing of bogus documents (invoices for work which had not been done) which had set in motion a chain of events resulting in a bank account being debited, may constitute a sufficient appropriation to amount to theft, in spite of the intervening acts of innocent agents (ie, employees of the company of which the appellant was the business manager), who had signed cheques without verifying his actions. There was no material distinction between leaving innocent agents to verify the appellant's actions and his ordering them to do so.

7. An exception: s. 3(2)

'Where property or a right or interest in property is or purports to be transferred for value to a person acting in good faith, no later assumption by him of rights which he believed himself to be acquiring shall, by reason of any defect in the transferor's title, amount to theft of the property': s. 3(2). Assume that X, a *bona fide* purchaser, *buys* a television from Y and learns later that it was stolen property, so that he, X, has no legal right to it. X decides, however, to keep it. Under s. 3(2) there is no 'later appropriation' by which he is guilty of theft. (It must be shown, of course, that X bought the property from Y in good faith.) It should be noted, however, that if, at a later date, X sells the television to Z, he (X) may be liable under the Theft Act 1968, s. 15 (*see* 17:7), for obtaining the price by deception, in that he impliedly represented that Z would obtain good title to it. *See R.* v. *Wheeler* (1991) (sale of stolen goods in market overt); *R.* v. *Adams* (1993) (protection of bona fide purchaser of stolen goods).

Appropriation following the owner's consent

8. The problem

May an act done with the authority or consent of the owner amount to an appropriation of goods for the purpose of the Theft Act 1968, where such authority or consent has been obtained by deception? The question was considered, and answered in the *affirmative*, by the House of Lords in *R.* v. *Gomez* (1993).

(a) *The facts.* X, an assistant manager of an electrical goods shop, obtained the consent of the shop manager to allow the delivery of goods from the shop to an acquaintance, Y, against two building society cheques, which X and Y knew to have been stolen. The manager's consent had been given when X told him that the cheques were 'as good as cash'. X was *convicted* for theft of the goods, the recorder having rejected his argument that there had been no appropriation within s. 1(1) because of the manager's authorisation of the transactions. X appealed.

(b) *Court of Appeal.* After an examination of *Lawrence* v. *MPC* (1972) and *R.* v. *Morris* (1984), in relation to the proper construction of ss. 1(1) and 3(1) (*see* 6 above), the Court of Appeal had *allowed* X's appeal. *Per* Lord Lane: 'We conclude that there was a *de facto*, albeit voidable, contract between the owners and Y, that it was by virtue of that contract that Y took possession of the goods, that accordingly the transaction of the goods to him was with the consent and express authority of the owner and that accordingly there was no lack of authorisation *and no appropriation'*. The Crown appealed from this decision. (The decisions in *Lawrence* and *Morris* are set out below.)

(c) *Lawrence* v. *MPC* (1972). X, a taxi driver, agreed to take Y, a newly-arrived student from overseas, a short distance, but pretended that Y's destination was a long way off and expensive to reach. When Y offered his wallet, X took £6, although the correct fare was a mere fraction of that sum. X was charged with theft.

(*i*) The House of Lords held that X *could* be convicted, even though Y had 'consented' to the taking. There were no grounds for concluding that the omission of the phrase 'without the consent of the owner' was inadvertent and deliberate. 'To read the subsection as if they were included is, in my opinion, wholly unwarranted. Parliament by the omission of these words has relieved the prosecution of the burden of establishing that the taking was without the owner's consent. That is no longer an ingredient of the offence': *per* Viscount Dilhorne.

(*ii*) It appeared to some writers, however, that the definition of 'appropriation' in *R.* v. *Morris* (1984) *did* import that phrase ('without the consent of the owner').

(d) *R.* v. *Morris* (1984). X had taken goods from a supermarket shelf and had replaced the price labels attached to them with labels showing lower prices. At the checkout point he had been asked for, and paid, the lower prices. He was convicted of theft. The House of Lords *dismissed appeals* from the decision of the Court of Appeal, upholding X's conviction. Lord Roskill made the following points:

(*i*) There can be no conviction for theft contrary to s. 1 unless appropriation is proved together with the other ingredients of the statutory offence. It was enough for the prosecution to prove the assumption by the accused of *any of the rights* of the owners of the property in question. On a fair reading of s. 3(1) it could not have been the intention that *every one* of the owner's rights, of which there were many, had to be assumed by the alleged thief.

(*ii*) The concept of appropriation involved *not an act expressly or impliedly authorised by the owner*, as where an honest customer took goods from a shelf to put on his trolley to take to the checkpoint, there to pay the proper price, *but an act by way of adverse interference with or usurpation of some right of the owner*.

(*iii*) The removal of goods from the shelf and the switching of labels evidenced adverse interference with or usurpation of the right of the owner and amounted to an appropriation.

(*iv*) The precise moment at which dishonest acts, not of themselves amounting to an appropriation, subsequently, because of some other and later acts, did bring about an appropriation within s. 3(1), would necessarily vary according to the particular case.

9. *R.* v. *Gomez* (1993): the House of Lords decides

The Crown's appeal from the Court of Appeal (*see* **8(b)** above) was *allowed*.

(a) Lord Keith noted that Viscount Dilhorne's speech in *Lawrence* (*see* **8(c)** above) contained two clear pronouncements: *first*, that it was no longer, after the passing of the 1968 Act, an ingredient of theft that the taking should be without the owner's consent; *second*, that an appropriation might occur even though the owner had permitted or consented to the property being taken.

(b) In *Morris* (*see* **8(d)** above) Lord Roskill had undoubtedly been *right* when he had said that the assumption by defendant of *any* of the rights of an owner could amount to an appropriation within s. 3(1), and that the removal of goods from the shelf and the changing of a price label had constituted the assumption of one of the rights of the owner and, hence, an appropriation within the meaning of the subsection. But some of the observations were *incorrect*.

(*i*) It seemed [to Lord Keith] that the label switch was *in itself* an assumption of one of the rights of the owner, whether or not it was accompanied by some other act, such as removing the article from the shelf and placing it in the trolley. No one but the owner had the right to remove a price label from an article or to place a price label on it. If anyone else did it, he did an act by way of adverse interference with, or usurpation of, that right. The label switching *in itself* constituted an appropriation, and so to have held would have been sufficient for dismissal of the appeal in *Morris*.

(*ii*) On the facts of the case, it had been unnecessary to decide whether the mere taking of the article from the shelf and placing it in a trolley amounted to the assumption of one of the rights of the owner and, hence, was an appropriation. There was much to be said in favour of the view that it did, in respect that doing so gave the shopper control of the article and the capacity to exclude any other shopper from taking it. But Lord Roskill had suggested that it did not: the concept of appropriation in the context of s. 3(1) 'involves not an act expressedly or impliedly authorised by the owner but an act by way of adverse interference with or usurpation of those rights. '

(*iii*) While it was correct to say that appropriation for purposes of s. 3(1) included the latter sort of act, it did *not* necessarily follow that no other action could constitute appropriation, and, in particular, that no act expressly or impliedly authorised by the owner could in any circumstances do so. *Lawrence* was a clear decision to the contrary because it laid down that an act might be an appropriation notwithstanding that it was done with the consent of the owner. A sensible distinction could *not* be made in that context between 'consent' and 'authorisation'.

(*iv*) In *Dobson* v. *General Fire and Life Assurance Corporation* (1990) – a civil case – the Court of Appeal had considered the apparent conflict of *Lawrence* and *Morris* and had applied *Lawrence*. There seemed to be no material distinction between the facts of *Dobson*, which had been correctly decided, and the present case. *Lawrence* had to be regarded as 'authoritative and correct'; there was no question of it being right to depart from it.

(*v*) X's conviction was *upheld*. (Note Lord Lowry's dissenting speech.)

10. The situation after *R. v. Gomez*

(a) The decision of the House of Lords in *Lawrence* is correct; but that in *Morris* is, in some of its aspects, incorrect. It is considered not possible, within the context of *Gomez*, to make a useful distinction between 'consent' and 'authorisation'. Essentially, therefore, a consent obtained by deception may constitute an appropriation for purposes of the Theft Act 1968.

(b) *Gomez* was applied by the Court of Appeal in *R. v. Atakpu and Roberts* (1993), in which it was held that if goods have once been stolen, they *cannot* be stolen again by the same thief exercising the same or other rights of ownership over the property; accordingly, if X steals property abroad and brings it into the UK for dishonest gain, the theft is nevertheless committed abroad and he may not be charged with theft in the UK.

    (*i*) *Per* Ward J: 'We find it more difficult to answer the question . . . as to whether or not theft is a continuous offence. On a strict reading of *Gomez*, any dishonest assumption of the rights of the owner made with the necessary intention constitutes theft and that leaves little room for a continuous course of action.'

    (*ii*) 'We would not wish that to be the law. Such restriction and rigidity may lead to technical anomalies and injustice. We would prefer to leave it for the commonsense of the jury to decide that the appropriation can continue for so long as the thief can sensibly be regarded as in the act of stealing . . .'

(c) *See* also *R. v. Gallaso* (1993).

Property

11. General definition

' "Property" includes money and all other property, real or personal, including things in action and other intangible property': s. 4(1).

(a) The term 'real property' includes land; 'personal property' refers to movable property, i.e. goods and chattels (and also leasehold interests in land). But note s. 4(2) at **12** below.

(b) 'Things in action' are rights to sue, i.e. rights of action enforceable by a court of law, e.g. on an insurance policy. For theft of a 'chose in action' (the right to have one's cheque honoured) *see R.* v. *Kohn* (1979). *See* also *Chan* v. *A.-G. of Hong Kong* (1988); *R.* v. *Wille* (1988) – by drawing cheques on an account at the bank and using the proceeds for his own purposes, the offender has assumed the rights of an owner and, therefore, appropriates the debt in question. 'When what the appellant did in this case is considered, it is hard to see what more he could do to assume the rights of the owner in respect of the account at Barclays to the extent of the amount for which the cheques were drawn, than to draw a cheque, issue the cheque, and then take steps which were designed to achieve that the company's account at the bank was debited with the amount of the cheque': *per* Woolf LJ.

(c) 'Intangible property' includes, for example, gas stored in a container or a system of pipes, patents, textile quotas (which were bought and sold freely. (It does *not* include the confidential information in an examination paper: *Oxford* v. *Moss* (1978).) *See R.* v. *Downes* (1983). (Because electricity does not constitute tangible property, it cannot be 'stolen' (but *see* 16:27).)

(d) In *R.* v. *Crick* (1993), the Court of Appeal held that a sum of money represented by a figure in an account falls within the phrase 'intangible property' in s. 4(1), so that a transaction effected by electronic means was an obtaining of intangible property.

12. Land and things forming part of the land

The general rule, under s. 4(2), is that a person cannot steal land, or things forming part of the land and severed from it by him or at his direction.

The qualifications to the rule in s. 4(2) are discussed in **13–17**. (Note, however, that land can be obtained dishonestly by deception – *see* 17:**12**.)

13. Trustees or personal representatives

The first exception to the general rule is in s. 4(2)(*a*), and refers to '. . . a trustee or personal representative . . . [who] appropriates the land or anything forming part of it by dealing with it in breach of the confidence reposed in him.'

(a) A trustee is a person who holds property on trust for another. Where he makes an unauthorised disposition of land, intending permanently to deprive the other of it, he may be guilty of theft.

(b) If the trustee, personal representative, or other person authorised to dispose of the land, sells or gives away a fixture or structure which forms part of the land (*see* **15(b)**) he may be guilty of theft.

14. Persons not in possession

The second exception is in s. 4(2)(*b*), and refers to a person who 'is not in possession of the land and appropriates anything forming part of the land by severing it or causing it to be severed, or after it has been severed'.

15. Tenants

The third exception is in s. 4(2)(*c*), and refers to a person who 'when, being in possession of the land under a tenancy . . . appropriates the whole or part of any fixture or structure let to be used with the land.'

(a) For the purposes of the subsection ' "tenancy" means a tenancy for years or any less period and includes an agreement for such a tenancy, but a person who after the end of a tenancy remains in possession as statutory tenant or otherwise is to be treated as having possession under the tenancy, and "let" shall be construed accordingly': s. 4(2).

(b) The problem of fixtures is this: is a chattel affixed to land or a building a part thereof? The general rule is that a chattel is not considered a fixture unless connected to the land or building in some substantial way and in circumstances which show that it was to be considered as part of the land. (*See* e.g. *Hulme* v. *Brigham* (1943); *Deen* v. *Andrews* (1985).)

(c) A tenant, therefore, cannot be guilty of theft if he digs and appropriates soil from the land of which he is in possession. But he may be guilty of theft if he removes without authorisation, say, a basin from a wall of a washroom in the house, or an ornamental stone fountain considered as part of the integral design of the house's grounds.

16. Things growing wild

'A person who picks mushrooms growing wild on any land, or who picks flowers, fruit or foliage from a plant growing wild on any land, does not (although not in possession of the land) steal what he picks, unless he does it for reward or for sale or other commercial purpose . . . "mushroom" includes any fungus, and "plant" includes any shrub or tree': s. 4(3).

17. Wild creatures

'Wild creatures, tamed or untamed, shall be regarded as property; but a person cannot steal a wild creature not tamed nor ordinarily kept in captivity, or the carcase of any such creature, unless either it has been reduced into possession by or on behalf of another person and possession of it has not since been lost or abandoned, or another person is in course of reducing it into possession': s. 4(4).

(a) The above has *no application* to a domestic animal, e.g. a dog or cat, which may be stolen like any other property.

(b) It is possible for X to steal, for purposes of the Act, a wild creature which has been reduced into Y's possession (where Y has not lost possession) or which Y is in the course of reducing into his possession, e.g. where X seizes a hare from Y who is poaching on Z's land. (NOTE: poaching is not an offence as such under the Theft Act: *See* the Night Poaching Acts 1828 and 1844; and the Theft Act 1968, Sched. 1, for the unlawful taking or killing of deer or fish. *See Jones* v. *Evans* (1978); *R.* v. *Smith* (1982).)

Property belonging to another

18. Definition
The term is given an extended meaning. 'Property shall be regarded as belonging to any person having possession or control of it, or having in it any proprietary right or interest (not being an equitable interest arising only from an agreement to transfer or grant an interest)': s. 5(1). *See Edwards* v. *Ddin* (1976). (X asked a garage attendant to fill his petrol tank. After this was done he drove off without paying. It was held that at the time of the appropriation, i.e. when X drove off, the petrol was not 'property belonging to another', because ownership in the petrol had been transferred from seller to buyer when it entered the tank. Hence, X was not guilty of theft. But see 'making off without payment', at 18:1.) *See* also *R.* v. *Cording* (1983), for the meaning of 'any proprietary right or interest'.

(a) *'Possession or control'.* Under this section, property may 'belong', not only to a person who 'possesses' it, but to one who 'controls' it, or to one whose right in it constitutes less than complete ownership. Assume that Z owns property which he lends to Y, and that X steals the property from Y. X has committed theft against both Y and Z.

(*i*) It follows, therefore, that a thief can steal property stolen by and in possession of another thief.

(*ii*) It follows, too, that X, the owner of property, may be guilty of stealing property which belongs to him if he takes it with dishonest intent from Y, who has possession of it. In *R.* v. *Turner* (1971) X took his car to be repaired by Y. Without telling Y, and to evade payment, X later took it dishonestly from Y's garage, where it was being repaired. X's appeal against conviction for theft was *dismissed*; it was held to suffice that the property was, in fact, in the possession or control of Y, from whom X had taken it. (*See*, however, *R.* v. *Meredith* (1973). In that case X's car had been impounded by the police. X retrieved it without authority from a police yard. It was held that X was *not* guilty of theft because he was not dishonest and the police had no right to detain the car in the particular circumstances.)

(*iii*) In *R.* v. *Bonner* (1970), it was held that a partner can be guilty of the theft of partnership property, since each partner has a proprietary right in that property.

(*iv*) Note *R.* v. *Woodman* (1974) – control of a site by excluding others from it is *prima facie* 'control' of articles on the site, within s. 5(1).

(b) '*Not being an equitable interest. . . .*' An equitable interest arising from an agreement to transfer or grant an interest is excluded from s. 5(1). With the exception of this type of equitable interest, owners of other equitable interests are within the protection of s. 5(1). (An example of such an equitable interest is a buyer's right to completion of an agreement to purchase, say, shares.) *See R.* v. *Shadrock-Cigari* (1988): a bank retains an equitable interest in a draft it has issued as the result of another's mistake, and that interest constitutes 'property' for purposes of the 1968 Act.

19. Trust property

By s. 5(2), 'where property is subject to a trust, the persons to whom it belongs shall be regarded as including any person having a right to enforce the trust, and an intention to defeat the trust shall be regarded accordingly as an intention to deprive of the property any person having that right'. Where there is no ascertainable beneficiary, the property is regarded as belonging to any person who has a right to enforce the trust. *See A.-G's Reference (No. 1 of 1989); R.* v. *Naylor and Clowes* (1993).

20. Property received on account of another

'Where a person receives property from or on account of another, and is under an obligation to the other to retain and deal with that property or its proceeds in a particular way, the property or proceeds shall be regarded (as against him) as belonging to the other': s. 5(3). *See R.* v. *Brewster* (1979) – agent using insurance premiums for his own purposes was convicted under s. 5(3).

(a) Assume that X, treasurer of a social club, collects weekly sums from members on the understanding that he will return the total amount paid in to him by each member on the following Christmas Day. X misappropriates the money. X would be guilty of theft under s. 5(3).

(b) Assume that £20 is given to X on the understanding that he will use it to buy wallpaper to decorate Y's house. X's subsequent appropriation of the money to his own use may be theft, since *there is an obligation* on X, in this case, to deal with the £20 in a particular way. *See R.* v. *Jones* (1948); *R.* v. *Hughes* (1956).

(c) In *R.* v. *Hall* (1973), a travel agent received money from clients for air flights which did not take place. He failed to repay clients' deposits. His conviction for theft was *quashed*. It was held that although he was under a contractual duty to provide tickets, there was, in this case, no evidence that the clients expected him to retain and deal with their money or its proceeds in a particular way. In relation to the money he stood as a debtor to the clients. *See* also *R.* v. *Robertson* (1977).

(d) In *R.* v. *Mainwaring* (1982), the Court of Appeal held that whether or not an obligation arises under s. 5(3) to retain and deal with property or its proceeds received from another in a particular way, is a matter of law, because the obligation is a legal obligation; but it will be for a jury to determine whether they find the facts and circumstances to be such that some legal obligation arises to which s. 5(3) applies.

(e) Non-payment of housing benefit by a tenant to his landlord, in direct satisfaction of rent arrears, was held *not* to be an offence under s. 5(3): *DPP* v. *Huskinson* (1988).

21. Receipt of property by a mistake

Note the following.

> 'Where a person gets property by another's mistake, and is under an obligation to make restoration (in whole or in part) of the property or its proceeds or of the value thereof, then to the extent of that obligation the property or proceeds shall be regarded (as against him) as belonging to the person entitled to restoration, and an intention not to make restoration shall be regarded accordingly as an intention to deprive that person of the property or proceeds': s. 5(4). (*See R.* v. *Davis* (1989).)

(a) Y intends to give X a £5 note, but, in the darkness, mistakes the nature of the note he is handling and gives him, instead, a £10 note. Later, when X discovers the mistake, he decides to keep the note. X is guilty of theft.

(b) Y intends to make a gift of a painting to X, believing that it is a poor imitation of a Renoir and of little value. X realises at once that it is a genuine Renoir and sells it at a later date to a dealer for £500,000. X is under no obligation to make restoration of the painting, or the proceeds, or the value, to Y, and, in this case, he has not committed theft.

(c)   Where X accepts money from a bookmaker, knowing that it is being paid by mistake, he has committed theft: *see R.* v. *Gilks* (1972), *See* also *R.* v. *Williams* (1979): X took obsolete foreign banknotes for exchange at a bureau de change, impliedly representing that they were valid currency, so that he was given the value of current banknotes. He was found guilty of obtaining by deception; there was a fundamental mistake operating on the cashier's mind, and property in the money handed to X had not passed to him.

(d)   Subject to proof of an appropriation and dishonesty, a person who does not repay to her employer money mistakenly credited to her bank account may be guilty of theft: *A.-G.'s Reference (No. 1 of 1983). See R.* v. *Doole* (1985).

(e) An employee who contracted with his employer to sell on his employer's premises only goods supplied by his employer and to retain and deal with the proceeds of such sales for the benefit of his employer, did *not* receive moneys on account of his employer within the meaning of s. 5(3) when they were paid to him by customers on the employer's premises for goods on these premises which he had secretly obtained from someone other than his employer: *A.-G.'s Reference (No. 1 of 1985)*.

> NOTE: For theft of *treasure trove* (defined in *A.-G. of Duchy of Lancaster* v. *Overton Farms* (1982)), *see R.* v. *Hancock* (1990). It is for the coroner's jury to determine whether the objects in question are in fact treasure trove and thus the property of the Crown. Defendant can be convicted only if the jury are sure that the objects (which must be gold or silver) had been *hidden* by persons who intended to retrieve them. *See* also the Coroners Act 1988, s. 30.

Progress test 14

1. What is the essence of the *actus reus* of theft?   **(3–5)**

2. Explain 'appropriation' under the Theft Act 1968.   **(6)**

3. Outline the decision of the House of Lords in *R.* v. *Gomez* (1993).   **(9,10)**

4. What is meant by 'property' under the 1968 Act?   **(11)**

5. How does the 1968 Act deal with 'things growing wild'?   **(16)**

6. Comment on *R.* v. *Turner* (1971).   **(18)**

7. Explain the decision in *R.* v. *Hall* (1973)   **(20)**

8. How does the 1968 Act deal with receipt of property by a mistake?   **(21)**

The essence of theft (2): *mens rea*

Essence of the offence: a reminder

1. Theft under s. 1

It should be remembered that a person is guilty of theft under s. 1 if he dishonestly appropriates property belonging to another with the intention of permanently depriving the other of it (*see* 14:1). It should be recalled, too, that the *actus reus* (*see* 14:3) is constituted by an appropriation of property belonging to another.

2. *Mens rea* outlined

The appropriation must have been made dishonestly *and* with the intention of permanently depriving the other person of the property. 'Dishonesty' is considered at **4–12**. 'Permanently depriving' is considered at **13–18**.

3. Section 1(2)

Note that it is immaterial that X's appropriation is not made with a view to gain, or is not made for X's benefit: s. 1(2).

'Gain' and 'loss' in the Act of 1968 are construed as extending not only to gain or loss in money or other property, but also to any such gain or loss whether temporary or permanent. 'Gain' includes a gain by keeping what one has, as well as a gain by getting what one has not. 'Loss' includes a loss by not getting what one might get, as well as a loss by parting with what one has: *see* s. 34(2)(*a*).

Dishonesty in relation to theft

4. Dishonesty: subjective or objective?

The problem for the court, in considering whether the accused has acted dishonestly, has been this: 'What test ought a jury to apply so as to determine the dishonesty of the accused? Should the jury apply a subjective or an objective test?'

(a) The 'subjective test' involves seeking an answer to the question: 'Did *the accused* believe that he was acting dishonestly?'
(b) The 'objective test' involves seeking an answer to the question: 'Would *a jury* consider the behaviour of the accused to be dishonest?'

(Note that the term 'dishonest' in the 1968 Act replaces the requirement of the Larceny Act 1916 that the accused should have acted 'fraudulently and without a claim of right made in good faith'.)

5. Some important decisions
The test of dishonesty has been considered in cases such as the following.

(a) *R.* v. *Gilks* (1972). X placed a bet on a horse with a bookmaker, Y. Although the horse was unplaced, Y paid X £106, acting under the mistaken belief that X had backed the winning horse. X knew that a mistake had been made, but kept the money, believing that when one deals with a bookmaker, 'if he makes a mistake you can take the money and keep it and there is nothing dishonest about it.' The Court of Appeal upheld X's conviction for theft. 'The deputy chairman having referred to evidence that the appellant had not hurried away from the betting shop after receiving this large sum, said: "It is a matter for you to consider, members of the jury, but try and place yourselves in [X's] position at that time and answer the question whether in your view he thought he was acting honestly or dishonestly." In our view that was in the circumstances of this case a proper and sufficient direction on the matter of dishonesty. On the face of it, [X's] conduct was dishonest; the only possible basis on which the jury could find that the prosecution had not established dishonesty would be if they thought it possible that [X] did have the belief which he claimed to have': *per* Cairns LJ.
(b) *R.* v. *Feely* (1973). X, branch manager of a betting firm, borrowed £30 from his employer's safe, in spite of rules forbidding this, and gave an IOU to cover the deficiency. He told police that he had borrowed the money intending to pay it back, but that his employers owed him £70, from which he wanted the £30 deducted. His appeal against a conviction for theft was allowed by the Court of Appeal. It was held that 'dishonestly' in s. 1(1) related only to *the state of mind* of the person who performed the act amounting to appropriation, and that, being a fact, should have been left to the jury. 'We do not agree that judges should define what "dishonestly" means. This word is in common use, whereas the word "fraudulently" which was used in the Larceny Act 1916, s. 1, had acquired as a result of case law a special meaning. Jurors, when deciding whether an appropriation was dishonest can be reasonably expected to, and should, apply the current standards of ordinary decent people. In their

own lives they have to decide what is and what is not dishonest. We can see no reason why, when in a jury box, they should require the help of a judge to tell them what amounts to dishonesty': *per* Lawton LJ.

(c)   *R.* v. *Greenstein* (1976). X had acted in share applications as a 'stag', applying for large quantities of shares (in the hope of selling out at a profit). He was convicted of obtaining letters of acceptance and 'return' cheques by deception. His appeal against conviction under s. 15(1) (*see* 17:7) was dismissed. The question of whether X had been guilty of dishonesty was *a question of fact for the jury.* 'In summing up the case to the jury the judge laid down the law in a way which is beyond criticism. He told the jury: "There is nothing illegal in stagging. The question you have to decide and what this case is all about is whether these defendants, or either of them, carried out their stagging operations in a dishonest way. To that question you apply your own standards of dishonesty. It is no good, you see, applying the standards of anyone accused of dishonesty, otherwise everybody accused of dishonesty, if he were to be tested by his own standards, would be acquitted automatically, you may think. The question is essentially one for a jury to decide and it is essentially one which the jury must decide by applying its own standards. " That was correct . . .': *per* Stephenson LJ.

6. A consideration of the 'dishonesty test'

In *R.* v. *Ghosh* (1982), the Court of Appeal considered the test of dishonesty under the 1968 Act. It held that the test was *both subjective and objective.* It is *subjective* in that it is the state of mind of the accused, and not his conduct, which must be considered. It is *objective* in that the standard of honesty to be applied is not that of the accused, but that of 'the reasonable and honest man'.

(a)   X, a surgeon, was alleged to have falsely represented that he performed an operation, and that money was due to him. In fact the operation had been carried out by someone else. He was charged with deception contrary to the 1968 Act, ss. 15(1) and 20(2) (*see* 17:7). X claimed that he had not acted dishonestly and that he was entitled to payment. The Court of Appeal *dismissed* X's appeal. 'Dishonesty' in s. 1 of the 1968 Act characterised a state of mind, not a course of conduct; if X's mind was honest it could not be deemed dishonest merely because the jury would have regarded that course of conduct as dishonest.

(b)   In so far as there was a misdirection as to honesty (the trial judge having directed the jury that they ought to apply contemporary standards of honesty and dishonesty in the context of all they had heard in the case in deciding whether X had been dishonest), the case was one in which the proviso (see Criminal Appeal Act 1968, s. 2(1)) should apply.

(c)   The following comments of Lord Lane LCJ should be noted.

(i)   'It is no defence for a man to say "I know that what I was doing is generally regarded as dishonest, but I do not regard it as dishonest. Therefore I am not guilty." What he is however entitled to say is: "I did not know that anybody would regard what I was doing as dishonest." He may not be believed, just as he may not believed if he sets up a claim of right. . . . But if he *is* believed, or raises a real doubt about the matter, the jury cannot be sure that he was dishonest.'

(ii) 'In determining whether the prosecution has proved that defendant was acting dishonestly, a jury must first of all decide whether according to the ordinary standards of reasonable and honest people what was done was dishonest. If it was not dishonest by those standards, that is the end of the matter and the prosecution fails. If it was dishonest by those standards, then the jury must consider whether the defendant himself must have realised that what he was doing was by those standards dishonest. In most cases, where the actions are obviously dishonest by ordinary standards, there will be no doubt about it. It will be obvious that the defendant himself knew that he was acting dishonestly. *It is dishonest for a defendant to act in a way which he knows ordinary people consider to be dishonest, even if he asserts or genuinely believes that he is morally justified in acting as he did.*'

NOTE: In *R.* v. *Vosper* (1990), the Court of Appeal stated that it was wise for a trial judge, when directing a jury on dishonesty on the lines set out in *R.* v. *Ghosh*, to use the identical words of Lord Lane. *See also R.* v. *Ravenshead* (1990).

7. Dishonesty: a summary

After *R.* v. *Ghosh*, which seems to have attempted a bringing together of the two 'tests', the proper test for dishonesty in theft (to be applied if s. 2 is not of assistance) is now of a *dual nature*: did the accused act dishonestly by the standards of 'ordinary decent people', *and, if so*, must *he* have realised that his acts were by those standards dishonest? The accused can be convicted only if the answer by the jury to *both* questions is affirmative. *See R.* v. *Kell* (1985); *R.* v. *Small* (1988) – it is a misdirection for a jury to be told on a charge of theft that an unreasonable belief that the property is abandoned cannot be an honest belief.

(a)   Lord Lane LCJ, in *R.* v. *Price* (1989), said that it was by no means in every case that the *Ghosh* direction should be given. In the majority of cases it was unnecessary and, indeed, misleading to give the direction. It was only desirable that it should be given when defendant was saying: 'I thought that what I was doing was honest but other people and the majority of people might think it was not honest.' *See R.* v. *Brennen* (1990).

(b) In *R.* v. *Green* (1992), the trial judge had given a *Ghosh* direction but had dealt *first* with defendant's state of mind *and then* with the test of how ordinary persons would judge his actions. He had also used an analogy of a person leaving a shop without paying for goods and used a witness who had been shocked by defendant's conduct as an example of a person to whose standards the jury might have regard. The Court of Appeal *allowed* an appeal against conviction (for deception), holding that the directions on dishonesty were confusing, and that if a *Ghosh* direction were appropriate in this particular case, the standards of ordinary, reasonable people should have been dealt with first. Further, the analogy and example employed by the trial judge were not appropriate.

8. Exclusion of some states of mind from 'dishonesty'
Under s. 2(1) some states of mind are excluded expressly from being considered as dishonest for purposes of the Act. 'A person's appropriation of property belonging to another is *not* to be regarded as dishonest' in the cases outlined at **9–11**. It should be noted that none of the beliefs involved in these exceptions needs to be 'reasonable', but the reasonableness of an alleged belief will be of significance *evidentially* when consideration is given to the genuineness of that belief.

9. A belief in a right in law
A person's appropriation of property belonging to another is *not* to be regarded as dishonest 'if he appropriates property in the belief that he has in law the right to deprive the other of it, on behalf of himself or a third person': s. 2(1)(*a*). Assume that Y owes money to X, based on a lawful business transaction, and that Y fails to pay. X, under the mistaken belief that the law allows him to recover in any way possible, seizes Y's goods. X's claim of right may be a defence to a charge of theft. In *R.* v. *Robinson* (1977), X was charged with robbery of Y, who owed him £7. X was convicted of theft, following a direction that the defence under the 1968 Act, s. 2(1)(*a*), required X's honest belief that he was entitled in law to get the money in a particular way. In allowing X's appeal, the Court of Appeal stated that it was *not* necessary for X to show an honest belief that he was entitled to take the money from Y in the way he did. Whether or not the belief was *reasonable* is relevant for deciding whether defendant had an honest belief: *see R.* v. *Holden* (1991).

10. Belief that the other person would consent
A person's appropriation of property belonging to another is *not* to be regarded as dishonest 'if he appropriates the property in the belief that he would have the other's consent if the other knew of the appropriation

and the circumstances of it': s. 2(1)(*b*). Where, therefore, X honestly (but not necessarily, reasonably) believes that Y would have consented to X's appropriation of Y's property in all the circumstances, X has *not* acted dishonestly within the Act. Assume that X, having forgotten to order a daily newspaper, and, knowing that his neighbour, Y, is away on holiday, takes a newspaper from Y's letter box and leaves the appropriate money there. If X can show that he honestly believed that Y would have consented to the appropriation in the circumstances, he has *not* acted dishonestly. (But s. 2(2) should be noted in this context: appropriation *may* be dishonest even though X is willing to pay for the property.)

(a) Note, on the interpretation of 'the other', for the purposes of s. 2(1)(*b*), *A.-G.'s Reference* (*No. 2 of 1982*), which points out that a person in total control of a limited liability company, by reason of his shareholding and directorship, or two or more such persons acting in concert, were capable in law of stealing the property of the company. *See R. v. Phillipou* (1989), in which the Court of Appeal held that where defendant and his co-accused were the sole directors and shareholders of a company, it *was* possible in law for them to steal from their own company.
(b) Note, also, the statement of Megaw LJ that a defendant's belief that he would have the other's consent, must be an honest belief in a true consent, honestly obtained. *See Lawrence v. MPC* (1972).

11. Belief that the owner cannot be traced

A person's appropriation of property belonging to another is *not* to be regarded as dishonest '(except where the property came to him as trustee or personal representative) *if* he appropriates the property in the belief that the person to whom the property belongs cannot be discovered by taking reasonable steps': s. 2(1)(*c*). Property which has been lost (but not abandoned) by Y continues to belong to Y. Where, therefore, X finds that property and honestly believes that it is not possible to trace its owner, and then appropriates it, the appropriation is *not* dishonest within the Act. If, however, at some time after the finding, X learns that the property belongs to Y, who can be traced easily, his continued appropriation amounts to acting dishonestly, for the purposes of the Act.

12. Willingness to pay for the property

'A person's appropriation of property belonging to another may be dishonest notwithstanding that he is willing to pay for the property': s. 2(2). Assume, therefore, that X covets goods belonging to Y, but knows that Y is not willing to sell, and that X then takes the goods, leaving money which represents (or even exceeds) their full market price. In such a case X has acted *dishonestly* and may be convicted of theft.

Intention of permanently depriving

13. The problem

It is for the prosecution to prove not *actual* permanent deprivation of Y's property by X, but rather that X, at the time he appropriated Y's property, intended to deprive Y permanently of it. The existence of such an intention is a question of fact: *see R.* v. *Lloyd* (1985). In many cases it is not difficult to prove that intention, e.g. when X takes money from Y's pocket and runs off, or when X takes goods from Y's shop and deliberately fails to pay for them on leaving the premises. Problems may arise, however, as where X takes Y's watch and pawns it, intending to redeem it at some later date. The problem is to show, from the nature of the property involved, from the act of appropriation by X, and his subsequent conduct, that X had an intention *permanently to deprive. See R.* v. *Velumyl* (1989), in which a manager took notes and coin from a safe at work, without permission, intending to replace them one week later. The Court of Appeal held that he had the intention *permanently to deprive* and had no intention to return the objects he had taken.

14. Determining the intent

Section 6 (which is set out in full at **15**) regards a person as having the appropriate intention:

(a) where he intends to treat the property as his own to dispose of regardless of another's rights;
(b) where he borrows or lends the property for a period of time and in circumstances considered as equivalent to an outright taking;
(c) where he parts with the property under a condition as to its return which he may not be able to carry out.

15. Section 6

By s. 6:

> '(1) A person appropriating property belonging to another without meaning the other permanently to lose the thing itself is nevertheless to be regarded as having the intention of permanently depriving the other of it if his intention is to treat the thing as his own to dispose of regardless of the other's rights; and a borrowing or lending of it may amount to so treating it if, *but only if,* the borrowing or lending is for a period and in circumstances making it equivalent to an outright taking or disposal. (2) . . . where a person having possession or control (lawfully or not) of property belonging to another, parts with the property under a condition as to its return which he may not be able to perform, this (if done for purposes of

his own and without the other's authority) amounts to treating the property as his own to dispose of regardless of the other's rights. '

16. Effect of s. 6(1)

Note the following comments of Lord Lane CJ in *R. v. Lloyd* (1985): '[The section] must mean, if nothing else, that there are circumstances in which a defendant may be deemed to have the intention permanently to deprive, even though he may intend the owner eventually to get back the object which has been taken.' (*Per curiam*: s. 6 should be referred to *in exceptional cases only*. In the vast majority of cases it need not be referred to or considered at all.)

(a) Note *R. v. Warner* (1970). X took Y's tools, but denied this when questioned by the police. At his trial, X admitted the taking but said that he had intended to return the tools after an hour, and that the police enquiry took place before he was able to do so. It was held that s. 6 did not vitiate the basic conception of s. 1 that, to constitute theft, the accused must intend permanently to deprive the owner of his property; the object of s. 6 is to prevent the accused raising a specious plea when it is obvious that he had intended to treat the property as his own. *Per* Edmund-Davies LJ: 'There is no statutory definition of the words "intention of permanently depriving"; but s. 6 seeks to clarify their meaning in certain respects. Its object is in no way to cut down the definition of "theft" contained in s. 1 . . . its apparent aim is to prevent specious pleas. But it is a misconception to interpret it as watering down s. 1.'

(b) *Per* Lord Lane CJ in *R. v. Lloyd* (1985): 'We would try to interpret s. 6 in such a way as to ensure that nothing is construed as an intention permanently to deprive, which would not prior to the 1968 Act have been so construed. Thus the first part of s. 6(1) seems to us to be aimed at the sort of case where a defendant takes things and then offers them back to the owner for the owner to buy if he wishes. If the taker intends to return them to the owner only on such payment, then, on the wording of s. 6(1), that is deemed to amount to the necessary intention permanently to deprive: *see*, for instance, *R. v. Hall* (1849).' *See* also *DPP* v. *Lavender* (1993).

17. Borrowing under s. 6(1)

A borrowing *may* amount to theft. The matter was discussed by the Court of Appeal in *R. v. Lloyd* (1985). In this case a film projectionist, X, had secretly removed films over a period of time and passed them to others for purposes of copying. X was convicted under the Criminal Law Act 1977, s. 1, of conspiracy to steal the films in breach of the Theft Act 1968, s. 1. X contended that he had not the necessary intention within s. 1(1) of the 1968 Act, since he had always intended to return the films within a short time of their removal from the cinema.

(a) The Court of Appeal held that borrowing or lending an article can only be deemed to amount to an intention of permanently depriving *if* the intention of the borrower or lender was to return the article to the owner in such a changed state that it had lost all its practical value. X's appeal was *allowed*.

(b) *Per* Lord Lane CJ: 'It seems to us that in this case we are concerned with the second part of s. 6(1) . . . "and a borrowing or lending of it may amount to so treating it if, but only if, the borrowing or lending is for a period and in circumstances making it equivalent to an outright taking or disposal." . . . Borrowing is *ex hypothesi* not something which is done with an intention permanently to deprive . . . A mere borrowing is never enough to constitute the necessary guilty mind *unless* the intention is to return the thing in such a changed state that it can be truly said that all its goodness or virtue has gone . . . Our view is that the films which were the subject of this alleged conspiracy had not themselves diminished in value at all . . . The borrowing, it seems to us, was not for a period, or in such circumstances, as made it equivalent to an outright taking or disposal. There was still virtue in the film.'

18. Inability to carry out a condition as to the return of property under s. 6(2)

Assume that X has undertaken to repair Y's antique clock, which he is holding for that purpose. X then pledges it to Z, without Y's authority, so as to secure a loan for his (X's) own private purpose. X's intention to permanently deprive Y of ownership may, under s. 6(2), emerge from his taking a chance of non-return of the clock to Y following the possibility that he (X) might be unable to repay the loan.

Conditional intent

19. The problem

X, examining the contents of Y's handbag (without Y's permission), may have in mind no specific property he wishes to steal; but he will steal only if articles of value can be discovered in the bag. His intention to deprive Y of her property is *conditional* on his finding something worth stealing.

In *R.* v. *Easom* (1971), X picked up a bag (placed as a trap by its owner, Y, a police officer) from the floor of a cinema. After opening the bag and examining its contents, X closed it and replaced it on the floor. He was convicted on an indictment charging theft of the bag, purse, notebook, etc. His conviction was *quashed*, the Court of Appeal holding that although X had appropriated the articles, *the appropriation was not accompanied by the intention of permanently depriving Y of her property.* 'What may be loosely described as a conditional appropriation will not do. If the appropriator has it in mind merely to deprive the owner of such of his property as, on examination, proves worth taking, and then, finding that the booty is valueless to the appropriator, leaves it ready to hand to be repossessed by the owner, the appropriator has not stolen': *per* Edmund-Davies LJ. *See* also *R. v. Husseyn* (1978).

20. *A.-G.'s References (Nos. 1 and 2 of 1979)*
The Court of Appeal has held that where (as in *R. v. Easom*) the accused had only a conditional intent to steal, he could be convicted of attempted theft provided the indictment did not particularise any specific objects (e.g. 'one purse') which, it was alleged, X intended to steal, but described the property generically (e.g. 'the contents of a handbag'). *See R. v. Smith and Smith* (1986).

(a) The principle of conditional intent remains available as the basis of a defence where X has been charged with stealing a particular specified item or items, and in such a case it is for the prosecution to show that X had the intent of stealing the item or items mentioned.
(b) Note that, as a result of the Criminal Attempts Act 1981 (*see* Chap. 8), it is an offence for X to attempt to steal from Y, even where the full offence is *physically impossible*.

Progress test 15

1. Comment on *R. v. Feely* (1973). **(5)**

2. Explain the 'dishonesty test' derived from *R. v. Ghosh* (1982). **(6,7)**

3. 'I took £20 from his desk because he owes my father that amount.' Discuss. **(9)**

4. Comment on *A.-G.'s Reference (No.2 of 1982)*. **(10)**

5. 'I confess to having taken the goods without paying for them, but I'm willing to pay for them here and now.' Discuss. **(12)**

6. Explain the decision in *R . v. Lloyd* (1985). **(17)**

16

Robbery, burglary and other offences

Robbery

1. At common law
Robbery was a capital offence at common law, constituted by the taking of goods from another by violence or by putting him in fear.

2. Under the Larceny Act 1916
Robbery was not defined by the Act. By s. 23, a person who, being armed with an offensive weapon or instrument, robbed, or assaulted with intent to rob, any person, or who robbed any person, and, at the time of, or immediately before or immediately after such robbery, used any personal violence, was guilty of a felony. (*Repealed* by the Theft Act 1968.)

3. Under the Theft Act 1968
'A person is guilty of robbery if he steals, and immediately before or at the time of doing so, and in order to do so, he uses force on any person or puts or seeks to put any person in fear of being then and there subjected to force': s. 8(1). 'A person guilty of robbery, or of an assault with intention to rob, shall ... be liable to imprisonment for life': s. 8(2). If the prosecution is to succeed, it must be shown that X has stolen property *and* that the theft took place in circumstances involving X's threat, or use, of force. *See R.* v. *Guy* (1991) – anyone guilty of robbery had to be guilty also of theft and anyone charged with robbery could be found not guilty of it but guilty of theft. For principles of sentencing *see R.* v. *O'Driscoll* (1986), *R.* v. *Bigby* (1993), and *A. -G.'s Reference (No. 26 of 1992)*. It is triable only on indictment.

4. 'If he steals'
The force, or threat of force, if it is to amount to robbery, must be used *in order that the accused person might steal*; hence, where a person does not steal, he cannot be convicted of robbery.

(a) Since the essence of robbery is theft, whatever defences are available to a person accused of theft will be available to one accused of robbery. A successful claim of right, therefore (*see* 15:**9**), may negate theft or robbery. *See R. v. Robinson* (1977), in which it was said by the Court of Appeal that the Theft Act 1968 had not altered the law as stated in *R. v. Skivington* (1968). *Per* Lord Goddard CJ: 'In the opinion of this court the matter is plain, namely that a claim of right *is a defence* to robbery . . . and that it is unnecessary to show that the defendant must have had an honest belief also that he was entitled to take the money in the way he did where X used a knife to threaten his wife's employer so that he could collect wages owing to her, which X had her authority to collect.'

(b) Where X uses force so as to take Y's motor van, but does not intend to deprive Y permanently of the van, X may be guilty of an offence under s. 12 (*see* **25**) (and also of assault), but he *cannot* be guilty of robbery.

(c) Where X is attacked by Y, and, in retaliation, knocks Y unconscious, *and then* appropriates money which he sees in Y's pocket, he may be charged with theft and an offence under the Offences against the Person Act 1861 (*see* Chap. 12), but *not* with robbery.

(d) In *R. v. Shendley* (1970), it was alleged that X attacked Y, took his goods and then forced him to sign a receipt purporting to show that X had bought the goods from him. (X alleged that, in fact, he had purchased the goods from Y.) X was convicted of robbery, but, on appeal, a verdict of theft was substituted. It was held that the trial judge's direction that . . . it would be open [to the jury] to find X guilty of robbery, that is robbery without violence' was wrong; under the Theft Act 1968 there is no such thing as 'robbery without violence.'

(e) In *Corcoran* v. *Anderton* (1980), the court considered the question: 'When is an appropriation complete?' X_1 and X_2 had agreed to steal Y's handbag. X_2 hit Y in the back and tugged at the bag so as to release it from her grasp. X_1 participated in this action. Y fell to the ground, releasing her bag. X_1 and X_2 ran off empty-handed and Y recovered her bag. X_1 was later convicted under s. 8 and appealed against conviction on the ground that neither he nor X_2 had sole control of the handbag at any time. The appeal was *dismissed*. It was held that *full control of the article was not necessary*: an appropriation had taken place when X_1 and X_2 snatched the bag from Y's grasp, since this was an unlawful assumption of Y's rights as an owner.

5. 'Immediately before or at the time'
Where force is employed so as to steal, it will constitute the offence of robbery only where it is employed at the very time of the stealing, or immediately before that event, but not some time after the event. In *R. v. Hale* (1978), X entered Mrs Y's house and, putting his hand over her mouth to stop her screaming, took jewellery from the house and then tied her

up. His appeal against conviction for robbery was *dismissed;* the force used in tying her up occurred 'immediately before or at the time of stealing', required under s. 8, since the act of appropriation can be a continuing one. The theft was not over when Y was tied up. 'The act of appropriation does not suddenly cease. It is a continuous act and it is a matter for the jury to decide whether or not the appropriation has finished': *per* Eveleigh LJ.

(a) Where X steals from Y, and, in attempting to escape after that event is completed, uses force against Y, this will *not* constitute robbery under the Act. (X could be charged, however, with both theft and assault, under the Offences against the Person Act 1861, s. 16.)

(b) Where X steals from Y, and, *later*, uses force or threats against Y, who is attempting to recover his property, this will *not* constitute robbery: *see* R. v. *Harman* (1620).

6. 'Uses force or seeks to put any person in fear'
The actual or threatened use of force against a person will suffice. (Note that the term 'force' is used, in contrast to 'violence' used in the 1916 Act.)

(a) The force may be minimal but must be *more than a slight physical contact*. Nor will a mere accidental use of force suffice.

(b) To constitute robbery, the force or threat of force must be *against a person*; hence, a threat by X to damage Y's property if Y does not hand it to him will *not* suffice. *See* R. v. *Donaghy and Marshall* (1981).

(c) The actual or threatened force can be *against any person*, and need not be against the person whose property is stolen. Thus, where X, in the process of stealing Y's purse, is interrupted by Z, who attempts to prevent the theft, and X uses or threatens force against Z, and goes on to complete the theft, X is guilty of robbery.

(d) The old common law rule that, to constitute robbery, the stealing must be from the person threatened or assaulted, or in his presence, *no longer applies*. In *Smith* v. *Desmond and Hall* (1965), X_1 and X_2 were convicted of robbery; they had attacked, tied and gagged Y and Z, a nightwatchman and engineer, and put them in a room, while they broke open a safe thirty yards away, out of the sight of Y and Z, but in their hearing. It was held on appeal that X_1 and X_2 had been properly convicted: it was enough that Y and Z were aware of the theft and were compelled by force to submit to it.

(e) Whether or not 'force' has been used in an alleged robbery is a question for the jury and there is no need for resort to the old authorities where the wording of the statute is clear: R. v. *Dawson* (1978) – X was convicted of robbery after he and two others approached Y in the street, and two of them stood on either side of Y, with the third behind him, while one nudged Y so that he lost his balance, enabling X to steal his

wallet. Note *R.* v. *Clouden* (1987), in which the Court of Appeal held that the old distinction between force on an actual person and force on property causing force on that person was *no longer relevant*. X had approached Y from behind and pulled her basket from her hands before running off with it. X's appeal against conviction of robbery was *dismissed*.
(f)   Where a *threat* of force is used, the question may arise: 'For how long does such a threat remain effective?' In *R.* v. *Donaghy and Marshall* (1981), Y, a taxi-driver, drove X_1 and X_2 from Newmarket to London at their demand after they had threatened his life. In London, X_1 stole money from Y. It was held that if X_1 and X_2 were to be convicted of robbery it would be necessary to satisfy the jury that the effect of the threat was continuing, to the knowledge of X_1 and X_2, and that they had deliberately used that effect to obtain money from Y, and that their manner was such that they had given the impression that the threat was continuing at the time of the theft.

Burglary

7. At common law
Burglary, in early law, was the breaking by night into a house, church, or the walls or gates of a town (*burgebreche* = breach of a borough). At common law it was described as the breaking and entering of a dwelling house by night with the intent to commit a felony therein, whether the felony was committed or not: *3 Co. Inst. 63.*

8. Under the Larceny Act 1916
This Act contained a complex definition (s. 25, *now repealed*), and its interpretation was beset with technical difficulties (*see* for example *R.* v. *Boyle* (1954)).

9. Under the Theft Act 1968
Section 9(1) says:

> 'A person is guilty of burglary if –

(a)   he enters any building or part of a building as a trespasser and with intent to commit any such offence as is mentioned in subsection (2); or
(b)   having entered any building or part of a building as a trespasser he steals or attempts to steal anything in the building or that part of it or inflicts or attempts to inflict on any person therein any grievous bodily harm'.

Most types of burglary are triable either way.

10. Two separate offences

There are two separate offences under s. 9(1). Both require proof of entry by the accused as a trespasser. Given the required intent, X commits an offence under s. 9(1)(*a*) at the very moment of entry; but an offence under s. 9(1)(*b*) is committed by X at the time the ulterior offence has been completed.

(a) For an offence under s. 9(1)(*a*), the prosecution must show that X intended to commit one of the offences mentioned in s. 9(2). For an offence under s. 9(1)(*b*), the prosecution must show that X has committed an offence specified under s. 9(1)(*b*).
(b) It will be observed that the range of offences to which s. 9(1)(*a*) refers is broader than that under s. 9(1)(*b*).

11. 'With intent to commit' an offence

The offences referred to in s. 9(1)(*a*) are:

(a) *stealing* anything in the building or part of the building in question: *see R. v. Walkington* (1979) (it was immaterial whether the theft was possible; it sufficed that the accused had an intent to steal, notwithstanding that there was nothing on the premises worth stealing);
(b) *inflicting grievous bodily harm* on any person therein; *see R. v. Jenkins* (1983) (the expression 'inflict grievous bodily harm' has not the same meaning as the expression in the Offences against the Person Act 1861, s. 20); the prosecution must prove the intention to inflict the harm, and the judge should withdraw from the jury any case where this is not done (*R. v. O'Neill, McMullen and Kelly* (1986));
(c) *raping* any woman therein: *see R. v. Burchill* (1977); *R. v. Moore* (1992);
(d) *doing unlawful damage* to the building or anything therein. *See* s. 9(2).

12. 'Enter'

The term 'enter' is not defined in the Act; presumably it has the specialised meaning attached to it in earlier cases under common law. The prosecution must show, for the purposes of s. 9, that the accused *did enter* the building.

(a) At common law there was a sufficient entry when any part of the body of the accused went over the threshold, e.g. a finger: *see R. v. Davis* (1823).
(b) There was also sufficient entry at common law by the mere insertion of an instrument which was to be used for effecting the ulterior offence, e.g. where a net on a cane was pushed in a window in order to take jewels from a room: *see R. v. Hughes* (1785). But *see R. v. Collins* (1973) at **(d)**.
(c) Insertion of an instrument solely for the purpose of gaining entry will *not* suffice: *see R. v. Rust and Ford* (1828).

(d) In *R.* v. *Collins* (1973), the Court of Appeal held that the entry must be 'effective and substantial'. In *R.* v. *Brown* (1985), the Court of Appeal considered a conviction of burglary. X had broken a shop window and 'rummaged about' with the top half of his body inside the window. X's appeal was dismissed; the Court held that since X had made an 'effective and substantial entry', he had entered the premises, for the purposes of s. 9.

13. 'Enters . . . as trespasser'

In general terms, trespass involves an entry on land without an invitation of any sort and without other lawful justification (*see Addie* v. *Dumbreck* (1929)), e.g. where X enters a house in Y's possession *intentionally, or recklessly* (in the *Cunningham* sense (*see* 3:**15**) in the case of a charge under s. 9(1)(*a*)), without Y's consent or any other lawful justification. *See R.* v. *Whiting* (1987).

(a) There is no trespass in the case of an involuntary entry.

(b) Entry under false pretences may constitute trespass, e.g. where X, intending to steal from Y's house, gains entry by pretending that he has authority to inspect Y's radio receiver: *see R.* v. *Boyle* (1954).

(c) Where the burglary charged involves entry as a trespasser 'with intent . . .', the intent must have existed at the time of that entry; the subsequent formation of an intention to steal from the premises after a trespassory entry will not suffice.

(d) In *R.* v. *Collins* (1973), it was held that there can be no conviction for entering premises as a trespasser, within the meaning of s. 9, unless the person entering knows that he is trespassing and, nevertheless, enters deliberately, *or* is reckless as to whether he is a trespasser. Hence, where X entertained an *honest belief* that he had consent to enter a building *before* effecting a substantial entry, he is not guilty of burglary under s. 9.

(e) 'A person is a trespasser for the purpose of s. 9(1)(*b*) if he enters premises of another knowing that he is entering in excess of the permission that has been given to him, or being reckless whether he is entering in excess of the permission that has been given to him to enter. Provided the facts are known to the accused which enable him to realise that he is acting in excess of the permission given or that he is acting recklessly as to whether he exceeds that permission, then that is sufficient for the jury to decide that he is in fact a trespasser': *R.* v. *Jones* (1976).

(f) The doctrine of trespass *ab initio* has no application to burglary: *R.* v. *Collins* (1973). (Under the doctrine, one who is entitled by law to perform an act and who abuses his authority, renders that act wrongful from the very beginning.)

(g) The unlawful act of X, charged with burglary by entering a building as a trespasser with intent to commit theft, does not end when he crosses the threshold or window sill. The unlawful act comprises the *entire* burglarious intrusion: *R.* v. *Watson* (1990).

14. 'Building or part of a building'
'Building' is not defined in the Act. The term covers, presumably, not only houses, but shops, offices, etc. Essentially, some degree of permanence of structure is required.

(a) References under s. 9 to 'a building' apply also 'to an inhabited vehicle or vessel, and shall apply to any such vehicle or vessel at times when the person having a habitation in it is not there as well as at times when he is': s. 9(3).
(b) 'Part of a building' is not defined in the Act. The term seems intended to cover, for example, two separate flats or rooms.
(c) Note *R.* v. *Walkington* (1979), in which the Court of Appeal held that a jury were entitled to conclude that a counter area within a shop was a 'part of a building' from which members of the public were excluded.

15. A.-G.'s References (Nos. 1 and 2 of 1979)
The A.-G. referred two cases, involving two questions concerning 'conditional intention', to the Court of Appeal. *See* 16:20.

(a) The first question asked whether a man who has entered a house *as a trespasser* with the intention of stealing money therein is entitled to be acquitted of an offence against s. 9(1)(*a*) on the grounds that his intention to steal is conditional upon his finding money in the house. The answer of the Court of Appeal was '*No*'.
(b) The second question asked whether a man who is attempting to enter a house *as a trespasser* with the intention of stealing anything of value which he may find therein is entitled to be acquitted of the offence of attempted burglary on the ground that at the time of the attempt his said intention was insufficient to amount to 'the intention of stealing anything', necessary for conviction under s. 9. The answer of the Court of Appeal was '*No*'.

Aggravated burglary

16. Under the Theft Act 1968
'A person is guilty of aggravated burglary if he commits any burglary and at the time has with him any firearm or imitation firearm, any weapon of offence, or any explosive': s. 10(1). *See* e.g. *R.* v. *Lemathy* (1991). It is triable only on indictment.

17. 'Firearm or imitation firearm'

'"Firearm" includes an airgun or air pistol, and "imitation firearm" means anything which has the appearance of being a firearm, whether capable of being discharged or not': s. 10(1)(*a*). (*See* the Firearms Acts 1968 and 1982, at Chap. 12.)

18. 'Weapon of offence'

'"Weapon of offence" means any article made or adapted for use for causing injury to or incapacitating a person, or intended by the person having it with him for such use': s. 10(1)(*b*). (This definition appears to be wider than that of an 'offensive weapon' in the Prevention of Crime Act 1953, s. 1(4): *see* 12:36.)

(a) *'Intended by the person having it with him for such use'*. This clause suggests that where the article possessed by X has not been made or adapted for use so as to injure or incapacitate a person, it may nevertheless be considered as a weapon of offence *if intended* by X for such use. It would seem that, in such a case, the prosecution will have to prove that X was carrying the article with him *with an intention* of using it to injure or incapacitate some person, should he feel that the circumstances necessitated such an action. The time of the intention necessary for a weapon not made or adapted for use as an offensive weapon to be such a weapon in considering the offence of aggravated burglary was during the period of the burglary itself: *R*. v. *Kelly* (1992).

(b) *'Having with him'* was considered in *R*. v. *Pawlicki* (1992) with reference to the Firearms Act 1968, s. 18(1) (*see* 12:**31**). The Court of Appeal held that the section imported an 'element of propinquity' which was not required for mere possession. The important factor was on the *accessibility of the guns* to the persons embarking on the commission of an indictable offence, rather than upon the precise distance between them and the guns. In this case the guns (in a motor vehicle parked outside the premises which were to be robbed) were readily accessible to defendants, who were convicted.

19. 'Explosive'

'"Explosive" means any article manufactured for the purpose of producing a practical effect by explosion, or intended by the person having it with him for that purpose': s. 10(1)(*c*).

20. 'At the time'

For X to be convicted of aggravated burglary, it is necessary to show that he had the firearm, etc. with him at the time he committed the burglary.

(a) Where X is charged with 'entering with intent' (*see* s. 9(1)(*a*)), 'at the time' refers to the time of actual entry.

(b) Where X is charged with committing a specific offence 'having entered' (*see* s. 9(1)(*b*)), 'at the time' will refer to the time of the commission by X of that specific offence.

(c) In *R. v. Francis* (1982), X gained entry to a house, armed with sticks. After discarding the sticks he stole property from the house. The Court of Appeal allowed an appeal from a conviction of aggravated burglary, and substituted one of simple burglary. The judge's direction that the prosecution need prove only that X was armed when he entered the premises was *incorrect*. Unless X intended to steal when he entered, he was guilty of aggravated burglary only if he had a weapon with him *at the moment when he stole*.

(d) The prosecution does *not* have to prove that X intended, if necessary, to use the weapon during the course of the burglary. It suffices that X was carrying the weapon with the intention of using it on some person. X's story that he intended to use the weapon on persons who, he thought, might attack him at some other time in circumstances totally unrelated to the burglary, was irrelevant. *See R. v. Stones* (1989).

Possession of articles for use in burglary, etc.

21. The offence

'A person shall be guilty of an offence if, when not at his place of abode, he has with him any article for use in the course of or in connection with any burglary, theft or cheat': s. 25(1). *See R. v. Ellames* (1974), in which the Court of Appeal held that to establish the offence of having an article for use in the course of burglary there must be evidence of some such burglary to be committed *in the future*. (*See* also *A.-G.'s Reference No. 1 of 1985*.)

(a) An offence under s. 12(1) (taking a conveyance without authority: *see* 25) is treated as theft for the purposes of this section; 'cheat' means an offence under s. 15 (*see* 17:7): *see* s. 25(5).

(b) There is no offence under the section where X is in possession of implements in his own home; the essence of the offence is possession elsewhere than at one's place of abode.

(c) In *R. v. Bundy* (1977), it was held that 'place of abode' means a fixed place, so that a car out on the road is *not* a place of abode.

(d) *See R. v. Doukas* (1978) – waiter in possession of bottles of his own wine, which he dishonestly intended to sell to hotel guests without revealing their true ownership, was held properly convicted of going equipped *to cheat*; *R. v. Corboz* (1984). *See* also *R. v. Cooke* (1986).

(e) *See Minor* v. *DPP* (1988) – a person who prepared in order to steal and *later* came into possession of equipment for theft *can* be convicted under s. 25(1).

22. Evidence

'Where a person is charged with an offence under this section, proof that he had with him any article made or adapted for use in committing a burglary, theft or cheat shall be evidence that he had it with him for such use': s. 25(3).

(a) Where the article has not been made or adapted for use in a burglary, theft or cheat, the mere fact of possession alone will not constitute *prima facie* evidence; but a jury is entitled to draw an inference from its nature and all the other circumstances as to its intended use: *see R. v. Harrison* (1970).

(b) In *R. v. Hargreaves* (1985) the judge directed the jury that they could convict X if satisfied that he *might* have used a piece of wire found on him, which had been adapted for the purpose of interfering with a gaming machine, even if not satisfied that he had a firm intention of doing so. The Court of Appeal allowed X's appeal against conviction under s. 25, holding that intention to use the article in the course of or in connection with theft had to be proved in order to justify a conviction.

23. Arrest

'Any person may arrest without warrant anyone who is, or whom he, with reasonable cause, suspects to be, committing an offence under this section': s. 25(4).

Other offences

24. Removal of articles from places open to the public
By s. 11(1):

> 'Where the public have access to a building in order to view the building or part of it, or a collection or part of a collection housed in it, any person who without lawful authority removes from the building or its grounds the whole or any part of any article displayed or kept for display to the public in the building or that part of it or in its grounds shall be guilty of an offence.'

The offence is triable either way.

(a) The creation of the offence took into account a notorious incident in which a Goya portrait was removed from a public art gallery by a person who did not intend permanently to deprive the gallery of it (and who, in fact, returned it after four years). He was found not guilty of larceny of the portrait, but guilty of larceny of the portrait's frame, which he had destroyed.

(b) 'Collection' includes a collection got together for a temporary purpose, but references in the section to a collection do not apply to a collection made or exhibited for the purpose of effecting sales or other commercial dealings: *see s.* **11 (1).**

(c) It is immaterial for the purpose of s. **11(1)** that –

'the public's access to a building is limited to a particular period or occasion; but where anything removed from a building or its grounds is there otherwise than as forming part of, or being on loan for exhibition with, a collection intended for permanent exhibition to the public, the person removing it does not commit an offence under this section unless he removes it on a day when the public have access to the building as mentioned in subsection (1)': s. 11(2).

See R. v. Durkin (1973) – removal of a painting from a municipal art gallery – in which it was held that for the purposes of s. 11(2) 'a collection intended for permanent exhibition to the public' means a collection intended to be permanently available to the public, whether or not it is regularly exhibited in its entirety.

(d) Where a person believes that he has lawful authority for the removal of the thing in question or that he would have it if the person entitled to give it knew of its removal and the circumstances, he does not commit an offence under the section: *see s.* 11(3).

25. Taking a conveyance without authority, or being carried by such a vehicle

'A person shall be guilty of an offence if, without having the consent of the owner or other lawful authority, he takes any conveyance for his own or another's use or, knowing that any conveyance has been taken without such authority, drives it or allows himself to be carried in or on it': s. 12(1). (The offence is concerned with *temporary deprivation only*; the intention to permanently deprive would fall within s. 1.) This is a summary offence under the Criminal Justice Act 1988, s. 37.

(a) '"Conveyance" means any conveyance constructed or adapted for the carriage of a person or persons whether by land, water or air . . .': s. 7(*a*). Conveyances constructed or adapted for use only under the control of a person not carried in or on them are excluded from s. 12. The section would not apply, therefore, to a goods trailer.

(b) No offence is committed by a person under the section 'by anything done in the belief that he had lawful authority to do it or that he would have had the owner's consent if the owner knew of his doing it and the circumstances of it': s. 12(6). It is for a jury to judge the accused's state of mind if he raises a defence under s. 12(6): *R. v. Clotworthy* (1981). *See R. v. Briggs* (1987).

(c) It is an essential ingredient of the offence that a movement (no matter how small) of the conveyance should take place: *see R. v. Bogacki* (1973). But s. 12 contains no requirement of 'driving away': *see R. v. Pearce* (1973). *See* also *Blayney* v. *Knight* (1975) (the taking must be intentional); *R. v. Bow* (1977), in which X parked his car while participating, so it was alleged, in poaching. When a gamekeeper parked his car to block X's exit, X entered the gamekeeper's car, and released the handbrake so that the car coasted for some few hundred yards. X was convicted, having taken the gamekeeper's car 'for his own use'.

(d) The prosecution does not have to prove a *specific intent* in addition to proving that the accused person took the conveyance without the owner's consent; accordingly a person can be guilty even if he was too drunk to form any intent: *see R. v. MacPherson* (1973).

(e) The prosecution does not have to prove absence of lawful authority on defendant's part *unless* there exists evidence showing that defendant believed he had lawful authority: *see R. v. Gannon* (1988).

(f) 'Use' of a vehicle necessarily involves use as a conveyance: *R. v. Stokes* (1983).

(g) A car abandoned by a thief and taken by another *could* be stolen a second time. A Divisional Court held that it could not be that offences under s. 12(1) were to be limited to facts where there had been one taking only. *See DPP* v. *Spriggs* (1993).

26. The Aggravated Vehicle-Taking Act 1992

The 1992 Act creates an *aggravated offence* in relation to the Theft Act 1968, s. 12(1), and introduces an amendment to the 1968 Act, in the form of s. 12A. The new offence is triable either way. See *R. v. Bird* (1993).

(a) A person is guilty of aggravated taking of a vehicle if he commits an offence under The Theft Act 1968, s. 12(1), in relation to a mechanically propelled vehicle, and it is proved that *after the vehicle was unlawfully taken (whether by him or another) and before it was recovered,* the vehicle was driven, or injury or damage was caused in one or more of the following circumstances: the vehicle was driven dangerously on a road or other public place; that, owing to the driving of the vehicle, an accident occurred causing injury to any person; that, owing to the driving of the vehicle, an accident occurred by which damage was caused to property other than the vehicle; that damage was caused to the vehicle: 1968 Act, s. 12A(1)(2).

(b) A person is not guilty of an offence under this section if he proves that the driving, accident or damage referred to in subsection (2) occurred *before* he committed the basic offence (an offence under s. 12(1)), *or* he was neither in nor in the immediate vicinity of the vehicle when that driving, accident or damage occurred: s. 12A(3).

(c) See also Bail (Amendment) Act 1993, s. 1(1).

27. Dishonest abstraction of electricity

'A person who dishonestly uses without due authority, or dishonestly causes to be wasted or diverted, any electricity shall on conviction on indictment be liable to imprisonment for a term not exceeding five years': s. 13. *See Low* v. *Blease* (1975); *Boggeln* v. *Williams* (1978), in which it was held that, in considering the offence of abstracting electricity without consent, whether the accused acted honestly is a question of fact which should be considered *subjectively*: *R.* v. *Hoar* (1982); *R.* v. *Western (1987). It would seem to suffice for s. 13 that the electricity is 'dishonestly wasted or diverted', so that it is not necessary to show that the accused used it for his own purposes. See* also *Collins and Fox* v. *Chief Constable of Merseyside* (1988); *R.* v. *McCreadie* (1993) (the use of electricity with no intention of paying for it will suffice to constitute the offence; there is no requirement that the electricity meter should have been tampered with in any way).

(a) 'This has to be a separate offence because owing to its nature electricity is excluded from the definition of stealing in . . . [s.] 1(1)': *Criminal Law Revision Committee Report*.
(b) It is an offence to use a licensed telecommunications system with intent to avoid payment: *see* the British Telecommunications Act 1984, s. 42, as amended.

Draft Criminal Code Bill

28. Burglary

'(1) A person is guilty of burglary if – (*a*) he enters a building or part of a building as a trespasser, intending to commit in the building or part of a building in question an offence of (*i*) theft; (*ii*) causing serious personal harm; (*iii*) rape; or (*iv*) destroying or damaging the building or any property therein; or (*b*) having entered a building or part of a building as a trespasser, he commits in the building or part of a building in question an offence of (*i*) theft or attempted theft; or (*ii*) causing, or attempting to cause, serious personal harm': cl. 147.

29. Commentary

'This clause takes the opportunity to correct a plain and unintended error in the Theft Act 1968, s. 9. Section 9(1)(*a*) expressly requires entry as a trespasser with intent to commit an "offence". But s. 9(1)(*b*) does not expressly require the infliction of grievous bodily harm, which may convert a trespassory entry into burglary, to be an offence; if para. (*b*) were taken literally, burglary could be committed accidentally by someone in a building as a trespasser . . . Our draft eliminates the error . . .': para. 16.8.

Progress test 16

1. What is the essence of the offence of robbery under the Theft Act 1968, s. 8? **(3)**

2. Comment on *Corcoran* v. *Anderton* (1980). **(4)**

3. Explain the decision in *R.* v. *Donaghy and Marshall* (1981). **(6).**

4. What is burglary under the Theft Act 1968, s. 9 ? **(9)**

5. What is the meaning of 'entering a building' in relation to burglary? **(12)**

6. Comment on *A.-G.'s References (Nos. 1 and 2 of 1979).* **(15)**

7. Outline the nature of aggravated burglary. **(16)**

8. Comment on *R.* v. *Pawlicki* (1992). **(18)**

9. What is the significance of *R.* v. *Durkin* (1973) ? **(24)**

10. State the gist of the Aggravated Vehicle-Taking Act 1992. **(26)**

Criminal deception under the Theft Acts 1968 and 1978

Criminal deception

1. Deception offences under the Theft Acts 1968 and 1978
The following offences relating to *deception* are created under the Theft Acts:

(a) *1968 Act:* obtaining property (s. 15: *see* **7**); obtaining a pecuniary advantage (s. 16: *see* **14**); procuring the execution of a valuable security (s. 20: *see* **20**).
(b) *1978 Act:* obtaining services (s. 1: *see* **24**); securing remission of a liability (s. 2(1)(*a*): *see* **32**); inducing a creditor to defer or forgo payment (s. 2(1)(*b*): *see* **33**); obtaining exemption from or abatement of liability to make a payment (s. 2(1)(*c*): *see* **34**).

2. Essence of the deception offences
These offences involve the *dishonest* obtaining of some kind of advantage (accruing from e.g. possession of property or the performance of a service) *as the result of a deception.* Each is an arrestable offence (*see* 1:**27**).

Fundamental features of the deception offences

3. Common elements
In all the offences enumerated at **1** the prosecution must prove that a false statement for which the accused, X, was directly responsible, which was made dishonestly, deliberately or recklessly, so operated on the mind of some person, Y, as to deceive him, with a result prohibited by the Theft Acts. In these offences the common fundamental features are X's *obtaining by a deception*, and his *dishonesty.* These elements are discussed below (*see* **4** and **5**).

4. Obtaining by deception
Consider the following cases. X offers to repair Y's television for £50 cash paid in advance, but he has no intention of performing any work, and he

absconds without carrying out the repairs. X utilises a cheque card, which he is not authorised to use, and obtains credit in this way from Y. By means of a fraudulent application, X obtains a passport and subsequently uses it: *R.* v. *Ashbee* (1989). In each of these cases there is a deception originating in a dishonest intent, as a result of which some advantage is obtained by X; i.e. there is a causal link of a direct nature between the deceptions practised by X and the prohibited effects of those deceptions. See *R.* v. *Miller* (1992) (the jury must consider the *entire course* of events leading to the loss suffered by the victim).

(a) *'Deception'* is defined in the 1968 Act, s. 15(4), and it has application to the 1968 Act, ss. 15, 16, 20(3), and to the 1978 Act, ss. 1, 2. *See* **10** below.

(b) *'Deliberate or reckless'*. *Deliberate deception* arises where the accused knew that what he represented as being true was, in fact, not true. *Reckless deception* arises where the accused made a false statement, 'being careless whether what he stated was true or false': *see Derry* v. *Peek* (1889). There is no offence under s. 15 where X makes a representation which he believes is true, but which he ought to have known, as a reasonable man, is untrue. Negligence is *not* to be equated with the dishonesty which characterises the offence of obtaining by deception. In *R.* v. *Staines* (1975) it was held that a deception, in order to be reckless within s. 15, must be more than merely careless or negligent, there must be indifference to or disregard of the feature of the statement's being true or false. *See R.* v. *Abdullah* (1982).

(c) *'By words or conduct'*. The words used may be *spoken or written*. Further, as in the case of obtaining by false pretences, the deception can result, not only from words, but from conduct. In *R.* v. *Barnard* (1837), it was held that X's wearing of cap and gown in a university town was sufficient, in itself, and without any words, to constitute a representation that he was a member of the university.

(d) Deception *by omission* seems possible, as where X acts so that Y is led to believe in the existence of a state of affairs which is later altered by X, and Y remains unaware of the alteration. *See* e.g. *DPP* v. *Ray* (1974), in which X ordered a meal in a restaurant and, after eating the main course, decided not to pay and ran off. It was held that his conduct in ordering the meal was a representation that he intended to pay, so that a subsequent decision not to pay, and his omission to correct the resulting misrepresentation as to his intentions, constituted a deception.

(e) X's representation must be shown to be *actually false* (*see* e.g. *R.* v. *Banaster* (1979)) and the falsity of the statement is for the jury to determine (*see R.* v. *Mandry and Webster* (1973)), and it *must deceive* some person, Y, with the result that X is allowed to obtain an advantage. But where Y is, in the event, aware of the falsity of X's representation and nevertheless allows X to obtain the advantage, no offence under ss. 15, 16 is committed.

(f) Note that a *human mind* must be deceived. 'Deception of a machine' for the purposes of ss. 15, 16 generally seems not possible.

(g) The false representation must affect the conduct of the person to whom it was made: *see R. v. Laverty* (1970). In *R. v. Collis-Smith* (1971), X obtained petrol by falsely representing to the garage attendant that he had his employer's permission to book it to his firm's account. The representation was made *after* possession of the petrol had been obtained by X, and it could not be said that it had operated on the mind of the garage attendant. X's misrepresentation was not, therefore, a cause of the petrol having been obtained. *See R. v. Silverman* (1987) (deception by silence in the process of making an exorbitant charge); *R. v. Miller* (1993).

(h) Where X draws a cheque in the knowledge that, because of inadequate funds, it will not be honoured, his action constitutes an implied representation which is false. In that event X's conduct is a deception. Where X draws a cheque backed by a cheque card which he is using after the bank has withdrawn authority for its use, his action constitutes a deception in that X deliberately misrepresents the bank's willingness to enter into the type of contract resulting from the use of such a card. *See Metropolitan Police Commissioner v. Charles* (1977); *R. v. Gilmartin* (1983) (in which defendant was charged under ss. 15, 16) – 'by the simple giving of a cheque, whether post-dated or not, the drawer impliedly represents that the state of facts existing at the date of handing over the cheque is such that in the ordinary course the cheque will, on presentation for payment, on or after the date specified in the cheque, be met.'

5. Dishonesty

Dishonesty must be proved in *all* deception offences. The word is not defined specifically for the purposes of ss. 15, 16. In *R. v. Woolven* (1984) it was held that in a case involving an attempt to obtain property by deception contrary to s. 15, a direction in accordance with *R. v. Ghosh* (1982) (*see* 15:6) would suffice to cover the situation.

6. Overlap of deception and theft

In *Lawrence v. MPC* (1972), the House of Lords considered: *'Whether the provisions of s. 15(1) and s. 1 of the Theft Act 1968 were mutually exclusive in the sense that if the facts proved would justify a conviction under s. 15(1) there cannot lawfully be a conviction under s. 1(1) on those facts.'* Per Viscount Dilhorne: 'In my opinion, the answer is, *No.* There is nothing in the Act to suggest that they should be regarded as mutually exclusive and it is by no means uncommon for conduct on the part of an accused to render him liable to conviction for more than one offence. Not infrequently there is some overlapping of offences. In some cases the facts may justify a charge under s. 1(1) and also a charge under s. 15(1). On the other hand there are cases which only come within s. 1(1) and some which are only within s. 15(1).'

Obtaining property by deception: 1968 Act, s. 15

7. Definition of the offence
'A person who by any deception dishonestly obtains property belonging to another, with the intention of permanently depriving the other of it, shall on conviction be liable to imprisonment . . .': s. 15(1). There is, therefore, an offence under s. 15, where X, an athlete, is given a longer start in a race than that to which he is entitled, following his deception, so that he wins the race and is awarded a money prize. *See* e.g. *R. v. Atwal* (1989). The offence is triable either way.

8. *Actus reus*
The following elements must be proved:

(a) a deception by X, which affects some person, Y;
(b) an obtaining (of control, possession, ownership) by X of property belonging to Y or some other person.

9. *Mens rea*
This comprises four elements:

(a) dishonesty;
(b) deliberation or recklessness in making the deception;
(c) an intention to obtain the property for oneself or another; and
(d) an intention to permanently deprive.

10. 'Deception'
The term is explained in s. 15(4) as 'any deception (whether deliberate or reckless) by words or conduct as to fact or as to law, including a deception as to the present intentions of the person using the deception or any other person.' *See R.* v. *Hamilton* (1990); *R.* v. *Bunche* (1993).

11. 'Obtains'
For the purposes of the section a person is treated as obtaining property 'if he obtains ownership, possession or control of it, and "obtain" includes obtaining for another or enabling another to obtain or retain': s. 15(2). It suffices for the purposes of s. 15, therefore, that X has obtained ownership of the property in question, or merely control, without necessarily having obtained its possession. *See R.* v. *Duru* (1973).

12. 'Property belonging to another'
'Property' in relation to s. 15 is as set out for the offence of theft in s. 4(1) (*see* 14:11): *see* s. 34(1). The qualifications set out in s. 4(2)–(4) (*see* 14:**13–17**) do *not* apply to s. 15, so that, in effect, almost all property may be the basis of an offence under the section. 'Belonging to another' in relation to s. 15 is as set out for the offence of theft in s. 4(1): *see* s. 34(1).

13. 'Intention of permanently depriving'
Section 15(3) provides that s. 6 (*see* 16:15) has application also to obtaining property by deception. *See Chan Wai Lam* v. *R.* (1981).

Obtaining a pecuniary advantage by deception: 1968 Act, s. 16

14. Definition of the offence
'A person who by any deception dishonestly obtains for himself or another any pecuniary advantage shall on conviction on indictment be liable to imprisonment for a term not exceeding five years': s. 16(1). There is, therefore, an offence under s. 16, where X, attempting to obtain advantageous terms on a policy of health insurance, states falsely that he is a non-drinker. *See* e.g. *R.* v. *Zemmel* (1985); *R.* v. *Melwani* (1989) (loans obtained by false statements as to the volume of imports). The offence is triable either way.

15. *Actus reus*
The following must be proved:

(a) a deception by X, which affects some person, Y; *and*
(b) an obtaining, not of property belonging to Y or some other person, but of an (intangible) pecuniary advantage.

16. *Mens rea*
This comprises:

(a) dishonesty;
(b) intention or recklessness in making the deception;
(c) an intention to obtain a pecuniary advantage for oneself or another.

17. 'Deception'
This term has the same meaning as in s. 15 (*see* 10): s. 16(3).

18. 'Pecuniary advantage'
The two cases in which a pecuniary advantage is to be considered in the context of s. 16 are set out in s. 16(2):

[**(a)** S. 16(2)(*a*): repealed by the Theft Act 1978];

(b) S. 16(2)(*b*): where a person is allowed to borrow by way of overdraft, or to take out any policy of insurance or annuity contract, or obtains an improvement of the terms on which he is allowed to do so. *Example*: X makes false statements to his banker, Y, to the effect that he has received large export orders, so that Y is induced to grant facilities for X's over-drawing; but note that in *R.* v. *Watkins* (1976) it was held that the offence under s. 16(2)(*b*) is committed where a deception causes only the granting of facilities for overdrawing without their being used.

(c) S. 16(2)(*c*): where a person is given the opportunity to earn remuner-ation or greater remuneration in an office or employment, or to win money by betting. *Example*: where a college tutor states falsely that he possesses a higher qualification so that he is promoted to a senior post. The words 'office or employment', within s. 16(2)(c), are to be considered in their ordinary sense rather than restricted to strictly defined contracts of service. Thus a self-employed accountant who had falsely represented himself as possessing an accountancy qualification fell within the subsec-tion. His appeal against conviction, on the ground that he had no 'office or employment' within the subsection, was dismissed by the Court of Appeal: *see R.* v. *Callender* (1992).

19. Deception by credit card
In *R.* v. *Lambie* (1981), X had been issued with a credit card with a limit of £200, but had exceeded the limit and had failed to return the card to the bank, using it for further transactions. She was charged under s. 16(1) with obtaining a pecuniary advantage by deception. She argued in the Court of Appeal against conviction by stating that there was no evidence to show that any deception had been operative, and her appeal was allowed. The House of Lords allowed the Crown's appeal, holding that X's presentation of the credit card in a shop constituted a representation of her authority to make a contract with the shop on the bank's behalf.

Procuring the execution of a valuable security: 1968 Act, s. 20(2)

20. Definition of the offence
The offence is committed when a person who 'dishonestly, with a view to gain for himself or another or with intent to cause loss to another, by any deception procures the execution of a valuable security': s. 20(2). Proof will be required of a causal connection between the deception and the *actus reus* of an offence under the section. The offence is triable either way.

21. 'Valuable security'

This includes any document creating, transferring, surrendering or releasing a right in or over property, or authorising the payment of money or delivery of any property, or the satisfaction of any obligation: *see* s. 20(3). In *R.* v. *Benstead* (1982), a letter of credit was held by the Court of Appeal to be a 'valuable security' under s. 20, because, when presented, a bank would have no right to refuse payment on the letter. *See R.* v. *Nanayakkara* (1987); *R.* v. *King* (1992) (a clearing house automated payment service order *is* a valuable security within s. 20); *R.* v. *Bolton* (1992) (neither a bank statement nor a telegraphic transfer is a valuable security within s. 20).

22. 'Deception'

This has the same meaning as in s. 15 (*see* **10**).

23. 'Procures the execution'

In *R.* v. *Beck* (1985), the Court of Appeal held that 'execution' was not to be construed in a technical sense. Hence, when a traveller's cheque was accepted as genuine by a payer who had paid its monetary value to the holder, he had 'executed' it. This was *disapproved* by the House of Lords in *R.* v. *Kassim* (1992).

(a) In *Kassim*, X had utilised a false name and address so as to open a bank account. He used the cheque book and cheque guarantee card which were issued to him and, as a result, was charged and convicted of offences under s. 20.

(b) *Per* Lord Ackner: 'It is clear from the legislative history of s. 20(2) that "execution" . . . has as its object a wide variety of documents including bills of exchange and other negotiable instruments. The subsection contemplates acts being done to or in connection with such documents. It does not contemplate and accordingly is not concerned with giving effect to the documents by the carrying out of the instructions which they may contain, such as the delivery of goods or the payment out of money'.

Obtaining services by deception: Theft Act 1978, s. 1

24. Definition of the offence

'A person who by any deception dishonestly obtains services from another shall be guilty of an offence': s. 1(1) of the 1978 Act. There is an offence, therefore, where X allows a barber, Y, to shave him, but has no intention of paying for Y's services, and does not do so. The offence is triable either way.

25. 'Obtaining of services'

'It is an obtaining of services where the other is induced to confer a benefit by doing some act, or causing or permitting some act to be done, on the understanding that the benefit has been or will be paid for': s. 1(2).

26. *Actus reus*

The following must be proved:

(a) a deception by X affecting Y;
(b) X's inducing Y to perform, cause or permit a service for X or a third party on the understanding that it has been or will be paid for;
(c) the obtaining of that service, which is a benefit to anyone.

27. *Mens rea*

This comprises:

(a) dishonesty;
(b) an intent by X to acquire for himself or another person a service and its benefits.

28. 'Deception'

The accused, X, must have obtained the service as the result of his deception. 'Deception' has the meaning given by the 1968 Act, s. 15: 1978 Act, s. 5(1). This means that X must *induce* Y to provide the service which confers a benefit. Some direct link must be shown between X's deception and the act from which X, or some other person, derives the benefit. There would be no offence under the section, therefore, where X secretly enters a theatre, thereby avoiding payment, for, in this case, there is no 'deception', in that X's entry is not known to the theatre owner and no one has been 'deceived'.

29. 'Services'

The term 'services' in s. 1 is not defined under the 1978 Act. The underlying concept seems to be some act performed or permitted by Y, which has conferred a benefit on X or some other person, the performance having been undertaken on the understanding that it has been or will be paid for. (The obtaining of gratuitous services is excluded.) Services must derive from some act, so that an omission will not suffice for the purposes of s. 1. The offence will be complete when Y does the act following X's deception. (Note *R. v. Halai* (1983) – provision of a mortgage advance *does not* constitute a 'service' for the purposes of s. 1. (But *see R. v. Teong Sun Chuah* (1991).) A hire-purchase agreement *does* constitute such a service: *R. v. Widdowson* (1986).)

30. 'Benefit'

The act performed, caused or permitted by Y need not necessarily benefit X; it suffices that it constitutes a benefit to any person. Where the 'benefit' is in itself a criminal offence it is highly unlikely to be considered as a benefit within s. 1.

Evading liability by deception: 1978 Act, s. 2

31. Definition of the offence

'2–(1) Subject to subsection (2) below, where a person by any deception–

(a) dishonestly secures the remission of the whole or part of any existing liability to make a payment, whether his own liability or another's; or
(b) with intent to make permanent default in whole or in part on any existing liability to make a payment, or with intent to let another do so, dishonestly induces the creditor or any person claiming payment on behalf of the creditor to wait for payment (whether or not the due date for payment is deferred) or to forgo payment; or
(c) dishonestly obtains any exemption from or abatement of liability to make a payment, he shall be guilty of an offence.' (*See R. v. Sibartie* (1983).)
The offence is triable either way.
'**(2)** For the purposes of this section 'liability' means legally enforceable liability; and subsection (1) shall not apply in relation to a liability that has not been accepted or established to pay compensation for a wrongful act or omission.
(3) For the purposes of subsection 1(*b*) a person induced to take in payment a cheque or other security for money by way of conditional satisfaction of a pre-existing liability is to be treated not as being paid but as being induced to wait for payment.
(4) For the purposes of subsection (1)(*c*) 'obtains' includes obtaining for another or enabling another to obtain.'

32. Securing the remission of a liability: s. 2(1)(*a*)

An offence is committed where X, as the result of a deception, secures the remission of an *existing, legally enforceable liability* in whole or part. Assume that X has borrowed money from a friend, Y, the amount to be repaid within six months. When payment is due, X tells Y an untrue story of a misfortune which makes it impossible for him to repay. Y is persuaded to forget the debt. X has committed an offence under s. 2(1)(*a*). *See R. v. Jackson* (1983) – use of a stolen credit card at a garage to obtain petrol and other goods led to the trader accepting it, so that he would look to the issuing authority for payment, thus allowing the defendant to secure the remission of an existing liability. In *R.* v. *Modupe* (1992), a Consumer Credit Act 1974 'regulated agreement' that was improperly executed (because of the use of a false name and because details of the total amount payable under a hire purchase agreement were not given) and was only enforceable with the leave of the court, *was* an 'existing liability' within the meaning of s. 2(1), notwithstanding the absence of such leave.

33. Inducing a creditor to wait for or to forgo payment: s. 2(1)(*b*)

An offence is committed where X, as the result of a deception, and intending to make *permanent default*, induces a creditor, Y, to abstain from demanding settlement of a debt legally due to him. The offence is committed, therefore, by X who returns bills to Y and marks them 'Gone away. Address unknown', so that Y is obliged to wait for payment; or by X who deceives Y, a grocer, into believing that goods supplied by Y to X have been paid for, so that X's account is marked as settled.

(a) In *R.* v. *Attewell-Hughes* (1991), X, a hotel manager, was convicted under s. 2(1) (b), on the grounds that he had issued worthless cheques which had induced creditors, including Y, to wait for payment. In fact, the liability to the creditors, including Y, was that of Z, the hotel owner, rather than of X. (The cheques were in payment of debts incurred by Z before X became hotel manager.) X was charged with acting 'with intent to make permanent default in whole or in part of an existing liability to pay £6347 to Y'.

(b) X appealed against conviction. The Court of Appeal observed that s. 2(1) (b) only covers an intention to make permanent default in repect of another's liability so long as the default is *by the person who is under that liability*. The existence of the second limb of the offence ('or with intent to let another do so') meant that the first limb, upon which X had been convicted, was confined to any liability of X. X had no liability in relation to the circumstances in question. His conviction was *quashed*.

34. Obtaining exemption from or abatement of liability to make payment: s. 2(1)(*c*)

It will be noted that this subsection does not require proof of any *existing* liability. The subsection will apply, for example, where X, who is not a student, deceives a travel company into allowing him a special student travelling rate. *See R.* v. *Firth* (1990) in which the Court of Appeal held that an offence under s. 2(1)(*c*) could be committed *irrespective* of whether the act was one of commission or omission, and could be committed *before* any liability to pay had come into existence.

False accounting and false statements by company directors

35. Definition of the offence of false accounting
'Where a person dishonestly, with a view to gain for himself or another or with intent to cause loss to another'

(a) destroys, defaces, conceals or falsifies any account or any record or document made or required for any accounting purpose; *or*
(b) in furnishing information for any purpose produces or makes use of any account, or any such record or document as aforesaid, which to his knowledge is or may be misleading, false or deceptive in a material particular:

he shall, on conviction on indictment be liable to imprisonment': Theft Act 1968, s. 17(1).

The offence is triable either way.

(a) *See R. v. Keatley* (1980). Note that a document is 'made or required' for an accounting purpose within s. 17(1)(*a*), although made for another purpose, if it was required for an accounting purpose as a subsidiary consideration: *A.-G.'s Ref. (No. 1 of 1980)*. Recklessness will suffice for the appropriate *mens rea*.
(b) *See R. v. Shama* (1990) – a document can be 'falsified' on a true construction of s. 17(1)(a) where there is a duty to complete one of a number of standard printed forms and no document was completed. (A telephone operator left unmarked certain forms which had to be completed for recording international calls.) In this case one of the standard printed forms could become a document 'required for an accounting purpose'.

36. Examples of the offence
The offence under s. 17 might be committed, for example:

(a) Where X falsifies his annual tax return so as to provide incorrect information for the Inland Revenue authorities.
(b) Where X, a taxi-driver, employed by the taxi-cab owner, Y, falsifies the readings on the taxi-meter, so as to give Y incorrect information concerning the amount of money collected in fares: *see R. v. Solomons* (1909).
(c) Where X, a turnstile operator at a football ground, admits two persons with one movement of the turnstile (thus recording the entry of one person only) having accepted payment from both of them: *Edwards v. Toombs* (1983).

37. 'Gain' or 'loss'

These terms bear the meaning set out in s. 34(2): *see* 15:3.

(a) In *R. v. Eden* (1971), the Court of Appeal held that the offence of false accounting, committed by a sub-postmaster who had made returns stating that he had paid out a larger number of pensions than were, in fact, covered by the vouchers submitted with the returns, could be based on an intention of *temporary gain*, e.g. 'putting off the evil day' of having to pay up so as to sort out the muddle.

(b) In *R. v. Golechha* (1989), X intending to induce a bank not to sue him because of some bills of exchange which had been discounted, presented further bills that were false, in that they purported falsely to show that they were supported by *bona fide* financial transactions. The Court of Appeal held that X's purpose *did not* amount to a view to gain for purposes of a charge of conspiracy to commit false accounting: the desired forebearance of the bank *did not* constitute getting or gaining of money or property. (*Per curiam*: X's conduct *could* fall within the 1968 Act, s. 16 (obtaining an overdraft by deception), *see* **14**, or the 1978 Act, s. 2 (evading liability by deception), *see* **31**.) *See also Lee Cheung Wing* v. *R.* (1992).

38. 'Falsifies'

For purposes of s. 17, 'a person who makes or concurs in making in an account or other document an entry which is or may be misleading, false or deceptive in a material particular, or who omits or concurs in omitting a material particular from an account or other document, is to be treated as falsifying the account or document': s. 17(2). In *R. v. Mallett* (1978) the Court of Appeal held that the prosecution need *not* show that the false 'material particular' is material to an accounting purpose, so long as the document itself (in this case a hire-purchase agreement) is for an accounting purpose.

39. 'Any account or record or document'

This phrase will include e.g. an automatic mechanism, such as a taximeter (*see* **36(b)**) or a computer, and possibly an electric- or gas-meter.

> NOTE: Where an offence under ss. 15, 16, 17 is committed by a body corporate with the consent or connivance of a director or other officer, that person as well as the company shall be guilty of that offence: *see* s. 18(1).

40. False statements by a company director

The offence is committed where the officer of a company, with intent to deceive its members or creditors about its affairs, 'publishes or concurs in publishing a written statement or account which to his knowledge is or may be misleading, false or deceptive in a material particular': s. 19. (For the false, deceptive or misleading statement in relation to an investment business, *see* the Financial Services Act 1986, s. 47(1). *See* also s. 200.) It is triable either way.

41. Dishonest suppression of documents
The offence is committed when a person who 'dishonestly, with a view to gain for himself or another or with intent to cause loss to another, destroys, defaces or conceals any valuable security, any will or other testamentary document or any original document of or belonging to, or filed or deposited in, any court of justice or any government department . . .': s. 20(1).

Progress test 17

1. What is the essence of the deception offences under the Theft Acts? **(2)**

2. Is 'deception by omission' possible? **(4)**

3. Comment on the overlap of 'deception' and 'theft'. **(6)**

4. Outline the Theft Act 1968, s. 15. **(7)**

5. Outline the Theft Act 1968, s. 16. **(14)**

6. Comment on *R. v. Callender* (1992). **(18)**

7. Explain the decision in *R. v. Lambie* (1981). **(19)**

8. What is the significance of *R. v. Beck* (1985)? **(23)**

9. Explain 'obtaining services by deception'. **(24–27)**

10. What is meant by 'evading liability by deception'? **(31)**

11. Comment on *R. v. Attewell-Hughes* (1991). **(33)**

12. Explain the decision in *R. v. Golechha* (1989). **(37)**

Making off, blackmail, and handling

Making off without payment

1. Essence of the offence

'. . . A person who, knowing that payment on the spot for any goods supplied or service done is required or expected from him, dishonestly makes off without having paid as required or expected and with intent to avoid payment of the amount due shall be guilty of an offence': Theft Act 1978, s. 3(1). This is a crime of specific intent: *see* 3:12. It is triable either way.

(a) *Actus reus.* The offence requires that X makes off from the spot where payment is required or expected from him in relation to some enforceable debt which he is avoiding; thus, X enters Y's taxi and, after the journey, leaves the taxi by running off, dishonestly, without paying the fare to Y.

(b) *Mens rea.* It must be shown that X's dishonesty was present at the time he made off; that he was aware of the requirement or expectation concerning payment; and that he intended to avoid payment.

(c) *What the prosecution must show.* Given the facts at **(a)** above, it will be necessary for proof of an offence under s. 3 to show:

(*i*) that X knew he was required to pay Y at the end of the journey;

(*ii*) that X made off from the spot where payment was required (i.e. the location of the taxi at the end of the journey);

(*iii*) that X was dishonest; and

(*iv*) that X's making off was accompanied by an intent to avoid payment to the taxi driver, Y.

Note that proof of deceit as such is *not* required.

(d) *Under s. 3(4) there is a statutory power of arrest.* 'A person may arrest without warrant anyone who is, or whom he, with reasonable cause, suspects to be, committing or attempting to commit an offence under this section.' Note *R.* v. *Drameh* (1983), where it was held that this power of arrest does *not* apply in the case of a person who has already committed the offence under s. 3(1).

2. 'Makes off'

This means making off from the spot where payment is required or expected, and what is 'the spot' will depend on the circumstances of the case: *see R.* v. *McDavitt* (1981). In *R.* v. *Brooks* (1983) the Court of Appeal approved the trial judge's statement that 'the essence of the offence is that people left, intending if they could, to get away without paying'. *See* also *Troughton* v. *Metropolitan Police* (1987) – X's conviction under s. 3 for making off without paying his taxi fare was quashed because the driver was in breach of contract, having failed to take X to his destination. See *Moberley* v. *Alsop* (1991) (payment required at more than one 'spot').

3. 'Dishonestly'

It must be shown that X was dishonest at the time when he made off, and this will be a question for a jury. The stealthy departure of X from the spot at which he was expected to pay may be viewed as evidence of dishonesty. If, however, the accused believed that he had no liability to pay for goods or services, this mistake of law might negate dishonest intention.

4. 'Without having paid'

A problem may arise where the accused, X, has made off after 'paying' Y by means of a cheque which he (X) knows to be worthless. It may be that, since Y requires and expects payment in this case by a good cheque, X has not carried out his obligation to pay Y 'as required or expected.'

5. 'Knowing that payment on the spot for any goods supplied or service done required or expected from him'

Where, for example, X_1 and X_2 are eating together in a restaurant, and X_1 makes off, believing that X_2 will pay for the meal, the offence under s. 3(1) is not committed, since X_1 does not act dishonestly and does not know that payment is required or expected from him: *see R.* v. *Brooks* (1983). Note s. 3(2): 'For the purposes of this section "payment on the spot" includes payment at the time of collecting goods on which work has been done or in respect of which service has been provided.' The subsection would cover, for example, X's making off without paying the garage mechanic who has repaired his car. But where X honestly believes, for example, that he is a 'credit customer' *and* does not know that payment on the spot is required, it would seem that no offence under s. 3(1) has been committed.

6. 'With intent to avoid payment'

In *R.* v. *Allen* (1985), the House of Lords held that on a charge of making off without payment, contrary to s. 3, there must be an intent *permanently* to avoid payment, and *an intent to merely delay payment is insufficient*. (In this case X had incurred a bill of £1,200 at a hotel and left without paying, having said that he expected to pay the bill later after some business had been transacted. It was held that the prosecution had to prove that X intended *permanently* to avoid paying his bill.)

7. 'Goods supplied or service done'

'Subsection (1) shall not apply where the supply of the goods or the doing of the service is contrary to law, or where the service done is such that payment is not legally enforceable': s. 3(3). Where, therefore, X 'makes off' from premises in which illegal business is being conducted and after engaging in a transaction resulting in an unenforceable debt (as where he has not paid a drug trafficker who has supplied him illegally with controlled drugs), there is *no offence* under s. 3.

Blackmail

8. Under the Theft Act 1968

The offences under earlier legislation (*see* the Larceny Act 1916, ss. 29–31) were replaced by a single offence of 'blackmail'. By s. 21(1):

> 'A person is guilty of blackmail if, with a view to gain for himself or another or with intent to cause loss to another, he makes any unwarranted demand with menaces; and for this purpose a demand with menaces is unwarranted unless the person making it does so in the belief –

(a) that he had reasonable grounds for making the demand; *and*
(b) that the use of the menaces is a proper means of reinforcing the demand.'

Note that 'gain or loss' includes gain or loss in money or other property: s. 34(2)(*a*). The offence is triable only on indictment.

9. Examples of the offence

The offence is committed, for example:

(a) Where X made a practice of picking up prostitutes in his car and, pretending to be a police officer, demanded money from them to avoid prosecution: *R. v. Cutbill* (1982).
(b) Where X, in severe pain, threatened to shoot Y, a doctor, if Y did not give him an injection of morphine: in this case X stands to gain the property contained in the injection, thereby making a gain for himself: *R. v. Bevans* (1988).
(c) Where X saw a newspaper photograph of Y, a total stranger to him, and wrote to Y demanding money with a threat to expose him as a homosexual, which he was not: *R. v. Christie* (1990).
(d) Where X wrote to a confectionery manufacturer threatening to

contaminate products unless the sum of £1 million was paid: *R.* v. *Telford* (1992).

10. *Actus reus*

The *actus reus* is the making of an unwarranted demand with menaces. It matters not that the demand is not complied with.

(a) 'Menaces' originally implied a threat of violence, but the term now has a wider meaning. 'The word "menaces" is to be liberally construed and not as limited to threats of violence but as including threats of any action detrimental to or unpleasant to the person addressed. It may also include a warning that in certain events such action is intended': *per* Lord Wright in *Thorne* v. *Motor Trade Association* (1937). *See R.* v. *Hoey* (1992) (demand for 'protection money').

(b) There need be no *express* threat; the demand may take any form; it may be explicit or implicit.

> 'You need not be satisfied that there was an express demand for money in words. You need not be satisfied that any express threat was made, but if the evidence satisfies you that, although there was no such express demand or threat, the demeanour of the accused and the circumstances of the case were such that an ordinary reasonable man would understand that a demand for money was being made upon him and that the demand was accompanied by menaces – not perhaps direct, but veiled menaces – so that his ordinary balance of mind was upset, then you would be justified in coming to the conclusion that a demand with menaces had been made . . .': *per* Pilcher J in *R.* v. *Collister* (1955).

(c) 'The nature of the act or omission demanded is immaterial, and it is also immaterial whether the menaces relate to action to be taken by the person making the demand': s. 21(2).

(*i*) It is immaterial whether the demand be in words or writing. 'When the demand is made by word of mouth it is usually made at one time and place. If the intended victim is too deaf to hear it or unable to understand it, it is nonetheless made': *per* Stephenson J in *Treacy* v. *DPP* (1971).

(*ii*) A written demand in the form of a letter is made where and when the letter is posted: *see Treacy* v. *DPP* (1971). 'Would a man say in ordinary conversation: "I have made a demand" when he had written a letter containing a demand and posted it to the person to whom the demand was addressed? My answer to that question is that it would be natural for him to say "I have made a demand" as soon as he had posted the letter, for he would have done all that was in his power to make the demand': *per* Lord Diplock in *Treacy* v. *DPP* (1971).

(d) The threat made must be such as would be likely to alarm an ordinary person of normal stability and courage, but it is not necessary to show that the intended victim did, in fact, become alarmed. In *R*. v. *Clear* (1968), X, a lorry driver employed by Y, had left his lorry for a time, during which its load was stolen. Following the commencement of an action by Y against the insurers, X approached Y and said that, unless he was paid money he would not give evidence that he had left his lorry secure. Y (who understood that, even if he lost the action, his insurers would pay for the value of the stolen goods) was in no way alarmed by the threat. X's conviction for blackmail was *upheld*, since it was sufficient on the facts as X believed them to be that an ordinary person would be likely to be influenced by the threat. In *R*. v. *Harry* (1974), in which the accused had sent letters to shopkeepers asking them to buy 'indemnity posters' in relation to a students' 'rag week', the judge, ruling that there was no evidence of any 'menace', cited *R*. v. *Clear* (1968): '"Menaces" must be of such a nature and extent that the mind of an ordinary person of normal stability and courage might be influenced or made apprehensive so as to concede unwillingly to the demand.' See *R*. v. *Cutbill* (1982); *R*. v. *Garwood* (1987).

(e) A judge need not explain the meaning of the word 'menaces' to a jury where, because of special knowledge in special circumstances, what would ordinarily be a menace is, in fact, not, or where the converse would be the case: *see R*. v. *Lawrence* (1971).

(f) 'There may be special circumstances unknown to an accused which would make the threats innocuous and unavailing for the accused's demand, but such circumstances would have *no bearing* on the accused's state of mind and of his intention. If an accused knew that what was threatened would have no effect it might be different': *per* Sellers J in *R*. v. *Clear* (1968).

(g) There can be no 'attempt to blackmail' – there is a complete offence or there is not. *See R*. v. *Moran* (1952).

11. *Mens rea*

The *mens rea* is the accused person's view to gain for himself or another, or his intent to cause loss, *and* a lack of belief, not only that his grounds for making the demand were reasonable, but that the menaces were 'proper' in the circumstances. (The Criminal Law Revision Committee, in its Eighth Report, suggested that 'proper' be interpreted in relation to 'what is morally and socially acceptable'.) In *R*. v. *Harvey*, (1981) X was charged with blackmail by making threats against Y's wife and child, and the Court of Appeal held that the question was whether the accused believed that the means he used were 'proper', in the sense of 'lawful'. The factual question of his belief should be left to the jury and it mattered not what a reasonable man believed, except in so far as it might throw light on what the accused believed. In *R. v. Cummings* (1986), the Court of Appeal held that it would always be a mitigating factor in blackmail that the offender believed himself to have some claim of right to the payment of the money he sought to enforce.

> NOTE: Harassment in relation to payment of a debt may be an offence under the Administration of Justice Act 1970, s. 40(1): 'A person commits an offence if, with the object of coercing another person to pay money claimed from the other as a debt due under a contract, he (*a*) harasses the other with demands for payment which, in respect of their frequency or the manner or occasion of making any such demand, or of any threat or publicity by which any demand is accompanished, are calulated to subject him or members of his family or household to alarm, distress or humiliation; (*b*) falsely represents, in relation to the money claimed, that criminal proceedings lie for failure to pay it; (*c*) falsely represents himself to be authorised in some official capacity to claim or enforce payment; or (*d*) utters a document falsely represented by him to have some official character which he knows it has not.' (For harassment in relation to residential occupiers of property, *see* Protection from Eviction Act 1977, s. 1(3), and *R. v. Burke* (1991), in which the House of the Lords held that harassment of a tenant need not be actionable in civil law in order to constitute an offence under s. 1(3).)

Handling under the Theft Act 1968

12. Definition of the offence
'A person handles stolen goods if (otherwise than in the course of the stealing) knowing or believing them to be stolen goods he dishonestly receives the goods, or dishonestly undertakes or assists in their retention, removal, disposal or realisation by or for the benefit of another person, or if he arranges to do so': s. 22(1).

The section replaced the earlier offence of 'receiving' by that of *handling*. A very important change is that the offence can be committed not only by a person who *knows*, but also by a person who *believes*, that the goods in question were stolen (*see* **21**). The offence is triable either way.

13. Examples of the offence
The offence is committed, for example:

(a) When X, who knows that Y or some other person has recently stolen a television receiver, helps Y to unload it from Y's van into a warehouse.

(b) When X discusses with Z the terms of a sale to Z of property which X knows to have been stolen by Y.

(c) When a person tells lies about stolen goods to protect a handler, so that he, too, handles, by dishonestly assisting in the retention of those goods for the benefit of another: *see R. v. Kanwar* (1982).

> NOTE: Section 23 created a further offence, which is committed where *'any public advertisement* of a reward for the return of any goods which have been stolen or lost uses words to the effect that no questions will be asked, or that the person producing the goods will be safe from apprehension or enquiry . . .' The person advertising the reward and the printer or publisher are liable, on summary conviction, to a fine. In *Denham* v. *Scott* (1984), the manager of a newspaper in which such an advertisement had been published was convicted although he had not checked it. It was held that the offence required no *mens rea*, and is, therefore, an offence of strict liability (*see* Chap. 4).

Handling outlined

14. 'Goods'
'Goods', for the purpose of s. 22, includes 'money and every other description of property except land, and includes things severed from the land by stealing': s. 34(2)(*b*). The Court of Appeal has held (*see A.-G.'s Reference No. 4 of 1979*) that things in action can be 'stolen goods' under s. 22. *See* **22**(d).

15. 'Dishonestly'
The offence requires that the accused shall have handled the goods dishonestly (and this will be a question of fact for the jury), knowing or believing them to be stolen. *See* also **21**.

(a) If, at the time X received goods stolen from Y by Z, he had the intention of returning them to Y, or handing them to the police, he would not be guilty of handling. If, however, he does decide to retain the goods he is guilty of theft.

(b) A claim of right may provide a defence.

(c) Merely *using* the stolen goods does not amount to retention: *R. v. Sanders* (1982). 'It must be proved in some way that the accused was assisting in the retention of the goods by concealing them, or making them more difficult to identify, or by holding them pending their ultimate disposal, or by some other act that was part of the chain of dishonest handling': *per* Dunn LJ.

(d) Note *Broom* v. *Crowther* (1985), in which X bought goods in good faith, but found later that they had been stolen. For one week he neither used nor attempted to dispose of the goods, since he was unable to decide what to do with them. It was held that he had not assumed the rights of the owner and, therefore, was not guilty of handling.

(e) In *R.* v. *Roberts* (1987), X, in response to an advertisement, used a false name and offered to return stolen paintings for a reward if no attempt were made to arrest him. His defence to a charge of handling was that he was 'an honest businessman' who had found out about the paintings by chance. Dismissing his appeal against conviction, the Court of Appeal held that 'dishonest' in s. 22(1) did not necessarily mean dishonest in relation to the loser of the goods, and unless X has raised the issue of whether he knew that anyone would regard what he did as dishonest, it was not necessary for the full subjective test set out in *R.* v. *Ghosh* (1982) (*see* **15:6**) to be mentioned in the summing up.

16. 'Handling'
The offence under s. 22 is a single offence: *see Griffiths* v. *Freeman* (1970). (Note, however, the seemingly conflicting statement of Lord Bridge in *R.* v. *Bloxham* (1982), that s. 22 creates *two offences*, namely, receiving, or arranging to receive, *and* an offence involving the other forms of handling (at (b) and (c) below). The reason is: 'receiving' (at (a) below) is the only offence under s. 22 that does not require to be undertaken 'by or for the benefit of another person'.) It can be committed in several ways (*see* s. 22(1) at 1):

(a) where X dishonestly *receives* stolen goods;
(b) where X dishonestly *undertakes to retain, remove, dispose of or realise* the goods by or for the benefit of another person;
(c) where X dishonestly *assists in the retention, removal, disposal or realisation* of the goods by or for the benefit of another person;
(d) where X *arranges to perform* any of the above acts.

17. 'Receiving'
Receiving does *not* require that X should have acted solely for the benefit of another person. Further:

(a) Receiving *the person* who has stolen the goods and has them in his possession does not, in itself, constitute a receiving of the goods.
(b) Where the thief retains control of the stolen goods (e.g. during negotiations with the accused) there is no receiving.
(c) Proof of receiving requires evidence that the accused person obtained control or possession of the stolen goods (or participated with others in obtaining such control or possession).
(d) It suffices that X's agent or servant received the stolen goods with X's authority.
(e) It was held in *R.* v. *Smythe* (1980) that 'receiving', in s. 22, indicates a single, finite act and not a continuing activity.

18. 'Undertakes or assists'

In the example under **13 (b)**, X may be said to have undertaken or assisted in the *disposal* of goods stolen by Y. In the example under **13(a)**, X has undertaken or assisted in the *removal* of stolen goods. A failure to reveal to the police the presence of stolen goods on the premises of the accused person does not necessarily amount to assisting in their *retention* (although it may constitute strong evidence).

(a) In *R.v.Pitchley* (1973), X was handed money by his son, Y, who asked him to look after it. The following day X deposited the money in his savings account. Five days later, X learned that the money was stolen property. He did not wish to take Y to the police and he permitted the stolen money to remain in his account until a few days later when the police interviewed him. His appeal against conviction of handling the money was *dismissed* by the Court of Appeal.

(b) *Per* Cairns LJ: 'In the course of argument, Nield J cited the dictionary meaning of the word "retain" – keep possession of, not lose, continue to have. In the view of this Court, that is the meaning of the word "retain" in this section . . . The meaning of the word "retention" in the section is a matter of law in so far as the construction of the word is necessary. It is hardly a difficult question of construction because it is an ordinary English word and in the view of this Court, it was no more necessary for the Deputy Chairman to leave to the jury the question of whether or not what was done amounted to retention, than it would be necessary for a judge in a case where goods had been handed to a person who knew that they had been stolen for him to direct the jury that it was for them to decide whether or not that constituted receiving . . .'

19. 'For the benefit of another person'

Where X is charged with a mode of handling other than receiving or arranging to receive, it must be shown that the handling has been performed by or for the benefit of another person. In *R. v. Bloxham* (1982), the House of Lords held that the category of 'other persons' contemplated by s. 22(1) is limited, and that a purchaser, as such, of stolen goods, is not 'another person' within the subsection.

20. 'Arranging'

The offence of handling is complete *immediately* the receipt of the stolen goods is arranged, or *immediately* an act of undertaking or assisting is arranged, e.g. where X makes an agreement to try to sell goods stolen by Y. In *R. v. Curbishley and Crispin* (1970), X_1 and X_2 telephoned Y to ask whether he needed help to remove stolen goods. The telephone was answered by a police officer (who had recovered the goods) and who pretended that assistance was required. X_1 and X_2 arrived by car and offered to help to remove the goods. It was held that this amounted to the offence of *attempting* dishonestly to assist in the removal or disposal of the goods. Note *R. v. Park* (1988) – an arrangement to handle stolen goods made *prior to the theft* of the goods was *not* an offence under s. 22(1).

21. 'Knowing or believing them to be stolen goods'
Formerly it was necessary that the accused person should have known that the goods had been stolen; his having had 'a pretty good idea', for example, did not suffice: *see R. v. Woods* (1969); *R. v. Reader* (1977) – 'to believe that the goods are *probably* stolen is not to believe that the goods *are* stolen.'

In *R. v. Hall* (1985), the Court of Appeal laid down guidelines on the directions to be given to the jury on the meaning of the phrase 'knowing or believing goods to be stolen' when the accused is charged under s. 22(1). 'We think that a jury should be directed along these lines. A man may be said to know that goods are stolen when he is told by someone with first hand knowledge (someone such as the thief or the burglar) that such is the case. Belief, of course, is something short of knowledge. It may be said to be the state of mind of a person who says to himself: "I cannot say I know for certain that these goods are stolen, but there can be no other reasonable conclusion in the light of all the circumstances, in the light of all that I have heard and seen." Either of these two states of mind is enough to satisfy the words of the statute. The second (that is, belief) is enough even if the defendant says to himself: "Despite all that I have seen and all that I have heard, I refuse to believe what my brain tells me is obvious. " What is not enough, of course, is mere suspicion: "I suspect that these goods may be stolen, but it may be on the other hand that they are not." That state of mind, of course, does not fall within the words "knowing or believing" . . .': *per* Boreham J. *See R. v. Harris* (1987) – in general, it is not necessary for the judge to define the meaning of 'knowledge' or 'belief' in s. 22; *R. v. Toor* (1987); *R. v. Brook* (1993).

Stolen goods

22. Scope of 'stolen goods'
The term refers to:

(a) goods stolen in England or Wales or elsewhere, provided that the stealing amounted to an offence where and at the time when the goods were stolen: *see* s. 24(1); *and*

(b) goods obtained in England or Wales or elsewhere either by blackmail (*see* s. 21) or by deception: *see* s. 15(1); *and*

(c) 'in addition to the goods originally stolen and parts of them (whether in their original state or not), any other goods which directly or indirectly represent or have at any time represented the stolen goods in the hands of the thief as being the proceeds of any disposal or realisation of the whole or part of the goods stolen or of goods so representing the stolen goods, and any other goods which directly or indirectly represent or have at any time represented the stolen goods in the hands of a handler of the stolen goods or any part of them as being the proceeds of any disposal or realisation of the whole or part of the stolen goods handled by him or of goods so representing them': s. 24(2)(*a*).

(d) *See A.-G.'s Reference (No. 4 of 1979)*, concerning a situation in which a thief pays stolen money into a bank account and *later* passes to the accused a cheque drawn on that account. The accused can be convicted under s. 24(2). Where the bank account has been credited with stolen money *and* money lawfully obtained, the prosecution must show that, at the time of receipt by the accused, the bank balance held by the thief included that which represented the proceeds of the stolen goods *and* that the receiver had received such proceeds, at least in part.

23. Goods which cease to be stolen
The offence of handling requires that the goods *shall have remained stolen at the time of such handling.*

> 'No goods shall be regarded as having continued to be stolen goods after they have been restored to the person from whom they were stolen or to other lawful possession or custody, or after that person and any other person claiming through him have otherwise ceased as regards those goods to have any right to restitution in respect of the theft': s. 24(3).

The question whether goods found and kept under observation by the police have been reduced into the lawful possession of the police so as to provide a defence under s. 24(3) is a question of fact depending primarily on the intentions of the police: *see A.-G.'s Reference No. 1 of 1974*. It was held in *Greater London Metropolitan Police Commissioner* v. *Streeter* (1980) that the marking and observation of stolen goods does *not* amount to restoration to the person from whom they were stolen or to other lawful possession or custody under s. 24(3).

The 'course of stealing' in s. 22

24. 'Otherwise than in the course of the stealing'
The person who has stolen the goods cannot himself be guilty of handling

them, since the handling must be 'otherwise than in the course of the stealing'.

(a) In *R.* v. *Pitham* (1976), the Court of Appeal held that once a dishonest appropriation has been completed, subsequent dealing with the goods will *not* be 'in the course of stealing' within s. 22(1).

(b) In *R.* v. *Cash* (1985), X was tried on an indictment comprising several counts of handling, having been found in possession of goods stolen at least nine days previously. He argued that it was for the prosecution affirmatively to prove that he was not the thief or party to the theft, in the light of the phrase 'otherwise than in the course of the stealing'. X's appeal against conviction was *dismissed*, the Court of Appeal holding that, there being no issue that X was the thief, there was no burden positively to disprove it. *See* also *A.-G. of Hong Kong* v. *Yip* (1988); *R.* v. *Foreman* (1991).

25. Joint theft

Where the theft is committed jointly by X₁ and X₂, neither can be guilty of *handling* the stolen goods even where he has given assistance to his partner.

Enforcement and procedure

26. Search for stolen goods

Where a justice of the peace concludes that there is reasonable cause to believe that any person has in his custody or possession, or on his premises, any stolen goods, he may grant a warrant to search for and seize them: *see* s. 26(1). A person authorised under s. 26 to search may enter and search and seize any goods he believes to be stolen: *see* s. 26(2). *See* also the Police and Criminal Evidence Act 1984, s. 19.

27. Procedure

'Any number of persons may be charged in one indictment with reference to the same theft, with having at different times or at the same time handled all or any of the stolen goods, and the persons so charged may be tried together': s. 27(1). Where two or more persons indicted for jointly handling stolen goods are being tried, the jury may find any of the accused guilty if satisfied that he handled all or any of the stolen goods, whether or not he did so jointly with the other accused or any of them: *see* s. 27(2). *See DPP* v. *Merriman* (1973), in which X₁ took stolen goods which he had received to X₂'s shop, where they were received by X₂. X₁ and X₂ were held to have been properly jointly indicted, even though both handlings were separate.

28. Evidence
Under s. 27(3), at any stage of the proceedings for handling, if evidence has been given that the accused had or arranged to have in his possession the goods, or had undertaken or assisted, etc. in their removal, disposition or realisation, the prosecution may adduce as evidence, for the purpose of proving that he knew or believed the goods to be stolen:

(a) evidence that he has had in his possession, or has undertaken or assisted in the retention, removal, disposal or realisation of, stolen goods from any theft taking place not earlier than twelve months before the offence charged: *see* s. 27(3)(a); *and*

(b) (provided that seven days' notice in writing has been given to him) evidence that he has within the five years preceding the date of the offence charged been convicted of theft or handling of stolen goods: *see* s. 27(3)(b).

29. Decisions relating to s. 27(3)
The following cases should be noted.

(a) *R.* v. *Davis* (1972). The Court of Appeal drew attention to the precise wording of s. 27(3)(a), emphasising that the material words were 'not earlier than the twelve months before the offence charged', and *not* 'within the period of twelve months before the offence charged.'

(b) *R.* v. *Wilkins* (1975). On a charge of handling, the admission of evidence of a conviction under s. 27(3) has relevance only to the question of *guilty knowledge*, and not to the question of possession. Where such evidence is allowed, the jury must be made to realise the issues to which it is relevant. *See R.* v. *Duffas* (1993).

(c) *R.* v. *Ball* (1983). 'The so-called "doctrine of recent possession" is misnamed. It has nothing to do with goods recently possessed. It concerns possession of goods recently stolen. It is not even a doctrine. It is in fact no more than an inference which a jury may, or may not, think it right to draw about the state of mind of a defendant who is dealing in goods stolen not long beforehand. It is based on commonsense': *per* McCullough J. Note also *R.* v. *Greaves* (1987) – the doctrine of recent possession is a rule of evidence in that it is an inference to be drawn *with the proper degree of certainty* from the evidence.

(d) *R.* v. *Powers* (1990). The Court of Appeal held that, in relation to a stolen car, the trial judge should have recognised that possession of a car, four to six months after its theft, could *not* amount to 'recent possession' from which the jury would be entitled to infer safely that the defendant was guilty of handling it, knowing or believing it to be stolen. In circumstances such as these the matter ought not to have been left to the jury.

30. Recent guidelines on theft and handling charged as alternatives

In *R.* v. *Shelton* (1986), the Court of Appeal enunciated guidelines in relation to cases where theft and handling might be charged as alternatives.

(a) The practice of charging theft and handling as alternatives should continue whenever there was a *real possibility* (not a fanciful one) that at a trial the evidence might support one rather than the other.

(b) There was a danger that juries might be confused by reference to second or later appropriations since the issue in every case was whether the defendant had in fact appropriated property belonging to another. If he had done so it was irrelevant how he came to make the appropriation provided it was in the course of theft.

(c) A jury should be told that a handler could be a thief, but he could *not* be convicted of being *both* a thief and a handler.

(d) Handling was the more serious offence, carrying a heavier penalty, because those who knowingly had dealings with thieves encouraged stealing.

Draft Criminal Code Bill

31. Handling

'A person is guilty of handling stolen goods if (otherwise than in the course of the stealing) knowing or believing them to be stolen goods, he dishonestly (*a*) receives or arranges to receive the goods; or (*b*) undertakes or arranges to undertake their retention, removal, disposal or realisation for the benefit of another; or (*c*) assists or arranges to assist in their retention, removal, disposal or realisation by another': cl. 172.

32. Commentary

'As the offence is currently drafted, a person may commit handling "if he dishonestly undertakes or assists in [the] retention, removal, disposal or realisation [of stolen goods] by or for the benefit of another" or "if he arranges to do so" (where "do so" also refers to receiving them). This clumsy expression has caused much unnecessary trouble. It seems clear that one may either (*i*) *undertake* a relevant act *for the benefit of another* or (*ii*) *assist in* the doing of a relevant act *by another*. Clause 172 is drafted accordingly': para. 16.**15**.

Progress test 18

1. What is meant by 'making off without payment'? **(1)**

2. Comment on *R.* v. *Allen* (1985). **(6)**

3. Give examples of blackmail under the terms of the Theft Act 1968, s. 21. **(9)**

4. Comment on *R.* v. *Clear* (1968). **(10)**

5. How is handling defined in the Theft Act 1968? **(12)**

6. Comment on *Broom* v. *Crowther* (1985). **(15)**

7. Outline the decision in *R.* v. *Pitchley* (1973). **(18)**

8. 'The offence of handling requires that goods shall have remained stolen at the time of such handling.' Explain. **(23)**

Criminal damage, trespass and related offences

The Criminal Damage Act 1971

1. General
The 1971 Act, which repealed the Malicious Damage Act 1861 almost entirely, revised and simplified the law relating to criminal damage to property. It created the following offences:

(a) a *basic* offence, covering the destruction of or damage to the property of another without lawful excuse (*see* 2);
(b) an *aggravated* offence, covering the destruction of or damage to property with intent to endanger the life of another (*see* 10);
(c) offences concerning threats to destroy or damage property, and possessing anything with intent to destroy or damage property (*see* 12, 13).

2. The basic offence: destroying or damaging the property of another
'A person who without lawful excuse destroys or damages any property belonging to another intending to destroy or damage any such property or being reckless as to whether any such property would be destroyed or damaged shall be guilty of an offence': s. 1(1). (This is an arrestable offence: Police and Criminal Evidence Act 1984, s. 24(1)(*b*).) It is triable either way (but *see* Magistrates' Courts Act 1980, s. 22 and Sch. 2).

3. 'Without lawful excuse'
Under s. 5(2)(a) a person accused under s. 1(1) is treated as having a lawful excuse if, at the time of the alleged commission of the offence, he believed that the person(s) whom he believed to be entitled to give consent to the destruction or damage had, or would have, given such consent. Under s. 5(2)(*b*) there is a lawful excuse if the accused person has carried out the destruction or damage so as to protect property in the belief that it was in immediate need of protection and that the means of protection were or would be reasonable having regard to all the circumstances. For the

purposes of s. 5 it is immaterial whether a belief is justified or not, if it is honestly held: s. 5(3).

(a) In *R.* v. *Hunt* (1977), X set fire to a bed in an isolated block of old people's flats to draw attention to the inadequacy of fire alarm apparatus. The Court of Appeal *dismissed his appeal* against conviction for arson (*see* 9), holding that his act was not one which did or could in itself protect property. *See R.* v. *Ashford* (1988).

(b) In *Jaggard* v. *Dickinson* (1981), X had damaged windows and curtains in an honest, although drunken, belief that the owner of the property would have consented to the act. Because of X's self-induced intoxication she had, in fact, entered the wrong house. X's appeal against conviction was *allowed*: it was held that s. 5(3) required consideration by the court of her *actual* belief, and that belief could be held *honestly*, even though resulting from self-induced intoxication.

(c) In *R.* v. *Denton* (1982), the Court of Appeal held that X was *not guilty* of arson by setting fire to his employer's property when he (X) believed that his employer had consented to the act in pursuance of a fraudulent insurance claim. (*See* also *R.* v. *Appleyard* (1985).)

(d) In *R.* v. *Hill* (1989), the Court of Appeal held that where, on a charge of criminal damage, or possession of an article with intent to damage property, the argument of defendant is that his purpose was to protect property which was in immediate need of protection, the test is *both subjective* (what was in 'defendant's mind' *and objective* (whether as a matter of law on the facts believed by defendant, his actions could amount to an action to protect property).

(e) In *Lloyd* v. *DPP* (1992), X, a motorist who had parked his car without permission on another's land, and who was fully aware that he ran the risk of the car's being clamped, had no lawful excuse to damage the clamp. It was held that he had been rightly convicted of criminal damage; the use of force could only be allowed if there were no reasonable alternative, but here X could have paid the penalty imposed, obtained the release of his car and sued later for return of the sum paid.

(f) In *Blake* v. *DPP* (1993), it was held that a genuine belief that he was doing the will of God did not provide defendant with a defence of lawful excuse to a charge of criminal damage. (He claimed to be carrying out a divine command by writing a Biblical quotation on a pillar at the perimeter of the Houses of Parliament.)

(g) Note s. 5(5). 'This section shall not be construed as casting any doubt on any defence recognised by law as a defence to criminal charges. ' Some general defences to criminal charges (*see* Chap. 6), e.g. insanity, self-defence, prevention of crime, apply, therefore, to offences within the 1971 Act. *See* e.g. *R.* v. *Orpin* (1980) (drunkenness accepted as a defence); *R.* v.

Hardie (1984) (involuntary intoxication resulting from soporific drug, preventing basic intent).

4. 'Destroys or damages'

Neither word is defined in the 1971 Act. 'To destroy' seems to imply, not necessarily demolition, but rather the rendering of property useless for its intended purpose. 'To damage' relates to non-trivial injury to property. 'The word . . . is sufficiently wide in its meaning to embrace injury, mischief or harm done to property, and that in order to constitute "damage" it is unnecessary to establish such definite or actual damage as renders the property useless or prevents it from serving its normal function': *per* Walters J in *Samuels* v. *Stubbs* (1972). (For earlier decisions on the meaning of these terms, *see* e.g. *Roper* v. *Knott* (1898).) *See R.* v. *Fancy* (1980) – motive for damage is generally irrelevant; *A.* v. *R.* (1978), in which it was held that spitting on a police officer's raincoat did not constitute 'damage' since the coat had not been rendered imperfect or inoperative; *Roe* v. *Kingerlee* (1986) – smearing mud graffiti on a police cell wall was held to be 'damage'. Damage need not be permanent to be 'criminal damage'.

(a) In *R.* v. *Whitely* (1991), the Court of Appeal held that an unauthorised impairment of the value of a computer disc to its legitimate user was capable of being 'damage' within the meaning of the 1971 Act. X, a computer hacker, had deleted files within a computer system, affecting the content of discs. The Court of Appeal *rejected* X's appeal against conviction, which involved an argument that it was only the intangible information contained on a particular disc, and not the disc itself, that had been affected. Interference with the magnetic particles on the disc, it was argued, could not amount to damage at law. The Court stated that what the 1971 Act required to be proved was that tangible property had been damaged, not necessarily that the damage itself should be tangible. There was no basis upon which the jury could properly have concluded that the discs were not capable of sustaining damage.

(b) X's actions had pre-dated the coming into force of the Computer Misuse Act 1990 (*see* 20:7). 'For the purposes of the Criminal Damage Act 1971, a modification of the contents of a computer shall not be regarded as damaging any computer or computer storage medium *unless* its effect on that computer or computer storage medium impairs its physical condition': 1990 Act, s. 3(6).

5. 'Property'

Under s. 10(1), 'property' means property of a tangible nature, whether real or personal, including money, wild creatures (but not wild flowers).

Land (which cannot be stolen: *see* 14:**12**) *can* come within the ambit of criminal damage. Intangible property (which can be stolen: *see* 14:**11**) does *not* come within the 1971 Act.

6. 'Belonging to another'

Destruction or damage under s. 1(1) relates only to property belonging to another. Under s. 10(2) property is treated as belonging to any person who has custody or control of it, or who has any proprietary right or interest, or who has a charge on it. X may be guilty of damaging his own property under the Act, therefore, where that property is in the custody of Y. *See R. v. Smith* (1974) (X, a tenant, damaged fixtures which he thought were his own). 'No offence is committed under s. 1 if a person destroys or causes damage to property belonging to another if he does so in the honest but mistaken belief that the property is *his own*, and, provided that the belief is honestly held, it is irrelevant to consider whether or not it is a justifiable belief': *per* James LJ.

7. 'Intending'

For 'intention', *see* 3:8. Intention is not to be equated with 'foresight of probable consequences' or 'recklessness'. X's intention to throw a small stone at Y's car is not *in itself* proof of his intention to damage the windscreen of that car. The taking of *deliberate steps to some desired end* may indicate an 'intended consequence'. It involves, therefore, a *mental state* in which a person wills those consequences which his conduct may possibly generate. (In *R. v. Hancock and Shankland* (1986), the House of Lords, in considering murder (*see* 9:28), stated that where questions relating to foresight and intention were left to a jury, this required that 'probability of a consequence' be drawn *specifically* to the jury's attention, as well as an explanation that the greater the probability of a consequence, the more likely it was that the consequence was foreseen, and that if it was foreseen, the greater the probability was that it was also intended.)

8. 'Reckless'

See 3:14–18. In *R. v. Caldwell* (1982), X, who had a grievance against Y, broke into Y's hotel and set fire to it. (For details, *see* 3:**16**.) On appeal, the House of Lords reviewed the meaning of 'recklessness' in the 1971 Act. (For pre-Caldwell decisions concerning 'recklessness', *see* e.g. *R. v. Briggs* (1977); *R. v. Stephenson* (1979).)

(a) '"Reckless" as used in the new statutory definition of the *mens rea* of these offences [damage to property] is an ordinary English word. It had not by 1971 become a term of legal art with some more limited esoteric meaning than that which it bore in ordinary speech – a meaning which surely includes not only deciding to ignore a risk of harmful consequences resulting from one's acts that one has recognised as existing, but also failing to give any thought to whether or not there is any risk in circumstances where, if any thought were given to the matter, it would be obvious that there was . . .': *per* Lord Diplock in *R*. v. *Caldwell* (1982).

(b) 'In my opinion a person charged with an offence under s. 1(1) is "reckless as to whether or not any property would be destroyed or damaged" if (1) he does an act which in fact creates an obvious risk that property will be destroyed or damaged and (2) when he does the act he either has not given any thought to the possibility of there being any such risk or has recognised that there was some risk involved, and has nonetheless gone on to do it. That would be a proper direction to the jury; cases in the Court of Appeal which held otherwise should be regarded as overruled': *per* Lord Diplock.

(c) In *Elliott* v. *C.* (1983), X, a backward fourteen-year-old schoolgirl, was charged under s. 1(1). Wandering about after a sleepless night, she had entered a shed and poured white spirit on the floor, which she then set alight, destroying the shed. She was acquitted; the magistrates found that she did not appreciate the inflammable nature of the white spirit, and, given her tired state, she did not give any thought to the risk of fire. Allowing the prosecutor's appeal, a Divisional Court held that the correct test is whether a *reasonably prudent person* would realise the danger of fire in those circumstances, even though the accused might not appreciate this. (A petition for leave to appeal to the House of Lords was refused.)

(d) In *R*. v. *R*. *(S.M.)* (1984), it was submitted at X's trial for arson that the degree of recklessness required ought to relate to someone of X's age (fifteen) and characteristics, not those of a prudent person of mature years. Rejecting this plea, the Court of Appeal held that the court was *not* obliged to equate the ordinary 'prudent man' with one who shared the age, sex and other specific characteristics of an accused person which might affect his recognition of risk.

(e) In *Chief Constable of Avon* v. *Shimmen* (1987), it was held that a person who recognises the risk involved in his action, but thinks that his prowess and control will minimise it, may be considered 'reckless' should damage result. *See* 3:19.

9. Arson

The *common law offence of arson* (maliciously and voluntarily burning the dwelling house of another) was *abolished* under the 1971 Act, s. 11.Under s. 1(3), however, it is stated that 'an offence committed under this section by destroying or damaging property by fire shall be charged as arson'. *See R*. v. *Aylesbury Crown Court, ex p. Simmons* (1972); *R*. v. *Cooper* (1991). The offence is triable either way.

In *R*. v. *Miller* (1983), the House of Lords considered the following

question: 'Whether the *actus reus* of the offence of arson is present when
a defendant accidentally starts a fire, and thereafter, intending to destroy
or damage property belonging to another being reckless as to whether
any such property would be destroyed or damaged, fails to take any steps
to extinguish the fire or prevent damage to such property by that fire.'
The answer was, *Yes. Per* Lord Diplock: 'In cases where an accused was
initially unaware that he had done an act which set in train events which,
by the time he became aware of them, obviously presented a risk that
property belonging to another would be damaged, he would be guilty of
an offence under s. 1(1) if, when he became aware that the events had
happened as a result of his own act, he did not try to prevent or reduce
the risk of damage.'

For attempted arson, *see R. v. Chamberlain* (1987); *A.-G.'s Reference (No.
3 of 1992)* (on a charge of *attempted arson* in the aggravated form contemplated in s. 1(2) (*see* below), in addition to establishing a specific intent to
cause damage by fire, it is sufficient to prove that defendant was reckless
as to whether life would thereby be endangered). For principles of
sentencing, *see R. v. Smith* (1993).

10. The aggravated offence: destroying or damaging property with intent to endanger life

'A person who without lawful excuse destroys or damages any property,
whether belonging to himself or another –

(a) intending to destroy or damage property or being reckless as to
whether any property would be destroyed or damaged; and
(b) intending by the destruction or damage to endanger the life of
another or being reckless as to whether the life of another would be
thereby endangered, shall be guilty of an offence': s. 1(2). It is triable only
on indictment.

11. The gist of s. 1(2)

The aggravated offence is concerned essentially with 'danger to the life
of another'. Hence, if X is to be charged under s. 1(2), it must be shown
that, in addition to the *mens rea* required for the basic offence (*see* 2), he
intended to endanger the life of another *or* was reckless as to whether the
life of another was endangered. The *actus reus* of an offence under s. 1(2)
is the same as that for s. 1(1), *but* under s. 1(2) the offence can be committed
in relation to property belonging to the accused. Note also that the defence
under s. 5(2)(a) (*see* 3) has no application to s. 1(2). *See R. v. Hoof* (1980); *R.
v. Hardie* (1984).

(a) In *R. v. Steer* (1987), X was charged under s. 1(2)(b). Following a
business disagreement with Y, he had fired shots at Y as he stood near a

bedroom window, which was smashed. X's appeal against conviction was upheld by the Court of Appeal and the Crown appealed. The House of Lords *dismissed* the Crown's appeal: s. 1(2)(*b*) was directed at danger to life caused by the damaged property, and *not* by the way in which it was damaged. Y's life had not been endangered by the damage caused to the window by X. The element of *mens rea* related to the endangering of life must refer to endangering resulting from the damage, as distinct from the means used to cause that damage.

(b) In *R*. v. *Sangha* (1988), X was charged under s. 1(2)(*a*)(*b*). He had set fire to furniture in a temporarily unoccupied flat. He submitted that there was no case since, if he knew that nobody was in the flat or did not know whether or not anyone was there, his act could not have created an obvious and serious risk to the life of another. The Court of Appeal *dismissed* X's appeal. The question was: 'Would an ordinary prudent bystander have perceived at the time the fire was started an obvious risk that property would be damaged and that life, as a result, would be endangered?' The special circumstances which prevented the danger from occurring were *irrelevant*.

(c) In *R*. v. *Dudley* (1989), X was charged under s. 1(2), having thrown a fire bomb at a house. The damage caused was trivial and X submitted that the jury should not convict since it could not be shown that the actual damage he had caused was intended or likely to endanger life. The Court of Appeal *rejected* X's appeal. The intention or recklessness required related not to the actual damage caused but to the damage *intended* by X.

(d) In *R*. v. *Parker* (1993), the Court of Appeal stated that the trial judge was correct in directing the jury that the prosecution had to prove that the accused had been reckless as to whether a life would be endangered, and that, in order to prove recklessness it must be proved that when accused set fire to the property (in this case by putting a lighted cigarette in a sofa) he was creating an *obvious risk* that a life would be endangered.

12. Threats to destroy or damage property

Under s. 2 it is an offence for a person without lawful excuse to make to another person a threat, intending that the other person would fear it would be carried out, to destroy or damage any property belonging to that other or a third person, or to destroy or damage his own property in a way which he knows is likely to endanger the life of that other or a third person. Note that the term 'reckless' does not appear in s. 2; the offence requires that the accused shall have *intended* that another person should fear the carrying out of the threat. The defence under s. 5 does not apply to an offence involving a threat under s. 2: *see* s. 5(1).

13. Possessing anything with intent to destroy or damage property

By s. 3 it is an offence for a person to have anything in his custody or under his control intending without lawful excuse to use it or cause or permit another to use it to destroy or damage any property belonging to some other person, or to destroy or damage his own or the user's property in a way which he knows is likely to endanger the life of some other person. The offence is triable either way. In *R. v. Buckingham* (1977), the Court of Appeal held that it did *not* suffice, for an offence under s. 3, that defendant realised that an article *may* be used for purposes of damaging or destroying property; he must *intend or permit* such use. But that use need not be immediate; intention to use, should it prove necessary, will suffice.

Trespass and related offences

14. Trespass: the general position

Trespass involves an unjustifiable interference with property. It is a *tort* involving 'direct and forcible injury' and, as such, is usually a matter for civil law. (For exceptional cases where trespass is an offence, *see* e.g. the Civil Aviation Act 1982, s. 39. For trespass relating to burglary under the Theft Act 1968, s. 9(1), *see R. v. Jones* (1976) (at 16:13).) By the Criminal Law Act 1977, a number of offences relating to the concept of trespass were created: some of these are outlined at 15–17 below.

15. Forcible entry

Under the 1977 Act, s. 6, any person who, without lawful authority, uses or threatens violence for the purpose of securing entry into any premises for himself or for any other person is guilty of an offence, provided that there is someone present on those premises at the time who is opposed to the entry which the violence is intended to secure *and* the person using or threatening the violence knows that this is the case.

(a) The fact that a person has an interest in or right to possession of premises does not, for the purposes of this section constitute lawful authority for the use of violence by him or anyone else for purposes of securing entry: s. 6(2).

(b) It is immaterial whether the violence is directed against persons or property: s. 6(4)(*a*).

(c) It is a defence for the accused to show that at the time of the alleged offence he or any other person on whose behalf he was acting was a displaced residential occupier of the premises in question: s. 6(3)(*a*). *See* also s. 6(3)(*b*). ('Any person who was occupying any premises as a residence immediately before being excluded from occupation by anyone who entered those premises, or any access to those premises, as a trespasser, is a displaced residential occupier of the premises for the purposes of this Part of the Act so long as he continues to be excluded from occupation of the premises by the original trespasser or by any subsequent trespasser': s. 12(3).)

(d) '''Premises'' means any building, any part of a building under separate occupation, any land ancillary to a building, the site comprising any building or buildings together with any land ancillary thereto . . .': s. 12(1)(*a*).

16. Adverse occupation of premises

Under the 1977 Act, s. 7, a person is guilty of an offence if he is on any premises as a trespasser after having entered as such *and* if he fails to leave after being required to do so by or on behalf of a displaced residential occupier of the premises or an individual who is a protected intending occupier: s. 7(1). A 'protected intending occupier' is one who has in the premises a freehold or leasehold interest with not less than twenty-one years to run and who acquired that interest as a purchaser for money or money's worth *and* who requires the premises for his own occupation as a residence *and* who is excluded from occupation by a trespasser: s. 7(2). It is a defence for the accused to prove that the premises are or form part of premises used mainly for non-residential purposes and that he was not on any part of the premises used wholly or mainly for residential purposes: s. 7(7).

17. Trespassing with a weapon of offence

Under the 1977 Act, s. 8, a person who is on premises as a trespasser, after having entered as such, is guilty of an offence if, without lawful authority or reasonable excuse, he has with him on the premises any weapon of offence: s. 8(1).

(a) 'Weapon of offence' means 'any article made or adapted for use for causing injury to or incapacitating a person, or intended by the person having it with him for such use': s. 8(2).

(b) Note also the offence of carrying and trespassing with firearms under the Firearms Act 1968, s. 20.

> NOTE: (1) Under the Criminal Justice and Public Order Bill, published in December 1993, the police would be given extended powers allowing them to order trespassers to leave land (including common land and minor highways) if they have brought more than six vehicles on it against the will of the owner. (Current legislation relates only to convoys of more than twelve vehicles.) The vehicles would be impounded. It would be an offence for a group of ten or more persons to gather to play loud music

during the night and to fail to comply with an order to leave. Vehicles and amplification equipment involved could be seized. Persons within a five-mile radius of the site of the intended performance could be turned back. (2) Criminal sanctions would be available to be used against squatters who fail to leave a building within 24 hours of the court's issuing an interim possession order.

Draft Criminal Code Bill

18. Destroying or damaging property
'(1) A person is guilty of an offence if he intentionally or recklessly causes the destruction of or damage to property belonging to another': cl. 180.

19. Intention or recklessness as to endangering life
(2) A person is guilty of an offence if he intentionally or recklessly causes the destruction of or damage to property (whether belonging to himself or another), intending by the destruction or damage to endanger the life of another or being reckless whether the life of another will be thereby endangered': cl. 180.

Progress test 19

1. What offences are created under the Criminal Damage Act 1971? **(1)**

2. Comment on *Lloyd* v. *DPP* (1992). **(3)**

3. What is meant by 'damage' under the 1971 Act? **(4)**

4. Comment on the term 'recklessness' in relation to the 1971 Act. **(8)**

5. Explain *R.* v. *Miller* (1983). **(9)**

6. Explain the decision in *R.* v. *Steer* (1987). **(11)**

7. Outline the Criminal Law Act 1977, s. 6. **(15)**

Forgery and counterfeiting

Forgery under the Forgery and Counterfeiting Act 1981

1. Essence of the 1981 Act
The Act repeated the Forgery Act 1913, and made fresh provision for England, Wales and N. Ireland with respect to forgery and kindred offences and to the counterfeiting of notes and coins and kindred offences. More specifically:

(a) the offence of forgery was *redefined* (*see* s. 1 at **2**);
(b) the Forgery Act 1913 and the Coinage Offences Act 1936 were *repealed* (*see* Sch. 1);
(c) 'the offence of forgery at common law is hereby *abolished* for all purposes not relating to offences committed before the commencement of this Act': s. 13.

2. The offence of forgery
'A person is guilty of forgery if he makes a false instrument, with the intention that he or another shall use it to induce somebody to accept it as genuine, and by reason of so accepting it to do or not to do some act to his own or any other person's prejudice': s. 1. The offence is triable either way.

(a) *'Instrument'*. Under s. 8(1), an 'instrument' means (for the purposes of Part I of the Act, which relates to forgery and kindred offences): any document, whether of a formal or informal character; any stamp sold or issued by the Post Office; any Inland Revenue stamp; any disc, tape, soundtrack or other device on or in which information is recorded or stored by mechanical, electronic or other means. It should be noted that a currency note (within the meaning of Part II of the Act – *see* **5** (a)) is *not* an 'instrument' for the purposes of Part I: s. 8(2).

(*i*) The instrument in question may be written on any kind of material, and the content of that writing may be in the form of words or other symbols.

(*ii*) A manufactured article, e.g. a portrait painting, is *not*, in itself, an 'instrument': *see* e.g. *R.* v. *Closs* (1858); *R.* v. *Douce* (1972).

(*iii*) Note the comments of the Law Commission: 'The essence of forgery, in our view, is the making of a false document intending that it be used to induce a person to accept and act upon the message contained in it, as if it were contained in a genuine document.'

(b) *'False'*. An instrument is false for the purposes of Part I if, for example, it purports to have been made: in the form in which it is made by a person who did not in fact make it in that form; in the form in which it is made on the authority of a person who did not in fact authorise its making in that form: s. 9. It is false if it purports to have been made or altered on a date on which, or at a place at which, or otherwise in circumstances in which, it was not in fact made or altered: s. 9(1)(*g*). See R. v. *Donnelly* (1984) at **4**; *R.* v. *Lack* (1987) (documents created after the liquidation of a company, but which purported to have been made by the company prior to that liquidation, are forgeries). It is false if it purports to have been made or altered by an existing person but he did not in fact exist: s. 9(1)(*h*). The following acts, are, therefore, *offences* under the 1981 statute.

(*i*) X, seeking employment, writes a reference purporting to have come from his former employer, Y; *see* s. 9(1)(*a*).

(*ii*) Y writes a cheque for £50, and X alters the figures so that it reads £80: *see* s. 9(1)(*c*).

(*iii*) Y gives his secretary, X, authority to write a cheque for £50, and X deliberately writes it out for £80: *see* s. 9(1)(*d*).

(c) *'Makes'*. 'A person is to be treated for the purposes of this part of this Act as making a false instrument if he alters an instrument so as to make it false in any respect (whether or not it is false in some other respect apart from that alteration)': s. 9(2).

(d) *'A person's prejudice'*. Under s. 10(1), an act or omission intended to be induced (*see* **(e)**) is to a person's prejudice if, and only if, it is one which, if it occurs, will result in his temporary or permanent loss of property, or in his being deprived of an opportunity to earn or increase remuneration, or in his being deprived of an opportunity to gain a financial advantage otherwise than by way of remuneration; or will result in someone being given an opportunity to earn or increase remuneration from him, or to gain a financial advantage from him otherwise than by way of remuner-ation; or will be the result of his having accepted a false instrument as genuine, or a copy of a false instrument as a copy of a genuine one, in connection with his performance of any duty: s. 10(1).

(*i*) An act which a person has an enforceable duty to do and an omission to do an act which a person is not entitled to do shall be disregarded for the purposes of this part of the Act: s. 10(2).

(*ii*) In this section, 'loss' includes not getting what one might get as well as parting with what one has: s. 10(5).

(*iii*) Note R. v. *Campbell* (1985). X had been tricked by Y into cashing a cheque made out to Z. X had done this by endorsing the cheque to herself and signing in the payee's name. The trial judge ruled that *dishonesty is no longer a necessary element of forgery*, and that there was an intention to do an act to the prejudice of another within s. 10(1)(*c*). The Court of Appeal held that the judge's ruling was *correct* in law.

(*iv*) Note *R. v. Utting* (1987), in which the Court of Appeal held that a person who makes a false instrument with the intention that the police should accept it as genuine and, therefore, not prosecute him, has *not* committed forgery under s. 1. Section 1 envisages that X, the forger, intends that Y will do, or omit to do, something, and that, as a result of Y's doing, or omitting to do, an act, Y will be prejudiced, or anyone else, other than X, will be prejudiced. There was no suggestion in this case that the omission of the police to prosecute prejudiced them or anyone else.

(e) '*Induce*'. In this Part of the Act, references to inducing somebody to accept a false instrument as genuine, etc., include references to inducing a machine to respond to the instrument or copy as if it were a genuine instrument or, as the case may be, a copy of a genuine one:s. 10(3).

> NOTE: A forged alteration to a document will not render it void *except where* that alteration is shown to go to the very essence or the whole of the document. See *Lombard Finance* v. *Brookplain Trading* (1991). X and Y were directors of B Ltd which wished to lease equipment from L Co. X and Y were signatories to a form of guarantee, guaranteeing the obligations of 'B Company Ltd' to L Co. At some later stage a person deleted the word 'company' in manuscript and added scrawls to the deletion which were intended to represent the signatures of X and Y and to indicate their agreement to the alterations. The Court of Appeal held that the alterations, although they constituted a forgery, did *not* render the document unenforceable.

3. Kindred offences

The following offences, kindred to forgery, are stated in the 1981 Act.

(a) *Copying a false instrument* (s. 2): making a copy of an instrument, which is, and which the person knows or believes to be, a false instrument, with the same intention as in s. 1. The offence is triable either way.

(b) *Using a false instrument and using a copy of a false instrument* (ss. 3, 4): using a false instrument known or believed to be false, and using a copy of an instrument, known or believed to be false, with the same intention as in s. 1. Note *R. v. Tobierre* (1986), in which the Court of Appeal held that, to prove an offence under s. 3, the prosecution must prove a double intention: that the defendant intended that some person should accept the forged instrument as genuine; *and* that there was an intention that the other person should act or omit to act to his own or someone else's prejudice. (*Per curiam*: the same construction applies to offences created by ss. 1, 2, 4, 5, reading these sections together with s. 10.) *See also R. v.*

Garcia (1988) – conspiracy to use false instruments. The offences are triable either way.

(c) *Possessing certain false instruments*: possessing false instruments and the implements and materials for making them. Thus, under s. 5(4), it is an offence for a person to make or to have in his custody or under his control machines or implements or paper or other material which to his knowledge is or has been specially designed or adapted for the making of the instruments to which s. 5 applies, without lawful authority or excuse. Those 'instruments' are: money and postal orders; UK postage, and Inland Revenue, stamps; share certificates; passports and similar documents; cheques, travellers' cheques; cheque and credit cards; certified copies relating to entries in registers of births, adoptions, marriages and deaths: s. 5(5).

4. The nature of a 'false instrument': recent decisions

In *R. v. Donnelly* (1984), the Court of Appeal considered the problem of 'falsity' under the 1981 Act. X, the manager of a jeweller shop, collaborated with Y so as to complete and sign a statement which purported to be a written valuation of jewellery items for insurance purposes. In fact, the items did not exist. X then handed the statement to another person, intending to defraud an insurance company. X was convicted under s. 1. The jury were directed that, following s. 9(1)(*g*) (*see* **2**), an instrument could be false if it purported to be made in circumstances in which it was not in fact made. X appealed.

(a) X argued that, *inter alia*, the written instrument was not a 'false instrument' under s. 9(1)(*g*); that it was no more than a 'lying instrument'; that an instrument could not be a forgery if it merely, on its face, told a lie, not being a lie as to what it was. The prosecution conceded that, at common law and under the Forgery Act 1913, the certificate would not have been considered a forgery. But the 1981 Act, it was argued, made new law, and in s. 9 what made an instrument 'false' was precisely enacted.

(b) The Court of Appeal declared that *the 1981 Act made new law*. It was intended to make 'fresh provision' with respect to forgery, and the words of s. 9(1)(*g*) 'expanded the ambit of the law beyond dates and places to any case in which an instrument purports to be made when it was not in fact made.' The valuation purported to have been made *after* X had examined the items; in fact the examination never took place because the items did not exist. That which purported to be a valuation after examination of the items was nothing of the kind; it was a worthless piece of paper and a forgery.

(c) It seemed therefore, as some legal writers pointed out, that the basic nature of the offence of forgery may have been changed. The fundamental concept of 'automendacity', by which a document had to 'tell a lie *about* *itself'*, as well as containing a false statement (*see* e.g. R. v. *Dodge and Harris* (1972)) was, apparently, no longer a feature of the offence of forgery.

(d) The decision in R. v. *Donnelly* can be questioned, however, in view of R. v. *More* (1987), which concerned, specifically, ss. 1, 9(1)(*h*). X stole a cheque and paid it into a building society in a false name (Y) in which he had opened that account. The House of Lords held that X was *not guilty* of forgery when he signed a form of withdrawal for the money in the name of Y. The withdrawal form had not 'told a lie about itself', it purported clearly to have been signed by the person who had originally opened the account (Y) and was, in itself, therefore completely accurate. The question of the Court of Appeal as to whether a person who had done as X did had made a 'false instrument', as defined in the Act, was to be answered in *the negative*.

Counterfeiting under the 1981 Act

5. Offences of counterfeiting notes and coins

Under s. 14: '(1) It is an offence for a person to make a counterfeit of a currency note or of a protected coin, intending that he or another shall pass or tender it as genuine. (2) It is an offence for a person to make a counterfeit of a currency note or of a protected coin without lawful authority or excuse.' For principles of sentencing *see* R. v. *Howard* (1986); R. v. *Page* (1992).

(a) *'Currency note'*. This means, in Part II of the Act (dealing with counterfeiting and kindred offences): any note lawfully issued in England and Wales, Scotland, N. Ireland, the Channel Islands, the Isle of Man and the Republic of Ireland, and is, or has been customarily used as money in the country of issue, and is payable on demand; or any note lawfully issued in some country other than those mentioned above and customarily used as money in that country: s. 27(1).

(b) *'Protected coin'*. This term means any coin which is customarily used as money in any country, or is specified in a treasury order for the purposes of Part II of the Act.

(c) *'Counterfeit'*. Under s. 28(1), a thing is a counterfeit of a currency note or protected coin if it resembles such a note or coin (whether on one side only or both) to such an extent that it is reasonably capable of passing for that note or coin, or if it has been altered so that it is reasonably capable of passing for a note or coin of some other description.

> NOTE: References in Part II of the Act to passing or tendering a counterfeit of a currency note or protected coin are not to be construed as confined to passing or tendering it as legal tender: s. 28(3).

6. Kindred offences

The following offences, kindred to counterfeiting, are stated in ss. 15–19.

(a) *Passing or delivering counterfeit notes and coins.* Under s. 15 it is an offence to pass or tender as genuine a counterfeit note or coin or to deliver such a counterfeit intending it to be passed or tendered as genuine, without lawful authority or excuse.

(b) *Having custody or control of counterfeit notes and coins.* Under s. 16, it is an offence for a person to have in his custody or under his control any thing which is, and which he knows or believes to be, a counterfeit note or coin intending to pass or tender it as genuine or to deliver it to another with the intention that he or another shall pass or tender it as genuine.

(c) *Making or having custody or control of counterfeiting materials and implements: see* s. 17.

(d) *Reproducing British currency notes, without lawful written authority* (s. 18) and making, selling or distributing imitation coins which are legal tender in any part of the UK, unless the Treasury has given written consent to the sale or distribution of such imitation British coins (s. 19).

Computer misuse

7. Unauthorised access to computer material

A person is guilty of an offence under the Computer Misuse Act 1990 s. 1, if he causes a computer to perform any function with intent to secure access to any program or data held in any computer; if the access he intends to secure is unauthorised; and he knows at the time when he causes the computer to perform the function that that is the case. The offence is triable summarily. Note *A.-G.'s Reference (No 1 of 1992)* – the offence in s. 1(1) does not require the use of two computers (allowing one to 'hack' into the other), but can be committed by *an individual* who secures access directly to the target computer.

8. Unauthorised access with intent to commit or facilitate commission of further offences

A person is guilty of an offence under s. 2 if he commits an offence under s. 1 with intent to commit the offence to which this section applies, or to facilitate the commission of such an offence (whether by himself or by any other person) and the offence he intends to commit or facilitate is referred to in this section as a 'further offence' (eg. offences of fraud and dishonesty): s. 2.

9. Unauthorised modification of computer material

A person is guilty of an offence under s. 3 if he does any act which causes an unauthorised modification of the contents of any computer and at the time when he does the act he has the requisite intention and the requisite knowledge. 'Requisite intent' is an intent to cause a modification of the contents of a computer, and by so doing, to impair the operations of a computer, to prevent access to any program or data held by the computer, to impair the operations of the program or the reliability of the data. 'Requisite knowledge' is the knowledge that any modification he intends to cause is unauthorised. The offence is triable either way.

Progress test 20

1. What is the essence of forgery under the Forgery and Counterfeiting Act 1981? **(2)**

2. What is an 'instrument' under the 1981 Act ? **(2)**

3. When is an instrument 'false' for the purposes of the 1981 Act? **(2)**

4. Comment on *R.* v. *Utting* (1987). **(2)**

5. Explain the decision in *Lombard Finance* v. *Brookplain Trading* (1991). **(2)**

6. Outline *R.* v. *Donnelly* (1984). **(4)**

7. What offences are created by the 1981 Act, s. 14? **(5)**

8. Outline the Computer Misuse Act 1990, s. 1. **(7)**

Part four

Offences against state security, public order, morals, and the administration of justice

21

Offences against the state and public order

General nature of the offences

1. Offences against the state

The need for the state to protect itself against enemies actual and potential within and without the realm is very important, and the offences covered in this chapter reflect that need. *Treason* (i.e. a breach of duty of allegiance owed to the Crown) is considered under **3–8**. The publication of seditious words, known as *sedition*, is considered under **9–12**. Offences related to terrorism are mentioned at **13**. The Official Secrets Acts, considered under **14–18**, cover offences which are thought to put at risk the very safety of the state. Offences against public order are noted under **25–31**.

2. Offences against international law and order

Four such offences are noted in this chapter. The first is *piracy* (*see* 19), which, with treason, remains a capital offence. The second and third have emerged from the conditions of the Second World War and its aftermath, and are based on international Conventions signed by Britain: *genocide* (*see* 20) and *hijacking* (*see* 21). The fourth concerns the *taking of hostages* (*see* 22).

Treason

3. The Statute of Treasons 1351
It is treason, for example:

(a) 'to compass or imagine the death of our lord the King or our lady his Queen or of their eldest son and heir';
(b) 'to levy war against our lord the King in his realm';
(c) 'to be adherent to the King's enemies in his realm, giving them aid and comfort in the realm or elsewhere'.
   The offence is triable only on indictment.

4. Compassing or imagining the death of the King
In spite of the word 'imagining' there must be proof of an overt act. In *R. v. Charnock* (1694) it was held that 'words of persuasion to kill the king' were sufficient to constitute an overt act of treason. 'Loose words, spoken without relation to any act or project,' would *not* suffice.

5. Levying war against the King in his realm
'War' does not refer exclusively to armed conflict against a foreign power; it includes disturbances within the realm involving the use of force by numbers of persons who intend by violence to usurp the functions of the government.

6. Adhering to the King's enemies in his realm, giving them aid and comfort in the realm or elsewhere
'We think that the meaning of these words is this: "giving aid and comfort to the King's enemies" are words in apposition; they are words to explain what is meant by being adherent to, and we think that if a man be adherent to the King's enemies in his realm by giving them aid or comfort in his realm, or if he be adherent to the King's enemies elsewhere, that is by giving to them aid or comfort elsewhere, he is equally adherent to the King's enemies, and if he is adherent to the King's enemies then he commits the treason which the statute of Edward III defines': *per* Darling J in *R. v. Casement* (1917).
   In this case, the accused, a British subject, went to Germany during the First World War and, while there, recruited British prisoners of war to join an 'Irish Brigade' which was part of the German armed forces. He was found guilty of treason, having adhered to the King's enemies by giving them aid and comfort, whether in his realm or elsewhere. *See R. v. Ahlers* (1915).

7. Misprision of treason
This common law offence is committed when a person knows, or has

reasonable cause to believe, that some other person has committed treason, and *fails*, within a reasonable time, to give this information to the appropriate authority. See *Sykes* v. *DPP* (1962).

8. Aliens and treason

The essence of treason is *a breach of duty of allegiance which is owned to the Crown*. An alien cannot generally commit treason, but, where he (or an alien enemy) has accepted the protection of the British Crown, he can be held to have committed treason under certain circumstances. In *Joyce* v. *DPP* (1946), an American citizen had obtained a British passport by misrepresenting himself as a British subject. He had assisted the enemy by broadcasting over the German radio during the war and was found guilty of treason.

> 'By his own act [i.e. having continued to possess a current British passport] he has maintained the bond which while he was in the realm bound him to his Sovereign . . . in these circumstances I am clearly of opinion that so long as he holds the passport he is, within the meaning of the statute, a man who, if he is adherent to the King's enemies in the realm or elsewhere, commits an act of treason': *per* Lord Jowitt LC.

Sedition

9. The essence of the offence

Sedition is a common law offence consisting of the *oral or written publication of words with a seditious intention*. It is triable only on indictment.

10. Public discussion and criticism

Reasonable criticism and public discussion are lawful. 'An intention to show that Her Majesty has been misled or mistaken in her measures, or to point out errors or defects in the government or constitution as by law established, with a view to their reformation . . . is not a seditious intention': Stephen J, cited by Cave J in R. v. *Burns* (1886).

11. Seditious intent

The accused person cannot be convicted of sedition in the absence of a seditious intent. 'In order to make out the offence of speaking seditious words there must be a criminal intent upon the part of the accused, they must be words spoken with a seditious intent': *per* Cave J in R. v. *Burns* (1886).

In R. v. *Chief Stipendiary Magistrate ex p Choudhury* (1990), a Divisional Court held that the seditious intention on which a prosecution for seditious libel must be founded is 'an intention to incite to violence or to create public disturbance or disorder against [Her] Majesty or the institutions of government. Proof of an intention to promote feelings of ill-will and hostility between different classes of subjects does not *alone* establish a seditious intention. Not only must there be proof of an incitement to violence in this connection but it must be violence or resistance or defiance for the purpose of disturbing constituted authority'.

12. Statutory enactments supplementing the common law
The following statutes have supplemented the common law on sedition.

(a) Incitement to Disaffection Act 1934, s. 1, by which it is an offence, maliciously and advisedly, to endeavour to seduce any member of the Forces from his duty or allegiance to the Crown. *See R. v. Arrowsmith* (1975). *See* also the Incitement to Mutiny Act 1797.

(b) Police Act 1964, s. 53, by which it is an offence to cause or attempt to cause or do any act calculated to cause disaffection among the members of a police force or to induce a policeman to commit a breach of discipline.

(c) Public Order Act 1986. *See* 24:**30**.

Offences related to terrorism

13. Prevention of Terrorism (Temporary Provisions) Act 1989
Events in Northern Ireland which were related to bombing attacks in England led to the Prevention of Terrorism (Temporary Provisions) Act 1974 which was superseded by the Acts of 1976, 1984, 1989.

(a) Terrorism is defined as '. . . the use of violence for political ends, and includes any use of violence for the purpose of putting the public or any section of the public in fear': s. 20(1). *See R. v. Governor of Durham Prison, ex p. Carlisle* (1979).

(b) It is an offence under the 1989 Act:

(*i*) to belong or profess to belong to a proscribed organisation (the Irish Republican Army or the Irish National Liberation Army), [but other organisations are proscribed under the Northern Ireland (Emergency Provisions) Act 1991] to solicit or invite support for such an organisation, to arrange or assist in the arrangement or management of meetings intended to further support for it (s. 2(1));

(*ii*) to solicit, or invite any other person to give or lend money or other property intending, knowing or suspecting that it will or may be applied or used in connection with acts of terrorism (s. 9) (*see also* Criminal Justice Act 1993, s. 49);

(*iii*) to solicit, or make available, money or other property for the benefit of a proscribed organisation (s. 10(1));

(*iv*) to fail without reasonable excuse to disclose information which may be of material assistance in preventing an act of terrorism or securing the apprehension, prosecution or conviction of a person for an act of terrorism (s. 18) (*see also* Criminal Justice Act 1993, s.51).

(c) The Home Secretary may make an *exclusion order* (ss. 4–8) against a person prohibiting him from being in or entering Great Britain, Northern Ireland or the United Kingdom, if he is satisfied that the person is or has been concerned 'in the commission, preparation or instigation of acts of terrorism'. The order expires three years after the day on which it was made: Sch. 2, s. 3(1)(2).

(d) Under s. 14 a constable may arrest without warrant any person whom he reasonably suspects to be guilty of certain offences under the Act, or of being concerned in acts of terrorism (including international terrorism) or of being subject to an exclusion order. The person arrested may not be detained for more than forty-eight hours in right of the arrest, but the Home Secretary may extend this for further periods of up to five days. *See R.* v. *Governor of Durham Prison, ex p. Carlisle* (1979); *Brannigan* v. *UK* (1993) (a decision of the European Court of Human Rights).

> NOTE: The Criminal Justice and Public Order Bill, published in December, 1993, contains proposals for the creation of new offences of possessing items intended for terrorist purposes, and possessing information likely to be of use to terrorists in planning acts of violence.

Official secrets

14. General purpose of the legislation
The general purpose of the legislation discussed under 15–18 is to guard the safety and interests of the State against enemies; the term 'enemy' includes a potential enemy: *see R.* v. *Parrott* (1913).

15. Official Secrets Act 1911, s. 1(1)
It is an offence if any person, for any purpose prejudicial to the safety or interests of the State:

(a) approaches, inspects, passes over or is in the neighbourhood of, or enters, any prohibited place within the Act, or

(b) makes any sketch, plan, model or note calculated or intended to be useful to an enemy.

The offence is triable only on indictment.

16. The mischief aimed at by s. 1

In *Chandler* v. *DPP* (1964), the accused persons, members of an organisation committed to nuclear disarmament, entered a prohibited place (an airfield), and admitted that, in doing so, they had intended to impede its functioning. They contended that they had not the necessary intention under s. 1, since their ultimate object was to benefit the State. They were convicted under s. 1, and their appeal dismissed. It was held by the House of Lords that:

(a) the mischief aimed at by s. 1 is not limited to espionage, but includes sabotage;
(b) if a person enters a prohibited place in order to cause obstruction and interference which is prejudicial to the defence dispositions of the country, an offence under s. 1 is committed, and the ultimate objects of that person are of no relevance; *and*
(c) the Crown's defence policy cannot be challenged in the courts.

17. Official Secrets Act 1920, ss. 1, 3, 7

It is an offence to make an unauthorised use of uniform or to make a false statement to gain admission to a prohibited place. It is an offence for any person who, in the vicinity of a prohibited place, interferes with the police or members of the Forces who are on guard. By s. 7, any attempt to commit an offence under the Acts of 1911 and 1920, or to solicit or incite or endeavour to persuade another to commit such an offence, is an offence, punishable as if the offence had been committed.

18. The 1989 Act

The following matters should be noted concerning the 1989 Act, which repeals the 1911 Act, s. 2.

(a) *Security and intelligence.* It is an offence for a member and former member of the security services to disclose, without lawful authority, any information, document or other article relating to security and intelligence which is or has been in his possession by virtue of his position as a member of those services: s. 1(1). It is an offence for a person who is or has been a Crown servant or government contractor to disclose without lawful authority, information which might cause damage to the security and intelligence services: s. 1(3). (For 'Crown servant', *see* SI 1990/200.)
(b) *Defence.* It is an offence for one who is or has been a Crown servant or government contractor, to make a damaging disclosure of any information, document or other article relating to defence: s. 2(1).
(c) *International relations.* It is an offence for an existing or former Crown

servant or government contractor to make a damaging disclosure of information relating to international relations: s. 3(1).

(d) *Crime and special investigation*. It is an offence for an existing or former Crown servant or government contractor to disclose information which results in the commission of an offence, or facilitates an escape from legal custody or impedes the prevention or detection of an offence: s. 4.

(e) *Information resulting from unauthorised disclosures*. It is an offence to disclose unlawfully information of this nature: s. 5. (For definition of 'unauthorised disclosure', *see* s. 7.)

Offences against international law and order

19. Piracy

Piracy *jure gentium* ('piracy against the law of nations') involves an *act of armed violence committed upon the high seas* within the jurisdiction of the Admiralty, and not being an act of war.

(a) The common law offence was supplemented by the Piracy Act 1837, by which piracy was made a capital offence: *see* s. 2.

(b) *See* also the Tokyo Convention Act 1967, the Aviation Security Act 1982 (relating to aircraft); *Athens Maritime Enterprises* v. *Hellenic Mutual War Risks Assn.* (1983).

20. Genocide Act 1969

A person commits the offence of genocide if, with intent to destroy in whole or in part, a national, ethnical, racial or religious group as such, he kills or causes serious bodily or mental harm to members of the group or deliberately inflicts on the group conditions of life calculated to bring about its physical destruction in whole or in part. *See* also the War Crimes Act 1991.

21. Aviation Security Act 1982: hijacking

The offence of hijacking is committed by a person on board an aircraft in flight who unlawfully, by the use of force or threats of any kind, seizes the aircraft or exercises control of it, whatever his nationality, whatever the State in which the aircraft is registered, and whether the aircraft is in the UK, or elsewhere: *see* s. 1(1). Where a person of whatever nationality does on board an aircraft wherever registered and while outside the UK, any act which, if done in the UK, would constitute the offence of murder, attempted murder, manslaughter, culpable homicide, assault or an offence within certain sections of the Offences against the Person Act 1861, his act constitutes that offence if it is done in connection with the offence of hijacking committed or attempted by him on board that aircraft: *see* s. 6. *See also* the Aviation and Maritime Security Act 1990, for hijacking of a ship or fixed platform.

22. Taking of Hostages Act 1982

It is an offence under s. 1(1) for a person, whatever his nationality, who, in the UK or elsewhere:

(a) detains any other person ('the hostage'); and
(b) in order to compel a state, international governmental organisation or person to do or abstain from doing any act, threatens to kill, injure or continue to detain the hostage.

The Public Order Act 1986

23. General effect of the Act

The 1986 Act made the following changes to the law relating to public order.

(a) *Some common law offences were abolished.* These include riot (*see* e.g. *Field* v. *Metropolitan Police District Receiver* (1907)), rout, unlawful assembly (*see* e.g. Wise v. *Dunning* (1902)), affray (*see* e.g. *R.* v. *Scarrow and Brown* (1968)). The Seditious Meetings Act 1817 and the Public Order Act 1936, s. 5, were repealed.
(b) Some new statutory offences were created. These include riot, violent disorder, affray, fear or provocation of violence, harassment, alarm or distress, commission of acts intended or likely to stir up racial hatred, possession of racially inflammatory material, offences of violence in relation to sporting events.
(c) *Other matters* New powers were created to control public processions and assemblies, and to direct trespassers to leave land.

24. Statutory interpretation of 'violence'

The essence of violence in the criminal law is *the unjust and unwarranted use of an unreasonable degree of force.* The 1986 Act, s. 8, states that 'violence' means 'any violent conduct, so that:

(a) except in the context of affray, it includes violent conduct towards property as well as violent conduct towards persons, *and*
(b) it is not restricted to conduct causing or intended to cause injury or damage but includes any other violent conduct (for example, throwing at or towards a person a missile of a kind capable of causing injury which does not hit or falls short).'

Riot, violent disorder and affray

25. Riot
The 1986 Act states: 'Where 12 or more persons who are present together use or threaten unlawful violence for a common purpose and the conduct of them (taken together) is such as would cause a person of reasonable firmness present at the scene to fear for his personal safety, each of the persons using unlawful violence for the common purpose is guilty of riot': s. 1(1).

(a) It is immaterial whether or not the 12 or more use or threaten unlawful violence simultaneously: s. 1(2).
(b) The common purpose may be inferred from conduct: s. 1(3).
(c) No person of reasonable firmness need actually be, or be likely to be, present at the scene: s. 1(4).
(d) Riot may be committed in private as well as in public places: s. 1(5).

26. Violent disorder
'Where 3 or more persons who are present together use or threaten unlawful violence and the conduct of them (taken together) is such as would cause a person of reasonable firmness present at the scene to fear for his personal safety, each of the persons using or threatening unlawful violence is guilty of violent disorder': s. 2(1). *See* e.g. *R.* v. *Rothwell* (1993).

(a) It is immaterial whether or not the 3 or more use or threaten unlawful violence simultaneously: s. 2(2).

27. Affray
'A person is guilty of affray if he uses or threatens unlawful violence towards another and his conduct is such as would cause a person of reasonable firmness present at the scene to fear for his personal safety': s. 3(1).

(a) Where two or more persons use or threaten unlawful violence, it is the conduct of them *taken together* that must be considered for purposes of s. 3(1): s. 3(2). It is not necessary to prove each separate allegation: *Cobb* v. *DPP* (1992).
(b) The use of words alone will not constitute a threat: s. 3(3). *See R.* v. *Dixon* (1993); *R.* v. *Robinson* (1993).
(c) No person of reasonable firmness need actually be, or be likely to be, present at the scene: s. 3(4). *See R.* v. *Davison* (1992).
(d) 'Violence' does *not* include, in the case of affray, violent conduct to property: s. 8.
(e) No affray is committed when violence is limited to those involved, and others present did not feel afraid for their own safety: *DPP* v. *Cotcher* (1992).

Fear or provocation of violence, and harassment, alarm or distress

28. Fear or provocation of violence

An offence is committed under s. 4(1) if a person uses towards another person threatening, abusive or insulting words or behaviour, or distributes or displays to another person any writing, sign or other visible representation which is threatening, abusive or insulting. The necessary intent is 'to cause that person to believe that immediate unlawful violence will be used against him or another by any person, or to provoke the immediate use of unlawful violence by that person or another, or whereby that person is likely to believe that such violence will be used or it is likely that such violence will be provoked.' *See Winn* v. *DPP* (1992).

(a) The offence may be committed in a public or private place: s. 4(2). *See Rukira* v. *DPP* (1993).
(b) A person is guilty of the offence only if he intends his words or behaviour, or the writing, etc., to be threatening, abusive or insulting or is aware that it may be so: s. 6(3).

29. Harassment, alarm or distress

A person is guilty of an offence under s. 5(1) if he uses threatening, abusive or insulting words or behaviour, or disorderly behaviour, or displays any writing, sign or other visible representation which is threatening, abusive or insulting, within the hearing or sight of a person likely to be caused harassment, alarm or distress thereby. *See DPP* v. *Orum* (1988).

(a) A person is guilty of the offence only if he *intends* his words or behaviour, or the writing, etc., to be threatening, abusive or insulting, or is aware that it may be so or (as the case may be) he intends his behaviour to be or is aware that it may be disorderly s. 6(4). (A *subjective* test should be applied by the court: *DPP* v. *Fidler* (1992).)
(b) It is a defence for the accused to prove that his conduct was reasonable, or that he had no reason to believe there was any person within sight or hearing likely to be caused harassment, alarm or distress, or that he was inside a dwelling and had no reason to believe that the words, behaviour, writing, etc., could be seen or heard outside that or any other dwelling: s. 5(3). *See Kwasi-Poku* v. *DPP* (1992).

Stirring up of racial hatred

30. Acts intended or likely to stir up racial hatred

The Act defines 'racial hatred' as 'hatred against a group of persons in

Great Britain defined by reference to colour, race, nationality (including citizenship) or ethnic or national origins': s. 17.

(a) It is an offence for a person to use threatening, abusive or insulting words or behaviour, or to display any written material which is threatening, abusive or insulting, if he intends thereby to stir up racial hatred or, having regard to all the circumstances, racial hatred is likely to be stirred up thereby: s. 18(1). The offence may be committed in a public or private place: s. 18(2). For defences, *see* s. 18(2) (4) (5).
(b) It is an offence for a person to publish or distribute written material which is threatening, abusive or insulting, if he intends thereby to stir up racial hatred, or having regard to all the circumstances racial hatred is likely to be stirred up thereby: s. 19(1). For defence, *see* s. 19(2).

31. Possession of racially inflammatory material
Under s. 23(1), a person who has in his possession written material which is threatening, abusive or insulting, with a view to (in the case of written material) its being displayed, published, distributed or broadcast, or (in the case of a recording) its being distributed, shown, played or broadcast, is guilty of an offence if he intends racial hatred to be stirred up thereby or, having regard to all the circumstances, racial hatred is likely to be stirred up thereby. For defence, *see* s. 23(3).

Offences relating to industrial action

32. Injury to persons or property arising from breach of contract
Under the Trade Union and Labour Relations (Consolidation) Act 1992, s. 240(1), it is an offence for a person, wilfully and maliciously, to break a contract of service or hiring, knowing or having reasonable cause to believe that the probable consequences of his so doing, either alone or in combination with others, will be to endanger human life or cause serious bodily injury, or to expose valuable property, whether real or personal, to destruction or serious injury.

33. Intimidation or annoyance by violence or otherwise
Under the 1992 Act, s. 241(1), a person commits an offence who, with a view to compelling another person to abstain from doing or to do any act which that person has a legal right to do or abstain from doing, wrongfully and without legal authority, uses violence to or intimidates that person, his wife or children, or injures his property, persistently follows that person, hides tools etc, belonging to that person, watches or besets that person's place of residence or work, follows that person with two or more other persons in a disorderly manner through a street.

Powers concerning processions and trespass

34. Processions and assemblies

Under s. 11, *written advance notice* must be given to the police of any proposal to hold a public procession intended to demonstrate support or opposition to the views or actions of any persons, to publicise a cause or campaign, or to mark or commemorate an event. It is an offence for the organisers to fail to satisfy the requirements as to notice or to change the date, time or route of the procession: s. 11(7). Conditions may be imposed by the police if there is a fear of public disorder or intimidation: s. 12(1). Similarly, public assemblies (of 20 or more persons) may involve the imposition of conditions on the organisers: s. 14(1).

35. Trespassers

The police are empowered under s. 39(1), in the case of *two or more trespassers* who are present on land with the common purpose of residing there for any period, and who have been asked to leave by or on behalf of the occupier, to direct those persons to leave the land where they have caused damage to property on the land or have used threatening, abusive or insulting words or behaviour to the occupier, *or* where they have brought twelve or more vehicles on to the land. It is an offence for a person to whom a direction to leave has been given to fail to leave as soon as reasonably practicable or who, having left, enters again as a trespasser within three months: s. 39(2). For defences, *see* s. 39(4). For construction of 'as soon as reasonably practicable', *see Krumpa* v. *DPP* (1989).

Public nuisance, and breach of the peace

36. Essence of the offence

Public nuisance is a *misdemeanour at common law*, constituted by an unlawful act or omission (*see R.* v. *Watts* (1703)) which inflicts damage or inconvenience on Her Majesty's subjects. It is triable either way: Magistrates' Courts Act 1980, s. 17, Sch. 1.

(a) Private nuisance usually necessitates a continuing state of affairs, but a public nuisance may be constituted by an isolated act.

(b) For a public nuisance to be established the prosecution must prove that the act complained of is unreasonable, substantial and affected a considerable body of people or a section of the public. It is actual rather than potential danger or risk that must be proved: *see R.* v. *Madden* (1975). The test is 'that a public nuisance is a nuisance which is so widespread in range or so indiscriminate in its effect that it would not be reasonable to expect one person to take proceedings on his own responsibility to stop it, but that it should be taken on the responsibility of the community at large': *A.-G.* v. *P.Y.A. Quarries* (1957). *See also* the Noise and Statutory Nuisance Act 1993.

(c) It is not necessary to show that the accused intended to create a public nuisance: *Lyons and Co.* v. *Gulliver* (1914).

(d) In *R* v. *Shorrock* (1993), X had agreed to hire out his field, but claimed that he did not know the type of event (an 'acid house party') which was planned. He was convicted of public nuisance as a result of what took place at the party. The Court of Appeal found that actual knowledge of the likely nuisance was not necessary; it sufficed that X knew or ought to have known, because the means of knowledge were available to him, that the consequence of granting a licence to use his field would be a public nuisance.

37. Obstruction of the highway
A highway is any way, e.g. path, road, bridge (or river: *see A.-G.* v. *Terry* (1874)), along which the public have a right to pass. The obstruction of such a highway constitutes a public nuisance.

(a) In order to constitute a nuisance, the obstruction must interfere with free passage in an appreciable way: *see R.* v. *Bartholomew* (1908).

(b) An appreciable obstruction will not constitute a nuisance if not prolonged for an unreasonable period of time: *see Nagy* v. *Weston* (1965).

(c) In *R.* v. *Moule* (1964) X was charged with causing a nuisance by sitting down in the highway (as a protest). It was held that his conduct constituted an unreasonable obstruction.

38. Statutory rules relating to obstruction of the highway
These may be found in, eg:

(a) Town Police Clauses Act 1847, s. 48, by which an offence is committed by any person who 'wilfully causes any obstruction in any public footpath or other public thoroughfare'. *See Waring* v. *Wheatley* (1951).

(b) Highways Act 1980, s. 137, by which it is an offence for any person without lawful authority or excuse wilfully to obstruct the free passage along a highway. *See Arrowsmith* v. *Jenkins* (1963) (an offence under the Highways Act 1959, s. 12(1), now s. 137 of the 1980 Act) in which the belief of the accused that she had a right to cause an obstruction was held to be of no relevance to this offence.

> NOTE: It is an offence, under the Highways Act 1980, s. 303, to wilfully obstruct a person acting in the execution of the Act. (This offence also constitutes the tort of wrongful interference with business and is liable to restraint by injunction: *Department of Transport* v. *Williams* (1993).)

39. Breach of the peace

This common law offence is described by Blackstone (*Commentaries*, **4**, 142) as 'breaking or disturbing the public peace by any riotous, forcible or unlawful proceeding'. Essentially, it involves *conduct related to violence*, real or threatened. A mere disturbance does not, in itself, constitute the offence unless it results from violence, real or threatened.

(a) In *R. v. Howell* (1982), the Court of Appeal held that there is a breach of the peace 'whenever harm is actually done or is likely to be done to a person or, in his presence, to his property, or a person is in fear of being so harmed through assault, affray, unlawful disturbance, riot or other disturbance':*per* Watkins LJ.

(b) A constable or any other person may arrest *without warrant* when the breach is committed in the presence of the person making the arrest, or where the arrestor reasonably believes that such a breach will be committed in the immediate future, or, where the breach has been committed and it is reasonable to believe that it will be renewed: *R. v. Howell* (1982). *See McConnell* v. *Chief Constable of Manchester* (1990) – a constable may arrest a person for conduct which he genuinely suspected might be likely to cause a breach of the peace even on private premises where no member of the public is present. For 'binding over' to keep the peace, see *Binding Over* (Law Comm., No. 222, 1994).

Progress test 21

1. Outline the essential features of treason.   **(3)**

2. What is involved in the offence of sedition?   **(9)**

3. What is the purpose of the Official Secrets Act 1989?   **(18)**

4. How does the Public Order Act 1986 define 'riot' and 'affray'?   **(25,27)**

5. What are the constituents of the offence involving 'fear or provocation of violence' under the 1986 Act, s. 4?   **(28)**

6. Outline the offence of stirring up racial hatred under the 1986 Act, s. 17.   **(30)**

7. How does the 1986 Act seek to deal with problems likely to arise from processions and assemblies?   **(34)**

8. What is the essence of 'public nuisance' and 'breach of the peace'?   **(36,39)**

Criminal libel, blasphemy and obscenity

Criminal libel

1. Elements of libel

A libel consists of the publication in writing, printing, pictures or other *permanent form*, of that which is calculated to injure the reputation of a person by lowering him in the estimation of right-thinking members of society generally. In essence, a libel vilifies a person, bringing him into *hatred, ridicule and contempt*.

(a) Libel is both a criminal offence *and* a tort; slander (defamation by words only) is a tort, not a crime.

(b) Libel is 'defamation crystallised into some permanent form'. Under the Defamation Act 1952, it is provided that the broadcasting of words by means of 'wireless telegraphy' is to be treated as publication in permanent form, and this is repeated in the Cable and Broadcasting Act 1984, s. 28(1). 'Words' includes pictures, visual images, gestures and other methods of signifying meaning: 1984 Act, s. 27(10).

(c) The publication of a criminal libel is a common law offence (and also a tort).

(d) Note the distinctions between civil and criminal libel. Unintentional libel is a tort, not a crime, since criminal libel requires appropriate *mens rea*. Further, some libels (e.g. blasphemous libel: *see* 5) are crimes, but not torts, since they defame no individual. For the requirement of publication to a third party in the case of civil, but not criminal, libel, *see* 2.

2. Publication of a criminal libel

The prosecution must prove publication. *See Vizetelly* v. *Mudie's Library* (1900). Essential to the offence is a tendency for publication of the libel to cause a breach of the peace (*see Thorley* v. *Lord Kerry* (1812)) and that the libel is serious (*see R.* v. *Wells Street Stipendiary Magistrate, ex p. Deakin* (1980)). The offence is triable only on indicment.

(a) It suffices that the libel is published to the prosecutor alone; publication to a third party (necessary in tort) is not essential: *see Clutterbuck* v. *Chaffers* (1816).

(b) The libel need not reach the prosecutor. In *R.* v. *Adams* (1888), X wrote a letter to Y containing immoral proposals, but it was intercepted by Y's mother. X was convicted; it was held that the sending of such a letter would probably *tend* to provoke a breach of the peace on Y's part, and on the part of persons connected with her.

3. The libellous nature of the published matter

Matter, the publication of which is calculated to provoke a breach of the peace, need not make any direct assertion. An assertion can be conveyed indirectly by insinuation or innuendo. In such a case *the judge* will say whether the language used can possibly bear the meaning alleged and whether such a meaning is capable of being defamatory; *the jury* will say whether it did bear such a meaning and was defamatory in fact: *see Capital and Counties Bank* v. *Henty* (1882). *See Desmond* v. *Thorne* (1983).

4. Defences

Certain defences are available to an accused person:

(a) *Fair comment on a matter of public interest.* Whether or not a matter is of 'public interest' will be decided by the judge: *see South Hetton Coal Co.* v. *NE News Association* (1894). The mode of expression must be fair, *and* the published opinion held honestly.

(b) *Justification.* Under the Libel Act 1843, s. 6, it is a defence to show that the libel was true *and* that its publication was for the benefit of the public.

(c) *Accidental or unauthorised publication.* Under the Libel Act 1843, s. 7, the accused person may show that publication was made without his knowledge, consent or authority *and* that it did not result from any lack of care on his part.

(d) *Absolute privilege.* Absolute privilege is attached to the following:

(*i*) Statements in Parliament and reports and papers produced by order of either House: *see* the Parliamentary Papers Act 1840.

(*ii*) Statements made in the course of judicial proceedings, and contemporaneous newspaper reports of those proceedings.

(*iii*) Communications made in the course of duty by one officer of state to another.

(e) *Qualified privilege.* This attaches to:

(*i*) Extracts from or abstracts of Parliamentary papers or reports, and fair and accurate reports of proceedings in Parliament or in courts of justice.

(*ii*) Statements made under some legal or social duty, or in pursuance of a common interest. *See* e.g. *Conerney v. Jacklin* (1985).

NOTE: (1) In the case of (e) above, the privilege is lost if publication is actuated by malice. (2) The publication of a libel known by the accused to be false is punishable under the Libel Act 1843, s. 4.

Blasphemy

5. Essence of the offence

Blasphemy is a common law offence, covering any scurrilous vilification of Christianity. Its essence appears to be 'indecent and offensive attacks on Christianity or the Scriptures, or sacred persons or objects, calculated to outrage the feelings of the general body of the community': *per* Lord Coleridge CJ in *R.* v. *Ramsay and Foote* (1883). It is immaterial whether the blasphemy be spoken or written. *See Bowman* v. *Secular Society Ltd* (1917); *R.* v. *Gott* (1922). The offence is triable only on indictment.

6. The law restated

The common law offence was considered obsolescent until the prosecution in 1977 of *Gay News* on a charge of publishing 'a blasphemous libel concerning the Christian religion, namely an obscene poem and illustration vilifying Christ in his life and in his crucifixion'. The Court of Appeal and the House of Lords *upheld* the subsequent conviction: *R.* v. *Lemon* (1979).

(a) Lord Scarman quoted with approval from Stephen's *Digest of the Criminal Law*: 'Every publication is said to be blasphemous which contains any contemptuous, reviling, scurrilous or ludicrous matter relating to God, Jesus Christ or the Bible, or the formularies of the Church of England as by law established.'

(b) The only *mens rea* required is an intent to publish the matter in question; an intent to blaspheme is *not* an ingredient of the offence. (Note the dissenting judgment of Lord Edmund-Davies: 'To treat as irrelevant the state of mind of a person charged with blasphemy would be to take a backward step in the evolution of a humane code.')

(c) The Law Commission (Report No. 79) has recommended the abolition of the common law offence of blasphemy.

(d) Suggestions that the law be extended so as to cover religions other than Christianity were rejected by a Divisional Court in *R.* v. *Bow St Magistrates ex p. Choudhury* (1990).

Obscenity: its nature and publication

7. The test of obscenity at common law

'I think the test of obscenity is this, whether the tendency of the matter charged as obscenity is to deprave and corrupt those whose minds are open to such immoral influences, and into whose hands a publication of this sort may fall': *per* Cockburn J in *R.* v. *Hicklin* (1868). *See R.* v. *Gibson* (1990).

8. The test of obscenity by statute

The essence of the common law test is retained in the Obscene Publications Act 1959, s. 1(1):

'For the purposes of this Act an article shall be deemed to be obscene if its effect or (where the article comprises two or more distinct items) the effect of any one of its items is, if taken as a whole, such as to tend to deprave and corrupt persons who are likely, having regard to all relevant circumstances, to read, see or hear the matter contained or embodied in it.'

(a)   The 1959 Act did not abolish the common law offence of obscene libel. Note, however, the 1959 Act, s. 2(4): 'A person publishing an article shall not be proceeded against for an offence *at common law* consisting of the publication of any matter contained or embodied in the article where it is of the essence of the offence that the matter is obscene'.

(b)   In *Calder Publications Ltd* v. *Powell* (1965), it was held that there is no reason whatever to confine obscenity and depravity to books dealing with sex, and that the book in question, which advocated drug-taking by stressing its allegedly favourable effects, was obscene within the 1959 Act, s. 1. Note that a publication may be obscene if only part of it is obscene: *Paget Publications* v. *Watson* (1952).

9. The offence of publishing an obscene article

It is an offence for a person to publish an obscene article whether for gain or not: *see* 1959 Act, s. 2(1). *See Gold Star Publications* v. *DPP* (1981).

(a)   For the purposes of the 1959 Act, a person publishes an article who distributes, circulates, sells, lets on hire, gives, or lends it, or who offers it for sale or for letting on hire, or in the case of an article containing or embodying matter to be looked at or a record, shows, plays, or projects it: *see* 1959 Act, s. 1(3).

(b)   In *R.* v. *Clayton and Halsey* (1963), X_1 and X_2, a bookshop owner and his assistant, were convicted of publishing obscene articles and conspiring to do so. The conviction of publishing was quashed; the evidence on that charge was that of a police officer who stated that, since it was part of his job to buy articles of that type, they aroused no feelings whatsoever in him. The test of a tendency to deprave and corrupt must be related to the susceptibility of the viewer of the article. (*See*, however, 10.)

(c)   The 'publication' of an obscene article was considered by the Court of Appeal on a reference by the Attorney-General: *see A. -G.'s Reference (No. 2 of 1975)*. The opinion was given that the words 'read, see or hear' in s. 1(1) of the 1959 Act (*see* 8) were to be defined as 'read, see or hear as a result of a publication by a person who publishes within the meaning of s. 1(3) of that Act [*see* (a)] and not otherwise'.

10. Having an obscene article for gain (whether gain to the accused or another)

It is an offence to possess an obscene article *for publication for gain*: Obscene Publications Act 1964, s. 1(1) (this amends, and adds to, the 1959 Act). Hence, a prosecution will not now fail under the circumstances of *R. v. Clayton and Halsey* (1963) (*see* 9 (b)); X_1 and X_2 could now be charged with having the article for publication for gain. *See R. v. Xenophon* (1992).

(a) By the 1964 Act, s. 1(3)(*b*), the question whether an article is obscene will be determined by reference to those circumstances of intended publication that 'it may reasonably be inferred [the accused person] had in contemplation and to any further implication that could reasonably be expected to follow from it . . .'

(b) 'A person shall be deemed to have an article for publication for gain if with a view to such publication he has the article in his ownership, possession or control': 1964 Act, s. 1(2).

11. 'An article'

By the 1959 Act, s. 1(2) 'article' had the meaning of 'any description of article containing or embodying matter to be read or looked at or both, any sound record, and any film or other record of a picture or pictures'.

(a) Note the 1964 Act, s. 2(1): 'the Obscene Publications Act 1959 (as amended by this Act) shall apply in relation to anything which is intended to be used, either alone or as one of a set, for the reproduction or manufacture therefrom of articles containing or embodying matter to be read, looked at or listened to, as if it were an article containing or embodying that matter so far as that matter is to be derived from it or from the set.'

(b) The term 'article' in the 1959 Act, s. 1(2), embraces a video cassette: *A. -G.'s Ref. (No. 5 of 1980). See* the Video Recordings Act 1984, ss. 2, 12.

12. Defences

The following defences are available:

(a) By the 1959 Act, s. 2(5), and the 1964 Act, s. 1(3)(*a*), the accused person may show:

(*i*) that he had not made any examination of the article in question, *and*

(*ii*) that he had no reasonable cause to suspect that his possession or publication of it would render him liable to be convicted of an offence under s. 2.

(b) By the 1959 Act, s. 4:

'(1) A person shall not be convicted of an offence against s. 2 of this

Act . . . if it is proved that publication of the article in question is justified as being *for the public good* on the ground that it is in the interests of science, literature, art or learning, or of other objects of general concern. (2) It is hereby declared that the opinion of experts as to the literary, artistic, scientific or other merits of an article *may be admitted* in any proceedings under this Act either to establish or negative the said ground.' *See R. v. Skirving* (1985).

(c)   In *R. v. Staniforth and Jordan* (1976), the Court of Appeal held that a defendant charged with possessing obscene articles for publication contrary to the 1959 Act, s. 2(1), may *not* call expert evidence in support of a defence under s. 4(1) that the publication had 'psychotherapeutic value'. The decision was upheld by the House of Lords in *DPP v. Jordan* (1977). (Lord Wilberforce noted that the judgment to be reached under s. 4(1), and the evidence to be adduced under s. 4(2), must be related to showing whether publication ought to be permitted in spite of obscenity, *not* to negative obscenity.) In the context of s. 4(1), 'learning' means 'a product of scholarship': *A.-G.'s Reference (No. 3 of 1977).*

(d)   The onus of proof of the matter put forward in defence rests on the accused person. *See Olympia Press v. Hollis* (1973).

13.   Forfeiture of obscene articles

Under the 1959 Act, s. 3, where an information is laid before a magistrate that there are reasonable grounds for suspecting that obscene articles are kept for publication for gain in any premises, a warrant may be issued for their seizure. Such articles must be brought before the magistrate who may issue a summons to the occupier of the premises to show cause why they ought not to be forfeited. Under s. 4(1) there is a defence of 'public good' in such proceedings. Note *Darbo v. DPP* (1991), in which a warrant authorising the search of premises for 'material of an explicitly sexual nature' was held bad because such articles are not, in themselves, necessarily 'obscene'. (*See* also the Video Recordings Act 1984, s. 21.)

14.   The Post Office Act 1953, s. 11

By this Act it is an offence to 'send or attempt to send or procure to be sent a postal packet which encloses any indecent or obscene print, painting, photograph, etc., or written communication, or any indecent or obscene article whether similar to the above or not . . .'

(a)   In *R. v. Anderson and Neville* (1972), it was held that in the Post Office Act 1953, s. 11, 'obscene' has its ordinary meaning (which includes 'shocking, lewd, indecent'), but that under the Obscene Publications Act 1959 the sole test of 'obscenity' is the tendency to deprave and corrupt.

(b)   In *R. v. Stamford* (1972), it was held that whether an article sent by post is indecent or obscene is a matter for the jury to decide without evidence from persons having views on the matter.

15. Malicious Communications Act 1988
It is an offence to send a letter or other article which conveys an indecent or gravely offensive message (or a threat or information which the sender knows is false) or any other article of an indecent or grossly offensive nature if the sender's purpose is to cause distress or anxiety to the recipient or any other person to whom he intends that it or its contents or nature should be communicated: s. (1).

16. Protection of Children Act 1978
Under s. 1(1) it is an offence for a person to take, or permit to be taken, any indecent photograph of a person under sixteen, or to distribute or show such a photograph, or to have such a photograph in his possession with a view to its being distributed or shown by himself to others, or to advertise that he distributes, shows or intends to show such a photograph. (*See also* proposals to increase maximum penalties, contained in the Criminal Justice and Public Order Bill, published in December 1993.)

17. Indecent Displays (Control) Act 1981
If indecent matter is publicly displayed, i.e. displayed in or so as to be visible from any public place, the person making the display or causing or permitting the display is guilty of an offence: s. 1(1), (2). 'Public place' includes any place to which the public have access (whether on payment or otherwise); it does not include part of a shop which the public can enter only after passing an adequate warning notice: s. 1(3), (6). Certain specified matter is excluded from the Act, e.g. that included in a TV broadcast, the display of an art gallery, a licensed film exhibition: s. 1(4) (as amended by the Cinemas Act 1985, Sch. 2).

18. Video Recordings Act 1984
The Act creates a category of 'excepted' video recordings (e.g. those designed to inform or instruct) but excludes from that category recordings which 'to any significant extent' depict 'human sexual activity or acts of force or restraint associated with such activity' or which are designed to stimulate or encourage such activity: ss. 1, 2. For general defences, see the 1984 Act, s. 14, and Video Recordings Act 1993, s. 2.

19. Cable and Broadcasting Act 1984
Under s. 25(1) an offence is committed by a person who provides a cable programme service which involves the publication of an obscene article. For defences (e.g. that the programme was 'for the public good'), *see* s. 25(6)–(8).

NOTE: In early 1994, the Home Office publicised suggestions concerning a redefinition of the term 'publication' in the Obscene Publications Act 1959 so as to include the electronic transmission of obscene materials between computers.

Progress test 22

1. What are the fundamentals of criminal libel? **(1)**

2. Outline the defences to a charge of criminal libel. **(4)**

3. Is blasphemy punishable today? **(5,6)**

4. Outline the meaning of 'article' under the Obscene Publications Act 1964. **(11)**

5. What is the essence of the Post Office Act 1959, s. 11? **(14)**

Misuse of drugs

The Misuse of Drugs Act 1971: classification and restrictions

1. The 1971 Act
The Misuse of Drugs Act 1971 reformed the law relating to the misuse of dangerous drugs. It replaced the Drugs (Prevention of Misuse) Act 1964 and the Dangerous Drugs Acts 1965 and 1967, and is now the governing statute.

2. Classification
Section 2 and Sch. 2 specify and classify those drugs controlled by the Act (known as 'controlled drugs').

(a) There are three classes of controlled drugs: A, B and C.
(b) The classification affects the maximum punishments for some offences under the Act: *see* Sch. 4 (as modified by the Controlled Drugs (Penalties) Act 1985, s. 1(1)). Thus, where a Class A drug is involved in the case of a person convicted of offences under the 1971 Act, ss. 4(2), (3), 5(3) (production, supply and possession with intent to supply), the penalty is life imprisonment or a fine, or both. For principles of sentencing *see R.* v. *Aramah* (1983) *R.* v. *Fleming* (1989); *A. -G'.s Reference (No. 16 of 1992).*
(c) By Order in Council, amendments may be made to Sch. 2, so as to add substances or products to the classification, to remove them, or to vary the grouping.
(d) For proof that a drug is 'controlled', *see R.* v. *Hunt* (1987).

3. Restriction of the import and export of controlled drugs
By s. 3, the import and export of controlled drugs, unless in accordance with a licence issued by the Secretary for State, are prohibited. *See R.* v. *Jakeman* (1983).

4. Restriction of the production and supply of controlled drugs
By s. 4, the production and supply of, or offer to supply, controlled drugs is rendered *unlawful* unless authorised by regulations made under s. 7 (see 9).

(a) 'Production' refers to producing the drug 'by manufacture, cultivation or any other method': s. 37(1). *See R.* v. *Thomas* (1981); *R.* v. *Russell* (1992) (the conversion of one type of Class A drug into another form of a similar genus can constitute 'production').

(b) 'Supply' must be 'to another': *see* s. 4(3)(b); hence, self-administration of a controlled drug is not within the section. *See R.* v. *Dempsey* (1986): 'supply' connotes an act designed to benefit the recipient, so the mere deposit of drugs for safekeeping did not constitute 'supply' under s. 4(3). *See R.* v. *Lubren* (1988) – 'another' meant someone not named on the indictment.

(c) Under s. 4(3)(c) it is an offence for a person 'to be concerned in the making to another' of an offer to supply a controlled drug (subject to s. 28). In *R.* v. *Blake* (1978), it was held by the Court of Appeal that the offence is widely drafted so as to include persons who may be some distance away at the time of making the offer.

(d) In *R.* v. *Gill* (1993), *the Court of Appeal held that to found a conviction of the offence of 'conspiracy to supply a controlled drug', it was not* necessary for the prosecution to show that the conspirators intended that the controlled drug should, pursuant to their offer, be supplied. Essentially, the offence of 'offering to supply a controlled drug' was complete *when the offer was made*, regardless of whether the offeror intended to carry the offer into effect by actually supplying that drug.

5. Restriction of cultivation of cannabis plant

By s. 6, subject to any regulations under s. 7, it is an offence to cultivate any plant of the genus *cannabis*. 'Cannabis' (a Class B drug) was redefined (*see* the 1971 Act, s. 37(1)) by the Criminal Law Act 1977, s. 52, thus: 'Cannabis (except in the expression "cannabis resin") means any plant of the genus Cannabis or any part of any such plant (by whatever name designated) except that it does not include cannabis resin or any of the following products after separation from the rest of the plant, namely – (*a*) mature stalk of any such plant, (*b*) fibre produced from mature stalk of any such plant, and (*c*) seed of any such plant.'

6. Unlawful possession

By s. 5(1), it is not lawful, subject to any regulations under s. 7, for a person to have a controlled drug in his possession. By s. 5(2) it is an offence, subject to s. 28 (*see* **12**, and to s. 5(4) (*see* **7**), for a person to have a controlled drug in his possession in contravention of subsection 1. *See R.* v. *Colyer* (1974). By s. 5(3) it is an offence, subject to s. 28, for a person to have a controlled drug in his possession, whether lawfully or not, with intent to supply it to another in contravention of s. 4 (*see* **4**): *see R.* v. *King* (1978). In *R.* v. *Maginnis* (1986), X was found with drugs in his car and said that his friend, Y, had left them there on the previous day, and that he was expecting Y to call for them. The judge decided that possessing drugs with the intention of returning them to their owner constituted possession with intent to supply, under s. 5(3). X was convicted and appealed. The Court of Appeal *allowed* X's appeal, holding that for there to be 'supply' there must be a transfer of physical control for the benefit of the recipient of the drugs. In the circumstances, Y's resumption of actual possession was not sufficient benefit to make the return to him of the drugs an actual act of supply.

(a) 'Possession' involves more than mere control; the person with control should *know* that the thing is in his control: see *Warner* v. *Metropolitan Police Commissioner* (1969) (*see* 4:3) For the purposes of s. 5(1) proof of possession entails proof of knowledge and the onus remains on the prosecution to show this: *R.* v. *Ashton-Rickhardt* (1977). Note *R.* v. *Martindale* (1986), in which the Court of Appeal held that a man who put a small quantity of cannabis in his wallet, knowing what it was, remained 'in possession' of it, even through his memory of the drug had faded or gone. Possession did not depend on the alleged possessor's powers of memory, and possession did not come and go as memory revived and faded.

(b) 'Possession with intent to supply' is distinguished from unlawful possession in the following ways:

    (*i*) whether the possession is lawful or not is *not relevant*;

    (*ii*) there must be some *ulterior intent* to supply to another.

(c) The fact that a quantity of drugs is too small for use does *not* preclude a conviction under s. 5(2). *See R.* v. *Boyesen* (1982), in which the House of Lords stressed that s. 5 creates an offence of *possessing* drugs, not using them, so that a person is guilty of the offence if he has in his possession any quantity, however small, that is visible, tangible and measurable. *See R.* v. *Hunt* (1987).

(d) On the interpretation of possessing a 'preparation' of a drug (*see* Sch. 2, Pt. I, para. 1), *see R.* v. *Cunliffe* (1986) – the word has to be given its ordinary meaning. In *Hodder* v. *DPP* (1990), the court stated that decided cases made clear that for a substance to be a 'preparation', a natural substance must have been subjected to some process by a human being which prepared the natural substance for future use as a drug. 'Prepare' meant 'to make ready or fit; to bring into a suitable state; to subject to a process for bringing it to a required state.'

7. Specific defences to a charge of unlawful possession

(NOTE: these defences are additional to those under s. 28: *see* **12.**) In any proceedings for an offence under s. 5(2) in which it is proved that the accused had a controlled drug in his possession, it is a defence for him to show that, knowing or suspecting it to be a controlled drug: he took possession of it for the purpose of preventing another from committing or continuing to commit an offence in connection with that drug and that as soon as possible after taking possession of it he took all such steps as were reasonably open to him to destroy the drug or to deliver it into the custody of a person lawfully entitled to take custody of it; or, he took possession of it for the purpose of delivering it into the custody of a person lawfully entitled to take custody of it and, as soon as possible, took steps to deliver it: *see* s. 5(4).

(a) The onus of proof relating to the defence rests on *the accused person*; the standard of proof is on *a balance of probabilities*.
(b) The defences have application only where the accused person knew or suspected at the time of taking possession of the controlled drug that it was such.

8. Authorisation of activities by the Secretary of State
Under s. 7(1) the Secretary of State may, by regulations, exempt certain controlled drugs from the provisions of the Act which relate to their import and export (s. 3), production and supply (s. 4), or possession (s. 5), and to other matters. Under s. 7(3) he must make regulations authorising doctors, dentists, veterinary surgeons and pharmacists to carry out their professional tasks as they relate to controlled drugs.

Other offences involving controlled drugs

9. Permitting certain activities on premises
A person commits an offence if, being the occupier or concerned in the management of any premises, he knowingly permits or suffers certain activities to take place on those premises, i.e. producing or attempting to produce a controlled drug in contravention of s. 4(1); supplying or attempting to supply a controlled drug to another in contravention of s. 4(1); or offering to supply a controlled drug to another in contravention of s. 4(1); smoking cannabis or opium: *see* s. 8. *See Taylor* v. *Chief Constable of Kent* (1981).

(a) '*Occupier of premises*'. In *R.* v. *Mogford* (1970), X_1 and X_2, sisters aged twenty and fifteen, were charged under the 1965 Act, s. 5, as the occupiers of premises, with permitting the premises to be used for the purpose of smoking cannabis. The parents of X_1 and X_2 were on holiday at the relevant time. It was held that X_1 and X_2 did not have sufficient control of the premises to be the occupiers. *See* also *R* v. *Tao* (1976), where it was held that a person is an 'occupier' of a room for the purposes of the 1971 Act if he is entitled to its exclusive possession, i.e. a room in a college hostel allotted to an undergraduate defendant, and his degree of control over the room is such that he is capable of excluding any person likely to commit an offence.

(b) *'Knowingly permits.'* 'The word "permits", used to define the prohibited act, in itself connotes as a mental element of the prohibited conduct knowledge or grounds for reasonable suspicion on the part of the occupier that the premises will be used by someone for that purpose and an unwillingness on his part to take means available to him to prevent it': *per* Lord Diplock in *Sweet* v. *Parsley* (1970) (a case under the 1965 Act) (*see* 4:3). *See R.* v. *Thomas* (1976).

10. Activities involving opium and drug administration kits etc.

It is an offence, subject to s. 28, for a person to smoke or otherwise use prepared opium, or to frequent a place used for that purpose, or to have in his possession utensils made or adapted for that purpose: *see* s. 9.

(a) Under s. 9A of the 1971 Act (inserted by the Drug Trafficking Offences Act 1986, s. 34(1)), a person who supplies or offers to supply any article which may be used or adapted to be used in the administration by any person of a controlled drug to himself or another, believing that the article, or the article as adapted, is to be used in circumstances where the administration is unlawful, is guilty of an offence.

(b) A person who supplies or offers to supply any article which may be used to prepare a controlled drug for administration by any person to himself or another, believing that the article is to be so used in circumstances where the administration is unlawful, is guilty of an offence: s. 9(A)3.

General defence

11. Application of the defence

The general defence under s. 28 applies to the following circumstances:

(a) unlawfully producing a controlled drug: *see* s. 4(2);

(b) unlawfully supplying or offering to supply a controlled drug: *see* s. 4(3);

(c) unlawfully possessing a controlled drug, or having a controlled drug in possession with intent to supply it in contravention of s. 4(1): *see* s. 5(2), (3);

(d) unlawfully cultivating cannabis: *see* s. 6;

(e) smoking opium: *see* s. 9.

12. The defence (s. 28(2), (3))

'(2) Subject to subsection (3) below, in any proceedings to which this section applies it shall be a defence for the accused to prove that he neither knew of nor suspected nor had reason to suspect the existence of some fact alleged by the prosecution which it is necessary for the prosecution to prove if he is to be convicted of the offence charged. (3) . . . The accused . . . shall be acquitted . . . if he proves that he neither believed nor suspected nor had reason to suspect that the substance or product in question was a controlled drug, or if he proves that he believed the substance or product in question to be a controlled drug, or a controlled drug of a description, such that, if it had been that controlled drug or a controlled drug of that description, he would not at the material time have been committing any offence to which this section applies. ' See R. v. *Ellis and Street* (1986).

(a) Nothing in s. 28 is to prejudice any defence which it is open to a person charged with an offence to which this section applies to raise apart from this section: *see* s. 28(4).

(b) In R. v. *Young* (1984), X, a soldier, was charged with possessing a controlled drug with intent to supply it to another. His defence, based on s. 28, was that he did not believe, suspect, or have any reason to suspect that what he had in his possession was a controlled drug. As to whether X's drunkenness could negate his belief or suspicion, the court-martial was directed that the test to be applied was that of the belief or suspicion of a 'reasonable and sober person'. The Court of Appeal *dismissed* X's appeal against conviction, holding that X's self-induced intoxication was *not* a factor relevant to whether he had reason to suspect that he had in his possession a controlled drug; that it was an unnecessary gloss to introduce the concept of the 'reasonable, sober person'; that a 'reason' was not something personal or individual, which called for a subjective consideration, but that it involved the wider concept of *'an objective rationality'*.

(c)   If the prosecution establishes that X had control of a box and knew that it contained something, then, if, in the event, the box contained unlawful drugs, it is up to X to show that he did not know of the contents, if he is to bring himself within the defence afforded by s. 28(3): R. v. *McNamara* (1988).

Drug addiction

13. Definition

'A person shall be regarded as being addicted to a drug if, and only if, he has as a result of repeated administration become so dependent upon the drug that he has an overpowering desire for the administration of it to be continued': SI 1973/799, as amended by SI 1989/1909. *See* Misuse of Drugs Act 1971, s. 10(2) (i).

14. Recent decisions

(a) *R.* v. *Bassett* (1985). Curing an offender of drug addiction is an improper reason for passing a long sentence of imprisonment.
(b) *R.* v. *Crampton* (1991). The admissibility as evidence of the interview of a drug addict suffering from withdrawal symptoms was questioned.

15. Addiction as a defence or in mitigation
Addiction is *no defence* to a criminal charge (not even in relation to mitigation). *See R.* v. *Lawrence* (1989) (offence committed so as to feed an addiction to heroin), in which the Court of Appeal stated: 'We cannot make too plain the principle to be followed. It is no mitigation whatever that a crime is committed to feed an addiction, whether that addiction be drugs, drink . . . or anything else.'

Drug trafficking offences

16. Definition
'Drug trafficking' means, under the Drug Trafficking Offences Act 1986, s. 38(1), doing or being concerned in any of the following:

(a) producing or supplying a controlled drug where this contravenes the 1971 Act, s. 4(1) or a corresponding law;
(b) transporting or storing a controlled drug where possession contravenes the 1971 Act, s. 5(1) or a corresponding law;
(c) importing or exporting a controlled drug where this is prohibited by the 1971 Act, s. 3(1) or a corresponding law;
(d) entering into or otherwise being concerned in an arrangement whereby the retention or control by or on behalf of another person of the other person's proceeds of drug trafficking is facilitated, or the proceeds of drug trafficking by another person are used to secure that funds are placed at the other person's disposal or are used for the other person's benefit to acquire property by way of investment.

17. Acquiring etc. property derived from drug trafficking
Under the 1986 Act, s. 23A(1), inserted by the Criminal Justice Act 1993, s. 16, a person is guilty of an offence if, knowing that any property is, or in whole or in part directly or indirectly represents, another person's proceeds of drug trafficking, he acquires or uses that property or has possession of it. Under s. 23A(2), it is a defence that the person charged acquired or used the property or had possession of it for adequate consideration. But the provision for any person of services or goods which

are of assistance to him in drug trafficking shall not be treated as consideration for the purposes of this section: s. 23A (4).

18. Assisting another to retain the benefit of drug trafficking

If a person enters into or is otherwise concerned in an arrangement whereby the retention or control by or on behalf of another (X) of X's proceeds of drug trafficking is facilitated (whether by concealment, removal from the jurisdiction, transfer to nominees or otherwise), or X's proceeds of drug trafficking are used to secure that funds are placed at X's disposal, or are used for X's benefit to acquire property by way of investment, knowing or suspecting that X is a person who carries on or has carried on drug trafficking or has benefited from drug trafficking, he is guilty of an offence; 1986 Act, s. 24(1).

19. Offences in connection with money laundering

The Criminal Justice Act 1993, s. 18, creates offences related to 'laundering' of the proceeds of trafficking (ie, the transfer of funds into apparently legitimate institutions in a manner intended to conceal their criminal origin), by inserting ss. 26B and 26C in the 1986 Act.

(a) A person is guilty of an offence if he knows, or suspects, that another person is engaged in drug money laundering, that the information, or other matter, on which that knowledge or suspicion is based came to his attention in the course of his trade, profession, business or employment, and he does not disclose the information or other matter to a constable as soon as is reasonably practicable after it comes to his attention: s. 26B.

(b) A person is guilty of the offence of 'tipping-off' if he knows or suspects that a constable is acting, or is proposing to act, in connection with an investigation which is being, or is about to be, conducted into drug money laundering, and he discloses to any other person information or any other matter which is likely to prejudice that investigation, or proposed investigation: s. 26C.

> NOTE: In this section, 'drug money laundering' means doing any act which constitutes an offence under s. 23A or 24 of the 1986 Act, or s. 14 of the Criminal Justice (International Co-operation) Act 1990 (concealing or transferring proceeds of drug trafficking), or in the case of an act done otherwise than in England and Wales, would constitute such an offence if done in England or Wales: 1986 Act, s. 26B(7), as inserted by the Criminal Justice Act 1993, s. 18. See SI 1993/1933.

20. Confiscation orders

Following conviction in the Crown Court of a drug trafficking offence, the court is obliged, under the 1986 Act, s. 1, to impose on the offender an order which recovers from him the proceeds of such trafficking. This is *in addition* to the sentence for trafficking. *See* e.g. *R.* v. *Osei* (1988). (A confiscation order is part of a sentence for purposes of appeal: *R.* v. *Johnson* (1990).) *See R.* v. *Rose* (1993).

(a) The amount in the order is the sum assessed by the court to be 'the value of the defendant's proceeds of drug trafficking': s. 4(1). That value is 'the aggregate of the values of payments or other rewards': s. 2(1)(b).
(b) The standard of proof required to determine any question arising under the 1986 Act as to whether a person has benefited from drug trafficking, or the amount to be recovered in his case in relation to a confiscation order, is that applicable in *civil proceedings*: s. 1(7A), as inserted by the Criminal Justice Act 1993, s. 7.

21. Investigation of a trafficker's financial dealings
Where there are reasonable grounds for suspecting that a person is or has been engaged in drug trafficking, a circuit judge may order, on application, the disclosure of information 'likely to be of substantial value (whether by itself or together with other material) to the investigation': *see* s. 27.

The Intoxicating Substances (Supply) Act 1985

22. The offence of supply of an intoxicating substance
Although this Act is not concerned with controlled drugs, it is mentioned here because the mischief it is intended to prevent arises from practices such as 'solvent abuse' (e.g. 'glue-sniffing') which, as in the case of misuse of drugs, tend to create addiction. It is an offence under the Act for a person to supply or offer to supply a substance other than a controlled drug [the term has the meaning of the 1971 Act] to a person under the age of eighteen whom he knows, or has reasonable cause to believe, to be under that age, or to a person who is acting on behalf of someone under that age, and whom he knows, or has reasonable cause to believe, to be so acting, if he knows or has reasonable cause to believe that the substance is, or its fumes are, likely to be inhaled by the person under the age of eighteen for the purpose of causing intoxication: s. 1(1). (Note, however, that 'solvent sniffing' is *not* 'drug abuse' for the purpose of a coroner's verdict: *R.* v. *Southwark Coroner ex p. Kendall* (1988).)

23. Defence
It is a defence for the accused person to show that at the time he made the supply or offer he was under the age of eighteen and was acting otherwise than in the course or furtherance of a business: s. 1(2).

Progress test 23

1. Outline the Misuse of Drugs Act 1971, s. 4.   **(4)**

2. Comment on *R. v. Maginnis* (1986).   **(6)**

3. What is meant by 'possession with intent to supply'?   **(6)**

4. Outline the specific defences to a charge of unlawful possession.   **(7)**

5. What is the nature of the general defence under s. 28?   **(12)**

6. What is meant by 'drug trafficking' under the Drug Trafficking Offences Act 1986, s. 38(1)?   **(16)**

7. Outline the offences in connection with money laundering in relation to drug trafficking.   **(19)**

Perjury and contempt of court

The nature of perjury

1. Definition of the offence
'If any person lawfully sworn as a witness or as an interpreter in a judicial proceeding wilfully makes a statement material in that proceeding, which he knows to be false or does not believe to be true, he shall be guilty of perjury . . .': Perjury Act 1911, s. 1(1). (A person who makes more than one false statement in a proceeding commits only one offence of perjury.) *See* also the Evidence (Proceedings in Other Jurisdictions) Act 1975, Sch. 1; the European Communities Act 1972, s. 11 (as amended by the Prosecution of Offences Act 1985, Sch.2); *R.* v. *Carroll* (1993). The offence is triable only on indictment.

In *R.* v. *Millward* (1985), the Court of Appeal, giving guidance for future cases, stated that, in order to establish the offence of perjury, the Crown must prove:

(a) that the witness was lawfully sworn as a witness;
(b) in a judicial proceeding;
(c) that the witness made a statement wilfully, i.e., deliberately and not inadvertently or by mistake;
(d) that the statement was false;
(e) that the witness knew it was false or did not believe it to be true;
(f) that the statement was, viewed objectively, material in the judicial proceeding.

2. Examples of the offence
At the trial of Y, X, lawfully sworn as a witness, is giving evidence on the vital question whether Y was in Manchester or Leeds on a certain day. X will be guilty of perjury if:

(a) he states that Y was in Manchester, knowing, in fact, that this was not so; *or*
(b) he states that Y was in Leeds, which, in fact, was true, but believing his statement to be untrue; *or*
(c) he states that Y was in Leeds, which in fact was true, but is reckless as to whether his statement is true, or not.

3. The subornation of perjury

'Every person who aids, abets, counsels, procures or suborns another person to commit an offence against this Act shall be liable to be proceeded against, indicted, tried and punished as if he were a principal offender': Perjury Act 1911, s. 7. *See R.* v. *Cromack* (1978). (Attempting to suborn the commission of an offence is now covered by the Criminal Attempts Act 1981, s. 1(4)(*b*).)

Interpretation of the Perjury Act 1911

4. 'Lawfully sworn as a witness'

For the purposes of the 1911 Act the forms and ceremonies used in administering an oath are immaterial if the court or person before whom it is taken has the power to administer an oath, and if it has been administered and accepted without objection by the person taking it, or declared by that person to be binding on him: *see* s. 15(1).

(a) The expression 'oath' includes affirmation and declaration (i.e. by persons who have no religious beliefs or who must not, because of religious beliefs, take such an oath): *see* s. 15(2); *see* also the Oaths Act 1978. An oath is valid if taken in a way binding and intended to be binding upon the conscience of a witness: *R.* v. *Chapman* (1980).

(b) Where it is not practicable to administer an oath in a manner appropriate to a person's religious beliefs, he can be required to make a solemn affirmation: Oaths Act 1978.

(c) Where a person is *not* a competent witness and has been sworn by mistake, he cannot be convicted of perjury: *see R.* v. *Clegg* (1868), where X deceived the court into hearing evidence by pretending to be his son, and was held not indictable for perjury.

5. 'Judicial proceeding'

This includes 'a proceeding before any court, tribunal, or person having by law power to hear, receive and examine evidence on oath': s. 1(2). The term includes not only courts of law and tribunals, but, for example, Commissioners of Income Tax hearing an appeal against assessment of taxes: *see R.* v. *Hood-Barrs* (1943).

6. 'Wilfully'

Wilfulness is an *essential element* in the offence. If, in 16, X states that Y was in Manchester, *honestly believing* that this is true, X has committed no offence.

(a) In *R.* v. *Millward* (1985) (*see* 1), the Court of Appeal discussed whether the word 'wilfully' in s. 1(1) requires proof by the prosecution of knowledge or belief by the accused that the questions asked and the answers to be given are material in the proceedings, so that no offence would be committed where a person makes a statement even though he knows it to be false and even though (in law) it is material, if he does so under the honest, but mistaken, belief that it is not material in those proceedings.

(b) The Court did not consider that the construction of s. 1(1) could bear such a meaning. 'The use of the word "wilfully" in s. 1(1) requires the prosecution to prove no more than that the statement was made deliberately and not inadvertently or by mistake': *per* Lord Lane.

7. 'A statement material in that proceeding'

'For if it be not material, then though it be false, yet it is no perjury, because it concerneth not the point in suit, and therefore in effect it is extrajudicial': Coke. *A statement is material if it is likely to influence the court in making any decision.*

(a) Whether a statement is material is a question of law which is to be determined by the court: *see* s. 1(6).

(b) In *R. v. Baker* (1895), X was charged with selling beer without a licence. In the course of his statement as a sworn witness he admitted a previous conviction for that offence, but stated falsely that, on that occasion, his solicitor had pleaded guilty without his authority. X's conviction for perjury was affirmed. *Per* Lord Russell CJ: 'The defendant's answers would affect his credit as witness, and all false statements, wilfully and corruptly made, as to matters which affect his credit, are material.'

(c) In *R. v. Sweet-Escott* (1971), X denied, in cross-examination as to credit, convictions relating to more than twenty years earlier (since when he had had no further convictions). X was acquitted of perjury, it being held that his answers were not material, since no reasonable magistrate would have been affected in his judgment of X's reliability by such matters.

(d) In *R. v. Millward* (1985) (*see* 1), the Court of Appeal held that there is an express *mens rea* requirement as to the falsity of a statement; but, on materiality, there is strict liability. What has to be considered is the materiality of the false statement not the materiality of the truth, if told. Attention was drawn to the importance of Lord Campbell's words in *R. v. Lavey* (1850): 'On the question whether what she falsely swore was material or not, you will consider whether her evidence in this respect might not influence the mind of the judge . . . in believing or disbelieving the other statements she made in giving her evidence.'

8. 'Knows to be false or does not believe to be true'

(a) Negligence will not suffice to constitute the *mens rea* of perjury.
(b) The expression of an opinion which is not genuinely held may constitute perjury: *see R. v. Schlesinger* (1867).

Offences akin to perjury and offences perverting the course of public justice

9. By the Perjury Act 1911
The following are offences under the 1911 Act:

(a) 'If any person being required or authorised by law to make any statement on oath for any purpose, and being lawfully sworn (otherwise than in a judicial proceeding) wilfully makes a statement which is material for that purpose and which he knows to be false or does not believe to be true . . .': s. 2(1).

(b) If any person wilfully makes a false statement relating to the registration of births or deaths: *see* s. 4(1).

(c) If any person knowingly and wilfully makes otherwise than on oath a statement false in any material particular in any oral declaration or answer which by Act of Parliament he is required to answer or in any abstract, account or balance sheet, or report: *see* s. 5.

10. Criminal Justice Act 1967, s. 89
It is an offence for any person in a written statement in criminal proceedings by virtue of the Act of 1967, or the Magistrates' Courts Act 1980, s. 102, wilfully to make a statement material in those proceedings which he knows to be false or does not believe to be true.

11. Offences aimed at perverting the course of public justice

(a) The nature and elements of this offence were reviewed by the Court of Appeal in *R.* v. *Thomas* (1979) (assisting a person to evade lawful arrest). The Court stated that it was well established that it is an offence at common law to do any act which had a tendency and was intended to pervert the administration of justice (and that included, as in the case under discussion, the arrest of suspected offenders). The offence was not confined to the use of dishonest, corrupt or threatening means. The Court asserted the independence of the common law offence from the statutory offences created by the Criminal Law Act 1967, ss. 4, 5. In *R.* v. *Bassi* (1985), the Court of Appeal held that it sufficed that conduct may lead and is intended to lead to a miscarriage of justice; it is not necessary that a miscarriage should actually occur.

(b) Examples of this type of offence are:

(i) *Interfering with witnesses.* It is an offence at common law to attempt to dissuade or prevent a witness from appearing or giving evidence: *see Shaw* v. *Shaw* (1861); *R.* v. *Postlethwaite* (1992). In *R.* v. *Toney* (1993), the Court of Appeal considered this matter and summarised the position thus: in the great majority of cases of perverting the course of justice by interfering with a witness, the *actus reus* would be accompanied by unlawful means (bribery, threats, improper pressure, etc.); the use of unlawful means was not, however an essential ingredient of the offence, and in cases where a defendant might otherwise have a defence of lawful excuse, he would nevertheless be liable if he employed unlawful means; 'unlawful means' in this context includes a threat to do an otherwise lawful act or to exercise a legal right; in all cases the prosecution must prove the necessary intent. (*See also* the Criminal Justice and Public Order Bill, published in December, 1993.)

(*ii*) *Fabricating false evidence with intent to mislead a judicial tribunal. See R. v. Firetto* (1991) (bogus samples of blood sent for analysis).

(*iii*) *Impersonating a juryman. See R. v. Clark* (1918).

(c) In *R. v. Rafique and Others* (1993), the Court of Appeal considered the question of an act committed *before* investigation of an offence had commenced. Three appellants, who knew that another person had been fatally shot accidentally, disposed of the gun and cartridges used before a police investigation had begun. It was held that they were rightly convicted of doing acts intended, and tending, to pervert the course of public justice. *Per* Lord Taylor: 'An act is not beyond the ambit of those tending to pervert the course of justice by reason of its being performed after the crime but before investigations into the alleged crime have begun . . .'

(*i*) 'Whether an act has a tendency to pervert the course of justice cannot depend upon whether investigation of the matter which may become the subject of court proceedings has begun . . .'

(*ii*) 'If an intention to pervert the course of justice in relation to that matter is proved, the act has the same quality whether performed before that alleged offence is investigated or even discovered as it would have been at a later stage.'

Background to contempt of court

12. Civil and criminal contempt

'The essence of contempt of court is action or inaction amounting to interference with or obstruction to, or having a tendency to interfere with or obstruct the due administration of justice': *see Re Dunn* (1906). (The power to commit for contempt of court has been a feature of the inherent jurisdiction of superior courts.) Contempt of court may be either of the following.

(a) *Civil contempt*, i.e. disobedience to the judgments and orders of courts made in civil proceedings. *See* e.g. *Home Office v. Harman* (1982), in which the House of Lords held that it is a *civil* contempt of court to allow journalists access to documents obtained in the course of discovery in litigation, even where the documents have been read out in open court. Note that the powers of the court to punish civil contempt are, in fact, *penal. See Guildford BC* v. *Valler* (1993).

(b) *Criminal contempt* (which is considered below) is based generally on a *common law offence*. (For a contempt based on *statute*, see, *e.g. R.* v. *Abdulaziz* (1989) – a person who, without just excuse, disobeys a witness order or summons to attend court is guilty of contempt of the court if he does not attend: see Criminal Procedure (Attendance of Witnesses) Act 1965, s. 3(1).)

13. Types of criminal contempt
Criminal contempt includes the following behaviour:

(a) Contempt in face of the court (*see* **14**).
(b) Conduct which scandalises the court (*see* **15**).
(c) Conduct calculated to interfere with, or obstruct, the due process of the court (*see* **16**).

14. Contempt in face of the court
This consists of words or actions in court which interfere with the course of justice. Examples are:

(a) directly insulting the judge: *see R.* v. *Davison* (1821);
(b) refusal by a witness to leave the court on being instructed to do so: *see Chandler* v. *Horne* (1842);
(c) interruption of proceedings by chanting slogans: *see Morris* v. *Master of the Crown Office* (1970).

15. Conduct which scandalises the court
This includes the publication of scurrilous abuse of a judge, in his capacity as a judge, with reference to his conduct of a case.

(a) *Per* Lord Russell CJ in *R.* v. *Gray* (1900): 'Any act done or writing calculated to bring a court or a judge of the court into contempt or to lower his authority is a contempt of court.' *See A.-G.* v. *BBC* (1981), approved in *Lutchmeeparsad Badry* v. *DPP* (1983) (contempt applies only to courts of justice properly called, and to judges of such courts (not e.g. to commissions)).
(b) Reasonable argument is not to be treated as contempt of court. 'No wrong is committed by any member of the public who exercises the ordinary right of criticising, in good faith, in private or public, the public act done in the seat of justice . . . Justice is not a cloistered virtue: she must be allowed to suffer the scrutiny and respectful, even though outspoken,

comments of ordinary men': *per* Lord Atkin in *Ambard* v. *A.-G. for Trinidad and Tobago* (1936).

(c) The intimidation of witnesses can be a criminal contempt. In *Moore* v. *Clerk of Assize (Bristol)* (1971), X's brother, Y, was charged with affray. Z, a fourteen-year-old girl, gave evidence against Y, after which X reproached her and made a threatening gesture. The judge trying the case against Y called X before him and sentenced him for contempt of court. It was held, on appeal, that X's behaviour *did* amount to contempt of court.

(d) Interference with a juror may constitute contempt of court. *See R.* v. *Giscombe* (1984) – the test for contempt is whether the accused *knowingly* did an act which was intended and calculated to interfere with the course of justice *and* was capable of having that effect.

16. Conduct interfering with or obstructing the due process of the court

This includes e.g. private communications to a judge with the intention of influencing him improperly; comments in newspapers. 'When an action is pending in the court and anything is done which has a tendency to obstruct the ordinary course of justice or to prejudice the trial, there is a power given to the courts . . . to deal with and prevent such matters': *per* Blackburn J in *Skipworth's Case* (1873).

(a) It is a defence for the publisher of a newspaper article to show that he did not know, and had no reason to suppose, that proceedings were pending: *see* the Contempt of Court Act 1981, s. 3.

(b) It is a contempt of court to publish the names of witnesses in defiance of the judge's direction: *see R.* v. *Socialist Worker Printers* (1975).

(c) It is a contempt of court for a newspaper to publish, with the intention to interfere with or impede the course of justice, extracts from a book at a time when other newspapers were restrained by injunction from publishing such material: *Times Newspapers Ltd* v. *A.-G.* (1991).

Contempt of Court Act 1981: the 'strict liability rule'

17. Meaning of the rule

In the 1981 Act, the phrase 'strict liability rule' means the rule of law whereby conduct may be treated as a contempt of court as tending to interfere with the course of justice, and in particular legal proceedings, *regardless of intent to do so*: s. 1. (*See A.-G.* v. *Newspaper Publishing Ltd* (1987) – 'intent' means 'specific intent'.) The term 'legal proceedings' includes proceedings before 'any tribunal or body exercising the judicial power of the state': s. 19.

18. Limitation of the scope of strict liability

The rule applies *only* to publications, i.e. any speech, writing, broadcast, cable programme (*see* the Cable and Broadcasting Act 1984, Sch. 5(39)), *or* other communication addressed to the public or any section of it: s. 2(1). It applies *only* to a publication 'which creates a substantial risk that the course of justice in the proceedings in question will be seriously impeded or prejudiced': s. 2(2). (In *A.-G.* v. *English* (1982), the House of Lords decided that where the risk of prejudice to legal proceedings occasioned by the publication of a newspaper article is merely an *incidental consequence* of a proper discussion of a point of general public interest, the publication is *not* a contempt of court.) The rule applies *only* to a publication if the proceedings in question are 'active': s. 2(3).

(a)   Criminal, appellate and other proceedings are 'active' from the relevant initial steps until concluded (Sch. 1, para. 3).

(b)   The 'initial steps' are: arrest without warrant; issue of warrant for arrest; issue of summons to appear; service of indictment or other document specifying the charge; oral charge.

(c)   Proceedings are 'discontinued' if: the charge is withdrawn or a *nolle prosequi* entered; in the case of proceedings commenced by arrest without warrant, the person charged is released, otherwise than on bail, without having been charged (Sch. 1, para. 7) or if proceedings are discontinued by virtue of the Prosecution of Offences Act 1985, s. 23 (1985 Act, Sch. 1, para. 4).

(d)   Proceedings are 'concluded': by acquittal or sentence; by any other verdict which puts an end to proceedings; by discontinuance or by operation of law (1981 Act, Sch. 1, para. 5).

> NOTE: In *A.-G.* v. *Guardian Newspapers* (1992), a Divisional Court held that when applying the strict liability rule under s. 2(2), a court must consider whether the publication created a serious, as opposed to a merely theoretical, risk that the course of justice would be seriously impeded or prejudiced.

19. Defence of innocent publication or distribution

A person is *not guilty* of contempt under the strict liability rule as publisher if he has taken *all reasonable* care at the time of publication *and* he does not know and has no reason to suspect that relevant proceedings are 'active' (*see* 18): s. 3(1). There is a similar defence in the case of distribution of a publication: s. 3(2).

20. Contemporary reports and discussion of public affairs

A person is not guilty of contempt in respect of a 'fair and accurate report of legal proceedings held in public, published contemporaneously and in good faith': s. 4(1). Under s. 4(2), the court may, where it appears to be necessary for avoiding a substantial risk of prejudice to the administration of justice in those proceedings (or in other proceedings, pending or imminent), order the postponement of publication. (*See R.* v. *Horsham Justices, ex p. Farquharson* (1982).) A publication made as part of a discussion in good faith of public affairs or other matters of general interest is not to be treated as contempt under the strict liability rule 'if the risk of impediment or prejudice to particular legal proceedings is merely incidental to the discussion': s. 5.

Other matters

21. Confidentiality of jury deliberations

It is a contempt of court to obtain, disclose or solicit any particulars of statements made, opinions expressed, arguments advanced or votes cast by members of a jury in the course of their deliberations in any legal proceedings: s. 8(1). This does not apply to disclosure of any particulars in the proceedings for the purpose of enabling the jury to arrive at their verdict: s. 8(2)(*a*).

22. Sources of information

No court may require a person to disclose, nor is any person guilty of contempt of court for refusing to disclose, the source of information contained in a publication for which he is responsible, *unless* it be established to the satisfaction of the court that disclosure is necessary in the interests of justice or national security or for the prevention of disorder or crime: s. 10.

(a) In *X Ltd* v. *Morgan-Grampian (Publishers) Ltd* (1990), the House of Lords held that an order for disclosure of a journalist's source under s. 10, on the ground that it was necessary in the interests of justice, was only to be made if the judge was satisfied that the interests of justice were of such preponderating importance as to override the statutory privilege.

(b) 'Interests of justice' was used in s. 10 in the sense that persons should be enabled to exercise important legal rights or to protect themselves from serious legal wrongs and was not confined to legal proceedings in a court of law. Lord Diplock's confining of the phrase to 'the technical sense of the administration of justice in the course of legal proceedings in a court of law' (*see Secretary of State for Defence* v. *Guardian Newspapers* (1985)) was 'too narrow': *per* Lord Bridge.

(c) Decisions as to whether disclosure was necessary were to be made by the courts and not by the journalist involved. There was no right of conscientious objection; such a doctrine entitled him to set himself above the law and 'was wholly unacceptable in a democratic society'.

23. Magistrates' powers

Under s. 12 a magistrates' court has jurisdiction to detain during its sitting or to sentence to imprisonment for up to one month or to fine, any person 'who wilfully insults the justice or justices, any witness before or officer of the court or any solicitor or counsel having business in the court, during his or their sitting or attendance in court or in going to or returning from the court, or wilfully interrupts the proceedings of the court or otherwise misbehaves in court': s. 12(1)(*a*)(*b*). *See Bodden* v. *CMP* (1989) – interruption from outside the court (by use of a loudhailer in the street) was held by the Court to constitute contempt within s. 12; *R.* v. *Powell* (1993) – wolf-whistling at a juror in court.

24. Publication of matters exempted from disclosure in court

In any case where a court allows a name or other matter to be withheld from the public, it is empowered under s. 11 to prohibit publication of such matter. *See R.* v. *Arundel Justices ex p. Westminster Press* (1985), where the purported prohibition of publication failed *solely* because the name had already been expressly mentioned in open court.

Progress test 24

1. How does the Perjury Act 1911 define 'perjury'? **(1)**

2. Give examples of the offence of perjury. **(2)**

3. 'Wilfulness is an essential element in perjury.' Comment. **(6)**

4. What is meant by 'perverting the course of justice'? **(9)**

5. Give examples of criminal contempt of court. **(13)**

6. What is the 'strict liability rule' under the Contempt of Court Act 1981? **(17)**

7. Comment on the confidentiality of jury deliberations. **(21)**

Appendix 1
Bibliography

(Students should use only the most up-to-date editions.)

Reference works
Archbold: Pleading, Evidence and Practice in Criminal Cases, Mitchell, Buzzard and Richardson (Sweet and Maxwell)
Blackstone's Criminal Practice, ed. Murphy (Blackstone Press)
Criminal Law: The General Part, Williams (Stevens)
A Theory of Criminal Justice, Gross (OUP)
A Criminal Code for England and Wales, Law Commission (HMSO) (Law Com. No. 177)
Report of the Royal Commission on Criminal Justice (HMSO) (Cm 2263)

Casebooks and other background material
A Casebook on Criminal Law, Elliot and Wood (Sweet and Maxwell)
Criminal Law: Cases and Materials, Smith and Hogan (Butterworths)
Criminal Law: Text and Materials, Clarkson and Keating (Sweet and Maxwell)
Crime, Reason and History, Norrie (Weidenfeld and Nicholson)

Textbooks
Criminal Law, Smith and Hogan (Butterworths)
Textbook on Criminal Law, Allen (Blackstone Press)
Introduction to Criminal Law, Cross, Jones and Card (Butterworths)
Principles of Criminal Law, Ashworth (OUP)
Law of Theft, Smith (Butterworths)
The Theft Acts 1968 and 1978, Griew (Sweet and Maxwell)

Appendix 2

Examination technique

1. The nature of first examinations in criminal law

First examinations in criminal law are usually designed so as to assess and evaluate a candidate's knowledge of basic principles and his ability to apply that knowledge to the comprehension, analysis and solution of simple legal problems. The ability to *understand principles*, the power to *reason* on the basis of those principles, the skill to *perceive relationships* among the data in a problem, and the capacity to recall relevant statutes and cases, are of much importance in this area of the law.

2. Pre-examination revision

A student's pre-examination preparation period should culminate in a relatively short spell of *methodical* revision. Timing is of the essence; in general, at least one month should be allowed for this important activity. The following points should be considered carefully.

(a) The revision period should be wide-ranging, but *selective*. A revision in detail is *not* recommended; the review should focus on *key principles and illustrations* rather than on minutiae. Hence the use of summaries and general headings is recommended.

(b) The selection of principles to be revised should include those which comprise the basic structure of criminal offences – *actus reus, mens rea*, participation, and general defences. A swift review of selected (offences against the person and property (e.g. unlawful homicide, theft, criminal damage) should be undertaken.

(c) During the revision period *powers of recall* should be exercised. Effective revision involves much more than the mere passive reading of text or notes; it requires a sustained active effort to recall principles and decisions of the courts without the use of external aids to the memory.

(d) Mere rote-learning (i.e. the memorisation, without comprehension, of lists of items) should be rejected at every stage of the student's learning programme, and particularly during revision. There should be concentration, rather, on the *patterns* which ought to have emerged during the basic study of the criminal law. There ought to be a review of, for example, the pattern of development in the law relating to murder and manslaughter. Other patterns in the evolution of the criminal law relating e.g. to strict liability or deception offences should be reviewed.

(e) A selection of questions picked from past papers of the relevant examinations authority should be answered *under examination conditions*. The problem of timing should be taken into account. Answers should be checked carefully.

(f) There should be a review of the *legal reasoning processes* by which a criminal court arrives at its decisions. A selection of leading cases should be re-read and particular attention given to the material facts, the reasoning leading to the court's conclusions; the essence of those particular conclusions should be related to the general structure of the criminal law.

3. Types of questions in criminal law first examinations
These tend to fall into two main groups, although overlap is common.

(a) *The question calling for a discussion*: eg,

'Clause 75 of the Law Commission's Draft Criminal Code Bill is as follows: "A person is guilty of assault if he intentionally or recklessly – (a) applies force to or causes an impact on the body of another; or (b) causes another to believe that any such force or impact is imminent, without the consent of the other or, where the act is likely or intended to cause personal harm, with or without his consent." Does this seem to you to be adequate?'

(b) *The question calling for a solution to a problem*: eg,

'In 1991 H married W. Six months later W made the first in a series of complaints to her friends concerning H's physical abuse of her. In early 1992 W complained to the police and H was interviewed, but no proceedings followed. In January 1993 H came home one evening and told W that he had been dismissed from his job, that she was responsible for his misfortunes and that he intended to kill her. W ran from the house and returned later to find H asleep in a drunken stupor. She deliberately turned on a gas tap in the room and left the house. When she returned H was dead. W has been charged with the murder of H and wishes to plead provocation. Advise W.'

4. The discussion question
Discussion ought to be based on a stratum of fact. The question calls for a careful analysis of clause 75, with attention directed in particular to words such as 'intentionally', 'recklessly', 'imminent', 'consent'. Leading cases, such as *Fagan* (1969), *Logdon* (1976), *Brown* (1993) (in which the House of Lords considered the question of consent to acts of violence) should be referred to. It should be noted that the clause does not treat common assault and battery as distinct offences; it implements the

recommendation that there should be a single offence of assault, whether or not there is a battery.

A structured answer is required, based upon a brief introduction, an analysis of aspects of the clause, comment on possible advantages and difficulties likely to attend its implementation, and a conclusion which deals with the matter of 'adequacy' in direct fashion.

5. The problem-solution question

This searching type of question requires the marshalling of appropriate principles, legislation and cases. Careful and repeated reading of the data is essential, and key words and phrases ought to be underlined.

An answer to the problem necessitates a consideration of the basis of the defence of provocation, ie, the test stated by Devlin J in *Duffy* (1949), (approved in *Ibrams* (1981)), the Homicide Act 1957, s. 3, the 'subjective' and 'objective' conditions which must be satisfied if the defence is to be made out, cases such as *DPP* v *Camplin* (1978), *Ahluwalia* (1992), and *Thornton* (1992). Matters such as the relationship between provocation and W's retaliation, the distinction between sudden loss of self-control and deliberate retribution, must be analysed.

The advice to W ought to be stated in systematic manner: a brief introduction to the defence and its constituent features should be followed by a review of the legislation and cases, which should lead to an application of principles to W's situation. A conclusion ought to present, in concise form, the precise advice to be given to W, given the circumstances of the case.

6. In the examination room

The following advice ought to be kept in mind.

(a) The instructions should be read with care – they may change from year to year and must not be taken for granted.

(b) The questions should be read with care, and a selection made, excluding those which are not to be attempted. Those in the latter group should be shut out from the candidate's mind, as far as that is possible.

(c) The allocation of time must be planned precisely. Each question must receive an appropriate allocation, thus ensuring that, because questions usually carry equal marks, no one question is rushed so as to give more time to another. Time must be allowed for a final check of the answer paper.

(d) Answers must be planned, preferably on the basis of a preliminary sketch. The order of presentation of the parts of an argument requires consideration.

(e) Clarity and methodical presentation in answers are highly desirable. In particular, examiners welcome indications as to *how* a candidate has arrived at his conclusions.

Appendix 3

Specimen test paper

The following questions are taken from papers in Criminal Law set by the University of London, whose kind permission to use them is acknowledged.

Instructions
1. Answer any *four* questions.
2. The time allowed for the test is *three hours*.

1. U, aged 67 years, saw V approaching and, believing that V was going to attack her, she shouted, 'He's going to attack me!' She then hit V over the head with her umbrella. V was a haemophiliac and he became concussed and seriously ill from the blow. He reeled in front of a passing car driven by W. W suffered from shock but was able to stop the car before suffering a severe heart attack. W recovered but V died in hospital.

Advise U. What difference, if any, would it make to your advice if U said she was Boadicea and, as an ardent feminist, she believed that she had the right to wipe out all men?

2. K was employed in a bank. One of his tasks was to take deposits from customers. K joined a religious sect which believed that money was tainted. K began to give customers excess payments and to strike out debits on customers' statements. K used the computer to add sums to customers' accounts and then wiped out the computer records which would have made it possible to trace these alterations. All the customers failed to report the additional credits to their account and some of them spent the excess. Also, K filled in credit application forms which K knew to be false. The advances which K received he gave to various charities who refused to return the proceeds.

Advise K and the charities.

3. 'Some defences negative a crime. Others provide an excuse for a fully constituted crime. In the former case the courts have no discretion

whether to allow the defence. In the latter case they are free to allow the defence, or to allow it subject to condition, or to refuse it.'

Discuss.

4. P hid a bomb aboard a plane. He telephoned the airline while the plane was on a transatlantic flight. He demanded payment of £1 million to tell them where the bomb was hidden. The airline refused to pay the money despite advice to the contrary from a security firm. As a result the plane was blown up and all the passengers and crew were killed.

Advise P of his criminal liability. What difference, if any, would it make to your advice if P believed that in demanding payment he was divinely inspired to raise the money to further his religious ends?

5. After a severe storm which damaged the roof of O's house, N asked O for £600 to repair the roof. N went onto the roof, repaired a few tiles, but did not do a thorough job. The next night, because of the inadequacy of the repair, the roof let in rain and O's furniture and fittings were damaged. N filled up his van with diesel at a local self service garage. He then decided to drive off as the attendant could not be contacted to take his money. He drove off, intending to return to pay when next in the area. As the attendant had not seen N fill his tank, N decided not to return. N stopped on the way home and ordered a meal at a fast food restaurant. Having consumed it, he told the waiter who he was and that he had decided not to pay. The waiter said that N could not leave the restaurant till he paid and N pushed past him.

Advise the parties of their criminal liability.

6. J, aged fifteen years, went into K's store and, while the assistant was in a back storeroom, J jumped over the counter and opened the drawer of an electric till, intending to steal the contents of the till. In fact, it was empty. J remained hidden behind the counter, intending to come out later to let in some friends to hold a party there and to enable them to use such items of dress as took their fancy. Later that night, J 'let in' fifty young teenagers for a 'rave' in the store. During the party several of the party-goers removed valuable items from the store. When the police arrived, J and friends barricaded the doors and effectively kept the police out for some time while many of them escaped through a passage at the back of the store. J fled with a model train set.

Advise J of his criminal liability.

7. P wanted to kill Q who P believed had attacked Q's daughter. P sent a letter to Q stating, 'Justice will be done sometime in the next five years! Take care! You will never know when.' From time to time P walked on the pavement outside Q's house without stopping or saying anything. P sent Q a postcard each week with a picture of a policeman on it. After six

months, Q had a nervous breakdown and attempted to commit suicide. Six months later, P locked Q in a lift to prevent Q speaking at a political rally. Q who suffered from claustrophobia had a heart attack.

Advise P.

Appendix 4

Report of the Royal Commission on Criminal Justice 1993 (Cm 2263)

1. Background

The Commission was set up in March 1991, and delivered its Report in July 1993. Its terms of reference required the Commission 'in effect, to examine the criminal justice system from the stage at which the police are investigating an alleged or reported criminal offence right through to the stage at which a defendant who has been found guilty of such an offence has exhausted his or her rights of appeal'.

2. Adversarial or inquisitorial system?

The Commission does not recommend a change to an inquisitorial system. 'We ourselves doubt whether the fusion of the functions of investigation and prosecution, and the direct involvement of judges in both, are more likely to serve the interests of justice than a system in which the roles of police, prosecutors, and judges are as far as possible kept separate and the judge who is responsible for the conduct of the trial is the arbiter of law but not of fact' (para.14).

A selection from some of the 352 recommendations of the Commission is given below. It is likely that some future reforms of the criminal law will be based upon the Report. (It should be noted that the Report did not receive universal acclamation: *see*, for example, the critical review by Professor Simon Lee in *The Times*, 27 July, 1993.)

3. Right of silence and confession evidence

The majority of the Commission believe that adverse inferences should not be drawn from silence at the police station and recommend retaining the present caution and trial direction (r.82). Investigators in serious fraud cases should retain their existing powers to require answers to questions(r.84). There should be a judicial warning in cases where confession evidence is involved. The precise terms of the warning should depend on the circumstances of the case. If it remains possible for a confession to be admitted without supporting evidence, the jury should be warned that great care is needed before convicting on the basis of the confession alone (r.89). The majority of the Commission believe that where a confession is credible and has passed the tests laid down in PACE, the jury should be able to consider it even in the absence of other evidence. The judge should in all such cases give a strong warning to the jury. The other evidence which the jury should be advised to look for should be supporting evidence in the *Turnbull* sense [*see R. v. Turnbull* [1977]QB 224] (r.90).

4. Prosecution
The CPS should be given the power to discontinue proceedings up to the beginning of the trial in both magistrates' courts and the Crown Court (r.97). Victims should so far as practicable be kept informed of the progress and outcome of cases, including decisions not to prosecute and, in some cases, the results of bail applications or successful appeals (r.101).

5. Pre-trial procedures in the Crown Court
Committal hearings in their present form should be abolished (r.116). Where sensitivity is not in issue, the prosecution's initial duty should be to supply to the defence copies of all material relevant to the offence or to the offender or to the surrounding circumstances of the case, whether or not the prosecution intend to rely upon that material (r.124). The prosecution should inform the defence at this stage of the existence of any other material obtained during the course of the inquiry into the offence in question (r.125).

Any defence disclosed to the prosecution in advance of the trial should not be disclosed to the jury until that defence, or an alternative, is advanced at the trial (r.133). The present system of sentence discounts should be more clearly articulated, with earlier pleas attracting higher discounts (r.156).

6. The trial
A rule should be introduced to enable judges to exclude evidence that, although relevant, may confuse the issues, mislead the jury, cause undue delay, waste time, or lead to needless presentation of cumulative evidence (r.181). Judges should be prepared, in suitable cases, to ask counsel why a witness has not been called and, if they think it appropriate, urge counsel to rectify the situation. In the last resort judges must be prepared to exercise their power to call the witness themselves (r.185). Hearsay evidence should be admitted to a greater extent than at present (r.189). The corroboration rules should be abolished (r.195).

7. Court of Appeal
In the view of the majority of the Commission, the present grounds of appeal should be replaced by a single broad ground which would give

the court flexibility to consider all categories of appeal. The correct approach is for the court to decide whether the conviction 'is or may be unsafe' (r.317). The majority of the Commission take the view that if the error [at the trial] would have made no difference to the safety of the conviction, the appeal should be dismissed. If the court believes that the error has rendered the conviction unsafe the appeal should be allowed. If the court believes that the conviction may be unsafe as a result of the error it should order a retrial (r.318).

In considering whether to receive fresh evidence the Court of Appeal should take a broad approach to the questions whether the fresh evidence was available at the time of the trial and if it was, whether there is a reasonable explanation for the failure to adduce it then or for any subsequent departure by a witness from the evidence given at the original trial (r.320). The test for receiving fresh evidence should be whether it is 'capable of belief' (r.322). In cases other than fresh evidence cases, where a retrial is desirable but not practicable a majority of the Commission consider that the court should automatically allow the appeal (r.324).

The requirement that before an appeal can be made to the House of Lords the Court of Appeal must certify that the case involves a matter of law of general public importance should be dropped. (r.328).

8. Correction of miscarriages of justice

The Home Secretary's power to refer cases to the Court of Appeal under the Criminal Appeal Act 1968, s. 17, should be removed and a new body ('the Authority') should be set up (r.331). The Authority's role should be to consider allegations put to it that miscarriage of justice may have occurred, to ensure that any further investigation called for is launched, to supervise that investigation if conducted by the police, and, where there are reasons for supposing that a miscarriage of justice might have occurred, to refer the case to the Court of Appeal (r.332). The Authority should be independent of the court structure (r.336).

Where the Authority believes that a case should be considered by the Court of Appeal, it should refer the case to that court, together with a statement of its reasons for so referring it and, at the same time, provide the Court with such supporting material as it believes to be appropriate and desirable, and which it believes may be admissible, though without any recommendation or conclusion as to whether or not a miscarriage of justice has occurred. The Court of Appeal should then treat any case so referred in the same way as an appeal from the Crown Court (r.337). The possible use of the Royal Prerogative of Mercy should be kept open for the exceptional case (r.339). There should be neither a right of appeal nor a right to judicial review in relation to decisions reached by the Authority (r.340).

Index